AMERICAN DREAMS

AMERICAN DREAMS

Readings for Writers

Paul Clee
Violeta Radu-Clee

TACOMA COMMUNITY COLLEGE

MAYFIELD PUBLISHING COMPANY

MOUNTAIN VIEW, CALIFORNIA

LONDON • TORONTO

Library of Congress Cataloging-in-Publication Data
Clee, Paul.
    American dreams : readings for writers / Paul Clee, Violeta Radu-Clee
        p.   cm.
    Includes index.
    ISBN 1–55934–377–X
    1. College readers.   2. English language—Rhetoric.   3. National characteristics, American—Problems, exercises, etc.   4. Success—Problems, exercises, etc.
5. Readers—United States.
I. Radu-Clee, Violeta.   II. Title.
PE1417.C6267   1995
808'.0427—dc20   95–34474
                                                                                              CIP

Manufactured in the United States of America
10 9 8 7 6 5 4

Mayfield Publishing Company
1280 Villa Street
Mountain View, CA 94041

Sponsoring editor, James Bull; production editor, Julianna Scott Fein; manuscript editor, Irina Raicu; art director, Jeanne M. Schreiber; text and cover designer, Anna George; art manager, Robin Mouat; manufacturing manager, Randy Hurst. The text was set in 10.5/12 Bembo by G & S Typesetters, Inc., and printed on 50# Buttes des Mortes by Banta Company.

Cover image: *Things to Come* by Virginia Maitland (acrylic on canvas, 60″ x 72″)

Acknowledgments and copyrights continue at the back of the book on pages 431–435, which constitute an extension of the copyright page.

 This book is printed on recycled paper.

To the Instructor

American Dreams introduces students to college writing by emphasizing those skills that have to do with writing about reading—from summarizing and responding to analyzing and synthesizing. The text includes a brief rhetoric and ten chapters of readings, which are unified by the overarching theme of the American Dream. The readings, both contemporary and historical, examine such questions as these: What is the American Dream? How is the idea of the Dream changing? What is the relation between the individual and society in America? What does the Dream mean to different individuals and groups within our society?

WHY THE AMERICAN DREAM?

We chose the theme of the American Dream for two reasons: First, as an ideal, the Dream has been, and still is, a powerful shaping force in American life. Recently it has gained new urgency, as the nation and world change, and as people ask whether the Dream is dead or alive and whether social changes—civil rights movements, immigration, growing diversity, global development—are killing it or reviving it. It is a theme that goes to the heart of much of what we regard as American, and it provides a revealing lens through which we can examine both the American past and contemporary issues.

Our second reason for choosing this theme is that it lends itself well to our goals as teachers of writing: It is broad enough to allow a wide variety of topics, yet focused enough to provide a sense of continuity; it encourages close reading, critical thinking, and thoughtful writing; and it engages students in issues that touch their lives in significant ways. As we have tested this material in our classes over the past few years, we have found that students respond to it with interest and enthusiasm. As they move through the book, there is a cumulative effect: Each chapter adds something to their knowledge and understanding. Thus they are able, as they progress, to bring greater knowledge and depth of thought to their writing. This emphasis on building writing skills through an intensive examination of a continuing theme is one of the unique features of this book.

HOW IS THE BOOK ORGANIZED?

The book is divided into two parts: a brief rhetoric (Chapters 1–4), and a thematically organized reader (Chapters 5–14). In Part I we begin with an explanation of active reading and give some exercises in summarizing and responding. Next, we move to the nature of the writing situation (writer, occasion, purpose, and audience), the process of writing, and the organization and development of essays. Here, we also introduce some principles of writing that "shows" (describes, narrates, illustrates) and writing that analyzes. We discuss the main features of each of these modes and talk about how they are used effectively in combination. The sample essay "Poker and the American Dream" provides a good example of how showing and analysis complement one another.

We also use "Poker and the American Dream" to demonstrate how ideas for writing can be generated from a reading selection. We pose not only the kinds of questions that might be asked of a piece of writing but also questions that might lead students to develop ideas of their own based on their reading.

One important feature of Part I is that we deal with the essay *before* the paragraph. Although this overturns the logic of a linear progression from simpler to more complex forms, we think that it makes better sense to consider the whole before the parts. Paragraphs seldom exist in isolation. So although we do touch on paragraphing when we talk about essays, we don't discuss it in detail until the end of the section on rhetoric. Thus when we come to paragraphs, students already have some understanding of the context in which they occur.

Finally, because we stress the connection between reading and writing throughout the book, we have included a section on working with sources.

In addition to providing information about writing, Part I also introduces the theme of the American Dream through examples and exercises.

Three interviews from Studs Terkel's *American Dreams: Lost and Found* set the stage by offering three personal views of the American Dream. Other examples in this section also bear upon the central theme.

Part II, the reader, contains ten chapters, each devoted to a distinct strand of the American Dream: success, individualism, the melting pot, working, and so on. Each chapter contains a variety of readings (six to eight) that bring different points of view to the chapter's theme, reflecting both a wide spectrum of opinion and the diversity of American society. We have chosen readings that play off one another in several ways, giving students ample opportunity to analyze, compare, and evaluate a range of approaches and ideas.

Each reading is preceded by an introductory note and a list of key vocabulary items and followed by questions for discussion. Each chapter includes, at the end, a broad selection of writing assignments. Some of them ask for analysis of the readings, and some of them ask students to relate what they have read to their own experience.

ACKNOWLEDGMENTS

Many friends, colleagues, and students contributed their suggestions and support to the shaping of this book. We would especially like to thank Debbie and John Kinerk, Gerry Shulenbarger, Dick Stein, and Thea Bennett and Michael Williams. We are grateful for the many valuable suggestions made by the reviewers: Cathryn Amdahl, Harrisburg Area Community College; Leslie Bradley, Pennsylvania State University; Tom Cameron, Austin Community College; Charles Fisher, Aims Community College; Debbie Kinerk, Tacoma Community College; Allison Smith, Western Washington University; and Edith Wollin, North Seattle Community College.

We are also indebted to the fine people at Mayfield who provided invaluable guidance in helping us organize this book and prepare it for publication. Many thanks to Jim Bull, Tom Broadbent, Julianna Scott Fein, Pamela Trainer, and Irina Raicu.

To the Student

This book provides instruction and practice in the kinds of writing you will have to do in many of your college courses. Because most college writing requires students to deal with material they have read, this is also a book about reading—careful, critical reading. In college work, reading and writing are inseparable.

We begin with short, simple assignments—writing summaries and short responses—then move on to longer and more complex essays and paragraphs. Along the way we will deal with questions of language, strategy, structure, and style. By the end of the course, you should be able to write short essays that demonstrate your ability to write about complex issues and your ability to use the conventions of written English effectively.

To give this book some unity of subject, we have chosen readings that all bear in a general way on a single theme—the American Dream. Thus, as you move through the book, the skills and knowledge you gain from working with the readings in one chapter can be applied to the next. We also hope that the reading and writing you do in this course will deepen your understanding of what it means to be alive in America today and of the choices and decisions you will face as you move out into the world.

"The American Dream" is an idea—a big one. It condenses in a brief phrase what the country is—or wants to be. Individuals have their own ideas of what the dream means to them, but most Americans also have the sense that there are, at bottom, some common elements of the Dream that unite all of us into a single community. What is this Dream? What does it mean? How do different people see it? How has it changed? How does it affect our hopes, our expectations, the way we live our lives? Does it still exist? Has it ever existed? These are some of the questions that the readings in this book explore. In each chapter, the readings address a particular issue from several points of view. You'll be asked to respond to these issues in a variety of ways, using the readings as a means to develop your own writing abilities.

Contents

8 Rugged Individuals   *201*

9 Working   *233*

I

ABOUT READING AND WRITING

1 Reading, Summarizing, Responding

ACTIVE READING

There is reading, and then there is *really reading*. When we read casually, we tend to read with the brain switched off, soaking up information like sponges or letting the words roll through our minds like a movie. A few days later we remember about a tenth of what we've read.

Reading with the brain switched on is different. It's active. Active readers conduct a running dialogue with the words on the page. They ask questions. They sort out the important from the less important. They look for connections, analyze evidence, ask how new knowledge fits with what they already know. In short, they bring themselves to the text.

To write well about what you read, you first have to understand a text thoroughly. This means reading the piece more than once, and it means using your brain as you read. There is a method to doing this, a method based on the way writers most often arrange their material.

With the exception of a few short stories and poems, most of the readings in this book are *expository* or *persuasive*. Expository writing seeks to inform and explain; persuasive writing, as the name suggests, seeks to persuade the reader of the writer's point of view. Both of these types of writing tend to follow a common underlying pattern: the main idea is placed near the beginning and is developed and supported in subsequent paragraphs. This pattern is not universal—sometimes considerations of audience and purpose will suggest a different order. But pay special attention to the beginnings and endings of articles, essays and paragraphs. Important ideas are most likely to appear in these positions.

Step 1: Previewing the Text

Before you actually start reading, get an aerial view of the terrain—a preview of what the whole piece is about. Read the first paragraph or two, then skim through the rest of the paragraphs, reading just the first couple of sentences in each one. Finally, read the concluding paragraph.

A quick survey of these key elements will give you a general idea of what the essay is about. You will find it is much easier to follow a writer's train of thought if you have the overall framework in mind before you start.

Step 2: Reading Closely and Marking the Text

On the second reading, fly closer to the ground, pen in hand. Underline words, phrases, and sentences that seem particularly important. When you come across something that seems *really* important, give it some kind of special mark: underline twice, put checks or stars in the margin, put parentheses or circles around key words and phrases.

Another technique is to write in the margins very brief summaries of key ideas. And you can also use the margins to write your own questions and responses.

We suggest you use a pen or pencil for this, rather than a highlighter. Why? With a pen or pencil you can annotate the text—write brief notes about it as you go. Annotations can serve as reminders of important ideas; they can indicate questions you might have about the text, and they can also record comments and reactions as you go along.

The first thing to strive for in marking the text is to pick out the main ideas. Pay special attention to introductions, conclusions, and the first few sentences of paragraphs. (However, keep in mind that main ideas in paragraphs may also be stated at the middle or the end, and in some cases not stated at all, but implied.)

Example of a Marked Text

The following example comes from a book entitled *American Dreams: Lost and Found,* written by the Chicago journalist Studs Terkel. To write the book, Terkel interviewed many people about what they thought of the American Dream, then transcribed the interviews. The interview we've included here is with Arnold Schwarzenegger, the famous body builder and film star.

As you read, notice how the text has been marked and annotated. Underlining is used to mark important points—general ideas, not examples.

Circles and parentheses draw attention to key words and phrases. Stars in the margins mark the beginnings of major divisions. Finally, annotations (marginal notes) briefly summarize each main section.

ARNOLD SCHWARZENEGGER

Call me Arnold.

I was born in a little Austrian town, outside Graz. It was a 300-year-old house.

When I was ten years old, I had the dream of being the best in the world in something. When I was fifteen, I had a dream that I wanted to be the best body builder in the world and the most muscular man. It was not only a dream I dreamed at night. It was also a daydream. It was so much in my mind that I felt it had to become a reality. It took me five years of hard work. Five years later, I turned this dream into reality and became Mr. Universe, the best-built man in the world.   *Desire to be best*

★ Winning is a very important word. There is one that achieves what he wanted to achieve and there are hundreds of thousands that failed. It singles you out: the winner.   *winning*

I came out second three times, but that is not what I call losing. The bottom line for me was: Arnold has to be the winner. I have to win more often than anybody else. I won the Mr. Universe title more often than anybody else. I won it five times consecutively. I hold the record as Mr. Olympia, the top professional body-building championship. I won it six times. That's why I retired. There was nobody even close to me. Everybody gave up competing against me. That's what I call a winner.

When I was a small boy, my dream was not to be big physically, but big in a way that everybody listens to me when I talk, that I'm a very important person, that people recognize me and see me as something special. I had a big need for being singled out.

Also my dream was to end up in America. When I was ten years old, I dreamed of being an American. At the time I didn't know much about America, just that it was a wonderful country. I felt it was where I belonged. I didn't like being in a little country like Austria. I did everything possible to get out. I did so in 1968, when I was twenty-one years old.   *Dreams of America*

If I would believe in life after death, I would say my before-life I was living in America. That's why I feel so good here. It is the country where you can turn your dream into reality. Other countries don't have those things. When I came over here to America, I felt I was in heaven. In America, we don't have an obstacle. Nobody's holding you back.

★ Number One in America pretty much takes care of the rest of the world. You kind of run through the rest of the world like nothing. I'm trying to make people in America aware that they should appreciate what they have here. You have the best tax advantages here and the best prices and the best products here.   *advantages of America*

One of the things I always had was a business mind. When I was in high school, a majority of my classes were business classes. Economics and accounting and mathematics. When I came over here to this country, I really didn't speak English almost at all. I learned English and then started taking business courses, because that's what America is best known for business. Turning one dollar into a million dollars in a short period of time. Also when you make money, how do you keep it?

Business

That's one of the most important things when you have money in your hand, how can you keep it? Or make more out of it? Real estate is one of the best ways of doing that. I own apartment buildings, office buildings, and raw land. That's my love, real estate.

Real estate / keeping money

I have emotions. But what you do, you keep them cold or you store them away for a time. You must control your emotions, you must have command over yourself. Three, four months before a competition, I could not be interfered by other people's problems. This is sometimes called selfish. It's the only way you can be if you want to achieve something. Any emotional things inside me, I try to keep cold so it doesn't interfere with my training.

controlling emotions

Many times things really touched me. I felt them and I felt sensitive about them. But I had to talk myself out of it. I had to suppress those feelings in order to go on. Sport is one of those activities where you really have to concentrate. You must pay attention a hundred percent to the particular thing you're doing. There must be nothing else on your mind. Emotions must not interfere. Otherwise, you're thinking about your girlfriend. You're in love, your positive energies get channeled into another direction rather than going into your weight room or making money.

You have to choose at a very early date what you want: a normal life or to achieve things you want to achieve. I never wanted to win a popularity contest in doing things the way people want me to do it. I went the road I thought was best for me. A few people thought I was cold, selfish. Later they found out that's not the case. After I achieve my goal, I can be Mr. Nice Guy. You know what I mean?

need to choose way of life early

California is to me a dreamland. It is the absolute combination of everything I was always looking for. It has all the money in the world there, show business there, wonderful weather there, beautiful country, ocean is there. Snow skiing in the winter, you can go in the desert the same day. You have beautiful-looking people there. They all have a tan.

California—essence of American Dream

I believe very strongly in the philosophy of staying hungry. If you have a dream and it becomes a reality, don't stay satisfied with it too long. Make up a new dream and hunt after that one and turn it into reality. When you have that dream achieved, make up a new dream.

I am a strong believer in Western philosophy, the philosophy of success, of progress, of getting rich. The Eastern philosophy is passive, which I believe in maybe three percent of the times, and the ninety-seven percent is Western, conquering and going on. It's a beautiful philosophy, and America should keep it up.

Belief in Western Philosophy

You may not agree with everything we've chosen to mark, but this example should give you an idea of what to look for and how much to mark. With practice, you will develop your own system.

SUMMARIZING

What Is a Summary?

A summary is a condensed version of a piece of writing. Summarizing will be nothing new for you; it's something you probably do every day. For example, if a friend asks you about a book you have read or a movie you have seen, or about a trip or a concert, you don't try to tell the whole thing from start to finish. You hit the high points, enough to give a general sense of the experience. You do this naturally and without really thinking about it. Summarizing a piece of writing is not much different; it just demands that you consider more carefully what you are going to say.

Why Summarize?

In many kinds of writing, including college papers, it is necessary to give the reader an idea of what various other writers have said about the subject. A summary is a way of providing a general understanding without quoting the original at length. It is a way of incorporating the ideas and information of others into your own work.

Tips on Writing a Summary

To write a summary, you have to do two things: First, locate the main ideas of the reading selection; second, put the author's ideas in your own words. Don't just copy sentences from the original. Stating the ideas of another writer in your own words shows that you understand those ideas, and it also gives you practice in expressing them in your own way. Sometimes you might use a key word or phrase from the original, but for the most part the wording and sentence structure should be your own. (If you do use words from the original, be sure to enclose them in quotation marks.)

The purpose of a summary is to give an accurate, objective representation of what the work says; you should *not* include your own ideas or interpretations. You will have a chance to do that later.

How Long Should a Summary Be?

The length of a summary depends on your purpose. For instance, if the purpose of a summary is to give the reader a general idea of the main point, a sentence or two would probably be enough. But if your purpose is to analyze a writer's position in detail, you would probably need to summarize all of the significant points in the piece you are working with. You will have practice in both.

Exercise: Writing Short Summaries

Write a *one-sentence summary* of each paragraph below. Look for the main idea, then write it in your own words. Since your purpose is to give a *general* idea of what the paragraph is about, you won't need to include details and examples.

PARAGRAPH 1

The importance of making it big, even making it big and greedy, is close to a given in today's society. Prevailing sentiment is widely recognized by eight in ten people and can be summed up thus: to make a lot of money is not only desirable, it is the "in" thing to do. To make money by skirting the intent and even the letter of the law is in itself a vicarious thrill. In a 1984 *Business Week/Harris Poll* 53% of all Yuppies admitted that they did their own income taxes so that they could cheat—no CPA or tax consultant would countersign their IRA returns. A big 82% of the entire adult population are convinced that if most Americans had the chance, they would engage in insider trading on Wall Street, even though it is illegal. A solid majority also agree with convicted Yuppie Dennis Levine, who justified his making $12.6 million from illegal insider trading by saying, "Why, everybody is doing it."

—LOU HARRIS
From *Inside America*

EXAMPLE of one-sentence summary: Most Americans today place a high value on making a lot of money, even if it means breaking the law.

PARAGRAPH 2

Today, a woman wants to be called ambitious the way she wishes to be called beautiful and bright. It has become an accolade, no longer synonymous with "aggressive," which was synonymous with "cold-hearted bitch." Of course, women have always been ambitious—but for social status, marriage and motherhood rather than fame and fortune. How things have changed, even in our

own lifetime: When we were girls, we talked about boys. Now
that we are women, we talk about work.

−KAREN HELLER
From "By Success Obsessed"

PARAGRAPH 3

There are two ways in which you can own a book. The first
is the property right you establish by paying for it, just as you pay
for clothes and furniture. But this act of purchase is only the prelude to possession. Full ownership comes only when you have
made it a part of yourself, and the best way to make yourself a part
of it is by writing in it. An illustration may make the point clear.
You buy a beefsteak and transfer it from the butcher's icebox to
your own. But you do not own the beefsteak in the most important sense until you consume it and get it into your bloodstream.
I am arguing that books, too, must be absorbed in your bloodstream to do you any good.

−MORTIMER ADLER
From "How to Mark a Book"

PARAGRAPH 4

One [American character trait] is the motivation that impels
Americans; their ambition is success and they measure their worth
as much by the upward distance they have traveled in society as by
the position they have reached. They think in terms of social mobility and movement along the social ladder rather than of com-
partmentalized classes or stability; as a result they are excessively
concerned with conformity, which seems essential to win the support of their peers needed for each upward move.

−RAY ALLEN BILLINGTON
From "The Frontier and the American Character"

PARAGRAPH 5

The American can endure almost all states except solitude. At
home in the world of material objects and gadgets, eager for the
company of others, he is restless and uneasy in the company of
himself. His society is crammed to the bursting point with clubs,
groups, associations, lodges, fraternities and sororities, organizations of every description which he joins in great numbers less to
be with his fellows than to get away from himself. He is an Elk,
Oddfellow, Shriner, Moose, Eagle or American Legionnaire. He
is a Rotarian, Kiwanian, Mason or Knight of Columbus. He attends church for reasons more social than religious. He joins

societies that seek to protect ownerless animals or aim at world government or rehearse the operettas of Gilbert and Sullivan. He attaches himself to the countless booster clubs that dot the civic landscape with posters advertising Belleville as the town of industrial opportunity, or Dead Lick as the biggest little city in the country. He attends innumerable conventions with unflagging enthusiasm. Bars, taverns, bowling alleys, poolrooms, gymnasiums, country clubs, are social centers that attract him in large clusters. When he is not in formal contact with others, he is listening to the radio, or sitting in front of a television set, or watching a movie, one in a dark crowd. He is never alone if he can help it.

–Leo Gurko
From *Heroes, Highbrows, and the Popular Mind*

Writing a Longer Summary

A longer summary gives *all* of the main ideas of the original. It is a condensed version of the whole. As an example, here is a summary of the Arnold Schwarzenegger interview.

When he was only ten years old, Arnold Schwarzenegger, who was born in Austria, dreamt of being the best at something. He became a body builder and, at the age of twenty, won the title of Mr. Universe. Winning became very important to him. To Schwarzenegger, a winner is someone who wins more championships than anyone else and wins by such a margin that no one is even close to him. But his dream was not just to be physically big; he wanted people to recognize him as an important, special person. Another part of his dream was to come to America, the country where, he says, "you can turn your dream into reality." In his view, America has no obstacles and has the best tax advantages, prices, and products. It's the best place to make a lot of money. To keep the money he has made, Schwarzenegger invests in real estate. "That's my love, real estate," he says. Next, Schwarzenegger talks about the need to choose at a young age whether to lead a "normal life" or to achieve something. To be an achiever, he believes, a person has to control emotion. While he is working toward a goal, he doesn't let emotions interfere, which makes him appear selfish and cold to some people. But once he has achieved his goal, he says, he can be "Mr. Nice Guy." Schwarzenegger has found the perfect place to realize his dreams—California. It has everything he has been looking for: money, show business, natural advantages and beautiful people. Finally, Schwarzenegger closes the interview with a statement of his beliefs. He believes in "staying hungry," always inventing new dreams, and he believes in the "Western philosophy of success, or progress, or getting rich. . . . conquering and going on."

From Summary to Response

Unlike a summary, a response is your own reaction to what you've read. Did you like it? Did you learn anything? Did it change your life? Did it leave you cold? What, exactly, did it do to you?

When we read about someone's ideas, we usually have an immediate, "gut" reaction—we like or we don't like, we are attracted or repulsed, interested or bored. Fine. These reactions are a starting point. But a written response asks for a little more thought, some pondering and head scratching, and a willingness to take a closer look at what made you react as you did.

Beginning writers sometimes have a hard time knowing what to say when they're asked to explain themselves. We can give you a few hints, but for the most part it's a matter of looking more closely at your opinions and asking yourself some questions. For instance, after reading the Arnold Schwarzenegger article, you probably have some general feeling that you like or dislike the man. The next step is to think about what *caused* that response. Ask yourself some questions: Do you admire Schwarzenegger? Hold him in contempt? Pity him? What personal qualities does he possess? What values does he hold? Is he a good or a bad model for people to emulate? Do you agree or disagree with his idea of success?

Asking and answering such questions—making notes to yourself as you do it—will give you material for a thoughtful, intelligent response. Try it.

Here are some other questions that could serve as springboards for a response. Dive in.

Did you learn anything that surprised or puzzled you? Why?

Did you find anything particularly interesting in the article? Why?

Was there anything that made you feel angry, optimistic, confused, concerned, bored?

Was there anything in the article with which you strongly identified? Why?

Whatever your reaction, give some reasons and examples, enough for the reader to understand how you came to your conclusions.

Here is an example of a student's response to the Arnold Schwarzenegger essay:

> I have to admire Arnold Schwarzenegger for what he has accomplished. He's one of those people who knows exactly what he wants and does everything he can to get it. He was determined and he worked hard to get where he is. But I wonder about his statement that he has to keep his emotions cold when he's working on his goal. It bothers me. I suppose that if you want the kind of success Arnold has, you have to keep yourself focused on your goal all the time and not let anything get in the way. But I can't imagine shutting off my feelings that way. Maybe I'm too much the other way. I tend to let people, especially my boyfriend, interfere when I really have work to do. I have to study hard if I want to reach my goal of becoming a biologist, but sometimes when friends stop by or call when I'm studying, I'll put off my work to spend time with them. I guess I'm just soft, but I don't want them to think I'm so concerned with getting ahead that I don't have time for friends. Is it really necessary, as Arnold says, to be selfish to accomplish anything? Maybe in some things it is. I don't know. I suppose it depends on what you call success. As they say, it's lonely at the top. Maybe there are other things more important than the top.

This response shows the writer thinking about what she has read. Her thoughts aren't completely worked out, so the response is more like thinking out loud, full of questions and changes in direction. But first responses will probably be like this. We're not looking for fully developed ideas here, just a first attempt to state a reaction to something in the reading.

Exercise: Readings for Summary and Response

The selections that follow are for practice in writing summaries and responses.

The first two selections are, like "Arnold Schwarzenegger," from Studs Terkel's book *American Dreams: Lost and Found*. The third is from another book, called *Habits of the Heart,* written by a group of five sociologists. All of the selections have to do with different views of the central theme of this book—The American Dream. For this exercise, read all three of the selections, and then pick the one to which you have the strongest reaction.

Before you begin this assignment, you might want to review quickly the sections on reading and marking the text (we hope you marked these sections). Then read several times the article you're going to write about, until you're satisfied that you have a grasp of all the important points and have marked them. Mark only the most important points—don't mark details, examples, or specific information. Your summary should include *only* the main points, and it should include them all. How long should it be? For the purpose of this exercise, try for a summary that is roughly one-fifth to one-fourth as long as the original—which means that a summary of a 1,000 word article would be about 200 to 250 words.

Keep in mind that this is a two-part exercise: summary and response. Write each part as a separate paragraph. The summary should present the main ideas of the reading objectively; don't let your own feelings creep in. Save your opinions for the second paragraph, the response. And when you write your response, try to give the reader a clear understanding of the reason you reacted as you did.

✍ **STUDS TERKEL**
Rosalie Sorrells

She is a traveling folk singer.

I think of the town I grew up in—Boise, Idaho—of my family and how they got there, and my own sense of place. I love the feeling of the country that you find in writers like Thomas Wolfe.

My grandparents were an adventurous kind of people. My grandfather was a preacher, wanted to live with the Indians, so he became a missionary to the Crow and the Sioux. He went to Montana. He crossed the Bad Lands all by himself. 1900. He's sort of mysterious to me except through the stories that my grandmother and my mother and father told me about him.

My father was born in Montana. They lived in tents and lodges. My father was one of four sons. My grandmother was a real good photographer. My mother still has some of those photographs. There's pictures of their first trek, this great long trek, with pack horses all strung out across the hill. They all went out on horseback.

They went on river trips. They didn't meet any hostile Indians. Everything they had to do with them was religious. Just the business of living in that time and place was dangerous, having babies in the wilderness and all those things. The trip took seven or eight years. . . .

I always thought of my father, until the day he died, as a young man. He was very handsome, had a little mustache and a light slender body. He was very alive, and I think of him with a lot of pleasure. He liked words, too. He loved Balzac and Rabelais. He turned me on to those things. He liked to play games with words and loved to tell stories always.

After I got married, I took up folk singing as a hobby. I collected old songs. So I'm not thinking of myself as a singer so much as someone who repeats old songs that they heard. I began to write, and I had this big repertoire of folk songs from Utah and Idaho that nobody else knew. I got invited to Newport in 1966. I'd never been east of Denver. When I drove into New York City at seven o'clock in the morning, it was like goin' to Mars. There was that skyline. I just flipped. I nearly had a heart attack, I was so excited. (Laughs.) We came into town—my brother was with me, and a couple of friends—it was too early to wake anybody up. We came to a bar. It was open at eight o'clock in the morning. Never saw a place that was open at eight o'clock in the morning. We had a bottle of champagne to celebrate the fact that we had finally arrived in New York City, and we went to the top of the Empire State Building. (Laughs.) Everyone always told me I'd hate it in New York because it was cold and awful and mean. I just loved it, every second of it. And I still do. (Laughs.) I'm a city junkie. I'd like to find out what makes each place so particular.

Boise hardly exists for me any more. All the things I remember with pleasure have been torn down and been replaced by bullshit. They want to make a mall of it. Downtown Boise, all covered, is like a cattle chute for customers, my mother says. All just for selling and consuming. I remember all those wonderful things that just aren't there any more. Boise is a corruption of "le bois." Trees. It used to be like a little cup of trees. A river runs right through the middle. You could hardly see more than two or three buildings. The statehouse and Hotel Boise. Just trees and this river. Oh, corridors of green. Trees so old and big that came together and made little corridors. It was against the law to shoot a squirrel, and the place was just all full of little brown squirrels. Old, old houses and a sense of community. None of that's there any more. They've cut down the trees, they tore down the old buildings. It's a real consumer town. What I remember with any pleasure is gone.

I was always a misfit, so I didn't have nice memories of, say, going to school. I didn't relate well to the kids 'cause I could read faster than they did. I was in third grade, and they had these reading tests, and I had very high scores. I didn't think I was that much smarter than anyone else. It's just that I read since I was a little bitty kid. You weren't supposed to be smart when you were a girl in 1949 in Boise, Idaho. You weren't supposed to let anybody know you knew anything. (Laughs.)

One day I got out of school, there were four or five big girls out there, fifth and sixth graders. They dragged me into the alley and knocked me down and told me I had to crawl home. They told me I shouldn't get such good scores any more. Like some kind of kid Mafia. (Laughs.) They're poking me with sticks. I lost my temper. I just became completely enraged, and I hurt a couple of 'em pretty bad. I hit one of 'em in the Adam's apple, and she had to stay out of school for a week. I kicked another in the groin, and she couldn't walk. And I ran home. I remember I threw up for about half an hour after I had gone into this terrible rage. I still think about it. I have not got used to the idea that somebody could do something like that to another person because that person was winning. Their sense was that I was winning. My sense was I wasn't competing.

I'm not trying to beat anybody out. I do what I do. It seems awful to me that anybody bases their whole life on winning. I always loved that song where Malvina Reynolds says:

I don't mind wearing raggedy britches
Because them that succeeds are sons of bitches.
I don't mind failing in this world.

There's another line:

I'll stay down here with the raggedy crew
If gettin' up there means steppin' on you.

I never thought of myself as being really poor because we had a house. We didn't have any money at all. But I think of myself as privileged because we had so many books and a place to live. . . .

Since 1966 I've been on my own. I've been so lucky in the friends that have come to me. People who've put me up across the country. I consider myself to be incredibly successful. I don't have any money, but I'm respected by those whose respect I crave. I'm given love by my audiences, and I make enough money to get along. I'd like it to be a little easier, but I do want my way.

I can't live with despair. I don't want to live with the notion that it's all downhill from here. I don't believe that. I don't have a sense of despair because I'm alive. When I'm dead, I don't expect to have a sense of anything. (Laughs.)

I look at my children and I could develop a sense of despair. My oldest son committed suicide. He went to some trouble to make me understand that that was not directed at me. But I can't figure out why I couldn't impart to him this sense of delight in being alive.

I look at a lot of these other children and I feel sorry for them. They get bored. I don't remember ever being bored. They're not curious. They practice alienation as if it was a thing to do. I think there's a giant conspiracy on the part of—who? ITT or them?—the rich, the powerful, the manipulators, to make us all the same. Make sure that we watch a lot of television. Make sure that we all have credit cards and cars and houses that are all kind of sleazy. We're so afraid we'll lose 'em that we'll do anything they want us to do to keep those things. I think that sense of values that measures a person's worth by how much they have is perpetrated by those rich and powerful people. To me, the most valuable people are the ones who kick and scream and won't go there. Who insist on being mavericks. Who refuse to go in that direction.

I have no intention of going under. I will play my drum my way.

✍ STUDS TERKEL
Rafael Rosa

He's a bellhop at a small theatrical hotel in Manhattan. He is forever smiling, eager to please, and quick to talk. He is the second youngest of ten brothers. He is nineteen.

"My parents were born in Puerto Rico. They been here a good seventeen years. My father works right here in the hotel, a houseman. My parents at home speak Spanish. I was born here in New York City, so when I went to school, my Spanish started turnin' poor. I figured it this way: I might as well hang on to both languages. Now when a Spanish-speaking person comes up to me, I like stutter. I made it to second year at high school."

My American Dream is to be famous. Like a big boss at a big firm, sit back, relax, and just collect. Oh, I treat my employees nice, pay 'em real good, don't overwork 'em too much, not like most bosses, they fire you right away.

I really would like to have a chauffeur-driven limousine, have a bar one side, color TV on the other. The chicks, the girls, oh yeah. Instead of coming in at eight in the morning and leavin' at eight in the afternoon. Maybe I'll invent something one of these days and wind up a millionaire. As for now, I'd really like to be chief pilot at the air force.

As I ride my bike here in New York, I see all these elegant-looking people, fancy-dressed, riding around in a limousine, just looking all normal. I figured if they can do, why can't I? Why can't I just go out there and get myself driven around for a while? I haven't hit it big yet, but I'm still working on it.

As I started growing older, I figured it's a jungle out there, you better grab a vine. So I grabbed a vine, and here I landed. (Laughs.) It's really hard out there in the city; you can't get a job any more. I would just like to be on TV, a newsman or something.

My friends are always talkin' about havin' a nice sheen. That's a nice car or van, something set up real nice on the inside with foldaway beds and wall-to-wall carpeting and paneling, fat tires, mufflers sticking out on the side, and speeding. Usually, they get together on this highway and they would race each other at the flat. It's really incredible. I don't see how these guys can do that. Drag racing.

I wanted to be a taxi driver. I figured it would be an exciting job, just riding around all day. Plus I had that driving fever. Most of the time, I dream I can fly, be all the way up there on the top. But I don't see how, unless I invent something, eh? Anti-gravity belt or something like that. It would cost a lot of loot just to make one of those. I'm a bicycle mechanic now. I ride 'em on one wheel also, but I don't think that's gonna get me far. I'd really like to be a motorcycle driver and explore the world.

Most of the time, I'm usually out in the streets, lookin' around. Scope on the nice women who pass by. I like their wardrobes and the way they walk, the way they talk. I should really be a gift to all women. I don't know how I'm gonna do it, but it's gonna be done somehow. (Laughs.)

My brother works in the post office, makin' some allright money. My other brother works in a factory, getting some good money as long as he can put in overtime. We're all in the same business, tryin' to move up, tryin' to see if we can get this "flat fixed" place or a grocery store. With the right location, we'll move up.

I would really like to invest in something *real big,* like in baby food. You can never run out of baby food. And cars. We'll never run out of cars as long as we don't run out of people. I could invest in tires. Where there's tires, there's automobiles. I guess I'm gonna have to hit it big.

People today are more like keepin' it to themselves. They don't let their emotions show. They're afraid to lose respect, cool. I'm open most of the time, I kinda like to turn off and on. I'm the kind of guy that gets along with everybody. I'm Puerto Rican and I got the complexion of a Negro, so I can fall to either side. I've been chased by whites a couple of times, but nothing special happens.

What's goin' on these days with all the violence, a person's gotta think twice of walking down the street. One time I got mugged in the

South Bronx. Three guys jumped me as I was walking down this dark street. One guy stops me for a cigarette, and as I go to give him one, two guys grab me from behind. They just started beatin' on me and took all my money and left me on the floor and fled. I recovered, and now I think twice about it. Before I was mugged, I walked down any street. I'd rather walk around a dark street than go through it, no matter how much time it's gonna take me to get there. If people call ya, I just keep on walking if I don't know the person. I look back and just keep walking.

I suggest: Don't walk alone at night. Walk with a stick to protect yourself. Don't get too high because it slows down your reflexes. You gotta keep your head clear. They say: Never look back. In real life, you gotta look back.

ℒ❤ ROBERT BELLAH, RICHARD MADSEN, WILLIAM M. SULLIVAN, ANN SWIDLER, STEVEN M. TIPTON

Joe Gorman

Joe has always lived in the small town where his father and mother have spent most of their lives: Suffolk, Massachusetts, a community of fewer than 20,000 people, about a half-hour's drive from Boston. Suffolk was founded in 1632, and about six months before one of us interviewed Joe Gorman, the town celebrated its 250th anniversary. Joe had taken charge of organizing the celebrations, although he had not originally been asked to do so. During the early phases of planning the anniversary festivities, the town manager appointed a committee of locally prominent townspeople that did not include Joe. But the problem was that practically none of its members had much experience in planning such a complicated event. To make matters worse, according to Joe, about half of them were more interested in getting their names in the paper than in doing much work. As a result, the first event in the long series of planned anniversary celebrations had been a fiasco—a large community dinner with only enough food for about half of the people who showed up. Joe Gorman knew that he had the ability to organize the celebrations successfully, and he felt a kind of duty to do whatever he could to help. So he got himself on the committee and became, in fact if not in name, its head.

Under Joe's direction, the anniversary celebration turned out to be a grand success. The festivities stretched out for nine months. There were parades, concerts, a carnival, athletic contests, dinners, dances, and ecumenical religious services, all well attended and smoothly organized. The fundamental meaning of the celebration was expressed for Joe in the slogan: "We are doing it together." As he put it, "That's so important—to work to get as many people as possible active." Another key theme was the importance of the family. The inspiration for many of the events came from the fact that that year had been proclaimed by the United Nations to be "the year of the family." For Joe, the highlight of the festivities was a softball tournament in which each team was made up of members of a different extended family. "We had eight clans—eight big families from Suffolk—in the tournament. In one of them some people came clear from Connecticut just to play softball on the side of their family. You know, for me the best time of the whole celebration was standing there back behind the bleachers after the softball games with members of the families that had played and talking with them about their families and drinking champagne. That to me was the ultimate. During the games between the clans, on many occasions, lots of people showed up besides the players to watch the game and see how people in the families were doing."

Another of the most inspiring events of the anniversary celebration was a day given over to the town's senior citizens. "We told people that this was their chance now to come together and see the people who had contributed to this town. They had an afternoon on the Common where they sold baked goods and made an awful lot of money." The whole series of anniversary celebrations was "so successful that the first thing that people said after it was over was, 'Why can't we have one every year?'" Accordingly, the town fathers decided to have an annual celebration and made Joe Gorman the head of the committee for the next year's celebration.

In Joe's vocabulary, *success* is a very important word. But throughout our conversation with him, it was consistently applied not to any status he had gained for himself or even to any accomplishment he had realized by himself. *Success* rather applied to the experience of togetherness the community had created partially through his efforts. "We had a lot of hassles [in organizing the anniversary celebration] and a lot of complaints that we had to deal with before we got it all rolling. But when it was over, the town was totally in favor of it. And even most of those people who had been opposed to various things came up to me and said that they were totally for having it again this year. So it was a great event, a great success, and it really brought the town together. If it's successful again this year, we're going to have it year after year. It was a great success. It was great for the community. But I didn't do it. The Suffolk family did it. Yes, it's the Suffolk family, and I love being a part of it."

This is not to say that Joe does not care about receiving personal rewards for his work within the community. What he considers to be one of the greatest events of his life happened to him several months after Suffolk's anniversary celebrations were finished. He was named Good Guy of the Year in Suffolk and a huge celebration was held for him by the business and civic leaders of the town. "It was a complete surprise for me. They got me to cooperate in it by telling me that they were putting on a benefit for someone else, one of my co-workers at the factory. It was really embarrassing because I was getting after some people thinking that they weren't doing enough in preparation for this celebration for this co-worker, and then I showed up and it was for me." Joe was immensely gratified at this expression of community affection. But it was important for him that it came as a surprise—that he experienced it as a reward he had not consciously worked for.

Besides enjoying the prestige the community has "spontaneously" given him, Joe also receives an income from his efforts on behalf of the community. It is, in fact, part of his profession to be a community "good guy." He is director of public relations for one of the large manufacturing companies located in Suffolk. Like most such companies, the firm that employs Joe wants to maintain good relations with the townspeople, and to do this it contributes money to community recreation programs and other charities. It is part of Joe Gorman's job to help his company decide how best to help the town. Even though much of it happens to be part of his job, however, Joe's community service work clearly remains a labor of love. He has been offered promotions to positions in his company's head office in Houston, but he has refused them. For him, his position in the community is more important than his status within his company. As he sees it, he works so hard for the town because he is a "natural citizen" of Suffolk. "I was born here. My father set up the athletic program at Suffolk High. Friendship alone with the people would keep me here. We will always stay here. It is my home."

2 The Writing Process

THINKING ABOUT AUDIENCE AND PURPOSE

When writers write, they do it for a reason—to inform, explain, persuade, entertain; to give advice, resolve a disagreement, solve a problem. To put it another way, the writer tries to do something to the reader, to move the reader in some way.

True, writing can be a private matter. In diaries and journals, we write for ourselves. We record impressions and try to put our thoughts and feelings into words. If this private writing is an end in itself, we don't need to consider anyone but ourselves. But when we go public *(publish)*, questions of purpose and audience enter the picture, and they play a crucial role in determining what we say and how we say it.

We all use language in different ways at different times, depending on how we feel about the subject and to whom we are talking. We don't talk the same way in a classroom as we do when we're home with friends. We don't use the same voice in a letter to a brother or sister as we do in an application for a scholarship. Purpose, attitude, and audience all enter into deciding what to say and how to say it.

In some situations, these elements are automatically present. For example, suppose you are angry with your representative in Congress for voting against a bill to provide money for student loans. You want to express your opinion in a letter. In a case such as this, you know why you are writing, you know what you want to accomplish, and you know who your reader is. Knowing these things helps to shape your letter. It influences the tone you take (you want to let the representative know you are upset, but you don't want to sound like a raving crank). And it influences what you say (your representative is familiar with the situation, so you don't need to explain it in detail).

All of these elements, working together, create the context for the writing. And it is the context that helps to determine things such as how to approach the reader, how much to say, how to say it, and how to arrange your material. As we write this, for instance, we have in the back of our mind a composite image of the students who have passed through our classes. Sometimes we'll even single out a particular student to act as our reader. A common affliction of teachers is that they are so familiar with their subject that they have trouble explaining it to a newcomer. They might gloss over points that need careful explanation, or not give enough examples, or not realize that a term needs to be defined. So in a real sense, our students are helping us write this book.

INVENTING A READER

Many writing situations, especially in school, are not as clear-cut as the example of the letter to the representative. Class assignments are often either practice exercises or proof that you have mastered the subject. The context is missing. You might not know exactly what you think and feel about a subject, or who your readers are, or how you want to affect them.

A good way to approach a situation like this is to start with what is called an exploratory, or discovery, draft. In other words, start by writing for yourself. Use writing to find out what you *do* think about the subject, why you hold a certain view, what kind of material you might include in your paper. Writing is not only a means of communication; it is also a tool for discovery. In a line that is often quoted, the English novelist E. M. Forster once remarked, "How do I know what I think until I see what I say?" When you write for yourself, you probe and question your own mind. Putting your thoughts and feelings and experiences in words can help you to see them more clearly, can raise issues you might not have considered, and can even lead you in directions you wouldn't have imagined otherwise.

Writing for yourself is a good way to begin. (If you want to sound like a raving crank, go ahead and sound like one.) But at some point, the reader has to be taken into account. If there isn't a real one, it might be necessary to invent one.

There are a couple of ways, depending on the situation, to think about the invented readers—as either a general audience or as readers with specific characteristics.

When you write for a group of your peers, people with a common interest, or a pen-pal in another country, you are writing for a specific audience. You have an idea of what your readers know, what their interests are, what kind of language will reach them. In other words, you have a sharp image of your reader in mind. But if you don't know exactly to whom you're writing, the image of the reader can become fuzzy, out of focus—or disappear altogether.

Good writers seem to have a built-in sense of audience—what the writer Robert Graves called "the reader over your shoulder." This sense of a reader is necessary to bridge the gap between what we, as writers, *know* we mean and what someone else might *think* we mean. The reader over your shoulder is a curious soul who is always saying things like, "What do you mean by that? Does that really say what you mean? I don't understand; give me an example. What has this got to do with that?"

One way to invent an audience is to ask and answer a few questions. For example, are you writing specifically for men, women, children, teenagers, fellow students, generation-X, middle-aged adults, senior citizens, other guitar players, computer hackers? Do your readers share your cultural background, or are they from a different culture? (In addition to national origin and race, cultural differences can include such divisions as city/country, east/west, north/south, rich/poor, and working class/managerial class.) How much do your readers already know about the subject? (How much do you need to explain?) Do your readers share your concerns and interests? Or do you need to *create* interest? What are your readers' moral, religious, and political beliefs? Are your readers likely to be hostile or friendly toward your point of view?

Answering these questions about your readers will help with decisions about how to approach them, how to arrange material, what information to include, what points to discuss, and what kind of language to use.

TAKING IT A STEP AT A TIME

The *worst* way to go about the job of writing is to try to do everything at once. The writer who tries to turn out a finished paper on the first try, sentence by sentence, from start to finish, is in for a frustrating time. There is simply too much to think about. Writing is a complex activity that involves a whole range of skills, from inventing an overall design to punctuating sentences and finding the right words. If you try to do all of this at once, you're most likely making the task more difficult than it needs to be.

There is a common misconception that good writers can sit down at a typewriter and knock off perfect copy every time. Not so. The finished product is the tip of the iceberg; what you don't see is the mass of material lurking beneath the surface. Try taking it a step at a time.

Each writer is different, so no single formula is going to work for everyone. Nevertheless, most writers know that a piece of writing grows and develops over time, and that it is a waste of energy to spend time at the beginning fiddling with sentences when some of them will probably need to be cut or revised later on. As you progress as a writer you will discover your own way of working. The process described below is meant to suggest a starting point; it is not set in concrete. You might find that skipping or rearranging some steps works best for you. Your temperament, your knowledge of the subject, your purpose, and your audience will all influence the way you approach any writing project. We recommend, however, that you begin by following this scheme; then experiment with different techniques, and make adjustments as you develop your skills.

Gathering Ideas

Students often tell us that the hardest part of writing is getting started. Most of the time, that's because they're trying to grind their way through the paper sentence by sentence, from beginning to end. So start somewhere else. Start at any point where you've got something to say and work from there. Don't always try to begin with the introduction. Often, the introduction is written last. How can you introduce something if you don't know what it is?

The first step in the writing process is sometimes called *prewriting*. As the name suggests, it is what the writer does before the actual writing. In this stage, don't be concerned with order, sentence structure, or mechanics. Banish them from your mind. The idea is to get as much as possible down on paper in any order it comes to you. Prewriting gets you going and eliminates worries about correctness. It *should* be messy.

Here are some techniques that will help you get started:

Listing

Probably the simplest way to get started is to make a list of ideas. Ideas don't have to be fully formed, and they don't have to be in any particular order. Just key words and phrases—enough to remind you of the idea—will do the job.

If you are writing about written sources, make notes about those parts of the sources that seem most important or that relate to the question on which you are writing. Note page numbers and write down key words that will remind you of what a particular passage says. Include notes on your own ideas and responses as you go along.

If you are writing from your own experience, jot down anything that comes to mind as you think about the topic. Put down everything you can think of as quickly as you can.

Brainstorming

Brainstorming is essentially making a list with other people. It should go quickly, without discussion of the merits of anyone's ideas. Visualize the word—*brain-storm*—and you should get some idea of what we mean. When you brainstorm, you put down ideas as they arrive, without judging or editing, even though they might seem stupid at the time. Ideas don't have to be expressed in full sentences, and they don't have to follow any kind of sequence. In short, at this stage, don't worry about any of the things that usually produce red marks from English teachers.

Freewriting

Freewriting is writing at a fairly fast pace, without stopping (even to think), for a set time—usually five or ten minutes. If, while you are doing this, you find yourself stumped for something to say, put down anything that comes to mind, regardless of whether it has anything to do with the subject. Put down nonsense. The important thing is to keep the pen moving, keep words coming.

Mapping

Writing is a *linear* process—you put one word after another, in a line. But this isn't the only way to gather ideas. Sometimes, it is easier to generate ideas if you use a non-linear approach. *Mapping* (or, as it is sometimes called, *clustering*) is a prewriting technique that frees the writer from linear thinking. Connections among ideas are represented by clusters of circles on a blank sheet of paper. The following example shows how thinking about the American Dream produces several clusters of ideas. Notice that in addition to the clusters, the writer has used some words that indicate specific kinds of connections: "but" indicates contrast; "contradiction?" indicates possible conflict. Words that suggest connections like these help to show how the writer is thinking about the subject.

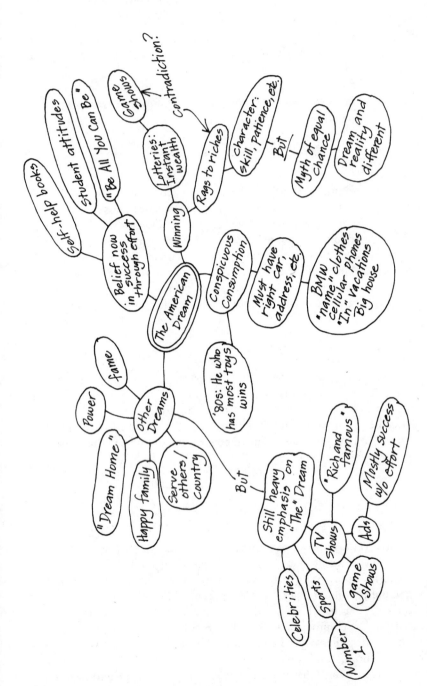

Figure 2.1 Mapping

Mapping can reveal relationships and ways of organizing material. Notice that in our example, the map suggests four main clusters of ideas. These clusters could be used as a framework for organizing a paragraph.

Although prewriting techniques are usually used at the beginning, they are also useful at other stages in the process. They can be used at any point, whenever you need to collect your thoughts or whenever you're stuck for what to do next.

Focusing and Planning

Once you have some words on paper, you can begin to think about how to focus and organize your paper. To focus means to clarify the scope and purpose of the paper. An organizational plan can be anything from a brief list of main points to a full-blown outline with Roman numerals, capital letters, numbers, and the rest of it.

Deciding on Your Main Idea

To start, you must answer one basic question: *What's the main point you want to make here?* Most writing, unless it is simply a report, has a single main point, the key idea the writer wants to convey. A statement of this will be your thesis. Your thesis might undergo some changes as you develop the paper, so at this point think of it as a *tentative* thesis.

Write your tentative thesis at the top of a sheet of paper.

Developing a Working Plan

Once you have written your thesis, the next step is to decide what reasons, arguments, and information you need to support it. To get an idea of where the whole paper is going, it is a good idea to make a *working plan*. A working plan is like a rough sketch of the paper, a diagram of its overall structure. A good way to begin is to look through your prewriting, marking the most important parts: probably just a few main points that you want to be sure to cover. You might even want to number them in the order you think they should appear in the paper. When you are trying to organize your material, look first for a natural order: *least important to most important, simple to complex, familiar to unfamiliar, problem to solution, before to after.* If you are working with a time sequence, such as describing a process or giving directions on how to do something, break the sequence into its major stages. If you are explaining a complex subject, think about what your readers need to know first, second, third, etc. Number the items on your list according to what you think is the best order.

Working plans, as we said, are rough sketches. They are especially useful in situations, like essay exams, where you have to write something quickly. Sometimes, though, you might be asked to write a more complete formal outline, which is done according to a standard form. We will explain this kind of outline later in this section.

To illustrate some of the different kinds of plans and outlines, we will use the example of a student's paper. This student wrote her response to two of the readings in the previous chapter: "Arnold Schwarzenegger" and "Rafael Rosa." Here is what she wrote.

Student Sample: Dreams and Realities

Arnold Schwarzenegger is a famous body builder and movie star. Rafael Rosa is a bellhop in a Manhattan hotel. Both of these men have big dreams, and both of them believe in the American Dream of fame and fortune. But that's where the similarity ends. Schwarzenegger has made it, while Rosa is still a bellhop. To realize his dream, Schwarzenegger pursued it with a single-minded dedication, while Rosa is still fantasizing about what he might be.

At an early age, Schwarzenegger learned to set his priorities, and throughout his career he let nothing distract him from his goal. When he was ten, he dreamt that he wanted to be the best in the world at something. At the age of fifteen, he dreamt that he wanted to be the best body builder. Five years later, he won the Mr. Universe contest. He was already famous when he came to the United States from Austria, but he knew he wanted more. So he set his sights on the movies. Schwarzenegger's attitude about achieving success is simple. He believes that he must control his emotions and feelings and not let anything distract him. He says, "Any emotional things inside me, I try to keep cold so it doesn't interfere with my training." Furthermore, he believes that a person must decide at an early age whether to live a "normal life" or "to achieve things you want to achieve."

Rafael Rosa also dreams of achieving great things, but he lacks the conviction and direction he needs to be successful. At the beginning of his interview he says, "My American Dream is to be famous." However, he seems very confused about what he really wants and needs to achieve his dream. During the interview he mentions a total of seven different things he wants to do, all of which would take considerable ambition and education to even begin. He wants to be a boss, a pilot, an inventor, an investor, and so on. But mostly he daydreams about the things he would like to have and the style in which he would like to live. He jumps from one thing to another like a bee flitting from flower to flower. In contrast to Schwarzenegger, he never talks about *how* he plans to get where he wants to go. Not everyone can be like Arnold Schwarzenegger. Not everyone would want to. Some would prefer a "normal" life. Rafael Rosa, however, has caught the dream of wealth and fame and power. Unfortunately, he has no idea of how to pursue it. He seems to know, sadly, that his only hope is to get lucky; "I guess I'm gonna have to hit it big," he says. I can see him standing in line every week to buy a lottery ticket. It's a shame. In a way, Rafael can be seen as a victim of the American Dream. It has filled his mind with fantasies of great things he will probably never have. But underneath all his daydreaming, Rafael sounds like a warm and friendly young man, someone who likes people and gets along well with them. Maybe for him a "normal" life would not be such a bad thing.

BLOCKING OUT   One of the simplest ways to put your material in order is to think of a paper as a series of blocks, each one dealing with a main supporting point. Figure 2.2 on page 30 is a block plan for the student's paper "Dreams and Realities."

THE WORKING OUTLINE   In drawing, an outline is a line that describes the overall shape of the subject. The same is true in writing. Any outline suggests two things: first, the relationship between main ideas and supporting information, and second, the order in which the material will be presented.

A working outline, like a block plan, should at least show the thesis and the main supporting points. It may also indicate the kind of specific information that will be included. Here is a working outline:

Dreams and Realities

Thesis: To realize his dream, Schwarzenegger pursued it with a single-minded dedication, while Rosa is still fantasizing about what he might be.

1. Schwarz.—set priorities early & always focused on goals.
   —knows what he wants when he's a boy
      —dream at age 10
      —dream at age 15
   —later, never allows distractions
      —keeps emotions cold
2. Rosa—doesn't have conviction or direction for success
   —dreams of fame
   —confused about how to achieve goals

BLOCKING OUT

Thesis: Arnold pursues goals
        Raphael fantasizes

Arnold
- Set priorities early
- focused on goals
  dreamed of being best
  dreamed of body building
  No distractions
  Kept emotions cold

Raphael
— No conviction or direction
— Dreams of fame
        — but —
No idea how to achieve
Mentions too many things
  he wants to be

Raphael "victim" of dream?
Maybe normal life OK

Figure 2.2   Blocking Out

THE TREE DIAGRAM   Another way to visualize the organization of a paper is the *tree diagram*. Like other kinds of plans, a tree diagram shows the thesis, the main supporting points, and the kind of information to be included. However, a tree diagram gives a different visual layout of the paper, which for some people makes it easier to see relationships. The main difference between a tree diagram and a block plan or working outline is that a tree diagram does not indicate the *order* in which the points will be presented in the paper. It simply indicates *levels* of support. Figure 2.3 is an example of a tree diagram.

Tree Diagram

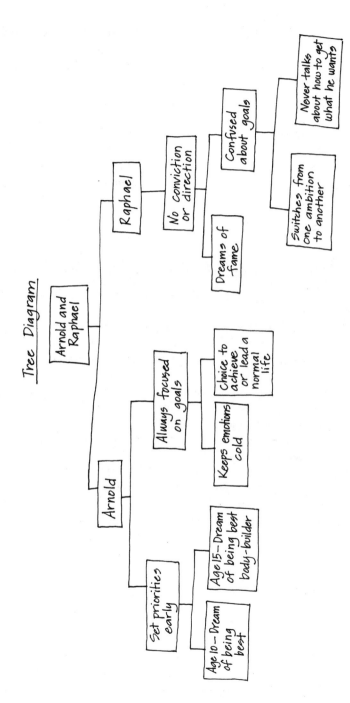

Figure 2.3   Tree Diagram

Whichever kind of plan you use, the guiding principle is the same: a plan reflects the relationship of the parts (supporting points) to the whole (thesis).

THE FORMAL OUTLINE   A formal outline is a more fully developed outline that is constructed according to a conventional system of notation. A formal outline begins with the title and thesis statement, and then indicates the points to be covered, using the following system: Roman numerals for the main points, capital letters for the main supporting points, then Arabic numbers and lower case letters for more specific information. Here is an outline of "Dreams and Realities":

Dreams and Realities

Thesis: To realize his dream, Schwarzenegger pursued it with a single-minded dedication, while Rosa is still fantasizing about what he might be.

    I. Schwarzenegger set his priorities early, and later in life always focused on his goal.
      A. When he was a boy, he knew he wanted to be the best.
        1. At the age of 10, he dreamt of being the best at something.
        2. At 15, he dreamt of being the best body builder.
      B. He never lets anything distract him from his goal.
        1. He keeps his emotions cold.
        2. He believes that a person must decide early whether to achieve goals or lead a "normal" life.
    II. Rosa lacks the conviction and direction needed for success.
      A. He dreams of fame.
      B. He's confused about how to achieve his goals.
        1. He mentions many things he'd like to be.
        2. He never talks about how to get what he wants.
Conclusion: Rafael Rosa could be seen as a victim of the American Dream.

Notice that the indentations in the outline reflect the *order* and *level* of points. For example, the indented capital "A" tells you that point will be the first one discussed after the main heading "I" and that it will support the main heading. The same is true of the other numbers and letters.

Notice also that there is always more than one number or letter. There is never an "A" without a "B" or a "1" without a "2." The reason for this is that the outline reflects the principle of *division;* in other words, the "A" and "B" say that main heading "I" is going to be divided into two parts. A subject can't be divided into just one part. If you find that in your outline there is just one number or letter, combine that item with the one above it. In other words, make it part of the larger heading.

ANOTHER APPROACH: THE DISCOVERY DRAFT   Here's a question some of you might be asking: "Do I *always* have to go through this series of steps? Is writing *always* that methodical? Not necessarily. Sometimes a different approach can work better. Sometimes the *act* of writing itself can be a way of discovering what you have to say. Putting thoughts into words, following them wherever they take you, can lead to unexpected and surprising places. For example, if you begin to write about a childhood experience, you very well might find that long-forgotten memories suddenly appear in vivid detail. Writing often works by a process of *association:* you write down one thought, which triggers another, which triggers another, which triggers another.

So if you are not sure where you are going, try writing a quick draft first to see what ideas come out of the process. Such a draft is called a *discovery draft,* and as the name suggests, its purpose is to find out what you think about a subject. A discovery draft should be written freely, without concern for organization, style, and correctness. It is for your eyes only.

After you have written a discovery draft, you can comb through it, pick out the main points you have raised, and *then,* if it needs reorganizing, make your plan. Getting started is difficult: if doing it one way doesn't work, try another.

Drafting

A first draft is an attempt to write a complete piece, from beginning to end. It should be done fairly quickly, following the plan and fleshing out your ideas. But don't concern yourself too much with anything that might block the flow of thought—things such as sentence structure, word choice, mechanics. Remember: The idea is to concentrate on one thing at a time; don't frustrate yourself by trying to do too much at once. In writing your first draft, work for an overall sense of beginning, development, and conclusion.

Revising and Editing

The first draft might be exactly what you want—or not. Probably not. It usually needs some tinkering. Look over your draft with the eyes of a reader coming to it for the first time. Are all of your points clearly and fully developed? Does the introduction entice a reader to continue reading? Would a different arrangement make the piece easier to follow or more forceful in its message? Does the conclusion re-emphasize the most important point? Is there anything that could be cut without loss of meaning or clarity?

Questions like these—questions of content and organization—are the kinds of questions to ask yourself during revision. Keep your thinking about the first draft loose. Remain open to new ideas. You might need a second or third draft before you get it right.

Until you are satisfied with your draft, it is not time to get out the handbook and dictionary. Working on the details comes in the next step—editing.

Editing is mainly work on sentence structure and wording. Could you make your point more clearly, more forcefully, more economically (in fewer words)? Could sentences be simplified or combined? Are sentences joined smoothly together (could a reader easily follow your thought from one sentence to the next)? Have you chosen the best words to convey your meaning?

Most editing concerns have to do with style—*how* you say what you say. For now, probably the best thing you can do is to read the paper aloud—either to yourself or to someone else. Notice how it sounds; language, after all, comes through the ear. As you read, note any passages that seem clumsy, wordy, or disconnected. Then try to rephrase them so that they read more easily.

Proofreading

The final step requires courage, determination, and a willingness to endure extreme boredom. It is menial labor. Check spelling—look up any words you are not sure of. Check to see that sentences are complete and correctly punctuated. If you know that you tend to make a particular error (such as sentence fragments or run-on sentences), read your paper over, looking for just that problem. Some writers even suggest reading the paper backwards, sentence by sentence, from the last to the first. This way it is easier to disregard meaning and concentrate on mechanics.

When you proofread, it is important to go word by word, sentence by sentence. You are not reading for meaning now; you are reading for craft. You probably won't want to do it. After you finish the final draft, you'll probably want to get rid of the paper as soon as you can. You'll be tired of it. Nevertheless, careful proofreading is as important as any other part of the process. A messy paper, full of misspellings and sentence errors, can negate all the work you've put into it.

As you work through these steps, try different approaches and see what works best for you. There is no *right* way to write. If you get stuck or something isn't working, try something else. The main lesson here is to break the job into parts that are more easily manageable. Don't try to do it all at once.

3 Writing Essays

In college, you will need to be able to write a number of different types of papers; you may be asked to report on a scientific experiment, to explain a psychological concept, to analyze a short story, to evaluate a candidate's position on a public issue, or to argue for or against a controversial proposal.

You have already done some reporting in the summaries you wrote in Chapter 1. But although reporting is an important part of college writing, you will usually have to do more than that. You will have to analyze information and ideas, draw conclusions, and develop and support your views. In this chapter we will look at different ways of discovering ideas, developing and shaping them into essays and paragraphs.

FROM TALKING TO WRITING

Suppose a friend asks you what you think of a movie you've just seen. Your first impulse would probably be to give it, like Siskel and Ebert, a "thumbs up" or a "thumbs down." In other words, you give your general impression. But most people wouldn't be satisfied with a simple yes or no, thumbs up or thumbs down. They would want to know why. They would want to know the *reasons* for your opinion.

This pattern is typical of much conversation: give an opinion, explain why you hold it. It's also the natural pattern of much writing. The difference—big difference—is that when you write you're talking to someone who isn't present. It's lonely work; no one is there to ask "Why?" or wrinkle a brow or raise an eyebrow. It's the job of the solitary writer to play both parts, to imagine a listener and to ask the questions a listener would ask.

Writing also makes you think more clearly about what you really mean and how you can best put it into words. And it allows you to order your ideas so that a reader can most easily follow the path of your thought, step by step.

ELEMENTS OF AN ESSAY

In this book we will deal primarily with writing intended to inform and explain (*expository* writing), and to some extent with writing intended to persuade and argue.

Most college writing, aside from simple reports and summaries, asks that you explain and support a particular view you have formed about the subject. You have to think about the subject, form a conclusion about it, and then explain *why* you came to that conclusion. This general pattern we will call *essay form:* making a point and developing it. As you will see, there are many ways of doing this.

The Introduction and Thesis

Traditionally, the essay is divided into three parts. The first part consists of an *introduction* and a statement of the essay's main point. The statement of the main point is called the *thesis*. In a short paper, it is usually a single sentence that comes at the end of a brief introductory paragraph; in a longer paper, it might come after several introductory paragraphs. There are exceptions to this, in which the thesis is saved for the end or developed in stages throughout the essay. Most often, however, it comes near the beginning. The thesis is often called the *controlling idea* because in large part it controls what kind of material goes into the rest of the essay.

The *introduction* can serve several purposes: it can stimulate the readers' interest, provide background information, or suggest why the topic is significant. The introduction sets the tone and establishes the context for the writer's thesis.

In the following example, from the student paper included in Part 2, Chapter 10, notice how the introduction presents the necessary background information for the reader. The writer introduces the essays to be discussed, gives short summaries of them, and at the end states her thesis (underlined).

Student Sample: Two Ways of Responding to Racism

Two African American writers describe very different ways of dealing with racism. In his essay "Black Men and Public Space," Brent Staples tells how he, a black man, inspires fear in white people when he encounters them in public places, particularly at night. Because he is black, people assume he is a dangerous character. Women cross the street to avoid him, and people in the subway move away. Staples deals with these situations by trying to portray himself as a harmless person. His way of handling racial prejudice is to change his behavior. The second writer, Zora Neale Hurston, shows us another way of dealing with racism. In "How It Feels to Be Colored Me," she describes how she faces racism directly through the strength of her own personality. Where Staples changes his behavior to avoid racial tension, Hurston doesn't change herself for anyone.

The Body

The second part of an essay, the *body,* can contain any number of paragraphs, all of which explain and support the thesis in various ways. In the thesis statement the writer makes a *claim* about the subject. To convince a reader that the claim is valid, the writer needs to give adequate reasons and information.

For example, in the essay that follows in this chapter, "Poker and the American Dream," Rex Jones analyzes the reasons why senior citizens play poker in some California poker clubs. His central claim is that they play in order to "pursue their vision of the American Dream." Such a statement raises questions, and these questions need to be answered in the body: how is poker similar to the American Dream? How do you know that people play for this reason and not for some other? Is the evidence strong enough to support the conclusion? (See the following chapter, "Writing Effective Paragraphs," for information on developing and organizing paragraphs.)

The Conclusion

Finally, an essay closes with a *conclusion* that returns in some way to the thesis, reminding the reader once again of the main point. It can also include such things as the writer's thoughts on the importance of the topic, speculations on the consequences of the writer's conclusions, suggestions for action, a strong final image, or an attempt to put the thesis into perspective. But whatever else it does, the conclusion gives the essay a sense of completion. Here, for instance, is the conclusion to the paper that we used as an example in discussing the introduction. In this conclusion, the writer does more than just summarize; she speculates on why these two people are so different.

> There are probably many reasons for these differences between the two writers. For one thing, Staples is a man, Hurston is a woman. Staples recognizes that "Women are particularly vulnerable to street violence, and young black males are drastically overrepresented among the perpetrators of that violence." Simply because he is a black male, Staples is seen as more dangerous, particularly in large, crime-filled cities like New York and Chicago. Moreover, Hurston was raised in a small Florida town where people were relatively friendly toward each other. Staples, who is from Chester, Pennsylvania, grew up "against a backdrop of gang warfare, street knifings, and murders." He learned to keep a low profile and stay out of fights. He says that his "shyness of combat has clear sources." Hurston describes herself as an outgoing, joyful child. She sat on the gatepost of her porch, waving and singing to people passing by. She felt that she belonged in her town. Staples never gives the feeling that he belonged anywhere. Hurston seems to belong wherever she goes. Staples is always a stranger.

Exercise: An Essay for Study

To study more closely how writers develop and organize essays, we will look at an example, an essay with the intriguing title "Poker and the American Dream." As you read the selection, apply the reading techniques you learned in the previous chapter.

1. Read the first two paragraphs (the quote from the advertising brochure is part of paragraph 1). Then read the last three paragraphs. This should give you a general idea of the main point—the author's thesis—and the overall structure of the essay. Try writing a statement of the thesis in your own words.

2. Read the whole essay carefully. As you read, ask yourself how each part helps to explain and support the author's thesis. Underline the main idea in each paragraph. Circle any words you don't know, then look them up in your dictionary and write short definitions in the margin.

After you have read the essay, see if you can answer the questions at the end ("Questions for Understanding").

✍ REX L. JONES

Poker and the American Dream

Poker is an American game. Its origins, style of play, and language are all American. The draw poker clubs of Gardena in southern California recognize this fact. An advertising brochure of one of the clubs states:

> Poker is America's favorite card game. Seventy million adults play cards and some 47 million prefer poker. Poker is as American as baseball and hotdogs. Many of our most famous Presidents were poker enthusiasts.

Poker is a pure expression of the American dream. Embodied in the action of the game is the ever-present notion that anyone with skill, individual initiative, patience, foresight, and a little luck can easily make the leap from rags to riches. In a recent article entitled "Who Dealt This Mess?" Barry Golson says that poker "is as perfect a microcosm as we have of the way a free-enterprise system is *supposed* to work, except that the rich don't necessarily get richer." He goes on to say that "in a limit game . . . a grocery clerk can humiliate an oil tycoon through sheer bravado—the object being, without exception, to bankrupt the bastard across the table."

Poker is an expression of the American dream in many other ways. We recognize the person who has achieved the American dream by conspicuous consumption. A house, a car, a color TV, a pocket full of credit cards, and a politician in the closet are some of the indications of success. In poker, the "winner" is easily recognized by diamonds, stickpins, car, clothes, bankroll, and the hangers on who flank him. He exudes rugged individualism—the winner at poker is his own man.

In the realization of the American dream, the arena is the system of free enterprise, where everyone has an equal chance; in the poker game, the arena is a system of free play, where all begin on equal footing. In the American dream, society is classless, anyone can play; it is the same with poker. In the American dream, the way to the top is up to you and you alone; in poker, too, winning is solely an individual effort. In the American dream, the winner takes all; in poker, there is no such thing as sharing the spoils.

The American dream and the game of poker thus have much in

common. The latter is the microcosm of the former. In Gardena, this melodrama is reenacted every day from 9 A.M. until 5 A.M. the next day. Most of the people who participate are the senior citizens of America—the retired, and the widowed, or that element of our society for whom the American dream has indeed become a living nightmare, because old age and retirement have made its realization next to impossible.

Daily, elderly men, living on their pensions and savings, and elderly women, living on inheritances and insurance premiums of their deceased husbands, frequent the poker clubs, often in shared taxis or cars, to pursue their vision of the American dream. They meet their friends, share stories of winning and losing, compare notes on racing forms, watch TV, eat, drink, and participate in the "action" with people from all walks of life. Small businessmen, bartenders, teachers, construction workers, doctors, students, hustlers, prostitutes, the unemployed, and tourists intermingle with the senior citizens, who all too often in our society are confined to the sterility of old-age homes or the loneliness of their rooms.

In Gardena, the poker clubs may be many things to many people, but to the aged they are—as expressed to me by an 83-year-old woman—a "godsend." In the clubs their lives attain a new meaning. In Gardena, few discuss their aches and pains or their imminent and inevitable deaths. The talk centers around poker and especially winning, which few if any are able to do consistently. No matter, there is always hope, and such hope is justified every day, when a few hit a big win. Winnings are remembered for years; losses are forgotten the next day. In the process, however, the American dream is perpetuated through poker play, and even the old can participate in the myth.

Poker Playing in Southern California

In California there are over 400 licensed and legalized draw-poker clubs. In Gardena, a sprawling suburb of about 50,000 people, located 10 miles south of downtown Los Angeles, poker is the major industry. The poker club payrolls amount to around $5 million annually. Thousands of southern Californians are attracted to its six poker parlors every year, most of them regular players. The Gardena clubs are the largest and best equipped of any of the California draw-poker clubs.

Each club is limited, by city law, to thirty-five tables; each table seats a maximum of eight players. In addition to the card tables, each club features a restaurant, lounge, and one or more color TV rooms. The restaurants serve decent food with diversified menus, at relatively low prices. Many serve weekly specials and buffets that attract hundreds of people who never sit at the poker tables. The clubs are tastefully decorated, by California standards, well lit, and provide free parking. They are located near major freeway systems and are therefore easily accessible to motor-crazed southern Californians.

Draw poker is still the number one attraction. In Gardena's clubs, as in most poker parlors in California, the house has no interest in the stakes of the games. The house provides the tables, cards, chips, game supervision, and other services, but the deal rotates among the players. Each player pays a "collection" to the house at the end of each half-hour of play, the amount being determined by the stakes of the table. The lower the stakes, the less the collection. The house then, essentially rents its services to those who wish to play poker. The collection, however, is no minor variable in terms of winning and losing.

Because of the collection at the end of each half-hour, a low-stakes game is a death wish. It took me some 1000 hours of poker playing to figure out this mathematical formula. In a game of, let's say, $1.00/$2.00 draw, the collection is $1.25 each half-hour. The "buy in," or the stakes that you are required to place in front of you on the table is $10.00. If all eight players at the table are of equal skill, and if at the end of 4 hours of play no player has won or lost at the card play, there will be no money on the table. Each and every player will be broke. Collectively, it costs $80.00 for 4 hours of play. The rent is not cheap.

As one moves to a higher-stakes game, the collection increases, but it increases disproportionately to the stakes of the game. For example, at a $10/$20 low draw game, the collection is $3.00 per half-hour. Collectively, at the end of 4 hours of play, it costs $192.00 per table to play. But the buy-in at $10/$20 low draw is $100.00. It would take from 16 to 17 hours, everything being equal, for the players at the table to go broke.

What this means for the regular players at Gardena is quite simple. Those who regularly play the low-stakes game, *even if they win at cards consistently,* will find it next to impossible to "beat the collection." They will lose money, not to the other players, but to the house. In 1970, I played regularly for 6 months in low-stakes games at Gardena, usually 1/2 high draw or 2/4 low draw. I played on the average of 50 hours a week, or a total of 1,500 hours. It cost me in collection fees an average of $3.00 per hour, or a total for 6 months of some $4,500. In tabulating the amount of money I spent at Gardena during that 6-month period, I estimated expenses of $2,000. Out of that $2,000 also came my food, transportation, and such other things as cigarettes and drinks. Any way I calculated it, I had won at cards. I estimate my winnings at close to $3,000, yet my bank account was some $2,000 short. What happened to the money? It went to the house.

I am convinced that this happens to every regular player at Gardena in low stakes games. This is substantiated by hundreds of interviews with people who play poker at Gardena and are aware that the house wins in the end. How else could the clubs meet a $5 million annual payroll, pay Gardena taxes, and also make a profit? . . .

The conclusion to my study is that the senior citizens who regularly play poker at Gardena lose money in one way or another. They spend their pensions or savings in order to frequent the clubs. The amount they lose is consistent with their income. The club owners recognize this, implicitly if not explicitly. As an example, last summer I played frequently at a $5/$10 low-draw game with a woman who was 76 years old and consistently lost money. In such a game, the losses can be heavy. An average win at a period of play in that game will range from $150 to $300. An average loss will amount to the same or more depending on the player. This woman knew this, because she had played the game in Gardena, in the same club, for over 20 years. She first began playing in the 1950s after moving to California from New York with her husband. Her husband, a successful businessman, died shortly after the move, leaving her with a fairly large income. After a period of boredom and loneliness, the woman soon discovered poker at Gardena, through a friend. Because she had the money, she rapidly moved to the high-stakes games, where the action was faster and more to her liking. During her play, she talked constantly, and frequently claimed that she had paid for the entire west wing of the club through collections over the years. She said that last year she had cashed $20,000 in checks at the cashier's window. At the end of the year, the owner of the club invited her into his office for a personal conference, and begged her to play at a lower-stakes game where she would not lose so much money. She refused, and said, "What else have I got to do with my money? Go on a goddamned world cruise with a bunch of old ladies? I'd rather lose it at poker!" . . .

It is my contention that the aged and retired play poker in Gardena for social and recreational reasons. They are reliving the American dream, which gives meaning to their lives. Poker functions to make them young again.

The Gardena clubs take the place of home life for the aged. They function quite simply as old-age homes, but offer a more exciting and stimulating environment than do regular institutions for the aged in our society. The clubs, unlike old-age homes, are not places to go and die but places to go and live. Here the aged, the retired, and the widowed are able to interact on a one-to-one basis with thousands of young people, who frequent the clubs simply to play cards. Here the regulars meet tourists from all over the United States and Canada. They meet and interact with people from all walks of life. The clubs offer something more to the regulars than the loneliness and passivity of old-age homes, where people spend most of their time thinking about illness, misfortune, and death. Such discussions are out of place in Gardena. . . .

As one 83-year-old woman put it at the end of an interview in which she systematically pointed out the evils and absurdities of playing poker at Gardena, "Son, if they closed Gardena tomorrow, I would die."

QUESTIONS FOR UNDERSTANDING

1. What are the specific similarities between poker and the American Dream discussed in paragraphs 3 and 4?

2. In paragraphs 5–7, the author focuses on the poker players. Why do the poker clubs appeal to elderly people? What does the author mean when he says at the end of paragraph 7, "even the old can participate in the myth"? What does the word "myth" suggest here?

3. In paragraphs 10–15, the author explains in great detail how "the collection" works. What is his main point concerning this practice—the main idea he wants the reader to understand? Can you conclude from this passage that the house is deceiving the players?

4. In paragraph 15, what is the author's reason for including the example of the woman who kept losing money? How does this example contribute to the thesis of the essay?

5. In the last two paragraphs, 17 and 18, what is the dominant *tone* (the author's attitude toward the clubs)? Is he giving an objective summary, or does he show that he favors or opposes the clubs?

ORGANIZING ESSAYS

In "Poker and the American Dream," Rex Jones follows the general pattern described earlier: He announces his thesis at the beginning, discusses it in detail, then returns to it and expands on it at the end.

Within this simple framework, Jones uses a variety of techniques to develop his thesis. He defines terms, describes people and places, presents factual information, illustrates his points with examples, and analyzes causes and motives. In this chapter, we will look at some of these common strategies that writers use to develop their ideas.

Showing, Not Telling: Describing, Narrating, Illustrating

An old saying among writers is "Show, don't tell." It underscores the difference between telling *about* an experience and describing it in such a way that readers can see it for themselves. This doesn't mean that writers never *tell*, but it does mean that telling is usually supported by showing. For example, Jones is *telling* when he says in paragraph 3, "Poker is an expression of the American dream in many other ways." In the rest of the paragraph he *shows* in what specific ways poker is an expression of the American Dream: conspicuous consumption and the marks by which a "winner" can be recognized.

Description, narration, and illustration are three ways of showing. Although we will discuss these techniques separately, in practice they often overlap. For example, an illustration might include within it bits of description or narration.

Description

A quick definition of description is "a picture in words." A good description creates a mental image; it grounds ideas in concrete reality.

For example, in paragraph 3, Jones begins with the claim that poker is an expression of the American Dream. He then shows us some of the *details* that constitute the evidence for his claim: "a house, a car, a color TV, a pocket full of credit cards, and a politician in the closet." This is a simple list of things the reader can visualize. Jones uses a similar list in paragraph 6, in which he details the people and activities in the clubs.

Descriptive writing engages not just the mind, but the senses as well. It makes the reader see, hear, feel, smell, taste. It evokes the world of bodily experience.

Narration

To *narrate* is to tell a story—a sequence of events in time. Works of fiction and feature films are often narratives. In daily life also, telling stories is one of the most natural human activities. A friend says, "Guess what happened to me today?" And off we go—telling a story.

Short narratives *(anecdotes)* are often used in essays as a way of making the writer's point more concrete, more real. In "Poker and the American Dream," Jones uses narrative to good advantage in paragraph 15—the story of the 76-year-old woman who had played poker for 20 years. The purpose of this narrative is to show that the elderly people who play in the clubs know very well they are losing money, but play for other reasons. In other words, the story is used to make a point, and it does so by putting that point in personal terms.

Illustration

When you think of an illustration, you probably think of a picture that depicts a scene from a book. The meaning is similar in writing. To illustrate means to give a specific *example* of a general statement.

A general statement is one that gives an overall impression; an example cites a specific instance. For example, Jones' statement that "the aged and retired play poker in Gardena for social and recreational reasons" is a *generalization;* he is making a claim about a whole group of people. The anecdote about the 76-year-old woman is an *example*—the story of one person who represents a general claim about many.

In fact, the club itself is an example. Jones uses it to represent all of the 400 poker clubs in California. It is important to ask, when you are using examples in this way, whether they are truly *representative*. Does the 76-year-old woman really represent all elderly poker players? Does the club represent all clubs? How do you know? In this case, it's a matter of whether you trust the author's judgment and honesty. Do you believe that he has studied the subject in enough depth and with enough objectivity to justify his conclusions?

The examples of the woman and the club are *extended examples;* that is, they are developed in detail. At other times, examples might only be mentioned—or *cited*. For instance, at the very end of the essay, Jones reinforces his point by citing the exclamation of an 83-year-old woman: "Son, if they closed Gardena tomorrow, I would die." Jones says that this statement came at the end of an interview, and he no doubt could have used this woman's story in a more extended example. But it probably would have duplicated the example of the 76-year-old. Besides, the older woman's words, set off by themselves, make a strong closing statement.

These techniques for showing are an important part of a writer's stock in trade. They demonstrate to the reader that the writer's ideas are firmly planted in the real world, the world of things and people and places. They also serve as *evidence* to show that the writer has factual backing for opinions, judgments and conclusions.

A Selection for Study

The selection below is the conclusion to N. Scott Momaday's book *The Way to Rainy Mountain*. The book is a long narrative of a journey that took Momaday from the mountains of Yellowstone to the plains of Southwest Oklahoma. Momaday, a writer and professor of English, is of Kiowa and Cherokee heritage. He grew up in New Mexico. Later in life, he undertook this journey to his ancestral homeland in a quest to discover for himself what it means to be a Kiowa. The end of his journey is his grandmother's grave at Rainy Mountain.

✍ N. Scott Momaday

From *The Way to Rainy Mountain*

Houses are like sentinels in the plain, old keepers of the weather watch. There, in a very little while, wood takes on the appearance of great age. All colors wear soon away in the wind and rain, and then the wood is burned gray and the grain appears and the nails turn red with rust. The window panes are black and opaque; you imagine there is nothing within, and indeed there are many ghosts, bones given up to the land. They stand here and there against the sky, and you approach them for a longer time than you expect. They belong in the distance; it is their domain.

Once there was a lot of sound in my grandmother's house, a lot of coming and going, feasting and talk. The summers there were full of excitement and reunion. The Kiowas are a summer people; they abide the cold and keep to themselves, but when the season turns and the land becomes warm and vital they cannot hold still; an old love of going returns upon them. The aged visitors who came to my grandmother's house when I was a child were made of lean and leather, and they bore themselves upright. They wore great black hats and bright ample shirts that shook in the wind. They rubbed fat upon their hair and wound their braids with strips of colored cloth. Some of them painted their faces and carried the scars of old and cherished enmities. They were an old council of warlords, come to remind and be reminded of who they were. Their wives and daughters served them well. The women might indulge themselves; gossip was at once the mark and compensation of their servitude. They made loud and elaborate talk among themselves, full of jest and gesture, fright and false alarm. They went abroad in fringed and flowered shawls, bright beadwork and German silver. They were at home in the kitchen, and they prepared meals that were banquets.

There were frequent prayer meetings, and nocturnal feasts. When I was a child I played with my cousins outside, where the lamplight fell upon the ground and the singing of the old people rose up around us and carried away into the darkness. There were a lot of good things to eat, a lot of laughter and surprise. And afterwards, when the quiet returned, I lay down with my grandmother and could hear the frogs away by the river and feel the motion of the air.

Now there is a funereal silence in the rooms, the endless wake of some final word. The walls have closed in upon my grandmother's house. When I returned to it in mourning, I saw for the first time in my life how small it was. It was late at night, and there was a white moon, nearly full. I sat for a long time on the stone steps by the kitchen door. From there I could see out across the land; I could see the long row of trees by the creek, the low light upon the rolling plains, and the stars of the Big Dipper. Once I looked at the moon and caught sight of a strange thing. A cricket had perched upon the handrail, only a few inches away. My line of vision was such that the creature filled the moon like a fossil. It had gone there, I thought, to live and die, for there, of all places, was its small definition made whole and eternal. A warm wind rose up and purled like the longing within me.

The next morning, I awoke at dawn and went out on the dirt road to Rainy Mountain. It was already hot, and the grasshoppers began to fill the air. Still, it was early in the morning, and birds sang out of the shadows. The long yellow grass on the mountain shone in the bright light, and a scissortail hied above the land. There, where it ought to be, at the end of a long and legendary way, was my grandmother's grave. She had at last succeeded to that holy ground. Here and there on the dark stones were ancestral names. Looking back once, I saw the mountain and came away.

Novelist Joseph Conrad once said that his purpose is to make you see. The purpose of description is to engage the reader through the senses: sight, smell, sound, taste, touch. Images that appeal to the senses are called *sensory details*. They draw the readers close, put them *in touch* with a place.

At its most basic level, a description moves through a scene naming things, naming actions. The more accurate and specific the name, the clearer the picture will be and the closer the reader will come. Momaday leads the reader, saying, "Look at that . . . and that": The "aged visitors . . . rubbed fat upon their hair and wound their braids with strips of colored cloth." See?

Naming shapes the framework, the outline, of a descriptive piece. But to draw the reader even closer, writers use words that engage the readers' senses—sight, sound, touch, taste, smell, and the sense of movement or pressure against the body. These words, or *images*, bring to mind particular colors, shapes, textures, sounds, odors, flavors, sensations. In Momaday's description, for example, the wood is "burned gray," the nails "turn red with rust," the window panes are "black and opaque."

When we try to describe something, we often compare it to something that is similar to it in some way. When Scott Momaday says that the houses are "like sentinels in the plain," he is using figurative language. (The houses are not really sentinels; sentinels are people who keep watch.) This kind of figure of speech is called a *simile*—a comparison of two things that uses "like" or "as." Although figures of speech are not literally true, they are, if well-chosen, true in some sense. The houses look like sentinels, and in a sense they seem to be standing watch.

Sometimes, rather than stating a comparison using "like" or "as," a writer will just *imply* that one thing is like another. For instance, when Momaday says that "the wood is burned gray," he does not mean that it has been in a fire; he is implying that the color is that of ashes. This kind of figure of speech—a comparison without "like" or "as"—is called a *metaphor.*

Figurative language such as this spices writing, creating images, suggesting similarities. It can be a compact way of suggesting a whole complex of qualities.

To make the reader see, the author not only uses the language of description but also presents the elements of the description in a particular order or pattern. Depending on the author's purpose, a description might be just a list of details (as in Rex Jones' description of the poker club), or it might draw a fuller, more complete picture, as in Momaday's first paragraph. Descriptions such as this usually have a point of focus and follow a pattern of some kind. In Momaday's paragraph, the opening sentence creates a *controlling image* that unifies the details in the passage. The houses are like "sentinels" (a guard; someone who watches over), and they are keeping a "weather watch." The description then focuses on the effects of weather in wearing down the houses. Finally, the paragraph returns to a picture of houses standing against the sky—a picture that echoes the opening image of the houses as sentinels.

The movement of the passage is controlled by a shifting sense of distance. Momaday begins from a point in the distance, moves closer (so close you can see the grain of the wood and the rust on the nails), then retreats to the distance again. It is a natural pattern of description (and drawing) to outline the subject first, then fill in the details. But whatever the approach, some logical order of details helps to move the reader smoothly through the scene. For example, a description of a landscape might move from foreground to background, from the center to the edges, or from right to left. A description of a room might move from near to far, or from important details to less important ones. A description of a person might move from overall size and shape to details of clothing to facial features, or from prominent features to less prominent ones.

In Momaday's description, each paragraph focuses on a particular point to be made about the subject. This point of focus, the main thing the writer wants the reader to understand, is called the *dominant impression*. For example, in Momaday's second paragraph, the dominant impression is one of life, excitement, vitality. The scene is lit by the bright light of day, and images of vivid color and sound prevail: braids bound with "bright strips of colored cloth," "loud and elaborate talk," "fringed and flowered shawls." The separate details of the paragraph, taken together, create a feeling of a unified whole.

Contrast the second paragraph with the third. Now it is night, and a mood of mourning shrouds the scene. "There is a funereal silence," and the moon casts a "low light across the plains." The world is still and somber. The paragraph closes with a beautiful image of a cricket against the full moon, a small thing seen whole by virtue of its position in Momaday's line of sight. It is a rich image, one that suggests, perhaps, the importance of Momaday's being in this very place for him to see his grandmother, and himself, fully and clearly.

The final paragraph completes the cycle from day to night to morning. Where the grasshopper in the third paragraph was a frozen image, a fossil, now "grasshoppers fill the air," birds sing, and the sun is hot and bright. Momaday's journey to his grandmother's grave is completed among images of life.

Looking beneath the Surface: Analyzing

How does something work? How do you do that? What does it mean? What caused it? What will its effects be? How is this different from that? How many kinds of it are there?

When we try to answer questions like these—How? What? Why?— we use the kind of thinking we call *analysis*. Analysis takes the subject apart and tries to understand what it really is or how it really works or what it really means.

"Poker and the American Dream" is essentially an analysis; it poses several questions, each one leading to a certain kind of analysis: Why do elderly people play in the clubs? How does the collection work? Why is poker like the American Dream? What is really going on here?

Analysis searches for the meaning behind appearances. For example, at first glance one might think that the clubs are cheating the elderly players. But on deeper analysis, it becomes clear that the players are fully aware of what's going on; so, Jones reasons, they must be motivated by something other than the desire to win. This insight leads to further analysis of the players' motives. If not to win, then why do they play? Well, says Jones, they play to regain the feeling of being young and of participating in the American Dream.

WORKING WITH SOURCES

As we explained earlier, the ability to summarize is an important first skill. In writing longer papers, you will often need to summarize parts of what you have read as you develop your own responses.

Analysis goes a step beyond summary. You put more of yourself into the writing: You clarify, explain, make connections; you use your judgment to question and evaluate an author's statements; you show how the parts relate to the whole.

Writing from a Single Source

The *analyst* acts as a mediator between author and audience, clarifying ideas, explaining the connections between evidence and conclusions, showing why the author has reached certain conclusions, evaluating the strengths of reasons and evidence. An analyst might also explain meanings that aren't apparent on the surface. For example, political analysts often analyze and interpret politicians' speeches to tell us, the ignorant public, what they really mean. Was the Senator's remark about the need for a stronger military really an expression of his principles? Or did it mean that the Senator has an army base in his district that he wants to protect?

Questions of analysis lead to a close examination of an author's ideas and information. Here are some examples of questions about "Poker and the American Dream" that ask for interpretive or analytical responses:

Explain Jones' reasons for his conclusion that elderly people play poker to feel that they participate in the American Dream.

What kinds of evidence does Jones give to back up his conclusion?

Do you agree with Jones' contention that "Poker is a pure expression of the American dream"? What are the strengths and weaknesses of his arguments?

In what ways does the example of the 76-year-old woman support Jones' conclusions?

What evidence is there in the essay that Jones thinks the clubs are good for elderly people? How strong is this evidence?

Writing from More Than One Source

Thus far in this chapter, we have dealt only with writing that uses a single source. But college writing usually requires that you use several sources. This means that you must analyze and compare differing points of view, show how one source agrees or disagrees with another, evaluate conflicting evidence, reasons, and arguments.

In each chapter of Part 2 of this book, we have chosen readings that focus on a particular theme related to the American Dream. The essays, stories, and poems in these chapters present a variety of points of view. Each selection reflects in some way upon the others, and many of the questions for writing ask you to analyze, compare, and evaluate these different points of view.

For example, let's consider "Poker and the American Dream" in connection with the readings included in the first chapter of this book. Since all of them have to do with a common subject, we can begin by asking general questions about their similarities and differences. In what specific ways do the writers agree or disagree about the meanings of the American Dream? If you have done a good job of marking the texts, you should be able to review the essays quickly, noting key points of difference and similarity.

Questioning the readings in this way is the starting point of a good analysis. In fact, a good question is usually the starting point of an essay. A good question provides a clear direction for development and a limited field for the writer to examine.

Here are some examples of questions for writing about the readings in this section.

Arnold Schwarzenegger's idea of the American Dream is obviously quite close to the description Jones gives in "Poker and the American Dream." In what specific ways are they alike? Although the two essays are apparently similar, are there any differences in the way they describe the characteristics of the American Dream?

Both Rosalie Sorrells and Joe Gorman hold views that differ from Jones' definition of the American Dream. In what specific ways are they different? What basic values underlie the ideas of Gorman or Sorrells, and how do they differ from the values described by Jones?

What satisfactions and rewards do Joe Gorman and the card players get from pursuing their versions of the American Dream? Are they entirely different, or are they in some ways similar?

Can you imagine Arnold Schwarzenegger spending his retirement years playing poker in a place like the Gardena club? Why or why not?

How many different kinds of American Dreams are represented in these readings? What are the most important differences between them?

Developing Your Own Ideas from Your Reading

So far, we've talked about writing that takes you further *into* a text or a group of texts. Another way to use reading as a basis for writing is to move *out of* the text to develop your own ideas about the subject.

We enter another dimension of reading when we examine issues raised by the text in light of our own observations, experiences, and beliefs. On one hand, reading leads us into the world of the writer; on the other, it leads us outward toward a fresh examination of our own views. We can think about the connection between reading and experience in several ways. Again, we begin with questions:

Do you agree or disagree with the author's conclusions? What reasons of your own would you give for your views?

In what ways did your reading change an opinion or belief that you previously held?

Does your own experience confirm or contradict the author's conclusions? Explain.

Did the reading cause you to think in more depth about an issue or problem that you hadn't really considered before?

Were there any statements in the reading that you found particularly enlightening, that made you look at something in a new way?

Are there any issues or details that the author *didn't* discuss, which you think should be considered before the reader comes to a conclusion?

What particular parts of the text did you find the most interesting, provocative, or puzzling? Why?

These are general questions that can be applied to any text. Those that follow illustrate the kinds of questions that might arise from thinking about a specific text in this way (once again, "Poker and the American Dream").

Notice that whenever Jones refers to "American dream," it is always *The* American Dream, not *an* American Dream or *one of* the American Dreams. Do you think he is justified in doing this? In what respects is the dream described in his essay *The* American Dream?

Jones says that in America "winners" are easily recognized by evidence of "conspicuous consumption." This statement could generate several questions:

> Can you think of examples from your own experience that would illustrate and support this statement?
>
> How would you define a "winner"? How could a "winner," as you define him or her, be recognized?
>
> What evidence do you see around you that Americans place a high value on winning? Consider your own experience as well as evidence from TV, films, magazines, and newspapers.

Do you know someone who exemplifies *your* idea of the American Dream? Explain your idea, then show how that person exemplifies it.

Do you agree with Jones that elderly Americans often feel left out of the American Dream? If so, why do you think this is true? If not, why not? What examples could you give to support your opinion?

Jones' essay implies that there are only two alternatives open to elderly people in American society: playing poker, or wasting away comparing ailments with their peers. Do you think this is really the case? Does American society provide so few options for the elderly?

What attitudes do you, or your family and friends, have about aging and the elderly? Do you respect and value elderly people, or do you consider them "over the hill," of no more use?

America is often charged with being a "youth culture." What evidence can you find in the media, particularly advertising, to support or contradict the idea that Americans value youth more than maturity?

If you define "The American Dream" differently than Jones does, what game or pastime could you use to illustrate your definition? What game or pastime would illustrate Joe Gorman or Rosalie Sorrells' idea of the American Dream?

Using Quotations

Whenever you repeat in your writing the words or ideas of someone else, you need to indicate that fact. In research papers, you have to document sources with notes and a bibliography (list of works used in the paper). But for now we will concentrate on using and marking passages that are quoted from a written source.

Elements that are quoted *verbatim* (word-for-word) are put within quotation marks (" "); passages that are summarized or paraphrased are not put in quotation marks, but are acknowledged in the text so that it is clear to the reader that they are someone else's thoughts. There are a number of ways of using quoted material in your own writing. Here are some of them.

Punctuating Quotations

1. A *comma* is put after the *dialogue tag*—a phrase like "She said," or "As Baker pointed out," or "According to Kuralt," that introduces the quotation. This comma is followed by the first quotation mark; then, at the end of the quotation, the period goes *inside* the final quotation mark.

2. Periods and commas at the end of a quoted passage always go *inside* the quotation mark.

3. *Colons* and *semicolons* always go *outside* the final quotation mark.

4. *Question marks* and *exclamation points* go *inside* the final quotation mark if they apply only to the words within the quotes. They go *outside* the final quotation mark if they apply to the whole sentence in which the quotation appears. For example:

St. Jean de Crevecoeur asked, "What is an American?"

(Only the words within quotes are a question.)

Was it Crevecoeur who said that "The American is a new man"?

(The whole sentence is a question.)

Was it St. Jean de Crevecoeur who asked, "What is an American?"

(Question within a question: one question mark inside the quotation marks.)

Quoting Complete Sentences

Suppose you want to use a complete sentence from the original after giving your own introduction. It would look like this:

Andrew Carnegie believes that the change from primitive to civilized conditions is easy to see. He says, "In the manufacture of products we have the whole story."

Sometimes, rather than putting the tag "He says" at the beginning of the quote, you might want to use it as an interruptor. For example:

> "In the manufacture of products," *says Carnegie,* "we have the whole story."

Note carefully the punctuation in the sentence above—particularly the placement of quotation marks and commas.

Quoting Longer Passages: Block Quotations

Although quotations should usually be kept as brief as possible, sometimes you might want to quote a passage of several sentences. For quotations longer than four of your typewritten lines *(block quotations),* use the following form:

- Indent the entire quotation ten spaces from the left-hand margin; leave the original right-hand margin.
- Introduce the quotation with a statement that ends with a *colon.*
- Do *not* use quotation marks.
- Double-space the quotation.

Here is an example, an introductory sentence followed by the quotation:

> When Rafael Rosa thinks about his future, he constantly skips from one thing to another:
>
> I really would like to have a chauffeur-driven limousine, have a bar one side, color TV on the other. The chicks, the girls, oh yeah. Instead of coming in at eight in the morning and leavin' at eight in the afternoon. Maybe I'll invent something one of these days and wind up a millionaire. As for now, I'd really like to be chief pilot at the air force.

Quoting Just a Word or Phrase

It is often unnecessary to quote a whole sentence or passage. You might need to use only a key word or phrase from the original. When you do this, the quoted words should be worked smoothly into your own sentence structure, so that the whole statement, including the quotation, reads well as a complete sentence. Here are some examples:

Carnegie doesn't want to discuss whether the change from primitive to civilized society is good or bad, for he views it as "a waste of time to criticize the inevitable."

(*Punctuation Note:* In the sentence above there is no punctuation between the writer's words and the quoted passage. The quotation is worked smoothly into the writer's own sentence structure.)

When you use this technique, be sure that the whole sentence, including the quotation, makes complete grammatical sense, and that your words and the quoted words work smoothly together.

Here is an example of a sentence in which the writer's words and the quotation *do not* fit together:

Carnegie doesn't want to discuss whether the change from primitive to civilized society is good or bad, for he views it as "It is a waste of time to criticize the inevitable."

This sentence uses Carnegie's exact wording, but the quoted passage doesn't fit grammatically with the writer's own words. *When you use quotations, read the whole sentence—including your words and the quotation. If it doesn't work, either change your own wording or use only part of the original. Don't change the wording of the original.*

Here is an example that uses only a few key words from the source:

Carnegie says that the "whole story" of the change from primitive to civilized conditions can be seen in "the manufacture of products."

(*Punctuation Note:* There are no commas.)

Giving Credit

You don't always need to quote verbatim. But even when you summarize or *paraphrase* (state in your own words) the ideas of another writer, you need to give credit to the source. The simplest way to do this is to state in your text where the idea or information came from. Note the following examples:

In "The Intellectual Savage," Jamake Highwater claims that people of different cultures see the world in fundamentally different ways.

Jeffrey Schrank, author of "Psychosell," says that many advertisements sell products by appealing to something that is lacking in consumers' lives.

According to Peter H. Schuck, many Americans are worried about the growing population of immigrants to this country. They believe, says Schuck, that the idea of *E Pluribus Unum* (one out of many) will be lost if minority groups become the majority.

The important thing is to make sure the reader knows when you are borrowing from a source and when you are using your own words and ideas.

WRITING ESSAYS OF ARGUMENT AND PERSUASION

Persuasive writing explains and defends the writer's position on a controversial issue—an issue to which there is more than one side, more than one position a reasonable person could take. A persuasive essay presents the writer's *conclusion* about the issue and gives *reasons* and *evidence* to back up the conclusion.

The terms *argument* and *persuasion* are often used interchangeably. Strictly speaking, an argument is a reasoned defense of the writer's position on an issue. But in popular usage, the word has been stretched to include everything from a playground shouting match to bickering over who pitched the final game of the 1951 World Series. For this reason, we prefer the term *persuasion*.

Persuasive writing shares many characteristics with expository writing. There is no clean line separating them. Most essays of analysis, for example, have an element of persuasion about them; the writer is trying to convince the reader that her interpretation has merit. Thus, much of what we have said about expository writing—its organization and development—applies also to persuasion. But persuasive writing requires closer attention to the relationships between conclusion, reasons, and evidence, to the possibility of other interpretations, and to the knowledge and attitudes of the reader.

In this section, we are restricting our discussion to *rational* persuasion: persuasion that attempts to convince by offering reasons and evidence. However, at the same time we recognize that most arguments are not settled by reason alone. If reason were the perfect road to truth and everyone could agree on certain rational principles, then all votes of Congress would be unanimous, all Supreme Court decisions would be 9–0, and we could all agree on eliminating nuclear weapons.

But the real world is not so simple. Emotions, beliefs, principles, temperament, and self-interest all play a part in the way we form our points of view. Nevertheless, we aspire to rationality, imperfect as it is, and the ability to think through difficult issues is an essential part of becoming educated.

In the section that follows, we will look at several strategies for developing a convincing persuasive essay.

Presenting and Explaining Reasons

The first question readers will ask about a writer's position on an issue is "Why?" Why do you hold this particular view rather than another? What are your reasons for taking this position? Expressing and explaining reasons is the first and most basic technique of persuasive writing.

In the following paragraph from his essay "Three Ways of Responding to Oppression" (included in full in Part 2, Chapter 10), Martin Luther King, Jr., explains why he opposes violence to achieve racial justice. In the opening sentence he gives two reasons for his position; he then explains them in the body of the paragraph.

Violence as a way of achieving racial justice is both impractical and immoral. It is *impractical* because it is a descending spiral ending in destruction for all. The old law of an eye for an eye leaves everybody blind. It is *immoral* because it seeks to humiliate the opponent rather than win his understanding; it seeks to annihilate rather than to convert. Violence is immoral because it thrives on hatred rather than love. It destroys community and makes brotherhood impossible. It leaves society in monologue rather than dialogue. Violence ends by defeating itself. It creates bitterness in the survivors and brutality in the destroyers. A voice echoes through time saying to every potential Peter, "Put up your sword." History is cluttered with the wreckage of nations that failed to follow this command.
       –MARTIN LUTHER KING, JR.
       From "Three Ways of Responding to Oppression"
       (the italics are ours)

Simply naming reasons is seldom enough. General words such as "impractical" and "immoral" might be interpreted differently by different readers. Therefore, it is necessary to explain *in what ways* violence is impractical and immoral. Whenever there is the possibility of more than one interpretation, explanation is necessary.

Presenting Evidence

Giving reasons identifies the *ground* on which an argument will be conducted. In the paragraph above, King is basing his argument on two grounds: practicality and morality. These are the two major grounds on which most arguments are based. From a practical point of view, we are interested in whether or not something will work; from a moral point of view, we are interested in whether it is right or wrong.

The next technique of persuasion takes us to a more specific level. Generally speaking, *evidence* is any specific material used to support the writer's judgment. Evidence includes verifiable facts and details, experience and observation, and the word of reliable authorities.

Facts and Details

For our purposes here, we will consider any information that is common knowledge or easily verified by reliable sources to be factual. The distinction between facts on the one hand and interpretations and opinions on the other is not always clear, particularly when you are dealing with material like statistics and public opinion polls. But that issue leads to problems that are too complex to take on here.

Here are some of the kinds of questions that can be answered factually:

In 1994, how many civilians in the United States were killed with assault rifles?

How much of the American budget is spent on entitlement programs like Social Security and Medicare?

What was the Teapot Dome scandal?

What percentage of American households owns more than one television set?

Personal Experience and Observation

Your own experiences and observations can play an important role in supporting your views. They establish your authority to deal with the issue, and they ground your arguments in the real world. Rex Jones' conclusions about poker players in "Poker and the American Dream," for example, are based entirely on his own observations of the poker clubs. Most of the writers included in Part 2 of this book make some use of their own experiences to support their views. In our earlier discussion of essays and paragraphs, we stressed the need for details and examples in expository writing. The same is true of persuasive writing. (If you review the sample paragraphs in the section on the paragraph, you will see that many of them are persuasive and that the writers use some kind of personal material: examples, anecdotes, observations.)

A student from Hong Kong wrote the following piece in a paper which argued that immigrants to the United States should not give up their native cultures:

> My best friend immigrated to America when he was twelve years old. After ten years, he took a vacation back to Hong Kong with his American fiancee. He spoke English all the time; he had almost forgotten how to speak Cantonese and how to follow the traditional customs. He did not know how to respect the elders (his grandparents), and treated them just like common friends. In addition, he had loose morals. Although he had a fiancee, he still went out with other girls.

Examples like this can strengthen a persuasive essay, but by themselves they are not usually enough. A reader could argue that this is just an isolated example, not typical of most immigrants, or that this person was just exposed to the worst elements of American life. Good examples are accurate, appropriate, and typical, and they usually need to be combined with a broader range of evidence to be effective.

The Judgments of Authorities

Authorities are people with extensive knowledge and experience in a particular field. They are usually recognized and respected by their colleagues and have published papers or books on important issues. Of course, not all experts in a field agree, and it is often difficult for amateurs to judge the credibility of an authority. Supreme Court judges, for example, are legal experts, yet few of their decisions are unanimous.

When you are using the judgments of authorities, it is important to know their qualifications. What education and experience have they had? Are their judgments widely accepted by others in the field? A number of reference books, like *Who's Who* and *Contemporary Authors* give short biographies of well-known people. A reference librarian can help you find such sources.

Modern advertising and publicity have confused the notion of authority. Film stars and athletes are used to sell everything from hair spray to presidents, though they probably have no more expertise than you or I. Check to see that the authorities you cite are really qualified to speak on the issue.

Organizing an Essay of Argument and Persuasion

Like expository writing, persuasive essays most often begin with an introduction that includes the writer's conclusion. The writer's conclusion is the thesis of the essay (in argumentation, the thesis is called the *proposition*). The rest of the paper develops the reasons and evidence that support the conclusion. This is a *conclusion-to-evidence* order of presentation.

The reverse of this order, *evidence-to-conclusion*, can sometimes be more effective, especially if you know the reader disagrees with your view. If you jump in right at the beginning with a strong statement of your proposition, the reader is likely to be put off. But if you can find evidence that you think the reader will accept, and work from there toward a conclusion, you improve your chances of getting a reader to consider what you have to say.

When you are deciding how to arrange your reasons and evidence, consider which of your points is strongest, which is weakest. It is usually best to move from *least important to most important*. This order creates a sense of increasing strength, carrying the reader along. (The end of the essay is the position of greatest emphasis.)

Anticipating Readers' Responses and Dealing with Counterarguments

Persuasive essays are written to move the readers in some way: to convince them to change their minds or to take action. It makes sense, then, that the writer needs to anticipate readers' responses and objections. It is best to imagine yourself writing for a skeptical reader, one who will examine your arguments closely and raise objections if reasoning or evidence is weak. To do this, you must familiarize yourself with the issues and be aware of arguments on both sides.

An example will help explain this point. Suppose you are arguing that smoking should be banned in restaurants. You base your case on practical grounds, citing evidence that second-hand smoke is harmful and that smoking bothers other customers. You think you have an airtight case. But no matter how strong your evidence is, your argument can be attacked on several other grounds. For instance, one argument often raised by restaurant owners is economic: What effect would a smoking ban have on restaurant profits? Another argument can be raised on the ground of individual rights and responsibilities: Is it the business of government to regulate everything that might be harmful to people. In other words, a reader could agree with all of your evidence that smoking is harmful but disagree with your proposition on the grounds that limiting government interference in private lives overrides other considerations. If you do not address this issue and answer it in some way, you will not change such a reader's mind.

Sample Essay of Argument and Persuasion

The following essay, "Smoke Signals," by Carll Tucker, addresses the issue of the regulation of smoking. Notice how Tucker arranges the parts of his argument to best advantage in order to convince a skeptical reader. Tucker's ultimate appeal rests not in a dislike of smoking, or even in evidence of its effects on health, but in general principles concerning the relationship between government and the individual. In other words, Tucker moves beyond his own preferences to examine the specific issue (banning smoking) in the light of larger issues of freedom and control.

The essay appeared in the *Saturday Review* in 1978.

ℒ❧ CARLL TUCKER
Smoke Signals

1. In recent weeks, the campaign against smoking has assumed new urgency and scored some impressive victories. A national No-Smoking Day evoked articles and editorials against the evil weed. The Civil Aeronautics Board has banned all cigar and pipe smoking on commercial airlines and has taken steps that could lead to the prohibition of cigarette smoking as well. Regulations against smoking in the Pentagon's dining halls and classrooms have been sent to the Army, Air Force, and Navy "for responses on how to implement them."

Introduction: background on the issue

2. Now I am not, nor have I ever been, a smoker. At the age of eight, I stole one of my father's cigars to share experimentally with a friend; fearful that our crime was about to be discovered by an approaching adult, I swallowed the lit butt. In college, unwilling to be considered uncool by classmates, I inhaled marijuana, but never with enjoyment. (Even in that era of "do your own thing," there were pressures to conform.) Shortly after graduation, I adopted a pipe in the belief that the first step toward being a writer was look-

Personal experience: identifies with opposing view

ing like one; but I soon abandoned it after finding that most of my reading time was spent trying to keep my tobacco on fire.

3. I am neither allergic to cigarette smoke nor fond of it. If at a lunch counter a woman asks in the middle of my meal would I mind if she smokes, I consider saying yes. I sit gratefully in the nonsmoking section of airplanes and movie houses.

Statement of the question to be examined

4. Nonetheless, I am troubled by the attitude and success of the campaigners against smoking. It is one thing to warn consumers that cigarette smoking may be hazardous to their health: living in a world of often invisible dangers, we should be grateful for the caution. It is even arguable that given the demonstrated ability of television and radio to reach below the intelligence and to sow subliminal "needs," cigarette advertising should be banished from the airwaves. But having alerted the consumer to the danger and having protected him from subliminal seduction, what arguments can be used to justify what the antismoking militants see as their eventual goal: the outlawing of cigarettes?

5. A recent editorial in *The New York Times* cited some reasons why the Carter administration ought not to be "resigned to a national addiction that will kill 300,000 Americans this year." Cost was one reason: according to Surgeon General Julius Richmond, ailments caused by smoking will cost the nation $20 billion this year. The will of the American smoker was another: eight out of ten smokers would like to quit, said Richmond, adding, "We must help them, and they want us to."

Summary of opposing arguments

6. Never having smoked, I do not comprehend the force or the invincibility of an addiction to tobacco, but I do know a number of less-than-Herculean Americans who have, albeit with some discomfort, managed to shake their addiction. I wonder what it is about the purported 80 percent of smokers who want to quit that prevents them from doing so. I also wonder whether the cost of treating a sickness should be used as an argument for removing the freedom to incur

Refutation of opposing arguments

the sickness and whether it is government's role to help citizens do something that they are not psychologically capable of doing themselves. (By this logic, government should limit the calories allowed to each American per day.)

7. The advantage of a democracy over various more or less organized methods of government is that it allows a citizen the maximum freedom to do as he pleases up to the point at which his freedom infringes on someone else's. As the world becomes more complex and people become more interdependent, our freedoms necessarily become more restricted. Speed limits were not needed before automobile and highway manufacturers created the opportunities for serious accidents. It was not necessary to prohibit homeowners from burning leaves until everyone's air became smoky.

8. What we must guard against, though, is using the excuse of interdependence to enact restrictions that, however desirable, are unnecessary. I suspect that the creation of nonsmoking sections in public places answers the complaints of most nonsmokers. To ban cigarettes altogether would be to do something that, however healthful, is not strictly necessary and that would limit the freedom of those who like to smoke. Government should resist the temptation to treat its citizens like children—making us wear seat belts that buzz if we don't fasten them, forbidding us marijuana or Laetrile or tobacco simply because they haven't been proved as safe as mother's milk (which nowadays isn't safe, either). Advise us, yes; restrict us when we threaten the essential freedoms of others. But do not attempt to protect us from all the dangers of existence. *[Thesis and supporting arguments]*

9. There are two sorts of freedom: freedom *from* and freedom *to*. Given the choice, democracy should favor the latter. Whether or not one likes smoking, the freedom to smoke is a more important right than freedom from smoking or its consequences. When usually thoughtful opinion shapers like *The New York Times* start advocating laws not because they are necessary for the preservation of our freedom but because they would be good for us, it is time to worry. *[Conclusion: summary and restatement]*

4 Writing Effective Paragraphs

HOW PARAGRAPHS WORK

A piece of writing more than a couple of hundred words long is generally divided into *paragraphs*. Paragraphs are not usually random divisions (except in newspaper articles where, because of the narrow columns, paragraphs are only a sentence or two long). In essays, magazine articles, and non-fiction books, there is some logic to paragraphing. A new paragraph usually marks the beginning of a new aspect of the topic: a new idea, another reason, a new body of information. An indented first line marks the break. In this way, paragraphing provides a key to the order of ideas and information. Each paragraph presents a new point that is related in some way to the main idea of the work.

Look at the sequence of opening paragraphs in "Poker and the American Dream."

1. Poker is an American game.

2. Poker is a pure expression of the American Dream.

3. Poker is an expression of the American Dream in many other ways.

4. In the realization of the American Dream, the arena is the system of free enterprise, where everyone has an equal chance; in the poker game, the arena is a system of free play, where all begin on an equal footing.

These sentences present in a clear and direct way the main points in the development of the essay. They also provide a unifying idea for each paragraph. Such sentences are called *topic sentences*. Like the thesis statement of an essay, the topic sentence states in condensed form the main idea of the paragraph.

A paragraph, then, is *a group of sentences that are unified by a single purpose or idea*. The material in the body of each paragraph contributes in some way to the further *development* of the idea: it gives reasons or evidence, it explains, it defines, it illustrates, it describes. For example, in the body of paragraph 2, the author explains some specific ways in which poker is an expression of the American Dream; he names particular characteristics to support the claim made in the topic sentence.

A CLOSER LOOK AT TOPIC SENTENCES

Placing the Topic Sentence

In the examples above, the topic sentence is the first sentence of the paragraph. There are good reasons for this. For one thing, readers pay closer attention to beginnings than to what follows. That's why newspaper reporters usually put the most important information at the top of the story. Second, it's easier to understand information if you know what the information is about. A topic sentence at the beginning tells the reader *why* the details that follow are important. Finally, a topic sentence at the beginning helps the writer, not just the reader. It provides a unifying idea for the material that follows, thus helping the writer to keep on track.

However, there may be reasons for placing the topic sentence somewhere else in the paragraph—or for having no topic sentence at all. In Jones' essay, for example, paragraphs 8 and 9 have no topic sentences, but the material in them is unified by a clear purpose that is there, even if unstated. Paragraph 8 demonstrates the extent and importance of poker playing in California and, specifically, Gardena; paragraph 9 sets the scene by describing the layout and facilities of the clubs. In other instances, a writer might save the topic sentence for the end (creeping up on it gradually, leading the reader along) or write a sentence or two of introduction before stating the topic sentence.

An experienced writer can vary paragraph structure in many ways. But for people learning to write, we strongly recommend starting every paragraph with a topic sentence. The exceptions to this are introductory, concluding, and transitional paragraphs. We'll talk about these later.

Writing a Good Topic Sentence

A good topic sentence does two things:

it names the subject

it makes a claim about the subject

SUBJECT   CLAIM

The Gardena clubs take the place of home life for the aged.

So, a topic sentence is a complete sentence (with a subject and predicate) that names the subject and says something about it. In doing so, the topic sentence provides the key words that give the paragraph *focus* (a sharp, limited subject) and *direction* (a suggestion of the kind of information that will be used to illustrate and support the main idea).

By providing focus and direction, effective topic sentences serve to hold the information in a paragraph together; they furnish a measure of control over the content. Or, to look at it another way, good topic sentences raise a question in the reader's mind—one that can be answered within the scope of the paragraph. In the example above, for instance, the sentence states that the Gardena clubs take the place of home life for the aged. A curious reader would probably ask, *In what ways is this true?* It is the writer's job to answer that question by demonstrating in detail how the clubs fulfill this function.

Considering how topic sentences are supposed to work, it is easy to see that some kinds of statements work better than others, Claims that are either too narrow or too broad make weak topic sentences. For example, "Joe Gorman lives in Suffolk, Massachusetts" is too narrow; it raises no questions in the reader's mind and gives the writer nowhere to go. On the other hand, sentences that just state a broad impression give the writer too much room to wander. For example, "Rosalie Sorrells is an interesting woman" could easily result in a disjointed, wandering paragraph.

When you are writing topic sentences, avoid general words like "interesting," "good," "neat," and "wonderful." Think about what makes Rosalie Sorrells interesting to you, then write a topic sentence that suggests the reason: "Rosalie Sorrells interests me because she is an independent woman who insists on doing things her own way." This sentence provides a much clearer focus for a paragraph.

Exercise: Writing Good Topic Sentences

The topic sentences below are either too broad or too narrow. Determine what the problem is, then write a revised version of each sentence. If the statement is too broad, narrow it by clarifying the specific claim being made; if it is too narrow, suggest a revision that makes a more general statement. We've revised the first one as an example. (Note: an experienced writer could probably begin paragraphs with the following sentences and make them work. We are asking you to do this exercise as a way of writing more sharply focused sentences to help develop and unify paragraphs.)

1. Joe Gorman is a hard worker.

   TOO BROAD.
   REVISION:
   Joe Gorman works hard to build a sense of community in his town.

2. Rosalie Sorrells talks a lot about her past.

3. Success is important to Joe Gorman.

4. Rafael Rosa dreams of having a chauffeur-driven limousine.

5. Arnold Schwarzenegger owns a lot of real estate.

6. Arnold Schwarzenegger deserves our admiration.

PUTTING MEAT ON THE BONES

Most people (including college professors) won't accept a simple, flat statement as true. They are likely to ask bothersome questions like *"Why?"* They want you to demonstrate that your statement is at least worth consideration. One feature of good thesis statements and topic sentences is that they provoke a question from a reader. "Poker is a pure expression of the American dream," says Jones. Oh, really. Why?

Everything after the topic sentence is the body, the meat of the paragraph. The body develops the main idea. It explains, it describes, it defines, it illustrates, it argues. It's a body; it packs flesh on the bones. It answers readers' questions and convinces the readers that the claim made by the topic sentence is worth listening to. In short, it makes them see.

Let's look at an example—this time from another essay, the one about Joe Gorman, from Chapter 1. As you read the following paragraph, pay attention to the way the author develops his point. The topic sentence is in italics.

> *Under Joe's direction, the anniversary celebration turned out to be a grand success.* The festivities stretched out for nine months. There were parades, concerts, a carnival, athletic contests, dinners, dances, and ecumenical religious services, all well attended and smoothly organized. The fundamental meaning of the celebration was expressed for Joe in the slogan: "We are doing it together." As he put it, "That's so important—to work to get as many people as possible active." Another key theme was the importance of the family. The inspiration for many of the events came from the fact that that year had been proclaimed by the United Nations to be "the year of the family." For Joe, the highlight of the festivities was a softball tournament in which each team was made up of members of a different extended family. "We had eight clans—eight big families from Suffolk—in the tournament. In one of them some people came clear from Connecticut just to play softball on the side of their family. You know, for me the best time of the whole celebration was standing there back behind the bleachers after the softball games with members of the families that had played and talking with them about their families and drinking champagne. That to me was the ultimate. During the games between the clans, on many occasions, lots of people showed up besides the players to watch the game and see how people in the families were doing."

That's a meaty paragraph. What does the body of the paragraph do? It answers in detail the question implied in the topic sentence: Why was the celebration a success? Moreover, it gives a concrete idea of what Joe Gorman means by success.

Now let's take the paragraph a piece at a time. First the topic sentence: "Under Joe's direction, the anniversary celebration turned out to be a grand success." This sentence contains the necessary parts: the *subject* and the *claim*. The subject is "the anniversary celebration"; the claim is "turned out to be a grand success." "Success" is the key word in the claim: it gives the paragraph focus and direction.

Now for the body. It begins with a sentence describing the content of the festivities, the parades, concerts, and so on. Then it moves on to the *meaning* of the event, which has two related parts: togetherness and the importance of family. Over half the paragraph is devoted to a detailed example that demonstrates the importance of family—the softball game. The space given to this description emphasizes that for Joe Gorman it was this sense of family that really made the whole thing a success.

Examples of Paragraph Development and Organization

There are many ways to develop the main idea of a paragraph. What follows is a selection of paragraphs that illustrate some common patterns of organization. Topic sentences are italicized. Most of the paragraphs here are taken from essays that appear in later chapters of this book.

Topic Sentence Illustrated by a Series of Examples

I am very much alienated by the way some ideas find their way into English words. For instance, when an English word is descriptive—like the word "wilderness"—I am often appalled by what is implied by the description. After all, the forest is not "wild" in the sense that it is something needing to be tamed or controlled and harnessed. For Blackfeet Indians, the forest is the natural state of the world. It is the cities that are wild and seem to need "taming." For most primal peoples the earth is so marvelous that their connotation of it requires it to be spelled in English with a capital "E." How perplexing it is to discover two English synonyms for Earth—"soil" and "dirt"—used to describe uncleanliness, *soiled* and *dirty*. And how upsetting it is to discover that the word "dirty" in English is also used to depict obscenities! Or take the English word "universe," in which I find even more complicated problems, for Indians do not believe that there is *one* fixed and eternal truth; they think there are many different and equally valid truths.

—JAMAKE HIGHWATER
From "The Intellectual Savage"

Work now pervades our non-working lives in unprecedented, widely accepted ways: cellular phones, answering machines, personal and portable computers. The career, for many people, has taken precedence over such time-honored human endeavors as building a strong family or seeking spiritual and philosophical truths. The person who works right up to the point of self-destruction is often accorded far more esteem than the person who seeks to lead a balanced life. Overworking is an American trait, much commented on by European observers; and it has become the hallmark of strenuous yuppies, whose chief complaint about life is "I don't have enough time."

—FRED MOODY
From "When Work Becomes an Obsession"

Topic Sentence Developed by One Extended Example

The household slice-of-life commercial is one of the classic offenders of the NARB [National Advertising Review Board] checklist. (Are sexual stereotypes perpetuated? You'd best believe it. Are the women portrayed stupid? And how.) Crisco's current campaign is a flawless example of this much-imitated genre, which has been developed and designed by Proctor & Gamble. In it various long-suffering husbands and condescending neighbors are put through the heartache of greasy, gobby chicken and fries, all because some unthinking corner cutter spent "a few pennies less" on that mainstay of American cookery, lard. These pound-foolish little women cause their loved ones to live through "disasters" and "catastrophes." At the cue word "catastrophe," our video crumples into wavy electronic spasms and thrusts us back to the scene of the crime; to that excruciating point in the Bicentennial picnic or the backyard cookout when Dad has to wrinkle his upper lip and take Mom aside for a little set-to about her greasy chicken. The moral, delivered by some unseen pedantic male announcer, is plain: "Ladies who've learned—buy Crisco."

—CAROL CALDWELL
From "You Haven't Come a Long Way Baby:
Women in Television Commercials"

Topic Sentence Developed by Listing Specific Characteristics of a General Concept

The essential elements of what Americans call free-enterprise capitalism came with the earliest settlers. The terms are not precise, but Americans have always believed they knew what "free market," "fair competition," "individual enterprise," and "equal opportunity" meant. And they have been equally sure that monopoly, socialism, and special privilege were beyond the bounds of acceptable economic behavior. The Puritans knew what was proper; central to their code of conduct was the notion that hard work was morally uplifting. Other Puritan virtues, such as thrift, perseverance, honesty, sobriety, punctuality, and initiative, conveniently brought profits as well as clean consciences. Anyone can develop these virtues; capacity, aptitude, and genes are less important than character, which alone limits a person's horizon.

—HENRY F. BEDFORD AND TREVOR COLBOURNE
From *The Americans: A Brief History*

Topic Sentence Developed by Stating and Explaining Reasons for the Author's Claim

Violence as a way of achieving racial justice is both impractical and immoral. It is impractical because it is a descending spiral ending in destruction for all. The old law of an eye for an eye leaves everybody blind. It is immoral because it seeks to humiliate the opponent rather than win his understanding; it seeks to annihilate rather than to convert. Violence is immoral because it thrives on hatred rather than love. It destroys community and makes brotherhood impossible. It leaves society in monologue rather than dialogue. Violence ends by defeating itself. It creates bitterness in the survivors and brutality in the destroyers. A voice echoes through time saying to every potential Peter, "Put up your sword." History is cluttered with the wreckage of nations that failed to follow this command.

                        –MARTIN LUTHER KING, JR.
              From "Three Ways of Responding to Oppression"

We demand difficulty even in our games. We demand it because without difficulty there can be no game. A game is a way of making something hard for the fun of it. The rules of the game are an arbitrary imposition of difficulty: When the spoilsport ruins the fun, he always does so by refusing to play by the rules. It is easier to win at chess if you are free, at your pleasure, to change the wholly arbitrary rules, but the fun is in winning within the rules. No difficulty, no fun.

                            –JOHN CIARDI
                 From "Is Everybody Happy?"

Other Arrangements

Not all paragraphs begin with the topic sentence. Here are some examples of paragraphs with the topic sentence placed elsewhere. See if you can discover a reason for the authors' choice of placement.

Topic Sentence at the End

My generation was the first to attend in great numbers both the ritual "schools" of our own cultures and the higher institutions of the white world. We grew up in two Americas—the ancient one that had existed for our ancestors for tens of thousands of years and the new one that is written about in history books. The tales of those two Americas are rarely compatible—and we quickly came to grasp our perilous situation. We had to make convincing use of our newly acquired intellectual skills in order to sustain our primal culture. We had to release a tide of communication between two worlds, and to do this we had to be a kind of people who had never before existed. *We had to abandon both Andrew Jackson's Wild Indians and Jean-Jacques Rousseau's Noble Savage and emerge as a new cultural mutant—the Intellectual savage—who was capable of surviving equally in two worlds by tenaciously retaining the ritual apparatus of primal people at the same time that we were attaining the intellectual and communications paraphernalia of the dominant societies.*

—JAMAKE HIGHWATER
From "The Intellectual Savage"

After dark, on the warrenlike streets of Brooklyn where I live, I often see women who fear the worst from me. They seem to have set their faces on neutral, and with their purse straps strung across their chests bandolier-style, they forge ahead as though bracing themselves against being tackled. I understand, of course, that the danger they perceive is not a hallucination. Women are particularly vulnerable to street violence, and young black males are drastically overrepresented among the perpetrators of that violence. *Yet these truths are no solace against the kind of alienation that comes of being ever the suspect, a fearsome entity with whom pedestrians avoid making eye contact.*

—BRENT STAPLES
From "Black Men and Public Space"

Topic Sentence After Introductory Information (the Second Paragraph in the Following Pair)

Compared with youth in the more turbulent late 1960's and early 1970's, high school seniors are seen to be quieter, less conspicuous in dress and behavior, and less radical in political views and actions. The flamboyant minority in previous decades has little counterpart today.

This evaluation comes from investigators at the University of Michigan's Institute for Social Research (ISR), who have questioned about 17,000 high school seniors annually during the past 10 years in the Monitoring the Future project. Researchers Jerald B. Bachman, Lloyd D. Johnston, and Patrick M. O'Malley have found that *teens have some concerns about attaining the American Dream.* The last few graduating classes, in fact, have placed increased emphasis on job status, income, and opportunities for advancement. Some of this attitude change may be attributed to recent high levels of unemployment. "For some, it may also reflect being at the tail end of the baby boom—they may face a crowded job market for much of their lifetime."

From "Teenagers Still Pursuing
the American Dream"

Topic Sentence in the Middle of the Paragraph, Preceded by a Definition and Followed by Discussion

Competition means to strive *against* others to achieve the same or similar goals. Cooperation means to strive *with* others to achieve the same or similar goals. A principle of the American way of life is the idea of competition. This takes the simple form of going out and doing better than the other even if you have to do him and his family injury in the process. *That* can be none of your concern. After all, you have your family to think of. This kind of indifference to the consequences to others of one's competitiveness is inherent in the principle of competition. *Our studies have shown us that this kind of competitiveness is extremely damaging to everyone and everything that comes within the orbit of its influence, to none more so than to the successful competitor, for the spoils, he finds in the end, do not belong to him; instead, he belongs to the spoils.* This is the kind of competition that leads to high frequencies of ulcers and nervous breakdowns; to high delinquency rates, divorce and separation rates, and homicide rates; and to violent crime rates that are the highest in the world—as they are in America.

—ASHLEY MONTAGU
From "Competition and Cooperation"

MAKING CONNECTIONS: IMPROVING COHERENCE

Student writers often complain that their writing doesn't "flow." What they mean by this, apparently, is that the writing doesn't move smoothly from one point, one sentence, one paragraph to the next. It is jerky, bumpy, disjointed, hard to follow.

The quality that people refer to as "flow" is called *coherence,* which means "sticking together." Coherence is the result of several elements working together. Here are some pointers for achieving it:

- *Group information and ideas in an orderly way.* Finish what you have to say about one thing before moving on to something else. Arrange ideas in some sort of natural progression: from general to specific, least to most important, simple to complex, easy to difficult, problem to solution.

- *Imagine yourself as audience.* Put yourself in the place of someone coming to your writing for the first time. One of the difficult things about writing is that you may know what you mean, but a reader might not understand in the same way what you've said, or may not see how one idea is connected with another unless you make the connection clear—explicit.

  Think about what a reader would need to know in order to understand the point you're making, and in what order the reader would need to know it. This is not easy to do. Feedback from your classmates and your instructor should help you develop this sense of audience.

- *Tell the reader how one thing is connected to another.* (Don't assume that the reader will automatically see a connection.) Two ways of doing this are by using *repetition* and *connecting expressions.*

- *Use repetition.* Use the same term, a similar term, or a pronoun to refer to an idea that is carried over from one sentence or paragraph to the next. Think of sentences as being hooked together, coupled like cars on a train. Sentences often contain, near the beginning, a key word or phrase that refers to something in the previous sentence. Not all sentences do this, but it is a good idea when you edit your own writing to ask whether a "hook" at the beginning of a sentence would help the reader to see a connection.

  Similarly, the opening sentences of paragraphs often do double duty. Not only do they state the main idea of the paragraph they belong to, but they also refer to the previous paragraph or to the main idea of the entire piece. For example, in his essay about how people respond to oppression, Martin Luther King, Jr., begins his fourth paragraph this way:

  A second way that oppressed people sometimes deal with oppression is to resort to physical violence and corroding hatred.

  Connecting statements like this are *explicit:* They state the connection in so many words (*A second way that . . .*). However, it is usually not necessary to be this explicit. Often, a key word or phrase will do the job. For example, one of the middle paragraphs in Jamake Highwater's "The Intellectual Savage" begins this way:

> This lesson in words and the ideas they convey is very difficult to understand, especially if we grow up insulated by a single culture and its single language.

If you read this statement in context, you will see that the first part of the sentence sums up the first part of the essay.

Statements that *summarize* (remind the reader of what has gone before) and statements that *forecast* (look ahead to what is coming) are important signposts for a reader. They remind the reader of important ideas, and they clarify how one thing is related to another.

- *Use transitional expressions.* Transitional expressions are those little words and phrases that tell us what connection a sentence has with the one that came before it or with the general organization of the whole piece—expressions such as "For example . . . ," "In addition . . . ," "On the other hand . . . ," "However . . . ," and "Finally. . . ." For a more complete list, see page 78.

- *Put orientational expressions at the beginnings of sentences.* Again, this is a general principle that doesn't always apply. But it is a good principle to observe unless there is a reason for breaking it.

  Orientational expressions establish such relationships as time, place, and position. They usually come at the beginning of a sentence and are often set off with a comma. Here are some examples (with the orientational expressions italicized):

> *In 1776,* the fledgling United States declared its independence from Britain. (*Time*)

> *In the alpine meadows of the Cascade Mountains,* spring doesn't come until July. (*Place*)

> *High above the stadium,* six skydivers joined hands to form a circle. (*Position*)

> Note: A comma is not used if the subject of the sentence comes after a linking verb that follows the orientational expression. For example:

> *On the corner of my desk* is a stack of file folders.
> *In my backyard pond* live four Japanese Koi.

Example of Paragraph Coherence

The following paragraph, the third one in Jamake Highwater's "The Intellectual Savage," uses both repeated terms and transitions. The repeated terms are in boldface and the transitions in bold italics. The first sentence uses repetition to link the paragraph to the previous one.

This perilous exploration of reality began for me in southern Alberta and in the Rockies of Montana when I was about five years old. *One day* I discovered a wonderful creature. **It** looked like a bird, but it was able to do things that many other birds cannot do. *For instance,* in addition to flying in the enormous sky, **it** swam and dove in the lakes and, sometimes, **it** just floated majestically on the water's silver surface. **It** would *also* waddle rather gracelessly in the tall grasses that grew along the shores. **That bird** was called *meksikatsi,* which, in the Blackfeet language, means "pink-colored feet." **Meksikatsi** seemed an ideal name for the versatile fly-swim **bird,** since **it** really did have bright pink feet.

The simple transitions "For instance" and "also" in this paragraph let you know that the sentences in which they occur give examples of the controlling idea—"it was able to do things that many other birds cannot do." In this way, they reinforce the relationship between details.

Transitional Expressions

There are many common transitional expressions. Here are some of the most often used, along with their meanings:

TO GIVE AN EXAMPLE:
    For example . . ., for instance . . .

TO MARK A SERIES OF EXAMPLES OR REASONS:
    First . . ., Second . . ., Third . . ., Finally . . .
    One . . ., Another . . ., Still another . . ., Finally . . .

TO SIGNAL AN ADDITION:
    In addition . . ., And . . ., Furthermore . . ., Also . . .,
    Moreover . . .

TO SUMMARIZE OR CONDENSE FOR EMPHASIS:
    In other words . . ., In short . . ., In brief . . .,
    On the whole . . ., To sum up . . .

To signal a contrast or turn of thought:
But . . . , Yet . . . , However . . . , On the other hand . . . ,
In contrast . . . , On the contrary . . . , Conversely . . .

To signal a cause or result:
Because . . . , Therefore . . . , Thus . . . , As a result . . . ,
So . . . , Consequently . . . , Due to . . .

To signal a conclusion:
In conclusion . . . , Finally . . . , Therefore . . .

Exercise: Writing Paragraphs

Choose one of the topics below, and write a paragraph of your own.

1. Review the questions in the section called "Working with Sources," (Chapter 3, "Writing Essays," pages 51–54). Respond to one of these questions in a paragraph of your own.

2. Write a paragraph explaining the different ideas of the American Dream represented in the selections you have read so far. Assume that you are writing for someone from another country who has only a vague idea of what the American Dream means.

3. Write a paragraph describing your own idea of the American Dream. You may use references to the readings if they help to explain your own views.

CHECKLIST: WRITING PARAGRAPHS

Start with some prewriting: list, freewrite, map.

Write a topic sentence that expresses your main idea.

Make a working plan.

Write a rough draft of the paragraph.

Revise, edit, and proofread the draft.

Write a final draft.

II

READINGS FOR WRITING

Part II of this book contains ten chapters, each one dealing with a separate topic on the general idea of the American Dream. Each chapter consists of a collection of readings—mostly essays, but some short stories and poems as well—that present a variety of views on the topic. We chose the readings for each chapter so that, in a sense, they speak to each other. Taken together, the readings in each chapter raise and illuminate certain common issues.

Each reading selection is followed by a list of "Questions for Discussion." The main purpose of these questions is to provide a starting point for class discussion; but they can also serve as a check on how well you have understood the piece, and as a stimulus for your own thinking.

The readings and writing topics can be used for either essays or paragraphs: the strategies are the same. The difference is a matter of how thoroughly the topic is developed. We have included several kinds of topics. Some of them ask that you stick close to the text or texts, summarizing or analyzing the authors' ideas. Others suggest ideas you can write about from your own experience and observation, using material from the readings as a prompt or a guide.

Canyon de Chelly, Arizona.

5 American Places:
Homeland, Heartland, Promised Land

We wonder whether the great American dream
Was the singing of locusts out of the grass to the west and the
West is behind us now:
The west wind's away from us:

We wonder if the liberty is done:
The dreaming finished

We can't say

We aren't sure

—ARCHIBALD MACLEISH
From *The Land of the Free*

Our lives and dreams are shaped by the places where we live. Arnold Schwarzenegger found his "dreamland" in California; Rosalie Sorrells longs for the town of Boise, Idaho, as it once was; Joe Gorman realizes his dream in Suffolk, Massachussets. The character of a place also reflects the character of the people who live there. We think of New Yorkers as being different from San Franciscans, Alaskans from Floridians, farm boys from city slickers. In a sense, the place and the people are inseparable: places shape people and people shape places.

The readings in this chapter represent some different ways of looking at places, and different ways of thinking and writing about them. Despite their different backgrounds and approaches, the writers included here share two important characteristics: They have observed and thought well about the places they describe; and they use the techniques of description—showing—to evoke a sense of place in the reader. As you read, pay attention not only to *what* these writers say, but also to *how* they create a sense of place.

JOHN MCPHEE
Anchorage, Alaska

John McPhee is a staff writer for the New Yorker, *and his work has appeared in many magazines. He has also written books on a wide variety of subjects, including the* Pine Barrens, Oranges, *and* Levels of the Game. *The selection below is from* Coming into the Country, *a book about life in Alaska and the Yukon.*

KEY VOCABULARY

A **FJORD** is a long, narrow sea inlet that runs between steep cliffs.

PASSAIC is a city in New Jersey. The name here refers to McPhee's contention that Anchorage is "that part of any city where the city has burst its seams and extruded Colonel Sanders."

QUEEN-POST TRUSSES are upright supporting posts set vertically between the rafters and central beam of a building.

QUOITS is a game in which rings of rope or iron are pitched at a stake in the ground.

SUTTON PLACE is a posh area in Manhattan, N.Y.

WALTER HICKEL was Governor of Alaska from 1966 to 1969 and U.S. Secretary of the Interior from 1969 to 1970, during Richard Nixon's presidency.

There are those who would say that tens of thousands of barrels of oil erupting from a break in the Trans-Alaska Pipeline would be the lesser accident if, at more or less the same time, a fresh Anchorage were to spill into the bush. While the dream of the capital city plays on in the mind, Anchorage stands real. It is the central hive of human Alaska, and in manner and structure it represents, for all to see, the Alaskan dynamic and the Alaskan aesthetic. It is a tangible expression of certain Alaskans' regard for Alaska—their one true city, the exemplar of the predilections of the people in creating improvements over the land.

As may befit a region where both short and long travel is generally by air, nearly every street in Anchorage seems to be the road to the airport. Dense groves of plastic stand on either side—flashing, whirling, flaky. HOOSIER BUDDY'S MOBILE HOMES. WINNEBAGO SALES & SERVICE. DISCOUNT LIQUORS OPEN SUNDAY. GOLD RUSH AUTO SALES. PROMPT ACTION LOCKSMITHS. ALASKA REFRIGERATION & AIR CONDITION. DENALI FUEL . . .

"Are the liquor stores really open Sundays?"

"Everything in Anchorage is open that pays."

Almost all Americans would recognize Anchorage, because Anchorage is that part of any city where the city has burst its seams and extruded Colonel Sanders.

"You can taste the greed in the air."

BELUGA ASPHALT.

Anchorage is sometimes excused in the name of pioneering. Build now, civilize later. But Anchorage is not a frontier town. It is virtually unrelated to its environment. It has come in on the wind, an American spore. A large cookie cutter brought down on El Paso could lift something like Anchorage into the air. Anchorage is the northern rim of Trenton, the center of Oxnard, the ocean-blind precincts of Daytona Beach. It is condensed, instant Albuquerque.

PANCHO'S VILLA, MEXICAN FOOD. BULL SHED, STEAK HOUSE AND SONIC LOUNGE. SHAKEY'S DRIVE-IN PIZZA. EAT ME SUBMARINES.

Anchorage has developed a high-rise city core, with glass-box offices for the oil companies, and tall Miamian hotels. Zonelessly lurching outward, it has made of its suburbs a carnival of cinder block, all with a speculative mania so rife that sellers of small homesites—of modest lots scarcely large enough for houses—retain subsurface rights. In vacant lots, **queen-post trusses** lie waiting for new buildings to jump up beneath them. Roads are rubbled, ponded with chuckholes. Big trucks, graders, loaders, make the prevailing noise, the dancing fumes, the frenetic beat of the town. Huge rubber tires are strewn about like **quoits,** ever ready for the big machines that move hills of earth and gravel into inconvenient lakes, which become new ground.

FOR LEASE. WILL BUILD TO SUIT.

Anchorage coins millionaires in speculative real estate. Some are young. The median age in Anchorage is under twenty-four. Every three or four years, something like half the population turns over. And with thirty days of residence, you can vote as an Alaskan.

POLAR REALTY. IDLE WHEELS TRAILER PARK. MOTEL MUSH INN.

Anchorage has a thin history. Something of a precursor of the modern pipeline camps, it began in 1914 as a collection of tents pitched to shelter workers building the Alaska Railroad. For decades, it was a wooden-sidewalked, gravel-streeted town. Then, remarkably early, as cities go, it developed an urban slum, and both homes and commerce began to abandon its core. The exodus was so rapid that the central business district never wholly consolidated, and downtown Anchorage is even more miscellaneous than outlying parts of the city. There is, for example, a huge J. C.

Penney department store filling several blocks in the heart of town, with an interior mall of boutiques and restaurants and a certain degree of chic. A couple of weedy vacant lots separate this complex from five log cabins. Downtown Anchorage from a distance displays an upreaching skyline that implies great pressure for land. Down below, among the high buildings, are houses, huts, vegetable gardens, and bungalows with tidy front lawns. Anchorage burst out of itself and left these incongruities in the center, and for me they are the most appealing sights in Anchorage. Up against a downtown office building I have seen cordwood stacked for winter.

In its headlong, violent expansion, Anchorage had considerable, but 15 not unlimited, space to fill. To an extent unusual among cities, Anchorage has certain absolute boundaries, and in that sense its growth has been a confined explosion. To the north, a pair of military bases establish, in effect, a Roman wall. To the west and south, **fjord**like arms of the Pacific—Knik Arm, Turnagain Arm—frame the city. Behind Anchorage, east, stand the Chugach Mountains, stunning against the morning and in the evening light—Mount Magnificent, Mount Gordon Lyon, Temptation Peak, Tanaina Peak, Wolverine Peak, the Suicide Peaks. Development has gone to some extent upward there. Houses are pushpinned to the mountainsides— a Los Angelized setting, particularly at night, above the starry lights of town. But the mountains are essentially a full stop to Anchorage, and Anchorage has nowhere else to go.

Within this frame of mountains, ocean, and military boundaries are about fifty thousand acres (roughly the amount of land sought by the Capital Site Selection Committee), and the whole of it is known as the Anchorage Bowl. The ground itself consists of silt, alluvium, eolian sands, glacial debris—material easy to rearrange. The surface was once lumpy with small knolls. As people and their businesses began filling the bowl, they went first to the knolls, because the knolls were wooded and well drained. They cut down the trees, truncated the hills, and bestudded them with buildings. They strung utility lines like baling wire from knoll to knoll. The new subdivisions within the bowl were thus hither and yon, random, punctuated with bogs. Anchorage grew like mold.

WOLVERINE ALUMINUM SIDING. ALASKA FOUR-WHEEL DRIVE. JACK BENNY'S RADIO-DISPATCHED CESSPOOL PUMPING.

Low ground is gradually being filled. The bowl has about a hundred and eighty thousand people now, or almost half of human Alaska. There are some in town—notably, Robert Atwood, of the *Times*—who would like to see Anchorage grow to seven hundred thousand. Atwood is a big, friendly, old-football-tackle sort of man, with whitening hair and gold-rimmed glasses. Forty years on the inside, this impatient advocate of the commercial potentialities of Alaska is said to be one of the two wealthiest people in the state, the other being his brother-in-law. "Idealists here in town see a need for a park in every housing development," Atwood told me one day. "They want to bury utility lines, reserve green belts, build bicycle paths. With these things, the bowl could only contain three hundred and fifty thousand. They're making it very difficult for man, these people. They favor animals, trees, water, flowers. Who ever makes a plan for man? Who ever *will* make a plan for man? That is what *I* wonder. I am known among conservationists as a bad guy."

In Anchorage, if you threw a pebble into a crowd, chances are you would not hit a conservationist, an ecophile, a wilderness preserver. In small ghettos, they are there—living in a situation lined with irony. They are in Alaska—many of them working for the federal government—because Alaska is everything wild it has ever been said to be. Alaska runs off the edge of the imagination, with its tracklessness, its beyond-the-ridge-line surprises, its hundreds of millions of acres of wilderness—this so-called "last frontier," which is certainly all of that, yet for the most part is not a frontier at all but immemorial landscape in an all but unapproached state. Within such vastness, Anchorage is a mere pustule, a dot, a minim—a walled city, wild as Yonkers, with the wildlife riding in a hundred and ninety-three thousand trucks and cars. Yet the city—where people are, where offices are—is perforce the home address of wilderness planners, of wildlife biologists, of Brooks Range guides.

The first few days I spent in Alaska were spent in Anchorage, and I 20 remember the increasing sense of entrapment we felt (my wife was with me), knowing that nothing less than a sixth of the entire United States, and almost all of it wilderness, was out there beyond seeing, while immediate needs and chores to do were keeping us penned in this portable **Passaic.** Finally, we couldn't take it any longer, and we cancelled appointments and rented a car and revved it up for an attempted breakout from town. A float plane—at a hundred and ten dollars an hour—would have been the best means, but, like most of the inmates of Anchorage, we could not afford it. For a great many residents, Anchorage is about all they ever see of Alaska, day after day after year. There are only two escape routes—a road north, a road south—and these are encumbered with traffic and, for some miles anyway, lined with detritus from Anchorage. We went south, that first time, and eventually east, along a fjord that would improve Norway. Then the road turned south again, into the mountains of Kenai—great tundra balds that reminded me of Scotland and my wife of parts of Switzerland, where she had lived. She added that she thought these mountains looked better than the ones in Europe. Sockeyes, as red as cardinals, were spawning in clear, shallow streams, and we ate our cheese and chocolate in a high

meadow over a torrential river of green and white water. We looked up to
the ridges for Dall sheep, and felt, for the moment, about as free. Anchorage
shrank into perspective. It might be a sorry town, but it has the greatest
out-of-town any town has ever had.

BIG RED'S FLYING SERVICE. BELUGA STEAM & ELECTRIC THAWING. DON'T
GO TO JAIL LET FRED GO YOUR BAIL.

There is a street in Anchorage—a green-lights, red-lights, busy street—
that is used by automobiles and airplanes. I remember an airplane in
someone's driveway—next door to the house where I was staying. The
neighbor started up its engine one night toward eleven o'clock, and for
twenty minutes he ran it flat out while his two sons, leaning hard into the
stabilizers, strained to hold back the plane. In Alaska, you do what you feel
like doing, or so goes an Alaskan creed.

There is, in Anchorage, a somewhat **Sutton Place.** It is an enclave,
actually, with several roads, off the western end of Northern Lights Boulevard, which is a principal Anchorage thoroughfare, a neon borealis. **Walter
Hickel** lives in the enclave, on Loussac Drive, which winds between curbs
and lawns, neatly trimmed, laid out, and landscaped, under white birches
and balsam poplars. Hickel's is a heavy, substantial home, its style American
Dentist. The neighbors' houses are equally expensive and much the same.
The whole neighborhood seems to be struggling to remember Scarsdale.
But not to find Alaska.

I had breakfast one morning in Anchorage with a man who had come
to Alaska from The Trust for Public Land, an organization whose goal is to
buy potential parkland in urban areas and hold it until the government,
whose legislative machinery is often too slow for the land market, can get
up the funds for the purpose. In overbuilt urban settings—from Watts to
Newark and back to Oakland—The Trust for Public Land will acquire
whatever it can, even buildings under demolishment, in order to create
small parks and gardens that might relieve the compressed masses. And now
The Trust for Public Land had felt the need to come to Anchorage—to the
principal city of Alaska—to help hold a pond or a patch of green for the
people in the future to have and see.

Books were selling in Anchorage, once when I was there, for forty- 25
seven cents a pound.

There are those who would say that the only proper place for a new
capital of Alaska—if there has to be a new one—is Anchorage, because
anyone who has built a city like Anchorage should not be permitted to
build one anywhere else.

At Anchorage International Airport, there is a large aerial photograph
of Anchorage formed by pasting together a set of pictures that were made
without what cartographers call ground control. This great aerial map is one

of the first things to confront visitors from everywhere in the world, and in bold letters it is titled "ANCHORAGE, ALASKA. UNCONTROLLED MOSAIC."

QUESTIONS FOR DISCUSSION

1. What is the "dominant impression" of McPhee's description? Can you find a sentence in the essay that sums up this impression?

2. In what ways does Anchorage exemplify "the predilections of the people in creating improvements over the land"?

3. Why does McPhee say that Alaska is not a frontier? Look up the word "frontier" and speculate about why McPhee thinks Alaska does not fit the definition.

4. Robert Atwood, one of the people McPhee interviews, complains about environmentalists. He says, "Who ever makes a plan for man?" What do you think he means by "a plan for man"?

5. In developing his description of Anchorage, McPhee uses a technique borrowed from film called "intercutting"—breaking up the description with signs from businesses and advertising slogans. And he closes the piece with a series of short, disconnected paragraphs. Do you think this technique is appropriate to the subject? Why?

6. To conclude the description, McPhee uses a caption from an aerial photograph at the airport: "ANCHORAGE, ALASKA. UNCONTROLLED MOSAIC." Why is this metaphor a particularly fitting conclusion?

✍ FRANCES FITZGERALD
From *Cities on the Hill*

*Frances FitzGerald is a freelance journalist whose work has appeared in many
magazines. In 1966 she spent a year as a freelance writer in Vietnam, and in
1967 she won the Overseas Press Club Award for the best interpretation of
foreign affairs. Drawing on material gathered in Vietnam, in 1972
FitzGerald published* A Fire in the Lake: The Vietnamese and
Americans in Vietnam, *for which she won several awards, including the
Pulitzer Prize and the National Book Award. She is also the author of*
America Revised, *a study of American history textbooks since the Civil
War, and* Cities on the Hill, *the book from which the following selection was
taken, which is a study of four visionary communities in the United States.*

KEY VOCABULARY

ARMISTEAD MAUPIN, a San Francisco writer and humorist, was Fitzgerald's
guide for part of the time she spent in the Castro.

SWISH is slang for "effeminate."

TOOTS SHOR'S was a famous restaurant in Manhattan whose walls were covered with photos of celebrities.

There were in fact four gay centers in San Francisco, each geographi-
cally distinct, each containing what appeared to be distinct subcultures or
culture parts.

The oldest gay center in the city lay in the Tenderloin—that triangle
of sleazy bars and cheap hotels bordered by the business district, the theater
district, and Market Street. The Tenderloin, like its counterparts in other
cities, was far from exclusively gay. The home of winos and bums, it was
the transit station for sailors and other impecunious travelers, and it harbored most of the prostitution, both gay and straight, for the entire city. In
the late afternoon female prostitutes, male hustlers, and transvestite whores
could be seen performing a complicated street corner ballet as they tried at
once to evade the police and sort out their initially undifferentiated customers. In the fifties the district had harbored most of the gay bars in the
city—but now only hustler and drag queen bars were left. The Kokpit,
owned by a queen called Sweet Lips, had been in operation for about a
decade. Now lined with trophies and photographs of countless drag balls,
it had become a kind of **Toots Shor's** of drag San Francisco. A few blocks

away there was a bar of a professional and much more highly specialized nature, where six- to seven-foot-tall black transvestites hustled white men in business suits, who were, necessarily, shorter.

Chronologically speaking, Polk Street, or Polk Gulch, was the second gay center of the city. It was the decorators' district, and in the sixties a number of gay bars had moved into the blocks lined with antique shops and furniture stores. Since then it had been the major site of the Halloween festivities. On that one night a year the police stood by, leaving the street to a carnival of witches, clowns, nuns on roller skates, and Jackie Kennedy look-alikes or Patty Hearst look-alikes with toy machine guns. Polk Street was a mixed neighborhood—both gay and straight people lived there, and its restaurants catered to both crowds. Its gay bars were thus not conspicuous except at night when groups of young hustlers stood out on the sidewalks around them. A number of them still catered to the stylish and the well-to-do. They had low lights, expensive furniture, and music by the old favorites: Marlene Dietrich, Noel Coward, and Judy Garland. Even to outsiders their patrons would be recognizable, for Polk Street was still the land of good taste and attitude: the silk scarf so perfectly knotted, the sentimentality, the witty little jab.

A newer gay center lay around Folsom Street in the old warehouse district south of Market. At night Folsom Street was the complement to Polk Street—the raw, as it were, to the cooked—for it was lined with leather bars: the Stud, the Brig, the Ramrod, the Black and Blue. Late at night groups of men in blue jeans, motorcycle jackets, and boots would circle around ranks of Triumphs and Harley-Davidsons, eyeing each other warily. The bars had sawdust on the floors, and men drank beer standing up, shoulder to shoulder, in a din of heavy metal and hard rock. In the Black and Blue some of them wore studded wristbands, studded neckbands, and caps with Nazi insignia; above the bar a huge motorcycle was suspended in a wash of psychedelic lights. On Wednesday nights the Arena bar had a slave auction: men would be stripped almost naked, chained up by men in black masks with whips, prodded, and sold off to the highest bidder. Such was the theater of Folsom Street. The men in leather came from Polk Street and other quiet neighborhoods, the money went to charity, and the "slave" put on a business suit and went to work the next day.

Folsom Street was a night town—the Valley of the Kings, it was called, as opposed to the Valley of the Queens in the Tenderloin and the Valley of the Dolls on Polk Street. But in addition to the leather bars, a variety of gay restaurants, discotheques, bathhouses, and sex clubs had moved into its abandoned warehouses and manufacturing lofts. It was an entertainment place, and few people lived there.

The Castro, by contrast, was a neighborhood. Though first settled by

gays—homesteaded, as it were—in the early seventies, it was now the ful-
crum of gay life in the city. At first glance it was much like other neighborhoods: a four-block main street with a drugstore, corner groceries, a liquor
store, dry cleaners, and a revival movie house whose facade had seen better
days. Here and there upscale money was visibly at work: a café advertised
Dungeness crab, a store sold expensive glass and tableware, and there were
two banks. But there was nothing **swish** about the Castro. The main street
ran off into quiet streets of two- and three-story white-shingle houses; the
main haberdashery, The All-American Boy, sold clothes that would have
suited a conservative Ivy Leaguer. In fact the neighborhood was like other
neighborhoods except that on Saturdays and Sundays you could walk for
blocks and see only young men dressed as it were for a hiking expedition.
Also the bookstore was a gay bookstore, the health club a gay health club;
and behind the shingles hung out on the street there was a gay real-estate
brokerage, a gay lawyer's office, and the office of a gay psychiatrist. The bars
were, with one exception, gay bars, and one of them, the Twin Peaks bar
near Market Street, was, so **Armistead** told me, the first gay bar in the
country to have picture windows on the street.

Armistead and his friends liked to take visitors to the Castro and point
out landmarks such as the Twin Peaks. But in fact the only remarkable-
looking thing on the street was the crowd of young men. Even at lunchtime
on a weekday there would be dozens of good-looking young men crowd-
ing the café tables, hanging out at the bars, leaning against doorways, or
walking down the streets with their arms around each other. The sexual
tension was palpable. "I'd never live here," Armistead said. "Far too intense. You can't go to the laundromat at ten A.M. without the right pair of
jeans on." The Castro was the place where most of the young gay men
came. Fifty to a hundred thousand came as tourists each summer, and of
these, thousands decided to settle, leaving Topeka and Omaha for good.
New York and Los Angeles had their Polk Streets and Folsom Districts, but
the Castro was unique: it was the first settlement built by gay liberation.

QUESTIONS FOR DISCUSSION

1. To distinguish Folsom Street from Polk Street, FitzGerald uses an analogy: Folsom is to Polk as the raw is to the cooked. What do you think
   she means by this analogy?

2. Each of the gay centers FitzGerald describes is marked by a distinct
   style. Summarize the essential style of each one.

3. FitzGerald says that the Castro, unlike the other three gay districts in San Francisco, is a neighborhood. From details in her description, what do you think FitzGerald means by "neighborhood"? What distinguishes a neighborhood from any other part of a city?

4. FitzGerald's description of the four gay centers is organized chronologically, from earliest to latest. In what ways does her description reflect an advance of the gay liberation movement?

𝒵❦ **ALFRED KAZIN**

From *A Walker in the City*

For over fifty years, Alfred Kazin has been a teacher and critic of American literature. He has taught at many colleges and universities, including the City College of New York, Harvard, and Hunter College. He has written several major works on American literature, beginning in 1942 with On Native Grounds. *This was followed by such books as* Contemporaries *(1962) and* A Writer's America *(1988). He has received numerous awards and fellowships. Kazin has also written personal memoirs, particularly about Jewish life in New York. The following selection is taken from* A Walker in the City, *a book about growing up in the Jewish neighborhood of Brownsville in the early part of the twentieth century.*

KEY VOCABULARY

BENITO MUSSOLINI was the Fascist dictator of Italy from 1922 to 1943. He joined with Germany and Japan in Word War II. Mussolini was executed in 1943.

DAGUERREOTYPES were, in the nineteenth century, photographs made on metal plates. In 1839, Jean Louis Daguerre received from the French Academy the first patent for a photographic process.

EL is an abbreviation for "elevated train"—a subway train that runs for all or part of its route on tracks raised above the ground.

A **FASCIST,** during the time in which Kazin's story takes place, is a follower of the Italian dictator Benito Mussolini. Fascism is a system of government characterized by one-party dictatorship, suppression of the opposition, and attitudes of nationalism and racism.

LA FORZA DEL DESTINO is an Italian phrase meaning "the force of destiny."

A **LITHOGRAPH** is a print made by a process of transferring an image to paper from a flat stone or metal plate.

TAMMANY COURT refers to Tammany Hall, a political organization in New York, founded in 1789. It held great power in New York politics, in part because of its willingness to help poor people and immigrants. It was also guilty of widespread corruption.

There was a new public library I liked to walk out to right after supper, 1
when the streets were still full of light. It was to the north of the Italians,

just off the **El** on Broadway, in the "American" district of old frame houses and brownstones and German ice-cream parlors and quiet tree-lined streets where I went to high school. Everything about that library was good, for it was usually empty and cool behind its awnings, and the shelves were packed with books that not many people ever seemed to take away. But even better was the long walk out of Brownsville to reach it.

How wonderful it was in the still suspended evening light to go past the police station on East New York and come out into the clinging damp sweetness of Italian cheese. The way to the borders of Brownsville there was always heavy with blocks of indistinguishable furniture stores, monument works, wholesale hardware shops. Block after block was lined with bedroom sets, granite tombstones, kitchen ranges, refrigerators, store fixtures, cash registers. It was like taking one last good look around before you said good-by. As the sun bore down on new kitchen ranges and refrigerators, I seemed to hear the clang of all those heavily smooth surfaces against the fiery windows, to feel myself pulled down endless corridors of tombstones, cash registers, maple beds, maple love seats, maple vanity tables. But at the police station, the green lamps on each side of the door, the detectives lounging along the street, the smell from the dark, damp, leaky steps that led down to the public toilets below, instantly proclaimed the end of Brownsville.

Ahead, the Italians' streets suddenly reared up into hills, all the trolley car lines flew apart into wild plunging crossroads—the way to anywhere, it seemed to me then. And in the steady heat, the different parts of me racing each other in excitement, the sweat already sweet on my face, still tasting on my lips the corn and salt and butter, I would dash over the tree-lined island at the crossroads, and on that boulevard so sharp with sun that I could never understand why the new red-brick walls of the Catholic church felt so cool as I passed, I crossed over into the Italian district.

I still had a certain suspicion of the Italians—surely they were all **Fascists** to a man? Every grocery window seemed to have a picture of **Mussolini** frowning under a feather-tipped helmet, every drugstore beneath the old-fashioned gold letters pasted on the window a colored **lithograph** of the Madonna with a luminescent heart showing through a blue gown. What I liked best in the windows were the thickly printed opera posters, topped by tiny photographs of singers with olive-bronze faces. Their long straight noses jutted aloofly, defying me to understand them. But despite the buzz of unfamiliar words ending in the letter *i,* I could at least make contact with **LA FORZA DEL DESTINO.** In the air was that high overriding damp sweetness of Italian cheese, then something peppery. In a butcher shop window at the corner of Pacific Street long incredibly thin sausage rings were strung around a horizontal bar. The clumps of red and brown meat dripping off those sausage rings always stayed with me until I left the Italians at Fulton Street—did they eat such things? Usually, at that hour of the early evening when I passed through on my way to the new library, they were all still at supper. The streets were strangely empty except for an old man in a white cap who sat on the curb sucking at a twisted Italian cigar. I felt I was passing through a deserted town and knocking my head against each door to call the inhabitants out. It was a poor neighborhood, poor as ours. Yet all the houses and stores there, the very lettering of the signs Avvocato Farmacia Latteria tantalized me by their foreignness. Everything there looked smaller and sleepier than it did in Brownsville. There was a kind of mild, infinitely soothing smell of flour and cheese mildly rotting in the evening sun. You could almost taste the cheese in the sweat you licked off your lips, could feel your whole body licking and tasting at the damp inner quietness that came out of the stores. . . .

Ahead of me now the black web of the Fulton Street **El.** On the other side of the Banca Commerciale, two long even pavements still raw with sunlight at seven o'clock of a summer evening take me straight through the German and Irish "American" neighborhoods. I could never decide whether it was all those brownstones and blue and gray frame houses or the sight of the library serenely waiting for me that made up the greatest pleasure of that early evening walk. As soon as I got out from under the darkness of the **El** on Fulton Street, I was catapulted into tranquility.

Everything ahead of me now was of a different order—wide, clean, still, every block lined with trees. I sniffed hungrily at the patches of garden earth behind the black iron spikes and at the wooden shutters hot in the sun—there where even the names of the streets, Macdougal, Hull, Somers, made me humble with admiration. The long quiet avenues rustled comfortably in the sun; above the brownstone stoops all the yellow striped awnings were unfurled. Every image I had of peace, of quiet shaded streets in some old small-town America I had seen dreaming over the ads in the *Saturday Evening Post,* now came back to me as that proud procession of awnings along the brownstones. I can never remember *walking* those last few blocks to the library; I seemed to float along the canvas tops. Here were the truly American streets; here was where they lived. To get that near to brownstones, to see how private everything looked in that world of cool black painted floors and green walls where on each windowsill the first shoots of Dutch bulbs rose out of the pebbles like green and white flags, seemed to me the greatest privilege I had ever had. A breath of long-stored memory blew out at me from the veranda of Oyster Bay. Even when I visited an Irish girl from my high school class who lived in one of those brownstones, and was amazed to see that the rooms were as small as ours, that a **Tammany court** attendant's family could be as poor as we were, that behind the solid "American" front of fringed shawls, Yankee rocking chairs, and oval **daguerreotypes** on the walls they kept warm in winter over an oil stove—even then, I could think of those brownstone streets only as my great entrance into America, a half-hour nearer to "New York."

I had made a discovery; I had stumbled on a connection between myself and the shape and color of time in the streets of New York. Though I knew that brownstones were old-fashioned and had read scornful references to them in novels, it was just the thick, solid way in which they gripped to themselves some texture of the city's past that now fascinated me. There was one brownstone on Macdougal Street I would stop and brood over for long periods every evening I went to the library for fresh books—waiting in front of it, studying every crease in the stone, every line in the square windows jutting out above the street, as if I were planning its portrait. I had made a discovery: walking could take me back into the America of the nineteenth century.

QUESTIONS FOR DISCUSSION

1. What is it that appeals to Kazin about 19th century America?

2. What kinds of sensory impressions dominate Kazin's descriptions of Brownsville, the Italian neighborhood, and the "American" neighborhood? Find some examples of each.

3. What clues are there in the reading to suggest that Kazin sees himself as not yet having arrived in America?

4. In what ways is the "American" neighborhood different from the others? Why do you think Kazin calls it the "American" neighborhood?

∞ EDDY HARRIS

From *The South of Haunted Dreams*

*Born in St. Louis, Missouri, Eddy Harris graduated from Stanford
University and studied in London. He has worked as a journalist and a
screenwriter. Harris has written three books, each one about a journey. His
first,* Mississippi Solo, *tells of his canoe trip down the Mississippi River.
His second,* Native Stranger, *is an account of a year spent travelling in
Africa. And the third,* South of Haunted Dreams, *from which the following
selection was taken, is the story of a motorcycle trip through the American
South. In all of these books, Harris explores the experience of Blackamericans
(his word) in the world today.*

KEY VOCABULARY

A **PARADOX** is a statement or circumstance that appears to be self-
contradictory but is nevertheless true.

I turned off the road I was on and headed up toward Tuskegee, where 1
the famous institute is.

By tradition an all-black college. Started in 1881 when Lewis Adams,
a former slave, and George Campbell, a former slave owner, persuaded the
state of Alabama that a college for blacks would be a good thing. Tuskegee
Institute illustrates the **paradox** of the South. A former slave working with
a former slave owner. The state of Alabama giving $2,000 for teachers' sala-
ries but nothing for land or buildings or equipment.

A falling-down church and an old wooden shack were the school until
the treasurer of another black college, Hampton Institute in Virginia, made
a personal loan of $200 to Tuskegee with which the school was able to buy
a hundred acres of abandoned farm-land. There are 268 acres now and 161
buildings. From 30 students in the first class the school has grown into an
academic community of 5,000—students, faculty, and staff. The campus is
a national historic site administered by the U.S. National Park Service. It is
a monument, a living museum.

For many of the old buildings on campus the bricks were made by
students, and the buildings themselves were built by students. It was the
philosophy of the school and its founder, Booker T. Washington, that
young blacks receive a practical education as well as a theoretical and cre-

101

ative one. To Booker T., who had been born a slave and who had worked his way through college as a janitor, graduating with honors, education was a total experience, meant to take place in the classroom and the workshop, but also in the dormitories and the dining halls. He wanted Tuskegee to be what he called a civilizing agent.

So the school taught agriculture, and the students ate the produce from   5
the school farm. Students made bricks and built buildings. And when they graduated, many students became educators, not only in the classroom. They went back, many of them, to the plantation areas to show people there how to put new energy and new ideas into farming and into life itself.

The buildings are old, some in need of repair; many wooden ones could use a coat of paint. And as I walked through the campus and into the buildings I felt nothing so much as the **paradox** of black/white life in America.

If not for donations from benefactors like Andrew Carnegie and John D. Rockefeller, Tuskegee would not exist. If not for segregation and the two societies, Tuskegee would not need to exist. And who knows if the Carnegies and the Rockefellers and the Huntingtons were so generous only as a way to keep blacks in schools for blacks and away from schools for whites?

The whole thing was making me crazy, giving me a headache, making me want to examine everyone's motives, everything's reasons. I went a mile or so down the road to the center of town and sat in the very center of a noisy little restaurant just off the town's main square. The sign read: PIERCE'S RESTAURANT. COUNTRY COOKING.

I talked to no one, just sat and watched the black people laughing and talking loud and loading down the country food. My spirits were lifted. I got an order of fried chicken, a side order of greens and one of black-eyed peas, some macaroni and cheese, and I ate until I couldn't eat any more.

The place was owned by a black man. The ladies behind the counter   10
were black. Most of the customers were black as well, but not all. There were many white people, farmers in overalls, laborers in blue jeans and dirty shirts, county bureaucrats in suits and ties. There were no private tables; you sat where you found a space. White people and black people sat shoulder to shoulder in this dusty southern town and ate greens and ham and sweet potatoes together. I don't know how close they sat—or even if they talked—once they left this two-room restaurant and the thousands of places like it in the South, but as James Anderman had said, in many ways blacks and whites are familiar with each other here. They may not be best friends, may not invite one another home for dinner, but they know each other. They are comfortable around each other in ways that they are not in the North. I cannot imagine a white lady sitting alone in a black restaurant in

Cleveland or in St. Louis. That woman in Saratoga Springs couldn't even walk on the same street with me without panicking. And yet here in the racist South, a lone white woman sits and reads a book and eats her lunch.

Lunch hour for most was over. All the white people had left by the time she arrived. But she came in and sat and ate.

She was a nurse, dressed all in white. Her hair was so gray, even it was white. Her name—so the tag pinned to her dress said—was Grace Comer. I did not talk to her. I didn't need to. I just watched her and I think she must have felt me watching, for she looked up from her book and smiled at me.

James Anderman thinks that if there's hope for this country, it's right here, right here in the South. And I begin to wonder.

There is plenty to remind you that evil still lives in the world. And so we leap at the little flickers of hope, as if we were moths and the flickers bright flames. A smile, a wave, a moment's kindness. Enough flickers and there will be flame, and the flame will become blaze.

I was falling in love with this place. I took the hour's ride from Tuske- 15 gee to Montgomery without the dread and rage that perhaps rightly ought to have been within me. So much had happened in Montgomery, so much started here, that it is easy to think the entire struggle for human rights began here. Let's not forget Booker T. and George Washington Carver, Sojourner Truth and Denmark Vesey and Harriet Tubman and Nat Turner and Ida Wells. These are the names we know. Let us not forget Rosa Parks, an ordinary woman, somebody's seamstress. She was simply tired one day—so the story goes—and refused to give up her seat to a white man. It was 1955. It wasn't that blacks had to sit at the back of the bus, as if there were a special section for them. It was simply that no black person was allowed to sit in front of a white person no matter where he sat. Rosa Parks was arrested for not surrendering her seat.

Some say she was just tired. Others claim the whole affair was planned. I am proud of her either way, proud of the blacks in Montgomery who refused to ride the buses as long as seating remained segregated. They made the necessary sacrifice. They walked to work and the buses ran empty for eleven months.

We like to think of them as ordinary people: Rosa and the black men and women who boycotted the buses; the college students in Greensboro and Nashville who sat at segregated lunch counters and endured the curs- ings and the beatings until the lunch counters were integrated; the men and women who marched peacefully for the right to vote; Elizabeth Eckford and eight black schoolmates who silently walked through a crowd of angry whites spitting at them, cursing them, hating them that first day blacks were allowed to go to Little Rock High School, and maybe every day afterwards.

They were not ordinary people but strong and brave, and we must never forget them and what they did for us.

Men like my father who hung his head in fear and shame to live and proudly tell the story. These are our heroes. Quiet heroes like Great-Grandfather Joseph and the many like him, men and women, whom we should remember if for no other reason than that they endured and that they survived and that they carried us one step farther, one step closer.

And while we are remembering, let us remember too the whites who 20 believed in racial equality and were cursed and beaten, arrested and killed alongside the blacks.

Let us never forget.

And let us lift every voice in praise.

QUESTIONS FOR DISCUSSION

1. What is the "paradox of the South" and how does the Tuskegee Institute illustrate it?

2. How were Booker T. Washington's ideas about education put into practice at the Tuskegee Institute?

3. Why does Harris' experience at Pierce's Restaurant strengthen his feeling that James Anderman is right when he sees "the hope for this country . . . right here in the South"?

4. Why was Harris expecting to feel rage during the trip to Montgomery?

5. What do Tuskegee and Montgomery symbolize for the United States?

☙ JUDITH ORTIZ COFER

From *Silent Dancing*

Judith Ortiz Cofer was born in Hormigueros, Puerto Rico, in 1952. Because her father was in the U.S. Navy, her family moved to Paterson, New Jersey, in 1954. While she was growing up, the family frequently travelled back and forth to Puerto Rico. Cofer received her M.A. degree from Florida Atlantic University in 1977. Today she teaches English at the University of Georgia. She has published three books of poetry and a collection of essays. Her novel Line of the Sun *(1989) was nominated for the Pulitzer Prize. The following selection is from* Silent Dancing: A Partial Remembrance of a Puerto Rican Childhood *(1990).*

KEY VOCABULARY

BARRIO is a Spanish word for "neighborhood."

CAFE-CON-LECHE is Spanish for "coffee with milk."

LA ISLA is Spanish for "the island" and here refers to the island of Puerto Rico.

We lived in Puerto Rico until my brother was born in 1954. Soon after, because of economic pressures on our growing family, my father joined the United States Navy. He was assigned to duty on a ship in Brooklyn Yard, New York City—a place of cement and steel that was to be his home base in the States until his retirement more than twenty years later. He left the Island first, tracking down his uncle who lived with his family across the Hudson River, in Paterson, New Jersey. There he found a tiny apartment in a huge apartment building that had once housed Jewish families and was just being transformed into a tenement by Puerto Ricans overflowing from New York City. In 1955 he sent for us. My mother was only twenty years old, I was not quite three, and my brother was a toddler when we arrived at *El Building,* as the place had been christened by its new residents.

My memories of life in Paterson during those first few years are in shades of gray. Maybe I was too young to absorb vivid colors and details, or to discriminate between the slate blue of the winter sky and the darker hues of the snow-bearing clouds, but the single color washes over the whole period. The building we lived in was gray, the streets were gray

105

with slush the first few months of my life there, the coat my father had bought for me was dark in color and too big. It sat heavily on my thin frame.

I do remember the way the heater pipes banged and rattled, startling all of us out of sleep until we got so used to the sound that we automatically either shut it out or raised our voices above the racket. The hiss from the valve punctuated my sleep, which has always been fitful, like a nonhuman presence in the room—the dragon sleeping at the entrance of my childhood. But the pipes were a connection to all the other lives being lived around us. Having come from a house made for a single family back in Puerto Rico—my mother's extended-family home—it was curious to know that strangers lived under our floor and above our heads, and that the heater pipe went through everyone's apartments. (My first spanking in Paterson came as a result of playing tunes on the pipes in my room to see if there would be an answer). My mother was as new to this concept of beehive life as I was, but had been given strict orders by my father to keep the doors locked, the noise down, ourselves to ourselves.

It seems that Father had learned some painful lessons about prejudice while searching for an apartment in Paterson. Not until years later did I hear how much resistance he had encountered with landlords who were panicking at the influx of Latinos into a neighborhood that had been Jewish for a couple of generations. But it was the American phenomenon of ethnic turnover that was changing the urban core of Paterson, and the human flood could not be held back with an accusing finger.

"You Cuban?" the man had asked my father, pointing a finger at his 5 name tag on the Navy uniform—even though my father had the fair skin and light brown hair of his northern Spanish family background and our name is as common in Puerto Rico as Johnson is in the U.S.

"No," my father had answered looking past the finger into his adversary's angry eyes, "I'm Puerto Rican."

"Same shit." And the door closed. My father could have passed as European, but we couldn't. My brother and I both have our mother's black hair and olive skin, and so we lived in El Building and visited our great-uncle and his fair children on the next block. It was their private joke that they were the German branch of the family. Not many years later that area too would be mainly Puerto Rican. It was as if the heart of the city map were being gradually colored in brown—*café-con-leche* brown. Our color. . . .

It became my father's obsession to get out of the **barrio,** and thus we were never permitted to form bonds with the place or with the people who lived there. Yet the building was a comfort to my mother, who never got over yearning for *la isla.* She felt surrounded by her language: the walls were thin, and voices speaking and arguing in Spanish could be heard all day. *Salsas* blasted out of radios turned on early in the morning and left on for company. Women seemed to cook rice and beans perpetually—the strong aroma of red kidney beans boiling permeated the hallways.

Though Father preferred that we do our grocery shopping at the supermarket when he came home on weekend leaves, my mother insisted that she could cook only with products whose labels she could read, and so, during the week, I accompanied her and my little brother to *La Bodega*—a hole-in-the-wall grocery store across the street from *El Building*. There we squeezed down three narrow aisles jammed with various products. Goya and Libby's—those were the trademarks trusted by her Mamá, and so my mother bought cans of Goya beans, soups and condiments. She bought little cans of Libby's fruit juices for us. And she bought Colgate toothpaste and Palmolive soap. (The final *e* is pronounced in both those products in Spanish, and for many years I believed that they were manufactured on the Island. I remember my surprise at first hearing a commercial on television for the toothpaste in which Colgate rhymed with "ate.") We would linger at La Bodega, for it was there that mother breathed best, taking in the familiar aromas of the foods she knew from Mamá's kitchen, and it was also there that she got to speak to the other women of El Building without violating outright Father's dictates against fraternizing with our neighbors.

QUESTIONS FOR DISCUSSION

1. Cofer describes her memories of life in Paterson in terms of sensory experiences: shades of gray, and banging and rattling pipes. What kind of feeling about her new surroundings do these sensory details suggest?

2. How does living in El Building compare with living in the family home in Puerto Rico? Give some examples from the text.

3. Were all of the family members affected the same way by the move to Paterson? Explain.

4. Was some of the racism and bigotry the family encountered in outsiders also present within the family? Explain.

5. Give some examples from the text to show how Cofer herself felt about life in Paterson. Was she more like her mother or her father?

In the following essay, an exchange student from Finland does a nice job of describing a Finnish sauna, as well as explaining its importance to the Finnish people. For this paper, she chose to write on question 7 from the list of topics included at the end of this chapter.

✍ STUDENT ESSAY:

The Finnish Sauna

The Finnish sauna is a traditional custom which is still alive in Finland today. When our Finnish ancestors first arrived at the site of their new homes and started to build, they began with the sauna, and there they at first lived. Nowadays there are saunas in many town houses in Finland, but it is absolutely essential to have one sauna at the summer cottage.

The best location for a sauna is on a lake or at the seashore, and, ideally, it should be built of logs. Smoke saunas, which have no chimneys, produce the best heat, but there are only a few of these left today because they produce too much soot.

Preparing for a sauna begins with chopping the wood, carrying it to the sauna, and kindling a fire in the boiler. To create steam, water is thrown on the rocks on top of the boiler. These rocks are heated by the fire underneath. The boiler also heats the water for washing. As soon as the fire is drawing well, it is time to go to the woods and break off sufficient birch twigs to make a sauna whisk, in Finnish called "vasta." These twigs are tied together into a whisk which will create a wonderful aroma in the sauna. When a whisk is used to slightly beat the skin, it makes blood flow more quickly. Also, birch leaves are full of vitamins, which are absorbed by the skin.

The sauna should be commenced lazily, and the water should be thrown carefully at the boiler, gradually building up the steam. As the steam builds up, the pores open and sweat begins to run. After being well-steamed, one can relax and cool off, first on the veranda of the sauna, then in the lake or the sea. Then the process can be repeated.

The Finnish sauna is very important to me, because at the end of a good sauna, I feel blissful—completely happy. I enjoy the leisure of the heat, peaceful relaxation in the sauna, and on the veranda afterwards, pleasant conversation and frequent plunges into the lake. Each of these is an integral part of the sauna.

But to Finns, the sauna is more than a pleasant experience; it is an important part of their culture, almost a ritual. The word "sauna" in Finnish means "to purify body and mind," and it is considered to be an important part of healthy living. Moreover, since the sauna was first a place to live, many people associate it with the home of their ancestors. Babies were born there. Meals were cooked on the hot stones. To me it is especially important because my grandparents were born in a sauna in 1905.

TOPICS FOR WRITING

1. In the selection from *Cities on the Hill*, Frances FitzGerald looks at how one of San Francisco's most celebrated districts has changed over time. Similarly, Judith Ortiz Cofer describes a neighborhood in transition—from Jewish to Puerto Rican.

   Choose a neighborhood in your community and describe the significant changes that have taken place within your lifetime. Like Fitz-Gerald, look for identifiable causes and general directions reflected by the changes you describe.

2. Alfred Kazin describes a walk that takes him through several neighborhoods in his city. Each neighborhood is distinctive in its own way. Take a similar walk in your town or city, going from one neighborhood to another, and describe the features that make the neighborhoods distinctive. Try to use several senses—sight, sound, smell, touch. Consider how the neighborhoods differ in age, economic class, and ethnic or racial composition.

3. As Eddy Harris does in the selection from *The South of Haunted Dreams,* describe a scene in a restaurant, or your campus cafeteria, for the purpose of showing how different groups of people either mingle or separate into groups. To what extent do people stay with others of similar backgrounds, interests, language, and so on?

4. Choose a famous or infamous location in your community and, using as many of the senses as possible, write a description of it. Select details to show the reader what makes the place famous or infamous.

5. Using details from John McPhee's "Anchorage, Alaska," write an explanation of what he means by the claim that "Anchorage . . . is the central hive of human Alaska, and in manner and structure it represents, for all to see, the Alaskan dynamic and the Alaskan aesthetic." Assume you are writing for a reader who has not read McPhee's piece.

6. Write a description of a place you have visited, trying to make someone else want to visit it. What is distinctive about the place? What features would appeal to your reader?

7. If you belong to a particular ethnic or racial group, write a description of a place that reflects the tastes or values of that group. Your subject could be a certain kind of building (church or temple, club, "hangout," home), a natural setting, or a sacred spot. Your purpose is to show someone who is not a part of your group why the place is important.

8. Arnold Schwarzenegger says that California is his "dreamland." What kind of place represents *your* idea of the American Dream? Describe

the place, choosing details that show the reader *why* you have chosen it and in what ways it represents your "dreamland."

9. Using any of the readings in this chapter, make a list of good examples of language used to create a *sense of place*. (You might want to review the section on description in Part I.) Then organize these examples into a paragraph of your own that explains this use of language.

10. Using any of the readings from this chapter, make a list of examples of language writers use to convey their *feelings* about a place. Then organize these examples into a paragraph of your own that explains this use of language.

Farmer showing soybeans that have and have not been grown in ground treated with lime.

6 Success, American-Style

Success is counted sweetest
By those who ne'er succeed.
—EMILY DICKINSON

In the nineteenth century, the American Dream solidified into the dream of success—moving upward. "From rags to riches," the inexhaustible theme of Horatio Alger's novels, became a household phrase. Success came to mean, in the minds of many Americans, climbing the ladder from bottom to top: a better job, more money, bigger house, prestige, and power.

In the American success story, improvement in one's standing required improvement of one's self. Self-help—the development of one's abilities and character—became the rage. In a tradition going back to the Puritans, hard work and an upright character paved the road to success.

The short poem printed on the next page appeared in *McGuffey's Newly Revised Eclectic Second Reader* (1853). This reader, compiled by the Ohio schoolmaster William Holmes McGuffey, was a collection of familiar readings and quotations that was used by practically every child in American schools. But it was more than just a school text; McGuffey's reader was a guidebook to character and success. The poem "Try, Try Again" expresses in a rousing, optimistic tone the American Dream of success: If you have the right attitude, work hard, and persevere, you can do anything.

ℒ Try, Try Again

Once or twice though you should fail,
    Try, Try Again;
If you would, at last, prevail,
    Try, Try Again;
If we strive, 'tis no disgrace,
Though we may not win the race;
What should you do in that case?
    Try, Try Again.
If you find your task is hard,
    Try, Try Again;
Time will bring you your reward,
    Try, Try Again;
All that other folks can do,
Why, with patience, should not you;
Only keep this rule in view:
    Try, Try Again.

The readings in this chapter examine the traditional American Dream of success and offer the views of several contemporary Americans on its meanings and its effects.

✍ FREDERICK LEWIS ALLEN

Horatio Alger

Frederick Lewis Allen was a journalist and writer of popular history. He joined Harper's Magazine *in 1923 and served as its editor-in-chief until 1953. He wrote five books, among them* Only Yesterday *(1932), a popular account of the 1920s, and* Since Yesterday *(1940), a history of the depression of the 1930s. The following selection is from* The Big Change *(1952), Lewis' last book, an informal history of the first half of the twentieth century.*

KEY VOCABULARY

FRUGALITY is the quality of thriftiness. A frugal person is careful about spending money.

A **PARADOX** is an apparent contradiction that is nevertheless true.

PERVASIVE means spread throughout, present everywhere.

INDUSTRY, as used here, is the quality of being industrious—hard-working.

VALIDITY is the quality of being based on truth or fact.

In 1899 there died in New York a man who, though he had never 1 made much of a study of economics and had a curiously immature mind, may have had a more **pervasive** influence on the thinking of American businessmen at the turn of the century than all the professors of economics put together. This man's name was Horatio Alger, Jr., and what he had done was to write more than a hundred books for boys—success stories called *Bound to Rise, Luck and Pluck, Sink or Swim, Tom the Bootblack,* and so forth—the total sales of which came to at least twenty million copies.

Horatio Alger was a creature of **paradox.** The unfailing theme of his books was the rise of earnest, hard-working boys from rags to riches; yet he himself did not begin life in rags and did not by any means achieve riches; during his later years he lived mostly in the Newsboys' Lodging House on one of New York's drearier streets. His paper-bound guides to success were, and are, generally regarded by educated readers as trash; they were literal, prosy, unreal, and unsubtle to a degree. Yet they were the delight of millions of American boys during the years between the Civil War and World War I, and it is possible that most of these boys got from Horatio Alger their first intelligible picture of American economic life.

The standard Horatio Alger hero was a fatherless boy of fifteen or thereabouts who had to earn his own way, usually in New York City. He was beset by all manner of villains. They tried to sell him worthless gold watches on railroad trains, or held him up as he was buggy-riding home with his employer's funds, or chloroformed him in a Philadelphia hotel room, or slugged him in a Chicago tenement. But always he was strong and shrewd and brave, and they were foolish and cowardly. And the end of each book found our hero well on the way toward wealth, which it was clear resulted from his diligence, honesty, perseverance, and thrift.

To the farmer's son, thumbing his copy of *Andy Grant's Pluck* by lamp-light on the Illinois prairie, or to the country banker's son, scanning the *Brave and Bold* series in a Vermont village, the lesson of Horatio Alger seemed clear: business was a matter of trading among individuals and small groups of men, and if you worked hard and saved your money, you succeeded. The basic principles of economic conduct were the same as those laid down by Benjamin Franklin's Poor Richard:

"God helps them that help themselves."

"Early to bed, and early to rise,
Makes a man healthy, wealthy, and wise."

"If we are industrious we shall never starve, for, as Poor Richard says, *At the working man's house, Hunger looks in; but dares not enter.*"

"A fat Kitchen makes a lean Will."

And, to sum up:

"In short, the way to wealth, if you desire it, is as plain as the way to market. It depends chiefly on two words, **industry** and **frugality.**"

There was no denying that the Alger thesis had a certain magnificent validity. Look at John D. Rockefeller, who had begun as a $4-a-week clerk in a commission merchant's house in Cleveland, and by the beginning of the twentieth century was becoming the richest man in the world. Look at Andrew Carnegie, who had begun at thirteen as a $1.20-a-week bobbin boy in a Pittsburgh cotton mill, and had become the greatest of steel manufacturers. Look at Edward H. Harriman, who had begun as a broker's office boy at $5 a week, and was building a railroad empire. And as for thrift, look at the great banker, George Fisher Baker, who not only had begun his career as a clerk, but during his early married life had imposed upon himself and his wife the discipline of living on half their income and saving the other half. These were only a few of the examples which proved the formula for success: begin with nothing, apply yourself, save your pennies, trade shrewdly, and you will be rewarded with wealth, power, and acclaim. To which the natural corollary was: poor people are poor because they are victims of their own laziness, stupidity, or profligacy.

Naturally it was pleasant for successful businessmen to believe that these were, in fact, the first principles of economics. But, one might ask, hadn't they learned in the classroom that economics is just a little more complex than that? To this question there are two answers. The first is that mighty few of the tycoons of 1900 had ever studied economics. Take, for instance, eight of the most successful of all: John D. Rockefeller, Carnegie, Harriman, and Baker, whom we have just mentioned; and also J. Pierpont Morgan, William Rockefeller, James Stillman, and H. H. Rogers. Of these eight, only Morgan had had anything approaching what we today would call a college education; he had spent two years at the University of Göttingen in Germany, where he had pretty certainly not studied anything that we would now classify as economics. And it is doubtful if even in the prime of life many of these men, or of their innumerable rivals and imitators, had much truck with economic science, or thought of professors of economics as anything but absurdly impractical theorists. A man who had come up in the world liked to describe himself as a graduate of the School of Hard Knocks. Education was all right in its way, and you sent your son to college if you could, if only because it was a good place to make useful contacts with the right people; but these college professors knew nothing about business, which was a battlefield for hard-shelled fighters. And anyhow the principles laid down by Ben Franklin, and somewhat foolishly simplified for boys by Horatio Alger, were fundamentally sound.

QUESTIONS FOR DISCUSSION

1. What does Lewis mean when he says, "Horatio Alger was a creature of paradox"?

2. Why, at the turn of the century, was Horatio Alger more influential than professional economists?

3. What are the main characteristics of the standard Horatio Alger hero?

4. How were Alger's methods of becoming successful related to popular standards of morality and folk wisdom?

5. What were the attitudes of successful 19th century businessmen, as well as Horatio Alger, toward formal education? Explain why they held such attitudes and why these attitudes are in tune with strong beliefs in individualism.

ℒ RUSSELL H. CONWELL

From *Acres of Diamonds*

Russell H. Conwell was a lawyer, clergyman, and author. After the American Civil War he practiced law in Minneapolis and Boston. In 1867 he became editor-in-chief of the Minneapolis Daily Chronicle; *in 1881 he was ordained a minister and was called to the Grace Baptist Church in Philadelphia. Three years later he founded Temple University. He died in 1925.*

Conwell is best known for his "Acres of Diamonds" speech, from which the selection below is taken. He delivered this speech over 6,000 times, making it one of the most popular speeches of the late nineteenth century.

I say you ought to be rich; you have no right to be poor. To live in   1
Philadelphia and not be rich is a misfortune, and it is doubly a misfortune, because you could have been rich just as well as be poor. Philadelphia furnishes so many opportunities. You ought to be rich. But persons with certain religious prejudice will ask, "How can you spend your time advising the rising generation to give their time to getting money—dollars and cents—the commercial spirit?"

Yet I must say that you ought to spend time getting rich. You and I know there are some things more valuable than money; of course, we do. Ah, yes! By a heart made unspeakably sad by a grave on which the autumn leaves now fall, I know there are some things higher and grander and sublimer than money. Well does the man know, who has suffered, that there are some things sweeter and holier and more sacred than gold. Nevertheless, the man of common sense also knows that there is not any one of those things that is not greatly enhanced by the use of money. Money is power. Love is the grandest thing on God's earth, but fortunate the lover who has plenty of money. Money is power; money has powers; and for a man to say, "I do not want money," is to say, "I do not wish to do any good to my fellow men." It is absurd thus to talk. It is absurd to disconnect them. This is a wonderfully great life, and you ought to spend your time getting money, because of the power there is in money. And yet this religious prejudice is so great that some people think it is a great honor to be one of God's poor. I am looking in the faces of people who think just that way. I heard a man once say in a prayer-meeting that he was thankful that he was one of God's poor, and then I silently wondered what his wife would say to that speech, as she took in washing to support the man while he sat and smoked on the veranda. I don't want to see any more of that kind of God's poor. Now, when a man could have been rich just as well, and he is now weak because he is poor, he has done some great wrong; he has been untruthful to himself; he has been unkind to his fellow men. We ought to get rich if we can by honorable and Christian methods, and these are the only methods that sweep us quickly toward the goal of riches.

QUESTIONS FOR DISCUSSION

1. According to Conwell, what is the relationship between wealth and morality?

2. What does Conwell imply when he says, "For a man to say, 'I do not want money,' is to say, 'I do not wish to do any good to my fellow men' "?

3. Conwell acknowledges that "there are some things higher and grander and sublimer than money." Yet he goes on to say that "the man of common sense" knows even these things are made better by money. What kinds of things do you think he is talking about here? How would they be "enhanced by the use of money"?

4. What do you think would be some characteristics of Conwell's "man of common sense"? What do you think common sense is?

$\mathscr{L}$ KAREN HELLER

By Success Obsessed

Karen Heller covers popular culture for the Philadelphia Inquirer, *where she has been a staff writer since 1986. Her articles have appeared in several national magazines.*

KEY VOCABULARY

An **ACCOLADE** is praise, approval.

AESTHETIC means, here, for reasons of beauty, looks.

BONHOMIE is a French word that means a pleasant disposition, good nature.

A **CHIMERA** was, in Greek mythology, a female monster, part lion, part goat, part serpent. More generally, the term refers to something imaginary or impossible, probably foolish.

An **ENIGMA** is something puzzling, obscure, or inexplicable.

FORTUITOUS means happening by accident or chance.

LEGION, originally a unit of the Roman army, means more generally a large number of something.

A **PROMONTORY** is a high ridge of land or a rock jutting out into a lake, sea, or river.

SALACIOUS means stimulating to the sexual imagination; lustful.

SALUTARY denotes something favorable: here, something conducive to health.

This is what has happened. We hit the streets before light; we go home 1 hours after the mad rush has ended. We miss the noise and the sun and the breeze, the constant parade of suits on the street. Nature has become an **enigma.**

We eat lunch, if we eat lunch at all, at our desks amid a mire of paper. We eat dinner at a sprinter's pace out of white paper cartons or boiled plastic bags. Our bodies are in fighting trim. The reason is neither **aesthetic** nor **salutary** but merely **fortuitous.** The cold, hard fact of the matter is that we do not have the time or, to use a crass word, the *leisure* that is required to put on weight.

During the woozy blur of the workweek, 120 hours of desperate living, we put ourselves in quarantine. Fun, once the leading player in the drama of our lives, has dropped out of the production and been replaced by a workhorse understudy called caffeine. We have cut out drink and cigarettes

and friends and drugs and sex and chocolate and, God knows, sleep, for that
elusive prize, success, a goal that we'll probably never achieve. We can see
it, though. It is out there on that far **promontory** with those other **chi-
meras:** wealth, happiness, power, and fame.

You see, there's a new, pure drug on the street. It is called ambition,
and the cost of addiction is sometimes dear. It feeds us. It fuels us. It can
make us flourish—or fester. The rewards are varied, the side effects **legion.**
The strain is too raw, too novel to predict its course from here. But one
thing is clear: Ambition, for many a bright young woman, has become
today's narcotic of choice.

As a narcotic, ambition is more like alcohol than heroin. It is legal. It 5
is always served up at swank parties. It can, when used properly, make us
feel lovely. (Unlike liquor, ambition is entirely condoned in the office; indeed, it is encouraged.) Control is the operative word with both substances.
With liquor, we prefer the company of social drinkers to the boozy presence of alcoholics. With ambition, we prefer people who know when to
stop striving to those who couldn't stop if they wanted to.

Ambition, like other habits, changes the way we live. Lovers and
love are penciled into expensive, bulging leather-covered calendars from
Britain—a place where they know about regimen. You think I'm kidding
about the scheduling; I am not. I have a friend who is so driven—a demanding job and a demanding child and one demanding husband—that
she routinely plans lovemaking in advance as Saturday night's primary
source of entertainment. Another cohort used to set the alarm for early in
the morning so she and her sweetheart could enjoy a little sweet pleasure
before their coffee. Unfortunately, they were usually too tired for the former, and too in need of the latter: The coffee always took precedence.

We are now amazed at evenings that last later than prime-time programming. Nocturnal rendezvous routinely end with this parting: "It's
been lovely, but I'm afraid I have a busy day ahead of me." Saturdays that
wash into Sundays are so unusual they are celebrated like holidays or com-
memorated like victorious battles: Bunker Hill, D day. Weeknights that
blur into weekdays are even rarer. But we brandish these bouts of pleasure
because, quite sadly, we know that they are the exceptions to the gruel.

If late nights are becoming obsolete, so are out-of-town weekends.
This past summer, many an ambitious friend announced that she was
spending July Fourth or Labor Day at the office: "No Cape Cod for me.
I'll be here in the city [long pause for full effect] *working.*" Invariably, the
word "working" was expressed as if it were synonymous with "saving
lives."

A woman like this is likely, even in summer, to sport a fluorescent-
soaked pallor, the current pigment of choice. Skin shielded from natural

light signifies drive, the new beauty ideal; a complexion the color of cara-
mel has lost its status. This is not because we have read that exposure to the
sun may hasten our demise or, even worse, age our appearance. No, it is
simply, strictly because we are just too damned busy working to spend that
much time outdoors.

The New Drug Is Drive

Today, a woman wants to be called ambitious the way she wishes to   10
be called beautiful and bright. It has become an **accolade,** no longer synonymous with "aggressive," which was synonymous with "cold-hearted
bitch." Of course, women have always been ambitious—but for social
status, marriage, and motherhood rather than fame and fortune. How
things have changed, even in our own lifetime: When we were girls, we
talked about boys. Now that we are women, we talk about work.

We talk about work all the time. It is our new pornography. I have seen
grown women grow **salacious** on the subject of salary review; salivate at
the mere mention of special projects; speak in hushed, breathy tones about
perks, mentors, and office power plays.

True story. Two attractive successful single Washington women, close
friends for a couple of years, are sitting in a bar, sipping scotch.

One turns to the other, with no humor at all intended, and asks: "Have
we ever discussed men before?"

"No, come to think of it, we haven't," says the other.

The first woman asks, now smiling at the absurdity of it, "Do you think   15
we should?"

Men, in this scheme of things, appear downright tertiary. I've known
women to move clear across the country, away from their boyfriends, to accept better jobs. I've seen women keep men waiting for hours in restaurants
while they checked those sales figures one more time. I've heard women
bore their sweethearts senseless while they talked shop with colleagues.

Of course, none of this is new: Men have been doing it for years. But
you have to wonder why women would want to follow suit.

It was in the cards or, more specifically, in the birthrate. Women in
their twenties, verging on 30, are baby-boomers, born at a time of so many
others and thus likely to have experienced rejection at an early age. It was
tough to get into special public schools, top private schools, upper-track
courses, rigorous after-school programs. I knew one girl who got turned
down by a summer camp. We knew that getting into the best college was
going to be a bitch. We studied diligently for standardized tests and ago-
nized over application essays. Such trying times made for tough skin, and
even tougher determination.

We were raised with the pervasive sense that there were too many of us out there taking up space, gasping for air. It wasn't true, of course, but when, finally, we were allowed to achieve, the sensation was not unlike that of three-year-olds at Churchill Downs held too long at the gate. And then the race was on.

Women with a Mission

Of all my friends, it is the women who are the most ambitious, the 20 most driven. They have everything, *everything*.

And do you know what they want?

More.

I have one friend, an artist, who is beautiful and bright and married to a terrific man and famous in her field and respected, and paid handsomely, too. And do you know what she wants? *More.* She's now trying her hand at a novel.

I have another friend, a writer, who is beautiful and bright and has several ardent admirers and is about to witness the culmination of her dreams, being published. And do you know what she wants? *More.* She continues to toil weekends and evenings; she cancels dates and trips to sit at the typewriter.

The business that I work in, the newspaper business, is a pyramid, like 25 a lot of other professions. Almost everyone is trying to reach the apex. Today, most of my newspaper friends are at the ten best papers in America, the exact place they have always wanted to be. And do you know what many of them talk about?

Less.

The other night, I was with a female friend who has one of the best jobs at one of the best big papers. "You know, maybe it's time to go to a smaller paper," she said. "I might be happier there." (Well, she's *been* at a smaller paper, a lot of smaller papers, and she didn't think she'd be happy until she got to a big one.) And another friend at a big-city daily dreams of chucking it all for a teaching job in a secluded setting. (Yes, you know and I know that she will be miserable there, but try telling *her* that.)

Ambition Overdose

Some women experience two disturbing side effects when getting high on pure, uncut ambition. One has to do with men; the other, with women.

Even if we were born to ardent feminists, we still expect to end up with men who are as ambitious as we are, or—and I know this doesn't sound particularly modern, but it's true—men who are even *more* driven than we are. If a woman goes looking for that overachiever, though, she may find that this kind of guy prefers the stay-at-home type or is already married or will always consider his career superior to hers or is so extremely ambitious that there's never time to see each other at all. But if she settles for a man who is more passive, it can drive her crazy or him crazy or, and perhaps this is preferable, both of them crazy. The successful woman wants both a modern career *and* an old-fashioned, career-oriented guy—which he's not. So she tries to spread some of her ambition onto him, hoping it works like the flu and, in a matter of days, he, too, will be infected.

It doesn't work. Ambition is a drug, not a germ. Most successful 30 women today sit around complaining not that their men are unfaithful or overweight, but that they're not ambitious. Often, in the end, it doesn't matter: These women are too busy to even see their beaux.

This is not the case, however, with other women. You will *always* see each other. The comparisons will be constant. Which is the second deadly side effect of too much drive. Nine times out of ten, when a talented woman reports trouble with a jealous colleague, the colleague is a young, ambitious woman.

This is awful. This is horrid. It is a male sexist's fantasy. It should not be allowed to happen. It happens all the time.

Often it will happen that one talented, bright, successful woman will hear about another. If she's an ambition junkie, her first question is always, without fail, the same: "How old is she?" If the rival is older, the ambition junkie is relieved. She has time to catch up. If the woman is younger, though—well, the Nazis couldn't have invented better torture.

If the pain is not too great, she will pose another question, which is invariably this: "Does she have a good social life?" If the answer is no, the ambition junkie might feel better, thinking of all those long, lonely Saturday nights. If the answer is yes, it will most likely be greeted with the same **bonhomie** with which Lee greeted Grant at Appomattox.

Competition among women can get mean and ugly. You could charge 35 admission and guys with big stogies would gladly pay the price. In the past three months, these disparaging words have been uttered by ordinarily rational, bright, attractive young women:

"Too bad Alice is bright *and* beautiful, I like her so much." (This comment made by three different women in one week.)

"If it makes you feel any better," says one friend about one of the most accomplished women she knows, "Rachel's love life is nonexistent, her self-esteem is low and her calves are fat."

Well, now, it didn't make me feel any better. (Well, *maybe* it could, but only on a really rotten day.) This is the language of ambition that has gotten out of control, when the narcotic has polluted the bloodstream and the brain and the body, when fear and jealousy have replaced dreams and de-sires. This is the language of addiction, and almost all of us have been guilty of using it. Honest, think about Jessica Lange. Can you really speak admir-ingly about a woman that talented, that ethereal, that lucky in love? When it gets this bad, there is only one thing to do: Dry up, come clean, get off the junk. You must take vacations, evacuate your office, ex-perience daylight. You must learn that there are happy people everywhere who don't give a damn about six-figure incomes or corner offices. You must remember that men have always been driven and they don't live as long as women do.

So, you understand all this. Now, turn off your desk lamp, pack up your 40 briefcase, put on your sneakers and depart for your long-neglected home.

QUESTIONS FOR DISCUSSION

1. Karen Heller acknowledges that both men and women can be driven by ambition, yet she only discusses the problems faced by ambitious women. Why?

2. Do you think the analogy between ambition and alcohol is a good analogy? In what ways is an obsession with ambition like alcoholism?

3. In paragraph 3, Heller points out that ambition has played a great role in our giving up many unhealthy habits; however, she doesn't sound very pleased with our reformed selves. Why?

4. What are the "two disturbing side effects" ambitious women are likely to experience "when getting high on pure, uncut ambition"?

5. Why is it a male sexist's fantasy that "nine times out of ten, when a talented woman reports trouble with a jealous colleague, the colleague is a young, ambitious woman"?

Stephen Cruz

The following selection, based on an interview with Stephen Cruz, is from Studs Terkel's book American Dreams: Lost and Found. *The interview was published in 1981.*

KEY VOCABULARY

An **EDICT** is a decree or command issued by an authority.

MAÑANA is a Spanish word meaning "tomorrow." It is often used to imply procrastination, putting things off until some indefinite time in the future.

SPUTNIK is the name of several satellites launched by the former Soviet Union. The first one, launched on October 4, 1957, shocked Americans, who had expected that America would win the space race.

VERBOTEN is a German word meaning "forbidden."

He is thirty-nine.
"The family came in stages from Mexico. Your grand-parents usually came first, did a little work, found little roots, put together a few bucks, and brought the family in, one at a time. Those were the days when controls at the border didn't exist as they do now."

You just tried very hard to be whatever it is the system wanted of you. 1
I was a good student and, as small as I was, a pretty good athlete. I was well liked, I thought. We were fairly affluent, but we lived down where all the trashy whites were. It was the only housing we could get. As kids, we never understood why. We did everything right. We didn't have those Mexican accents, we were never on welfare. Dad wouldn't be on welfare to save his soul. He woulda died first. He worked during the depression. He carries that pride with him, even today.

Of the five children, I'm the only one who really got into the business world. We learned quickly that you have to look for opportunities and add things up very quickly. I was in liberal arts, but as soon as **Sputnik** went up, well, golly, hell, we knew where the bucks were. I went right over to the registrar's office and signed up for engineering. I got my degree in '62. If you had a master's in business as well, they were just paying all kinds of bucks. So that's what I did. Sure enough, the market was super. I had four-teen job offers. I could have had a hundred if I wanted to look around.

I never once associated these offers with my being a minority. I was aware of the Civil Rights Act of 1964, but I was still self-confident enough to feel they wanted me because of my abilities. Looking back, the reason I got more offers than the other guys was because of the government **edict.** And I thought it was because I was so goddamned brilliant. (Laughs.) In 1962, I didn't get as many offers as those who were less qualified. You have a tendency to blame the job market. You just don't want to face the issue of discrimination.

I went to work with Procter & Gamble. After about two years, they told me I was one of the best supervisors they ever had and they were gonna promote me. Okay, I went into personnel. Again, I thought it was because I was such a brilliant guy. Now I started getting wise to the ways of the American Dream. My office was glass-enclosed, while all the other offices were enclosed so you couldn't see into them. I was the visible man.

They made sure I interviewed most of the people that came in. I just 5 didn't really think there was anything wrong until we got a new plant manager, a southerner. I received instructions from him on how I should interview blacks. Just check and see if they smell, okay? That was the beginning of my training program. I started asking: Why weren't we hiring more minorities? I realized I was the only one in a management position.

I guess as a Mexican I was more acceptable because I wasn't really black. I was a good compromise. I was visibly good. I hired a black secretary, which was **verboten.** When I came back from my vacation, she was gone. My boss fired her while I was away. I asked why and never got a good reason.

Until then, I never questioned the American Dream. I was convinced if you worked hard, you could make it. I never considered myself different. That was the trouble. We had been discriminated against a lot, but I never associated it with society. I considered it an individual matter. Bad people, my mother used to say. In '68 I began to question.

I was doing fine. My very first year out of college, I was making twelve thousand dollars. I left Procter & Gamble because I really saw no opportunity. They were content to leave me visible, but my thoughts were not really solicited. I may have overreacted a bit, with the plant manager's attitude, but I felt there's no way a Mexican could get ahead here.

I went to work for Blue Cross. It's 1969. The Great Society is in full swing. Those who never thought of being minorities before are being turned on. Consciousness raising is going on. Black programs are popping up in universities. Cultural identity and all that. But what about the one issue in this country: economics? There were very few management jobs for minorities, especially blacks.

The stereotypes popped up again. If you're Oriental, you're real good 10 in mathematics. If you're Mexican, you're a happy guy to have around, pleasant but emotional. Mexicans are either sleeping or laughing all the time. Life is just one big happy kind of event. *Mañana.* Good to have as part of the management team, as long as you weren't allowed to make decisions.

I was thinking there were two possibilities why minorities were not making it in business. One was deep, ingrained racism. But there was still the possibility that they were simply a bunch of bad managers who just couldn't cut it. You see, until now I believed everything I was taught about the dream: the American businessman is omnipotent and fair. If we could show these turkeys there's money to be made in hiring minorities, these businessmen—good managers, good decision makers—would respond. I naïvely thought American businessmen gave a damn about society, that given a choice they would do the right thing. I had that faith.

I was hungry for learning about decision-making criteria. I was still too far away from top management to see exactly how they were working. I needed to learn more. Hey, just learn more and you'll make it. That part of the dream hadn't left me yet. I was still clinging to the notion of work your ass off, learn more than anybody else, and you'll get in that sphere.

During my fifth year at Blue Cross, I discovered another flaw in the American Dream. Minorities are as bad to other minorities as whites are to minorities. The strongest weapon the white manager had is the old divide and conquer routine. My mistake was thinking we were all at the same level of consciousness.

I had attempted to bring together some blacks with the other minorities. There weren't too many of them anyway. The Orientals never really got involved. The blacks misunderstood what I was presenting, perhaps I said it badly. They were on the cultural kick: a manager should be crucified for saying "Negro" instead of "black." I said as long as the Negro or the black gets the job, it doesn't mean a damn what he's called. We got into a huge hassle. Management, of course, merely smiled. The whole struggle fell flat on its face. It crumpled from divisiveness. So I learned another lesson. People have their own agenda. It doesn't matter what group you're with, there is a tendency to put the other guy down regardless.

The American Dream began to look so damn complicated, I began to think: Hell, if I wanted, I could just back away and reap the harvest myself. By this time, I'm up to twenty-five thousand dollars a year. It's beginning to look good, and a lot of people are beginning to look good. And they're saying: "Hey, the American Dream, you got it. Why don't you lay off?" I wasn't falling in line.

My bosses were telling me I had all the "ingredients" for top management. All that was required was to "get to know our business." This term comes up all the time. If I could just warn all minorities and women whenever you hear "get to know our business," they're really saying "fall in line." Stay within that fence, and glory can be yours. I left Blue Cross disillusioned. They offered me a director's job at thirty thousand dollars before I quit.

All I had to do was behave myself. I had the "ingredients" of being a good Chicano, the equivalent of the good nigger. I was smart. I could articulate well. People didn't know by my speech patterns that I was of Mexican heritage. Some tell me I don't look Mexican, that I have a certain amount of Italian, Lebanese, or who knows. (Laughs.)

One could easily say: "Hey, what's your bitch? The American Dream has treated you beautifully. So just knock it off and quit this crap you're spreading around." It was a real problem. Every time I turned around, America seemed to be treating me very well.

Hell, I even thought of dropping out, the hell with it. Maybe get a job in a factory. But what happened? Offers kept coming in. I just said to myself: God, isn't this silly? You might as well take the bucks and continue looking for the answer. So I did that. But each time I took the money, the conflict in me got more intense, not less.

Wow, I'm up to thirty-five thousand a year. This is a savings and loan 20 business. I have faith in the executive director. He was the kind of guy I was looking for in top management: understanding, humane, also looking for the formula. Until he was up for consideration as executive v.p. of the entire organization. All of a sudden everything changed. It wasn't until I saw this guy flip-flop that I realized how powerful vested interests are. Suddenly he's saying: "Don't rock the boat. Keep a low profile. Get in line." Another disappointment.

Subsequently, I went to work for a consulting firm. I said to myself: Okay, I've got to get close to the executive mind. I need to know how they work. Wow, a consulting firm.

Consulting firms are saving a lot of American businessmen. They're doing it in ways that defy the whole notion of capitalism. They're not allowing these businesses to fail. Lockheed was successful in getting U.S. funding guarantees because of the efforts of consulting firms working on their behalf, helping them look better. In this kind of work, you don't find minorities. You've got to be a proven success in business before you get there.

The American Dream, I see now, is governed not by education, opportunity, and hard work, but by power and fear. The higher up in the organization you go, the more you have to lose. The dream is *not losing*. This is the notion pervading America today: Don't lose.

When I left the consulting business, I was making fifty-thousand dollars a year. My last performance appraisal was: You can go a long way in this business, you can be a partner, but you gotta know our business. It came up again. At this point, I was incapable of being disillusioned any more. How easy it is to be swallowed up by the same set of values that governs the top guy. I was becoming that way. I was becoming concerned about losing that fifty grand or so a year. So I asked other minorities who had it made. I'd go up and ask 'em: "Look, do you owe anything to others?" The answer was: "We owe nothing to anybody." They drew from the civil rights movement but felt no debt. They've quickly forgotten how it happened. It's like I was when I first got out of college. Hey, it's really me, I'm great. I'm as angry with these guys as I am with the top guys.

Right now, it's confused. I've had fifteen years in the business world as 25 "a success." Many Anglos would be envious of my progress. Fifty thousand dollars a year puts you in the one or two top percent of all Americans. Plus my wife making another thirty thousand. We had lots of money. When I gave it up, my cohorts looked at me not just as strange, but as something of a traitor. "You're screwing it up for all of us. You're part of our union, we're the elite, we should govern. What the hell are you doing?" So now I'm looked at suspiciously by my peer group as well.

I'm teaching at the University of Wisconsin at Platteville. It's nice. My colleagues tell me what's on their minds. I got a farm next-door to Platteville. With farm prices being what they are (laughs), it's a losing proposition. But with university work and what money we've saved, we're gonna be all right.

The American Dream is getting more elusive. The dream is being governed by a few people's notion of what the dream is. Sometimes I feel it's a small group of financiers that gets together once a year and decides all the world's issues.

It's getting so big. The small-business venture is not there any more. Business has become too big to influence. It can't be changed internally. A counterpower is needed.

QUESTIONS FOR DISCUSSION

1. What does the phrase "get to know your business" really mean to Stephen Cruz?

2. Why did Stephen Cruz leave each of his well-paying jobs? Identify specific reasons for each job, as well as the underlying reason common to them all.

3. What role did a tradition of hard work and the belief in the American

Dream play in Cruz's professional success? List the details from his story that reveal the role of hard work.

4. Although he first studied the liberal arts, Cruz switched to engineering and then went on for a Master's degree in business as well. What historical event influenced his decision? Why?

5. Summarize Stephen Cruz's relations with other members of minority groups. Are these relations what you might have expected? Explain.

6. What are Stephen Cruz's feelings about the American Dream at the time of this interview?

✍ WILLIAM ZINSSER

The Right to Fail

William K. Zinsser has written for many magazines, including Life *and* Look. *He has also written several books, including* Pop Goes America *(1966),* The Lunacy Boom *(1970), and On* Writing Well *(1980). Since 1970, he has been on the faculty of Yale University.*

KEY VOCABULARY

FRUMENTUM is a Latin word that means "grain," especially wheat.

GAIUS JULIUS CAESAR (100−44 B.C.) was a Roman statesman, general, historian, and dictator who was finally assassinated.

GEORGE ELIOT is the pen name of Mary Ann Evans (1818−1880), an English novelist.

THE HELVETII were a Celtic people inhabiting Helvetia (approximately modern-day Switzerland) during the time of Julius Caesar.

T. S. ELIOT (1888−1965) was an American-born poet, critic, and playwright, best known for his long poem *The Wasteland.* Eliot lived most of his life in England.

VISTA is an acronym for Volunteers in Service to America, an organization sponsored by the U.S. Office of Economic Opportunity. It is composed of volunteers dedicated to educating and teaching skills to the poor.

I like "dropout" as an addition to the American language because it's 1 brief and it's clear. What I don't like is that we use it almost entirely as a dirty word.

We only apply it to people under twenty-one. Yet an adult who spends his days and nights watching mindless TV programs is more of a dropout than an eighteen-year-old who quits college, with its frequently mindless courses, to become, say, a **VISTA** volunteer. For the young, dropping out is often a way of dropping in.

To hold this opinion, however, is little short of treason in America. A boy or girl who leaves college is branded a failure—and the right to fail is one of the few freedoms that this country does not grant its citizens. The American dream is a dream of "getting ahead," painted in strokes of gold wherever we look. Our advertisements and TV commercials are a hymn to material success, our magazine articles a toast to people who made it to the top. Smoke the right cigarette or drive the right car—so the ads imply—and girls will be swooning into your deodorized arms or caressing your expensive lapels. Happiness goes to the man who has the sweet smell of achievement. He is our national idol, and everybody else is our national fink.

I want to put in a word for the fink, especially the teen-age fink, because if we give him time to get through his finkdom—if we release him from the pressure of attaining certain goals by a certain age—he has a good chance of becoming our national idol, a Jefferson or a Thoreau, a Buckminster Fuller or an Adlai Stevenson, a man with a mind of his own. We need mavericks and dissenters and dreamers far more than we need junior vice-presidents, but we paralyze them by insisting that every step be a step up to the next rung of the ladder. Yet in the fluid years of youth, the only way for boys and girls to find their proper road is often to take a hundred side trips, poking out in different directions, faltering, drawing back, and starting again.

"But what if we fail?" they ask, whispering the dreadful word across the Generation Gap to their parents, who are back home at the Establishment nursing their "middle-class values" and cultivating their "goal-oriented society." The parents whisper back: "Don't!" 5

What they should say is "Don't be afraid to fail!" Failure isn't fatal. Countless people have had a bout with it and come out stronger as a result. Many have even come out famous. History is strewn with eminent dropouts, "loners" who followed their own trail, not worrying about its odd twists and turns because they had faith in their own sense of direction. To read their biographies is always exhilarating, not only because they beat the system, but because their system was better than the one that they beat.

Luckily, such rebels still turn up often enough to prove that individualism, though badly threatened, is not extinct. Much has been written, for instance, about the fitful scholastic career of Thomas P. F. Hoving, New York's former Parks Commissioner and now director of the Metropolitan Museum of Art. Hoving was a dropout's dropout, entering and leaving schools as if they were motels, often at the request of the management. Still, he must have learned something during those unorthodox years, for he dropped in again at the top of his profession.

His case reminds me of another boyhood—that of Holden Caulfield in J. D. Salinger's *The Catcher in the Rye,* the most popular literary hero of the postwar period. There is nothing accidental about the grip that this dropout continues to hold on the affections of an entire American generation. Nobody else, real or invented, has made such an engaging shambles of our "goal-oriented society," so gratified our secret belief that the "phonies" are in power and the good guys up the creek. Whether Holden has also reached the top of his chosen field today is one of those speculations that delight fanciers of good fiction. I speculate that he has. Holden Caulfield, incidentally, is now thirty-six.

I'm not urging everyone to go out and fail just for the sheer therapy of it, or to quit college just to coddle some vague discontent. Obviously it's better to succeed than to flop, and in general a long education is more helpful than a short one. (Thanks to my own education, for example, I can tell **George Eliot** from **T. S. Eliot,** I can handle the pluperfect tense in French, and I know that **Caesar** beat the **Helvetii** because he had enough **frumentum.**) I only mean that failure isn't bad in itself, or success automatically good.

Fred Zinnemann, who has directed some of Hollywood's most hon-   10
ored movies, was asked by a reporter, when *A Man for All Seasons* won every prize, about his previous film, *Behold a Pale Horse,* which was a box-office disaster. "I don't feel any obligation to be successful," Zinnemann replied. "Success can be dangerous—you feel you know it all. I've learned a great deal from my failures." A similar point was made by Richard Brooks about his ambitious money loser, *Lord Jim.* Recalling the three years of his life that went into it, talking almost with elation about the troubles that befell his unit in Cambodia, Brooks told me that he learned more about his craft from this considerable failure than from his many earlier hits.

It's a point, of course, that applies throughout the arts. Writers, playwrights, painters and composers work in the expectation of periodic defeat, but they wouldn't keep going back into the arena if they thought it was the end of the world. It isn't the end of the world. For an artist—and perhaps for anybody—it is the only way to grow.

Today's younger generation seems to know that this is true, seems willing to take the risks in life that artists take in art. "Society," needless to say, still has the upper hand—it sets the goals and condemns as a failure everybody who won't play. But the dropouts and the hippies are not as afraid of failure as their parents and grandparents. This could mean, as their elders might say, that they are just plumb lazy, secure in the comforts of an affluent state. It could also mean, however, that they just don't buy the old standards of success and are rapidly writing new ones.

Recently it was announced, for instance, that more than two hundred thousand Americans have inquired about service in **VISTA** (the domestic Peace Corps) and that, according to a Gallup survey, "more than 3 million American college students would serve **VISTA** in some capacity if given the opportunity." This is hardly the road to riches or to an executive suite. Yet I have met many of these young volunteers, and they are not pining for traditional success. On the contrary, they appear more fulfilled than the average vice-president with a swimming pool.

Who is to say, then, if there is any right path to the top, or even to say what the top consists of? Obviously the colleges don't have more than a partial answer—otherwise the young would not be so disaffected with an education that they consider vapid. Obviously business does not have the answer—otherwise the young would not be so scornful of its call to be an organization man.

The fact is, nobody has the answer, and the dawning awareness of this 15 fact seems to me one of the best things happening in America today. Success and failure are again becoming individual visions, as they were when the country was younger, not rigid categories. Maybe we are learning again to cherish this right of every person to succeed on his own terms and to fail as often as necessary along the way.

QUESTIONS FOR DISCUSSION

1. In paragraph 6, Zinsser says, "Failure isn't fatal." In paragraph 5, he gives some examples of men with "minds of their own." Based on these examples, what is the connection between Zinsser's idea of "failing" and developing a mind of one's own?

2. According to Zinsser, in what ways can success be dangerous?

3. How does the "generation gap" become apparent when we look at attitudes toward failure and success? How about the gap between society's attitudes and an individual's aspirations?

4. What does this essay say about the role of college, or education in general, in the making of a successful human being?

🖎 SYLVIA RABINER

How the Superwoman Myth
Puts Women Down

Sylvia Rabiner was born in New York in 1939. She was educated at Hunter College and New York University. Rabiner is a teacher and freelance writer who has written for such magazines as Mademoiselle, Working Mother, *and* The New Republic.

KEY VOCABULARY

ASTUTE means having keen judgment; sharp.

BED.-STUY. is an abbreviation of Bedford-Stuyvesant, a poor district in New York City.

DESULTORY means jumping from one thing to another; disconnected; rambling.

To **EMULATE** means to strive to be like, or to equal, someone or something. Emulating is not quite the same as "copying" or "imitating."

A **VANGUARD** (originally a military term), is the foremost member or group; the one out in front.

Sunday afternoon. I'm making my usual **desultory** way through the 1 *Sunday Times* when I come upon Linda Kanner. Ms. Kanner is prominently on display in The National Economic Survey, where she is referred to as a woman "in the **vanguard** of women taking routes to the executive suite that were formerly traveled by men." A quick run-through of the article reveals that she is a marketing consultant with an M.B.A. degree from Harvard and a degree from The Simmons School of Social Work. She is married to a physician who has an M.B.A., too. Somewhere along the way she has managed to find time to produce two sons, and all this glory is hers at age 31.

Well, there goes my Sunday afternoon. After reading about Ms. Kanner, I will be in a muddy slump until nightfall at least. Every time I come across one of these proliferating articles about the successful woman of today, I am beset by feelings of self-contempt, loathing, and failure. Moreover, I hate Ms. Kanner, too, and if she were in my living room at the moment, I would set fire to her M.B.A. I am a six-year-old child once again, listening while my mother compares me to one of my flawless cousins.

Let me tell you, it's getting harder all the time to be a successful woman. In the old days, a woman was usually judged by the man she had ensnared. If he was a good provider and she kept the house clean, was a good cook, and raised a few decent children, she was well regarded by her peers and most likely by herself as well. Now the mainstream Women's Movement has thrust forth a new role model: the capitalist feminist. The career woman with a twist, she's not your old-time spinster who sacrificed marriage and motherhood for professional advancement, but a new, trickier model who has it all—a terrific career, a husband with a terrific career, and a couple of children as well.

We have Isabel Van Devanter Sawhill, successful economist, wife of New York University president John, and mother; or Letty Cottin Pogrebin, successful author, editor, activist, wife of lawyer Bert, and mother. A recent article in *Newsweek* investigated the life-styles of working couples with children. Their random democratic sampling included Kathy Cosgrove, vice-president of a public relations firm, wife of Mark, an advertising executive; Consuelo Marshall, Superior Court commissioner, wife of George, Columbia Pictures executive; Charlotte Curtis, associate editor of the *New York Times,* wife of William Hunt, neurosurgeon; and Patricia Schroeder, congresswoman, wife of lawyer Jim. Patricia, the article gushed, managed at 35 to "gracefully combine career, marriage, and family." The article was capped by a description of Carla Hills, Secretary of Housing and Urban Development, presidential possibility for the supreme court, wife of Roderick, chairman of the Securities and Exchange Commission, and mother of four. There was a photograph of Mrs. Hills presiding over her impeccable family at the dinner table. The article was swingy and upbeat. If they can do it, how about you? . . . Another afternoon ruined.

I turned for instruction to Letty Cottin Pogrebin, embodiment of the 5 success game. Letty is now an editor at *Ms.* and author of two books— "How to Make It in a Man's World" and "Getting Yours." Those titles reveal Letty's commitment to self-advancement. She doesn't hesitate to tell her readers that she is a woman to **emulate.** Letty was an executive at 21. She married a man whom she adores and has three "happy, well-behaved, bright, and spirited kids." I gleaned all this from Letty's first book. Since Letty was also gracefully combining career, marriage, and family, I thought I might get some pointers from her.

Letty Cottin arrived at Bernard Geis in 1960. After six months she was promoted to the position of director of publicity, advertising, and subsidiary rights. She met her husband at a party and married him a couple of months later. She proceeded to have her first children (twins) as planned "early in marriage but after one full year as unencumbered newlyweds." Their next baby fit in perfectly after the three-year space between children which they deemed most desirable. She sums up: "It's better to be working than not working; it's better to be married than single; it's better to be a mommy as well as a Mrs. But it's best to be all four at once!"

Now, where does that leave me? My thumbnail autobiography follows: I am a child of my times, definitely more the rule than the exception to it. Raised in the '40s and '50s, the words *career* and *goal* were not spoken when I was in the room. I got the standard New York City College Jewish Parental Advice to Daughters. "Take a few education courses. Then if . . . God forbid . . . anything should happen, you can always take care of yourself." Nora Ephron said that she always knew she wanted to write (Dorothy Parker was her idol). When her less motivated college friends went off after graduation and got married, Nora went off and wrote. A few remarkable women like Nora and Letty undoubtedly knew at the age of 18 or younger what profession they wanted to pursue, but most of us at Hunter College, as I recall, were thundering off in a herd to stand under the marriage canopy. A bunch of simpletons, you say? Not so. We had produced the school plays, edited the school newspapers, put together the creative publications, belonged to Arista, and frequently had our names on the honor roll. What was happening, then? Well, let's call it economics. We were the children of immigrant or near immigrant parents. Hard-working, uneducated or self-educated, they didn't know how to guide their bright daughters. The depression had been deeply felt and was well remembered. Their watchword was security. Dorothy Parker was my idol, too, but to my parents, writing was not a job. With encouragement from neither parents nor teachers, most of us sought security in marriage or teaching.

Now, I married neither wisely nor well, which to judge by current divorce statistics, proves me to be obstinately average. I worked to put my husband through graduate school, traveled where his career dictated, had two children as a matter of course and in the fall of 1969, although I had felt suffocated by my marriage, I protestingly and hysterically suffered its demise. My child support settlement would have done nicely to keep me in a cozy little tenement on Avenue C and 5th Street. I wanted to remain part of the middle class so I had to work: I had two children under the age of five and couldn't possibly pay a housekeeper. And I didn't really want a day-care center or babysitter with my boys eight or nine hours a day while I was at work. I wanted to be with them, so I found a job teaching night classes, and I tended home and sons during the day. A divorced woman with kids has a lot of things to think about. She is usually racing around trying to pay bills, do her job reasonably well, have some kind of social life, and be a loving mother too.

After 1969 I noticed that I never walked down a street; I ran. I ate standing up. I screamed at my sons a lot. The **astute** reader will detect here the subtle differences between Letty's life and mine. I admit I was failing in being a successful woman; I didn't have a terrific career, and I didn't have a husband with a terrific career. Where were all those dynamic, achieving wonderful men that the women in the news stories found and married? Not in the playgrounds and supermarkets where I spent my days, not in the classrooms where I spent my evenings, and not in any of the other places I checked out with varying degrees of enthusiasm on the weekends when I had a babysitter. As for my long-range career goals—well, to tell the truth, I was grateful to have my teaching contract renewed each semester. My concession to getting ahead was to return to graduate school to earn my M.A. degree. I was able to indulge in this luxury only because the university at which I taught offered me free tuition. At $91 a credit, graduate school is hardly a priority of the divorced working mother. It appears that in addition to all my other errors in judgment, I've made the mistake of living in New York City during a recession. Last June I lost the teaching job that was supposed to be my security in case . . . God forbid . . . anything happened. After collecting unemployment insurance for five months, I am now typing, filing, and serving my boss his coffee four times a day.

Now, I ask you—do I need to read about the triumphant lives of Helen 10 Gurley Brown or Mary Wells Lawrence? Statistics currently indicate that there are 7.2 million families headed by women. Most of us are clerks, secretaries, waitresses, salesgirls, social workers, nurses, and—if lucky enough to still be working—teachers. For us, the superwoman who knits marriage, career, and motherhood into a satisfying life without dropping a stitch is as oppressive a role model as the airbrushed Bunny in the *Playboy* centerfold, or That *Cosmopolitan* Girl. While I struggle to keep my boat afloat in rough waters with prevailing high winds, I am not encouraged to row on by media hypes of ladies who run companies, serve elegant dinners for 30, play tennis with their husbands, earn advanced degrees, and wear a perfect size eight. They exist, I know, a privileged, talented minority, but to encourage me by lauding their achievements is like holding Sammy Davis, Jr., up as a model to a junior high school class in **Bed.-Stuy.** What does it really have to do with them?

Women are self-critical creatures. We can always find reasons to hate ourselves. Single women believe they are failing if they don't have a loving, permanent relationship; working mothers are conflicted about leaving their children; divorced women experience guilt over the break-up of their marriages; housewives feel inadequate because they don't have careers; career women are wretched if they aren't advancing, and everyone is convinced she is too fat!

It is ironic that feminism, finally respectable, has been made to backfire in this way. The superwoman image is a symbol of the corruption of feminist politics. It places emphasis on a false ideal of individual success. We are led to believe that if we play our cards right, we'll get to the top, but in the present system it won't work; there just isn't that much room up there. And in our class society, those at the top probably were more than halfway up to start with. The superwoman image ignores the reality of the average working woman or housewife. It elevates an elite of upper-class women executives. The media loves it because it is glamorous and false. In the end it threatens nothing in the system. In fact, all it does is give women like me a sense of inferiority.

QUESTIONS FOR DISCUSSION

1. How do the standards by which women were judged in the "old days" compare with the standard by which they are judged today?

2. Why does the author feel that the superwoman myth put forth in the media is unfair to the vast majority of working women?

3. Do you agree with the author that feminism and its goals for women are finally respectable? Why or why not?

4. What kind of advice would you give your daughter as she begins to make career and personal choices? Give some specific examples.

5. How does your situation and the situations of your female friends and relatives compare with the two scenarios contrasted in this essay? Explain.

✑ E. B. WHITE

The Second Tree from the Corner

Elwyn Brooks (E. B.) White was on the staff of the New Yorker *magazine for many years. He is best known for his essays that appeared in "The Talk of the Town" section of that magazine. These essays have been collected in* The Wild Flag *(1946) and more recently in* Writings from The New Yorker. *He is also familiar to many readers as the author of the children's books* Stuart Little *and* Charlotte's Web. *Widely recognized for his mastery of English prose style, in 1959 White published, along with William Strunk, the influential manual* The Elements of Style. *White died in 1985.*

KEY VOCABULARY

CONSUMPTION means, here, tuberculosis—a communicable disease that causes lesions of the lungs, bones, and other parts of the body.

ESCAPISM is the habit of escaping from unpleasant realities through self-deceiving fantasy or entertainment.

RÉSUMÉ is a French term meaning "summary."

A **SÉANCE** is a meeting of people who hope to receive messages from spirits. As used in this story, the word suggests useless sessions.

UNREGENERATE means, here, unrepentant; stubborn or obstinate.

"Ever had any bizarre thoughts?" asked the doctor.   1
Mr. Trexler failed to catch the word. "What kind?" he said.
"Bizarre," repeated the doctor, his voice steady. He watched his patient for any slight change of expression, any wince. It seemed to Trexler that the doctor was not only watching him closely but was creeping slowly toward him, like a lizard toward a bug. Trexler shoved his chair back an inch and gathered himself for a reply. He was about to say "Yes" when he realized that if he said yes the next question would be unanswerable. Bizarre thoughts, bizarre thoughts? Ever have any bizarre thoughts? What kind of thoughts *except* bizarre had he had since the age of two?
Trexler felt the time passing, the necessity for an answer. These psychiatrists were busy men, overloaded, not to be kept waiting. The next patient was probably already perched out there in the waiting room, lonely, worried, shifting around on the sofa, his mind stuffed with bizarre thoughts and amorphous fears. Poor bastard, thought Trexler. Out there all alone in

141

that misshapen antechamber, staring at the filing cabinet and wondering whether to tell the doctor about that day on the Madison Avenue bus.

Let's see, bizarre thoughts. Trexler dodged back along the dreadful cor- 5 ridor of the years to see what he could find. He felt the doctor's eyes upon him and knew that time was running out. Don't be so conscientious, he said to himself. If a bizarre thought is indicated here, just reach into the bag and pick anything at all. A man as well supplied with bizarre thoughts as you are should have no difficulty producing one for the record. Trexler darted into the bag, hung for a moment before one of his thoughts, as a hummingbird pauses in the delphinium. No, he said, not that one. He darted to another (the one about the rhesus monkey), paused, considered. No, he said, not that.

Trexler knew he must hurry. He had already used up pretty nearly four seconds since the question had been put. But it was an impossible situation—just one more lousy, impossible situation such as he was always getting himself into. When, he asked himself, are you going to quit maneuvering yourself into a pocket? He made one more effort. This time he stopped at the asylum, only the bars were lucite—fluted, retractable. Not here, he said. Not this one.

He looked straight at the doctor. "No," he said quietly. "I never have any bizarre thoughts."

The doctor sucked in on his pipe, blew a plume of smoke toward the rows of medical books. Trexler's gaze followed the smoke. He managed to make out one of the titles, "The Genito-Urinary System." A bright wave of fear swept cleanly over him, and he winced under the first pain of kidney stones. He remembered when he was a child, the first time he ever entered a doctor's office, sneaking a look at the titles of the books—and the flush of fear, the shirt wet under his arms, the book on t.b., the sudden knowledge that he was in the advanced stages of **consumption,** the quick vision of the hemorrhage. Trexler sighed wearily. Forty years, he thought, and I still get thrown by the title of a medical book. Forty years and I still can't stay on life's little bucky horse. No wonder I'm sitting here in this dreary joint at the end of this woebegone afternoon, lying about my bizarre thoughts to a doctor who looks, come to think of it, rather tired.

The session dragged on. After about twenty minutes, the doctor rose and knocked his pipe out. Trexler got up, knocked the ashes out of his brain, and waited. The doctor smiled warmly and stuck out his hand. "There's nothing the matter with you—you're just scared. Want to know how I know you're scared?"

"How?" asked Trexler. 10

"Look at the chair you've been sitting in! See how it has moved back away from my desk? You kept inching away from me while I asked you questions. That means you're scared."

"Does it?" said Trexler, faking a grin. "Yeah; I suppose it does."

They finished shaking hands. Trexler turned and walked out uncertainly along the passage, then into the waiting room and out past the next patient, a ruddy pin-striped man who was seated on the sofa twirling his hat nervously and staring straight ahead at the files. Poor, frightened guy, thought Trexler, he's probably read in the *Times* that one American male out of every two is going to die of heart disease by twelve o'clock next Thursday. It says that in the paper almost every morning. And he's also probably thinking about that day on the Madison Avenue bus.

A week later, Trexler was back in the patient's chair. And for several weeks thereafter he continued to visit the doctor, always toward the end of the afternoon, when the vapors hung thick above the pool of the mind and darkened the whole region of the East Seventies. He felt no better as time went on, and he found it impossible to work. He discovered that the visits were becoming routine and that although the routine was one to which he certainly did not look forward, at least he could accept it with cool resignation, as once, years ago, he had accepted a long spell with a dentist who had settled down to a steady fooling with a couple of dead teeth. The visits, moreover, were now assuming a pattern recognizable to the patient.

Each session would begin with a **résumé** of symptoms—the dizziness in the streets, the constricting pain in the back of the neck, the apprehensions, the tightness of the scalp, the inability to concentrate, the despondency and the melancholy times, the feeling of pressure and tension, the anger at not being able to work, the anxiety over work not done, the gas on the stomach. Dullest set of neurotic symptoms in the world, Trexler would think, as he obediently trudged back over them for the doctor's benefit. And then, having listened attentively to the recital, the doctor would spring his question: "Have you ever found anything that gives you relief?" And Trexler would answer, "Yes. A drink." And the doctor would nod his head knowingly.

As he became familiar with the pattern Trexler found that he increasingly tended to identify himself with the doctor, transferring himself into the doctor's seat—probably (he thought) some rather slick form of **escapism**. At any rate, it was nothing new for Trexler to identify himself with other people. Whenever he got into a cab, he instantly became the driver, saw everything from the hackman's angle (and the reaching over with the right hand, the nudging of the flag, the pushing it down, all the way down along the side of the meter), saw everything—traffic, fare, everything—through the eyes of Anthony Rocco, or Isidore Freedman, or Matthew

Scott. In a barbershop, Trexler was the barber, his fingers curled around the comb, his hand on the tonic. Perfectly natural, then, that Trexler should soon be occupying the doctor's chair, asking the questions, waiting for the answers. He got quite interested in the doctor, in this way. He liked him, and he found him a not too difficult patient.

It was on the fifth visit, about halfway through, that the doctor turned to Trexler and said, suddenly, "What do you want?" He gave the word "want" special emphasis.

"I d'know," replied Trexler uneasily. "I guess nobody knows the answer to that one."

"Sure they do," replied the doctor.

"Do you know what you want?" asked Trexler narrowly.   20

"Certainly," said the doctor. Trexler noticed that at this point the doctor's chair slid slightly backward, away from him. Trexler stifled a small, internal smile. Scared as a rabbit, he said to himself. Look at him scoot!

"What *do* you want?" continued Trexler, pressing his advantage, pressing it hard.

The doctor glided back another inch away from his inquisitor. "I want a wing on the small house I own in Westport. I want more money, and more leisure to do the things I want to do."

Trexler was just about to say, "And what are those things you want to do, Doctor?" when he caught himself. Better not go too far, he mused. Better not lose possession of the ball. And besides, he thought, what the hell goes on here, anyway—me paying fifteen bucks a throw for these **séances** and then doing the work myself, asking the questions, weighing the answers. So he wants a new wing! There's a fine piece of theatrical gauze for you! A new wing.

Trexler settled down again and resumed the role of patient for the rest   25 of the visit. It ended on a kindly, friendly note. The doctor reassured him that his fears were the cause of his sickness, and that his fears were unsubstantial. They shook hands, smiling.

Trexler walked dizzily through the empty waiting room and the doctor followed along to let him out. It was late; the secretary had shut up shop and gone home. Another day over the dam. "Goodbye," said Trexler. He stepped into the street, turned west toward Madison, and thought of the doctor all alone there, after hours, in that desolate hole—a man who worked longer hours than his secretary. Poor, scared, overworked bastard, thought Trexler. And that new wing!

It was an evening of clearing weather, the Park showing green and desirable in the distance, the last daylight applying a high lacquer to the brick and brownstone walls and giving the street scene a luminous and intoxicating splendor. Trexler meditated, as he walked, on what he wanted.

"What do you want?" he heard again. Trexler knew what he wanted, and what, in general, all men wanted; and he was glad, in a way, that it was both inexpressible and unattainable, and that it wasn't a wing. He was satisfied to remember that it was deep, formless, enduring, and impossible of fulfillment, and that it made men sick, and that when you sauntered along Third Avenue and looked through the doorways into the dim saloons, you could sometimes pick out from the **unregenerate** ranks the ones who had not forgotten, gazing steadily into the bottoms of the glasses on the long chance that they could get another little peek at it. Trexler found himself renewed by the remembrance that what he wanted was at once great and microscopic, and that although it borrowed from the nature of large deeds and of youthful love and of old songs and early intimations, it was not any one of these things, and that it had not been isolated or pinned down, and that a man who attempted to define it in the privacy of a doctor's office would fall flat on his face.

Trexler felt invigorated. Suddenly his sickness seemed health, his dizziness stability. A small tree, rising between him and the light, stood there saturated with the evening, each gilt-edged leaf perfectly drunk with excellence and delicacy. Trexler's spine registered an ever so slight tremor as it picked up this natural disturbance in the lovely scene. "I want the second tree from the corner, just as it stands," he said, answering an imaginary question from an imaginary physician. And he felt a slow pride in realizing that what he wanted none could bestow, and that what he had none could take away. He felt content to be sick, unembarrassed at being afraid; and in the jungle of his fear he glimpsed (as he had so often glimpsed them before) the flashy tail feathers of the bird courage.

Then he thought once again of the doctor, and of his being left there all alone, tired, frightened. (The poor, scared guy, thought Trexler.) Trexler began humming "Moonshine Lullaby," his spirit reacting instantly to the hypodermic of Merman's healthy voice. He crossed Madison, boarded a downtown bus, and rode all the way to Fifty-second Street before he had a thought that could rightly have been called bizarre.

QUESTIONS FOR DISCUSSION

1. Why does Mr. Trexler deny ever having had "bizarre thoughts"?
2. When Mr. Trexler realizes that "he increasingly tended to identify himself with the doctor," it is nothing new to him. Why do you think he says this?
3. On his fifth visit, Mr. Trexler takes over the doctor's questioning role. What happens when he does this? What do we learn about the doctor?

4. When he tries to explain what he wants, Mr. Trexler remembers "that it was deep, formless, enduring, and impossible of fulfillment, and that it made men sick, and that when you sauntered along Third Avenue and looked through the doorways into the dim saloons, you could sometimes pick out from the unregenerate ranks the ones who had not forgotten, gazing steadily into the bottoms of the glasses on the long chance that they could get another little peek at it." Do you see a connection between whatever this "it" is and Mr. Trexler's "second tree from the corner"? What do they have in common? (In exploring this question, compare Trexler's wants with the doctor's wants.)

5. In this story, "the second tree from the corner" is a *symbol*—an object that stands for something else, usually something intangible and hard to define. Look closely at the description of the tree and see if you can express what it represents to Trexler. What qualities does it have that he admires?

6. How do you interpret the final sentence in the next-to-last paragraph? Why is Trexler "content to be sick, unembarrassed at being afraid"? What do you think the image of "the bird courage" says about Trexler?

The following essay summarizes Karen Heller's "By Success Obsessed," then follows with the student's own response to some of the ideas in the article. The summary does a good job of condensing Heller's main ideas. In the response to the first topic from this chapter's list, the student considers her own desire for success in light of the women Heller describes.

✍ STUDENT ESSAY:

A New Drug for Women

In her essay "By Success Obsessed," Karen Heller argues that modern working women have become obsessed with success. This obsession, she says, is like an addiction, similar to alcohol: "Ambition, for many a bright young woman, has become today's narcotic of choice." Furthermore, addiction to ambition, like other addictions, "changes the way we live." Heller paints a picture of the young professional woman as a workaholic who has given up everything—including sex, sleep, and chocolate—that might take time away from her climb up the ladder of success. Heller blames this addiction on the "baby-boom," which produced a generation of women who were "raised with the sense that there were too many of us out there taking up space, gasping for air." As a result, these women grew up in an atmosphere of intense competition, with tough skins and "tougher determination." Now, even if they have achieved success in their chosen fields, these women can't get enough. They always want more. This "ambition overdose" has "two disturbing side effects. . . . One has to do with men; the other with women." Ambitious women, says Heller, want men who are as ambitious as they are. But a man like this more than likely wants a "stay-at-home type or is already married or will always consider his career superior to hers or is so extremely ambitious that there's never time to see each other at all." On the other hand, if the woman chooses a passive man, she will probably drive them both crazy by trying to infect him with some of her ambition. The other side effect of too much ambition is mean and ugly competition among women. Successful women disparage colleagues who are younger, better looking, or have a successful social life. In conclusion, Heller urges women to stop this behavior. She advises women to kick their addictions, take time for themselves, and realize that people can be happy without "six-figure incomes or corner offices."

I think this essay gives a realistic view of how women are now. They feel that they need to accomplish something in their lives, and they finally have the opportunity to do it. Many doors have been opened to women that were closed to them in the past. It is understandable that they would want to take advantage of the new opportunities. As Heller says, "The sensation was not unlike that of three-year-old colts at Churchill Downs held too long at the gate." I also think that part of this addiction to ambition comes from the feeling that to be successful, women have to perform better than men. They have to be more ambitious, more driven, more competitive. I understand these feelings. I want to be successful too, but I have not yet felt addicted to ambition. Maybe I just don't know it. But I wonder whether ambition has to be a drug. I know plenty of successful people (at least I consider them successful) who also have families and a good social life. For me, the definition of success includes these things. In my case, much of my drive for success comes from my family. It's not that they put a lot of pressure on me. But the only successful people in my family are my uncles, who have achieved their goals of becoming an advertising executive and bank president. I have a strong desire to become the first successful woman in my family, and I want to work hard for that. Successful women should be proud they have the ambition, drive, and ability to succeed. But they also need to be aware of the pitfalls Heller talks about. As much as I want success in the business world, I also want a happy life at home. I know it's difficult to do both, but if I learn when to say "enough!" then I might be able to lead a balanced life.

TOPICS FOR WRITING

1. Pick one of the readings from this chapter that triggers a strong response in you. Write a summary of the reading, then follow it with an explanation of your own thoughts and feelings. (See "Writing a Longer Summary" and "From Summary to Response," Chapter 1.)

2. In his essay about the Horatio Alger stories, Fred Allen discusses the qualities of character that, according to these stories, a young man should have in order to become successful. Summarize the main character traits of a successful young man as Horatio Alger sees them; then discuss whether you think those traits would ensure success for a young person today. What *do* you see as being necessary for success in the world today?

3. Karen Heller compares ambition to alcoholic addiction. This kind of comparison is called an *analogy*. Try to explain your idea of ambition or success, using an analogy of your own invention.

4. Do Stephen Cruz and the ambitious women in Karen Heller's article have anything in common? Do they have the same ambitions, expectations, or problems? Does it seem to you that women and minorities face similar difficulties, or are they different in some ways?

5. Using the information in "By Success Obsessed," write a letter to a young woman just graduating from high school, telling her about the effect an obsession with ambition might have on her life.

6. Try to explain to a puzzled reader why, in E. B. White's "Second Tree from the Corner," the tree is an appropriate symbol for the "it" that Mr. Trexler wants. What is it about the tree that catches his attention and represents, for him, his desire?

7. Which of the readings in this chapter would you recommend to a young person just starting out on a career? Describe the kind of person you are writing to, and explain why you would recommend the reading you have chosen. In your paper, include a summary of the main points of the reading.

8. Based on what you have read so far in this book, write an essay that discusses the different ideas of success present in American society.

State your general purpose in the introduction, and write a paragraph for each type of success you present. You may include ideas that the readings *don't* mention. Imagine that you are writing for someone who has just arrived from another country.

9. The word "dropout" usually has a negative connotation. Referring to some of the material in William Zinsser's "The Right to Fail," write a letter to the parents of a high school dropout, assuring them that dropping out may not be the disaster they think it is.

10. The last part of the "Stephen Cruz" interview and the ideas in "The Right to Fail" touch on some common ground. What similar thoughts about success do they express? Are there any differences between their views?

11. If your definition of success is different from any of those presented in this chapter, write your own definition, explaining how and why you see success in a different way.

12. Why, do you think, did Stephen Cruz give up his career in business? Write a summary of the reasons for his decision.

13. Do you think Stephen Cruz made a wise choice? Or did he give up his career too easily?

14. Does Stephen Cruz fit the pattern of a Horatio Alger character? Explain how you think he fits the pattern and how you think he differs from it.

15. Conwell's "Acres of Diamonds" is a sermon, evidently addressed to an audience of church-going people. Summarize the main points of the sermon excerpt included in this chapter. Then explain whether or not you think Conwell successfully reconciles Christian values with the idea that everyone should try to get rich.

16. Write an essay in which you summarize the similarities you see in the way Karen Heller ("By Success Obsessed") and Sylvia Rabiner ("How the Superwoman Myth Puts Women Down") view the new role of women and their attitudes toward success.

17. Isolate one of the characteristics of the "Superwoman" in Sylvia Rabiner's essay, and write an essay arguing that this characteristic is actually making life more difficult for modern women.

18. Write a letter to your children (real or imagined) in which you give them advice on how to be successful in life. From the readings, use whatever information serves your purpose. Use language that a young person could understand.

European immigrants on Ellis Island in New York harbor.

7 In and Out of the Melting Pot

Give me your tired, your poor
Your huddled masses yearning to breathe free,
The wretched refuse of your teeming shore.
Send these, the homeless, tempest-tost to me,
I lift my lamp beside the golden door.
—EMMA LAZARUS
Inscription on the base
of the Statue of Liberty

The first Americans arrived somewhere between 20,000 and 50,000 years ago, making their way from Siberia to Alaska across a land bridge. The land was theirs until the seventeenth century, when the immigrations from Europe began, changing the character of American life forever.

In America, everyone is from somewhere else. The story behind modern America is largely a story of arrivals, of a country shaped by an unprecedented mixing of peoples and cultures. Waves of immigration over several centuries have also shaped the way we think about America. The image of this country that most older Americans grew up with was *the melting pot.* This term was first used in 1908 as the title of a play by Israel Zangwill, but the idea was suggested much earlier in St. Jean de Crevecoeur's *Letters from an American Farmer,* written in 1782. An excerpt from Crevecoeur's book is included in this chapter.

The melting pot soon became a popular metaphor for the way America would "melt down" immigrants from many lands into a homogenous product called "an American." It implied that in a generation or two the new arrivals would shed all traces of their country of origin—their language and customs—and blend into the great American mainstream.

The melting pot was never a very accurate metaphor—less accurate for some than for others. Even though it was relatively easy for most Europeans to blend in, many of them held on to some of their "Old World" ways and retained a sense of where they came from. And for those whose skin was black or brown or yellow, the idea of a melting pot never held much meaning.

The question of how we should best view American society is a live issue in the country today. Some people think that it is most important to keep a sense of a common culture, while others argue that the multi-cultural make-up of American society should be recognized and respected. This issue has bred a host of new proposals for images to replace the melting pot, among them a salad bar, a mosaic, and a boulliabaise. The argument for these new images is that they all represent something which is unified, but in which the ingredients remain distinctly themselves; they are not blended together to the point where they lose their identity. In a salad, for example, a tomato is still a tomato, a cucumber still a cucumber.

The reading selections in this chapter examine life in the American melting pot—or mosaic, or salad bar. We have chosen them to give a wide range of opinions and perspectives. As you read, think about each selection in the context of the general theme. What differences and similarities do you see in the views presented here?

ℒ DUDLEY RANDALL

The Melting Pot

*Dudley Randall was born in 1914 in Washington, D.C., but has lived most
of his life in Detroit. Before entering college, he was a foundry worker at the
Ford Motor Company and a letter carrier for the post office. He served in the
South Pacific during World War II and entered college after the war, earning
an M.A. in library science from the University of Michigan. He has been a
librarian in the Detroit city libraries and a librarian and poet-in-residence at
the University of Detroit. In addition to his own writing, Randall has been
influential as a publisher. In 1965 he founded the Broadside Press, which has
published over thirty books by black poets.*

There is a magic melting pot   1
where any girl or man
can step in Czech or Greek or Scot,
step out American.

Johann and Jan and Jean and Juan,   5
Giovanni and Ivan
Step in and then step out again
all freshly christened John.

Sam, watching, said, "Why, I was here
even before they came."   10
And stepped in too, but was tossed out
before he passed the brim.

And every time Sam tried that pot
They threw him out again.
"Keep out. This is our private pot.   15
We don't want your black stain."

At last, thrown out a thousand times,
Sam said, "I don't give a damn.
Shove your old pot. You can like it or not,
but I'll be just what I am."   20

QUESTIONS FOR DISCUSSION

1. What is common to the nationalities mentioned in the first stanza and the names listed in the second?

2. What does Sam mean in stanza 3 when he says, "Why, I was here/even before they came"? To whom, exactly, is he referring?

3. What is Sam's attitude in the final stanza? Has he given up? Is he beaten down? Angry? Determined? Resigned?

4. What do you think a young man like Sam, feeling the way he does, might do? How would he act on his feelings? What choices are open to him?

✑ St. Jean de Crèvecoeur

Letter III: What Is an American?

St. Jean de Crèvecoeur was born in France in 1755. He immigrated to Canada during the French and Indian wars, then travelled in Canada and the Eastern United States, finally settling in Orange County, New York. Most of his book Letters from an American Farmer *was written during the quiet years preceding the American Revolution. As a Loyalist (supporter of the British during the revolution), he fled to France in 1780. In 1785 he returned to America as the French Consul. He returned to France in 1790 and lived out the remainder of his life in his native country.*

KEY VOCABULARY

APPELLATION means name or title.

An **ARISTOCRACY** is a social and political system controlled by a privileged, hereditary ruling class.

ECCLESIASTICAL DOMINION means domination, or control of people's lives, by the church.

EMBRYO usually refers to a living being in an early stage of development; here, it is used metaphorically in the same way as "the seeds of . . ."

ERE means "before."

FACTIONS are groups that are in conflict with one another within a country, usually over political or religious issues.

INDIGENCE means poverty.

A **METAMORPHOSIS** is a change from one form to another.

NATIONAL GENIUS refers to the idea that people from different countries have special talents and abilities characteristic of their own nation.

PENURY means poverty.

UBI PANIS IBI PATRIA, in Latin, means "home is where the bread is."

An **UNLETTERED MAGISTRATE** is an illiterate judge.

I wish I could be acquainted with the feelings and thoughts which must   1
agitate the heart and present themselves to the mind of an enlightened Englishman, when he first lands on this continent. He must greatly rejoice
that he lived at a time to see this fair country discovered and settled; he
must necessarily feel a share of national pride, when he views the chain of
settlements which embellishes these extended shores. When he says to

157

himself, this is the work of my countrymen, who, when convulsed by **factions,** afflicted by a variety of miseries and wants, restless and impatient, took refuge here. They brought along with them their **national genius,** to which they principally owe what liberty they enjoy, and what substance they possess. Here he sees the industry of his native country displayed in a new manner, and traces in their works the **embryos** of all the arts, sciences, and ingenuity which flourish in Europe. Here he beholds fair cities, substantial villages, extensive fields, an immense country filled with decent houses, good roads, orchards, meadows, and bridges, where an hundred years ago all was wild, woody, and uncultivated! What a train of pleasing ideas this fair spectacle must suggest; it is a prospect which must inspire a good citizen with the most heartfelt pleasure. The difficulty consists in the manner of viewing so extensive a scene. He is arrived on a new continent; a modern society offers itself to his contemplation, different from what he had hitherto seen. It is not composed, as in Europe, of great lords who possess everything, and of a herd of people who have nothing. Here are no **aristocratical** families, no courts, no kings, no bishops, no **ecclesiastical dominion,** no invisible power giving to a few a very visible one; no great manufacturers employing thousands, no great refinements of luxury. The rich and the poor are not so far removed from each other as they are in Europe. Some few towns excepted, we are all tillers of the earth, from Nova Scotia to West Florida. We are a people of cultivators, scattered over an immense territory, communicating with each other by means of good roads and navigable rivers, united by the silken bands of mild government, all respecting the laws, without dreading their power, because they are equitable. We are all animated with the spirit of an industry which is unfettered and unrestrained, because each person works for himself. If he travels through our rural districts he views not the hostile castle, and the haughty mansion, contrasted with the clay-built hut and miserable cabin, where cattle and men help to keep each other warm, and dwell in meanness, smoke, and **indigence.** A pleasing uniformity of decent competence appears throughout our habitations. The meanest of our log-houses is a dry and comfortable habitation. Lawyer or merchant are the fairest titles our towns afford; that of a farmer is the only **appellation** of the rural inhabitants of our country. It must take some time **ere** he can reconcile himself to our dictionary, which is but short in words of dignity, and names of honor. There, on a Sunday, he sees a congregation of respectable farmers and their wives, all clad in neat homespun, well mounted, or riding in their own humble wagons. There is not among them an esquire, saving the **unlettered** magistrate. There he sees a parson as simple as his flock, a farmer who does not riot on the labor of others. We have no princes, for whom we toil, starve, and bleed: we are the most perfect society now existing in the world. Here man is free as he ought to be; nor is this pleasing equality so transitory as many others are. Many ages will not see the shores of our great lakes replenished with inland nations, nor the unknown bounds of North America entirely peopled. Who can tell how far it extends? Who can tell the millions of men whom it will feed and contain? for no European foot has as yet traveled half the extent of this mighty continent! . . .

In this great American asylum, the poor of Europe have by some means met together, and in consequence of various causes; to what purpose should they ask one another what countrymen they are? Alas, two thirds of them had no country. Can a wretch who wanders about, who works and starves, whose life is a continual scene of sore affliction or pinching **penury,** can that man call England or any other kingdom his country? A country that had no bread for him, whose fields procured him no harvest, who met with nothing but the frowns of the rich, the severity of the laws, with jails and punishments; who owned not a single foot of the extensive surface of this planet? No! Urged by a variety of motives, here they came. Everything has tended to regenerate them; new laws, a new mode of living, a new social system; here they are become men: in Europe they were as so many useless plants, wanting vegetative mold and refreshing showers; they withered, and were mowed down by want, hunger, and war; but now by the power of transplantation, like all other plants they have taken root and flourished! Formerly they were not numbered in any civil lists of their country, except in those of the poor; here they rank as citizens. By what invisible power has this surprising **metamorphosis** been performed? By that of the laws and that of their industry. The laws, the indulgent laws, protect them as they arrive, stamping on them the symbol of adoption; they receive ample rewards for their labors; these accumulated rewards procure them lands; those lands confer on them the title of freemen, and to that title every benefit is affixed which men can possibly require. This is the great operation daily performed by our laws. From whence proceed these laws? From our government. Whence the government? It is derived from the original genius and strong desire of the people ratified and confirmed by the crown. This is the great chain which links us all, this is the picture which every province exhibits. . . .

What attachment can a poor European emigrant have for a country where he had nothing? The knowledge of the language, the love of a few kindred as poor as himself, were the only cords that tied him: his country is now that which gives him land, bread, protection, and consequence: *Ubi panis ibi patria* is the motto of all emigrants. What then is the American, this new man? He is either a European, or the descendant of a European, hence that strange mixture of blood, which you will find in no other country. I could point out to you a family whose grandfather was an Englishman, whose wife was Dutch, whose son married a French woman, and whose present four sons have now four wives of different nations. *He* is an American, who, leaving behind him all his ancient prejudices and manners, receives new ones from the new mode of life he has embraced, the new government he obeys, and the new rank he holds. He becomes an American by being received in the broad lap of our great *Alma Mater.* Here individuals of all nations are melted into a new race of men, whose labors and posterity will one day cause great changes in the world. Americans are the western pilgrims, who are carrying along with them that great mass of arts, sciences, vigor, and industry which began long since in the east; they will finish the great circle. The Americans were once scattered all over Europe; here they are incorporated into one of the finest systems of population which has ever appeared, and which will hereafter become distinct by the power of the different climates they inhabit. The American ought therefore to love this country much better than that wherein either he or his forefathers were born. Here the rewards of his industry follow with equal steps the progress of his labor; his labor is founded on the basis of nature, *self-interest;* can it want a stronger allurement? Wives and children, who before in vain demanded of him a morsel of bread, now, fat and frolicsome, gladly help their father to clear those fields whence exuberant crops are to arise to feed and to clothe them all; without any part being claimed, either by a despotic prince, a rich abbot, or a mighty lord. Here religion demands but little of him; a small voluntary salary to the minister, and gratitude to God; can he refuse these? The American is a new man, who acts upon new principles; he must therefore entertain new ideas, and form new opinions. From involuntary idleness, servile dependence, penury, and useless labor, he has passed to toils of a very different nature, rewarded by ample subsistence—This is an American.

QUESTIONS FOR DISCUSSION

1. Crevecoeur published his *Letters from an American Farmer* in 1782. In what ways was Crevecoeur's America different from Europe at the time he was writing?

2. According to Crevecoeur, what power enabled the poor and oppressed of Europe to be transformed into free citizens of America?

3. What does Crevecoeur mean when he says Americans are the "Western pilgrims"? What place in the development of civilization does he envision for America?

4. Crèvecoeur says that in America a person's labor is founded on the "basis of nature." What is this "basis of nature"? From your reading of the essay, can you explain in more detail what Crèvecoeur means by it?

5. In his final paragraph Crèvecoeur asks the question, "What then is the American, this new man?" How does he answer that question? What are the characteristics of this "new man"?

6. What are some ways in which America in Crèvecoeur's time differs from America today?

ℒ⌄ JAMAKE HIGHWATER

The Intellectual Savage

Jamake Highwater is a Native American of Blackfoot/Cherokee heritage. He has written many reviews and articles, as well as novels and books about Native American culture. In 1978 he won the Newberry Honor Award for his book Anpao: An American Indian Odyssey, *and in 1979 he received the Peace Book Award for* The Sun, He Dies, *a novel about the end of the Aztec world. The book from which this essay is taken is* The Primal Mind: Vision and Reality in Indian America, *published in 1981.*

KEY VOCABULARY

ANDREW JACKSON'S *WILD INDIANS* refers to the Old West stereotype of the Indian as a wild, uncivilized savage.

JEAN-JACQUES ROUSSEAU'S *NOBLE SAVAGE* refers to another image of tribal people that was popular in the 18th century. Rousseau was a French philosopher who believed that people were by nature good and that it was civilization that had corrupted them. Thus the "noble savage" was held up as an example of humanity in its unspoiled state.

MULTIFACETED means having many sides, or "faces."

A **MUTANT** is an offspring that is significantly different from its parents.

A **PARADOX** is a statement that seems to be self-contradictory, but is nevertheless true.

The greatest distance between people is not space but culture. 1

When I was a child I began the arduous tasks of exploring the infinite distance between peoples and building bridges that might provide me with a grasp of the mentality of Native Americans as it relates to the worldview of other civilizations. I had to undertake this task in order to save my life; for had I simply accepted the conventions by which white people look at themselves and their world I would have lost the interior visions that make me an Indian, an artist, and an individual.

This perilous exploration of reality began for me in southern Alberta and in the Rockies of Montana when I was about five years old. One day I discovered a wonderful creature. It looked like a bird, but it was able to do things that many other birds cannot do. For instance, in addition to flying in the enormous sky, it swam and dove in the lakes and, sometimes, it just floated majestically on the water's silver surface. It would also waddle rather gracelessly in the tall grasses that grew along the shores. That bird was called *méksikatsi,* which, in the Blackfeet language, means "pink-colored feet." Méksikatsi seemed an ideal name for the versatile fly-swim bird, since it really did have bright pink feet. When I was about ten years old my life changed abruptly and drastically. I was placed in an orphanage because my parents were destitute, and eventually I was adopted by a non-Indian foster father when my own parent was killed in an automobile accident. I found myself wrenched out of the world that was familiar to me and plunged without guidance into an entirely alien existence. I was told to forget my origins and try to become somebody I was not.

One day a teacher of English told me that méksikatsi was not really 5 méksikatsi. It didn't matter that the word described the bird exactly for me or that the Blackfeet people had called it méksikatsi for thousands of years. The bird, I was told, was called duck.

"DUCK?"

Well, I was extremely disappointed with the English language. The word "duck" didn't make any sense, for indeed méksikatsi doesn't look like the word "duck." It doesn't even sound like the word "duck." And what made the situation all the more troublesome was the realization that the English verb "to duck" was derived from the actions of the bird and not vice versa. So why do people call méksikatsi *duck?*

This lesson was the first of many from which I slowly learned, to my amazement, that the people of white America don't *see* the same things that Indians see.

As my education in the ways of non-Indian people progressed, I finally came to understand what duck means to them—but I could never forget that méksikatsi also has meaning, even though it means something fundamentally different from what duck means.

This lesson in words and the ideas they convey is very difficult to un- 10 derstand, especially if we grow up insulated by a single culture and its single language. In fact, it has been the most complicated lesson of my life. As I have gained experience and education in both the dominant culture and that of Indians, I have found it progressively more difficult to pass from one world to the other. I had to discover a place somewhere between two worlds. It is not simply a matter of language, for, as everyone knows, it is possible to translate with fair accuracy from one language to another without losing too much of the original meaning. But there are no methods by which we can translate a mentality and its alien ideas.

I am very much alienated by the way some ideas find their way into English words. For instance, when an English word is descriptive—like the word "wilderness"—I am often appalled by what is implied by the description. After all, the forest is not "wild" in the sense that it is something needing to be tamed or controlled and harnessed. For Blackfeet Indians, the forest is the natural state of the world. It is the cities that are wild and seem to need "taming." For most primal peoples the earth is so marvelous that their connotation of it requires it to be spelled in English with a capital "E." How perplexing it is to discover two English synonyms for Earth— "soil" and "dirt"—used to describe uncleanliness, *soiled* and *dirty*. And how upsetting it is to discover that the word "dirty" in English is also used to depict obscenities! Or take the English word "universe," in which I find even more complicated problems, for Indians do not believe in a "*uni*-verse," but in a "*multi*-verse." Indians don't believe that there is *one* fixed and eternal truth; they think there are many different and equally valid truths.

The late Hannah Arendt has given a vivid depiction of this concept of Indian reality, though she did not intend to clarify anything but the **multi-faceted** nature of reality itself. She said in her last book, *The Life of the Mind,* that the impulse behind the use of reason is not the discovery of truth but the discovery of meaning—and that truth and meaning are not the same things.

If we can accept the **paradox** that the real humanity of people is understood through cultural differences rather than cultural similarities, then we can make profound sense of our differences. It is possible that there is not one truth, but many; not one real experience, but many realities; not one history, but many different and valid ways of looking at events.

At the core of each person's life is a package of beliefs that he or she learns and that has been culturally determined long in advance of the person's birth. That is equally true for Indians and for white people. The world is made coherent by our description of it. Language permits us to express ourselves, but it also places limits on what we are able to say. What we call things largely determines how we evaluate them. What we see when we speak of "reality" is simply that preconception—that cultural package we inherited at birth. For me it was méksikatsi; for an English-speaking child it was duck.

Indian children have long been urged by educators to see things and to name them in terms of the cultural package of white people, though such training essentially divests Indians of their unique grasp of reality, of their own dissimilar cultural package. Children of the dominant society are rarely given the opportunity to know the world as others know it. Therefore they come to believe that there is only one world, one reality, one truth—the one they personally know; and they are inclined to dismiss all other worlds as illusions. 15

Evidence that Indians have a different manner of looking at the world can be found in the contrast between the ways in which Indian and non-Indian artists depict the same events. That difference is not necessarily a matter of "error" or simply a variation in imagery. It represents an entirely individual way of seeing the world. For instance, in a sixteenth-century anonymous engraving of a famous scene from the white man's history an artist depicted a sailing vessel anchored offshore with a landing party of elegantly dressed gentlemen disembarking while regal, Europeanized Indians look on—one carrying a "peace pipe" expressly for this festive occasion.

The drawing by an Indian, on the other hand, records a totally different scene: Indians gasping in amazement as a floating island, covered with tall defoliated trees and odd creatures with hairy faces, approaches.

When I showed the two pictures to white people they said in effect: "Well, of course you realize that what those Indians thought they saw was not really there. They were unfamiliar with what was happening to them and so they misunderstood their experience." In other words, there were no defoliated trees, no floating island, but a ship with a party of explorers.

Indians, looking at the same pictures, pause with perplexity and then say, "Well, after all, a ship is a floating island, and what really are the masts of a ship but the trunks of tall trees?" In other words, what the Indians saw was real in terms of their own experience.

The Indians saw a floating island while white people saw a ship. Isn't it also possible—if we use the bounds of twentieth-century imagination— that another, more alien people with an utterly different way of seeing and thinking might see neither an island nor a ship? They might for example see the complex networks of molecules that physics tells us produce the outward shapes, colors, and textures that we simply *see* as objects. . . .

Today we are beginning to look into the ideas of groups outside the dominant culture; we are finding different kinds of "truth" that make the world we live in far bigger than we dreamed it could be. . . .

My generation was the first to attend in great numbers both the ritual "schools" of our own cultures and the higher institutions of the white world. We grew up in two Americas—the ancient one that had existed for our ancestors for tens of thousands of years and the new one that is written about in history books. The tales of those two Americas are rarely compatible—and we quickly came to grasp our perilous situation. We had to make convincing use of our newly acquired intellectual skills in order to sustain our primal culture. We had to release a tide of communication between two worlds, and to do this we had to be a kind of people who had never before existed. We had to abandon both **Andrew Jackson's** *Wild Indians* and **Jean-Jacques Rousseau's** *Noble Savage* and emerge as a new cultural **mutant**—the *Intellectual Savage*—who was capable of surviving equally in two worlds by tenaciously retaining the ritual apparatus of primal people at the same time that we were attaining the intellectual and communications paraphernalia of the dominant societies.

QUESTIONS FOR DISCUSSION

1. What does Highwater mean when he says he had to undertake his exploration to "save his life"?

2. What meaning does Highwater find in the word *méksikatsi* that he does not find in *duck?*

3. Highwater begins his essay with a discussion of language. Why do you think language is so important to him?

4. What reasons and examples does Highwater give to back up his claim that people's view of reality is determined by their "cultural package"? Are his arguments sound? Can you think of other instances where cultural preconceptions might influence a person's view of the world?

5. Highwater argues that "the real humanity of people is understood through cultural differences rather than cultural similarities." But another commonly-held view is that despite cultural differences, people of different races and nationalities are actually more alike than different— that we all share the same basic needs, desires, and human qualities. Do you think Highwater makes a good case for his point of view? Which view do you think is more valid? Why?

6. Explain the title of this essay—"The Intellectual Savage."

7. What do you think Highwater would have to say about Crevecoeur's statement that in America "individuals of all nations are melted into a new race of men"?

✍ JOSEPH BRUCHAC
Ellis Island

Joseph Bruchac was born in 1942 in Saratoga Springs, New York. His father's family was Slovak, and his mother was Anaki Native American. Bruchac was raised by his maternal grandfather. He holds a B.A. degree in creative writing from Cornell University and an M.A. from Syracuse University. For three years, he taught in Ghana; then he taught creative writing at Skidmore College. He has published two books of poetry: Indian Mountain *and* The Buffalo in the Syracuse Zoo. *He is also the founder and editor of the* Greenfield Review, *a literary magazine. Bruchac lives in Greenfield Center, New York, with his wife and two sons.*

KEY VOCABULARY

ELLIS ISLAND is an island in Upper New York Bay. It was the leading American immigration center from 1892 to 1943, the first place where most European immigrants stepped onto American soil.

To **QUARANTINE** is to keep isolated from others. To reduce the chance of disease being brought into the country, immigrants were held on Ellis Island until the authorities could certify their good health.

Beyond the red brick of **Ellis Island**   1
where the two Slovak children
who became my grandparents
waited the long days of **quarantine,**
after leaving the sickness,   5
the old Empires of Europe,
a Circle Line ship slips easily
on its way to the island
of the tall woman, green
as dreams of forests and meadows   10
waiting for those who'd worked
a thousand years
yet never owned their own.

Like millions of others,
I too come to this island,   15
nine decades the answerer
of dreams.

Yet only one part of my blood loves that memory.
Another voice speaks
of native lands within this nation.   20
Lands invaded
when the earth became owned.
Lands of those who followed the changing Moon,
knowledge of the seasons
in their veins.   25

QUESTIONS FOR DISCUSSION

1. Joseph Bruchac is descended from both immigrant and Native American parents. Based on the poem, do you think he feels closer to one side of his heritage than the other? Or is he divided between them?

2. The idea of *ownership* is mentioned twice in the poem—in the first stanza and the third. What attitude toward ownership is reflected in each of these stanzas?

3. What differences between the culture of Europeans and the culture of Native Americans does Bruchac emphasize in this poem?

✎ ANZIA YEZIERSKA

America and I

*Born in Russia, Anzia Yezierska immigrated to the United States in 1901.
In her first book,* Hungry Hearts, *she described life in New York's sweat-
shops and ghettos. She wrote a number of novels, including* Salome of the
Tenements *(1922) and* Children of Loneliness *(1923). Her autobiography,* Red Ribbon on a White Horse, *was published in 1950.*

KEY VOCABULARY

DUMB in this story means "unable to speak."

A **GHETTO** was originally a section of a European city to which Jews were
restricted. The word has come to mean any slum section of a city, usually
occupied by minority groups.

GOTTUNIU (also spelled "Gotenyu") is a Yiddish expression meaning "Dear
God!" It is an outburst that can signify joy, affection, or misery.

OI-I WEH (also spelled "Oy Veh") is also a Yiddish expression, meaning literally "Oh, pain!" In effect, it means "Oh, woe is me!"

A **SWEAT-SHOP** is a factory where workers work long hours for low pay,
under bad conditions.

A **UTOPIA** is a perfect, ideal society.

As one of the **dumb,** voiceless ones I speak. One of the millions of 1
immigrants beating, beating out their hearts at your gates for a breath of
understanding.

Ach! America! From the other end of the earth where I came, America
was a land of living hope, woven of dreams, aflame with longing and desire.

Choked for ages in the airless oppression of Russia, the Promised
Land rose up—wings for my stifled spirit—sunlight burning through my
darkness—freedom singing to me in my prison—deathless songs turning
prison-bars into strings of a beautiful violin.

I arrived in America. My young, strong body, my heart and soul pregnant with the unlived lives of generations clamoring for expression.

What my mother and father and their mother and father never had a 5
chance to give out in Russia, I would give out in America. The hidden sap
of centuries would find release; colors that never saw light—songs that died
unvoiced—romance that never had a chance to blossom in the black life of
the Old World.

169

In the golden land of flowing opportunity I was to find my work that was denied me in the sterile village of my forefathers. Here I was to be free from the dead drudgery for bread that held me down in Russia. For the first time in America, I'd cease to be a slave of the belly. I'd be a creator, a giver, a human being! My work would be the living joy of fullest self-expression.

But from my high visions, my golden hopes, I had to put my feet down on earth. I had to have food and shelter. I had to have the money to pay for it.

I was in America, among the Americans, but not of them. No speech, no common language, no way to win a smile of understanding from them, only my young, strong body and my untried faith. Only my eager, empty hands, and my full heart shining from my eyes!

God from the world! Here I was with so much richness in me but my mind was not wanted without the language. And my body, unskilled, un-trained, was not even wanted in the factory. Only one of two chances was left open to me: the kitchen, or minding babies.

My first job was as a servant in an Americanized family. Once, long   10
ago, they came from the same village from where I came. But they were so well-dressed, so well-fed, so successful in America, that they were ashamed to remember their mother tongue.

"What were to be my wages?" I ventured timidly, as I looked up to the well-fed, well-dressed "American" man and woman.

They looked at me with a sudden coldness. What have I said to draw away from me their warmth? Was it so low from me to talk of wages? I shrank back into myself like a low-down bargainer. Maybe they're so high up in well-being they can't any more understand my low thoughts for money.

From his rich height the man preached down to me that I must not be so grabbing for wages. Only just landed from the ship and already thinking about money when I should be thankful to associate with "Americans."

The woman, out of her smooth, smiling fatness assured me that this was my chance for a summer vacation in the country with her two lovely children. My great chance to learn to be a civilized being, to become an American by living with them.

So, made to feel that I was in the hands of American friends, invited to   15
share with them their home, their plenty, their happiness, I pushed out from my head the worry for wages. Here was my first chance to begin my life in the sunshine, after my long darkness. My laugh was all over my face as I said to them: "I'll trust myself to you. What I'm worth you'll give me." And I entered their house like a child by the hand.

The best of me I gave them. Their house cares were my house cares. I got up early. I worked till late. All that my soul hungered to give I put into the passion with which I scrubbed floors, scoured pots, and washed clothes. I was so grateful to mingle with the American people, to hear the music of the American language, that I never knew tiredness.

There was such a freshness in my brains and such a willingness in my heart that I could go on and on—not only with the work of the house, but work with my head—learning new words from the children, the grocer, the butcher, the iceman. I was not even afraid to ask for words from the policeman on the street. And every new word made me see new American things with American eyes. I felt like a Columbus, finding new worlds through every new word.

But words alone were only for the inside of me. The outside of me still branded me for a steerage immigrant. I had to have clothes to forget myself that I'm a stranger yet. And so I had to have money to buy these clothes.

The month was up. I was so happy! Now I'd have money. *My own, earned* money. Money to buy a new shirt on my back—shoes on my feet. Maybe yet an American dress and hat!

Ach! How high rose my dreams! How plainly I saw all that I would do with my visionary wages shining like a light over my head!

In my imagination I already walked in my new American clothes. How beautiful I looked as I saw myself like a picture before my eyes! I saw how I would throw away my immigrant rags tied up in my immigrant shawl. With money to buy—free money in my hands—I'd show them that I could look like an American in a day.

Like a prisoner in his last night in prison, counting the seconds that will free him from his chains, I trembled breathlessly for the minute I'd get the wages in my hands.

Before dawn I rose.

I shined up the house like a jewel-box.

I prepared breakfast and waited with my heart in my mouth for my lady and gentleman to rise. At last I heard them stirring. My eyes were jumping out of my head to them when I saw them coming in and seating themselves by the table.

Like a hungry cat rubbing up to its boss for meat, so I edged and simpered around them as I passed them the food. Without my will, like a beggar, my hand reached out to them.

The breakfast was over. And no word yet from my wages.

"*Gottuniu!*" I thought to myself. Maybe they're so busy with their own things they forgot it's the day for my wages. Could they who have everything know what I was to do with my first American dollars? How could they, soaking in plenty, how could they feel the longing and the fierce hunger in me, pressing up through each visionary dollar? How could they know the gnawing ache of my avid fingers for the feel of my own, earned dollars? *My* dollars that I could spend like a free person. *My* dollars that would make me feel with everybody alike!

Breakfast was long past.

Lunch came. Lunch past.   30

Oi-i weh! Not a word yet about my money.

It was near dinner. And not a word yet about my wages.

I began to set the table. But my head—it swam away from me. I broke a glass. The silver dropped from my nervous fingers. I couldn't stand it any longer. I dropped everything and rushed over to my American lady and gentleman.

"*Oi weh!* The money—my money—my wages!" I cried breathlessly.

Four cold eyes turned on me.   35

"Wages? Money?" The four eyes turned into hard stone as they looked me up and down. "Haven't you a comfortable bed to sleep, and three good meals a day? You're only a month here. Just came to America. And you already think about money. Wait till you're worth any money. What use are you without knowing English? You should be glad we keep you here. It's like a vacation for you. Other girls pay money yet to be in the country."

It went black for my eyes. I was so choked no words came to my lips. Even the tears went dry in my throat.

I left. Not a dollar for all my work.

For a long, long time my heart ached and ached like a sore wound. If murderers would have robbed me and killed me it wouldn't have hurt me so much. I couldn't think through my pain. The minute I'd see before me how they looked at me, the words they said to me—then everything began to bleed in me. And I was helpless.

For a long, long time the thought of ever working in an "American"   40 family made me tremble with fear, like the fear of wild wolves. No—never again would I trust myself to an "American" family, no matter how fine their language and how sweet their smile.

It was blotted out in me all trust in friendship from "Americans." But the life in me still burned to live. The hope in me still craved to hope. In darkness, in dirt, in hunger and want, but only to live on!

There had been no end to my day—working for the "American" family.

Now rejecting false friendships from higher-ups in America, I turned back to the **Ghetto.** I worked on a hard bench with my own kind on either side of me. I knew before I began what my wages were to be. I knew what my hours were to be. And I knew the feeling of the end of the day.

From the outside my second job seemed worse than the first. It was in a **sweat-shop** of a Delancey Street basement, kept up by an old, wrinkled woman that looked like a black witch of greed. My work was sewing on buttons. While the morning was still dark I walked into a dark basement. And darkness met me when I turned out of the basement.

Day after day, week after week, all the contact I got with America was 45 handling dead buttons. The money I earned was hardly enough to pay for bread and rent. I didn't have a room to myself. I didn't even have a bed. I slept on a mattress on the floor in a rat-hole of a room occupied by a dozen other immigrants. I was always hungry—oh, so hungry! The scant meals I could afford only sharpened my appetite for real food. But I felt myself better off than working in the "American" family, where I had three good meals a day and a bed to myself. With all the hunger and darkness of the sweat-shop, I had at least the evening to myself. And all night was mine. When all were asleep, I used to creep up on the roof of the tenement and talk out my heart in silence to the stars in the sky.

"Who am I? What am I? What do I want with my life? Where is America? Is there an America? What is this wilderness in which I'm lost?"

I'd hurl my questions and then think and think. And I could not tear it out of me, the feeling that America must be somewhere, somehow— only I couldn't find it—*my America,* where I would work for love and not for a living. I was like a thing following blindly after something far off in the dark!

"*Oi weh!*" I'd stretch out my hand up in the air. "My head is so lost in America! What's the use of all my working if I'm not in it? Dead buttons is not me."

Then the busy season started in the shop. The mounds of buttons grew and grew. The long day stretched out longer. I had to begin with the buttons earlier and stay with them till later in the night. The old witch turned into a huge greedy maw for wanting more and more buttons.

For a glass of tea, for a slice of herring over black bread, she would buy 50 us up to stay another and another hour, till there seemed no end to her demands.

One day, the light of self-assertion broke into my cellar darkness.

"I don't want the tea. I don't want your herring," I said with terrible boldness. "I only want to go home. I only want the evening to myself!"

"You fresh mouth, you!" cried the old witch. "You learned already too much in America. I want no clock-watchers in my shop. Out you go!"

I was driven out to cold and hunger. I could no longer pay for my mattress on the floor. I no longer could buy the bite in the mouth. I walked the streets. I knew what it is to be alone in a strange city, among strangers.

But I laughed through my tears. So I learned too much already in 55

America because I wanted the whole evening to myself? Well America has yet to teach me still more: how to get not only the whole evening to myself, but a whole day a week like the American workers.

That sweat-shop was a bitter memory but a good school. It fitted me for a regular factory. I could walk in boldly and say I could work at something, even if it was only sewing on buttons.

Gradually, I became a trained worker. I worked in a light, airy factory, only eight hours a day. My boss was no longer a sweater and a blood-squeezer. The first freshness of the morning was mine. And the whole evening was mine. All day Sunday was mine.

Now I had better food to eat. I slept on a better bed. Now, I even looked dressed up like the American-born. But inside of me I knew that I was not yet an American. I choked with longing when I met an American-born, and I could say nothing.

Something cried **dumb** in me. I couldn't help it. I didn't know what it was I wanted. I only knew I wanted. I wanted. Like the hunger in the heart that never gets food.

An English class for foreigners started in our factory. The teacher had 60 such a good, friendly face, her eyes looked so understanding, as if she could see right into my heart. So I went to her one day for an advice:

"I don't know what is with me the matter," I began. "I have no rest in me. I never yet done what I want."

"What is it you want to do, child?" she asked me.

"I want to do something with my head, my feelings. All day long, only with my hands I work."

"First you must learn English." She patted me as if I was not yet grown up. "Put your mind on that, and then we'll see."

So for a time I learned the language. I could almost begin to think with 65 English words in my head. But in my heart the emptiness still hurt. I burned to give, to give something, to do something, to be something. The dead work with my hands was killing me. My work left only hard stones on my heart.

Again I went to our factory teacher and cried to her: "I know already to read and write the English language, but I can't put it into words what I want. What is it in me so different that can't come out?"

She smiled at me down from her calmness as if I were a little bit out of my head. "What *do you want* to do?"

"I feel. I see. I hear. And I want to think it out. But I'm like **dumb** in me. I only feel I'm different—different from everybody."

She looked at me close and said nothing for a minute. "You ought to join one of the social clubs of the Women's Association," she advised.

"What's the Women's Association?" I implored greedily.   70

"A group of American women who are trying to help the working-girl find herself. They have a special department for immigrant girls like you." I joined the Women's Association. On my first evening there they announced a lecture: "The Happy Worker and His Work," by the Welfare director of the United Mills Corporation.

"Is there such a thing as a happy worker at his work?" I wondered. Happiness is only by working at what you love. And what poor girl can ever find it to work at what she loves? My old dreams about my America rushed through my mind. Once I thought that in America everybody works for love. Nobody has to worry for a living. Maybe this welfare man came to show me the *real* America that till now I sought in vain.

With a lot of polite words the head lady of the Women's Association introduced a higher-up that looked like the king of kings of business. Never before in my life did I ever see a man with such a sureness in his step, such power in his face, such friendly positiveness in his eye as when he smiled upon us.

"Efficiency is the new religion of business," he began. "In big business houses, even in up-to-date factories, they no longer take the first comer and give him any job that happens to stand empty. Efficiency begins at the employment office. Experts are hired for the one purpose, to find out how best to fit the worker to his work. It's economy for the boss to make the worker happy." And then he talked a lot more on efficiency in educated language that was over my head.

I didn't know exactly what it meant—efficiency—but if it was to make the worker happy at his work, then that's what I had been looking for since I came to America. I only felt from watching him that he was happy by his job. And as I looked on this clean, well-dressed, successful one, who wasn't ashamed to say he rose from an office-boy, it made me feel that I, too, could lift myself up for a person.

He finished his lecture, telling us about the Vocational-Guidance Center that the Women's Association started.

The very next evening I was at the Vocational-Guidance Center. There I found a young, college-looking woman. Smartness and health shining from her eyes! She, too, looked as if she knew her way in America. I could tell at the first glance: here is a person that is happy by what she does.

"I feel you'll understand me," I said right away.

She leaned over with pleasure in her face: "I hope I can."

"I want to work by what's in me. Only, I don't know what's in me. I only feel I'm different."

She gave me a quick, puzzled look from the corner of her eyes. "What are you doing now?"

"I'm the quickest shirtwaist hand on the floor. But my heart wastes away by such work. I think and think, and my thoughts can't come out."

"Why don't you think out your thoughts in shirtwaists? You could learn to be a designer. Earn more money."

"I don't want to look on waists. If my hands are sick from waists, how 85 could my head learn to put beauty into them?"

"But you must earn your living at what you know, and rise slowly from job to job."

I looked at her office sign: "Vocational Guidance." "What's your vocational guidance?" I asked. "How to rise from job to job—how to earn more money?"

The smile went out from her eyes. But she tried to be kind yet. "What *do* you want?" she asked, with a sigh of last patience.

"I want America to want me."

She fell back in her chair, thunderstruck with my boldness. But yet, in 90 a low voice of educated self-control, she tried to reason with me:

"You have to *show* that you have something special for America before America has need of you."

"But I never had a chance to find out what's in me, because I always had to work for a living. Only, I feel it's efficiency for America to find out what's in me so different, so I could give it out by my work."

Her eyes half closed as they bored through me. Her mouth opened to speak, but no words came from her lips. So I flamed up with all that was choking in me like a house on fire:

"America gives free bread and rent to criminals in prison. They got grand houses with sunshine, fresh air, doctors and teachers, even for the crazy ones. Why don't they have free boarding-schools for immigrants— strong people—willing people? Here you see us burning up with something different, and America turns her head away from us."

Her brows lifted and dropped down. She shrugged her shoulders away 95 from me with the look of pity we give to cripples and hopeless lunatics.

"America is no **Utopia.** First you must become efficient in earning a living before you can indulge in your poetic dreams."

I went away from the vocational-guidance office with all the air out of my lungs. All the light out of my eyes. My feet dragged after me like dead wood.

Till now there had always lingered a rosy veil of hope over my emptiness, a hope that a miracle would happen. I would open my eyes some day and suddenly find the America of my dreams. As a young girl hungry for love sees always before her eyes the picture of lover's arms around her, so I saw always in my heart the vision of Utopian America.

But now I felt that the America of my dreams never was and never could be. Reality had hit me on the head as with a club. I felt that the

America that I sought was nothing but a shadow—an echo—a chimera of lunatics and crazy immigrants.

Stripped of all illusion, I looked about me. The long desert of wasting   100 days of drudgery stared me in the face. The drudgery that I had lived through, and the endless drudgery still ahead of me rose over me like a withering wilderness of sand. In vain were all my cryings, in vain were all frantic efforts of my spirit to find the living waters of understanding for my perishing lips. Sand, sand was everywhere. With every seeking, every reaching out I only lost myself deeper and deeper in a vast sea of sand.

I knew now the American language. And I knew now, if I talked to the Americans from morning till night, they could not understand what the Russian soul of me wanted. They could not understand *me* anymore than if I talked to them in Chinese. Between my soul and the American soul were worlds of difference that no words could bridge over. What was that difference? What made the Americans so far apart from me?

I began to read the American history. I found from the first pages that America started with a band of Courageous Pilgrims. They had left their native country as I had left mine. They had crossed an unknown ocean and landed in an unknown country, as I.

But the great difference between the first Pilgrims and me was that they expected to make America, build America, create their own world of liberty. I wanted to find it ready made.

I read on. I delved deeper down into the American history. I saw how the Pilgrim Fathers came to a rocky desert country, surrounded by Indian savages on all sides. But undaunted, they pressed on—through danger—through famine, pestilence, and want—they pressed on. They did not ask the Indians for sympathy, for understanding. They made no demands on anybody, but on their own indomitable spirit of persistence.

And I—I was forever begging a crumb of sympathy, a gleam of   105 understanding from strangers who could not sympathize, who could not understand.

I, when I encountered a few savage Indian scalpers, like the old witch of the sweat-shop, like my "Americanized" countryman, who cheated me of my wages—I, when I found myself on the lonely, untrodden path through which all seekers of the new world must pass, I lost heart and said: "There is no America!"

Then came a light—a great revelation! I saw America—a big idea—a deathless hope—a world still in the making. I saw that it was the glory of America that it was not yet finished. And I, the last comer, had her share to give, small or great, to the making of America, like those Pilgrims who came in the *Mayflower*.

Fired up by this revealing light, I began to build a bridge of understanding between the American-born and myself. Since their life was shut out from such as me, I began to open up my life and the lives of my people to them. And life draws life. In only writing about the **Ghetto** I found America.

Great chances have come to me. But in my heart is always a deep sadness. I feel like a man who is sitting down to a secret table of plenty, while his near ones and dear ones are perishing before his eyes. My very joy in doing the work I love hurts me like secret guilt, because all about me I see so many with my longings, my burning eagerness, to do and to be, wasting their days in drudgery they hate, merely to buy bread and pay rent. And America is losing all that richness of the soul.

The Americans of to-morrow, the America that is every day nearer 110 coming to be, will be too wise, too open-hearted, too friendly-handed, to let the least last-comer at their gates knock in vain with his gifts unwanted.

QUESTIONS FOR DISCUSSION

1. At the beginning of the story, what is Yezierska's idea of the American Dream? How does she think life in America will be different from life in Russia?

2. Yezierska's story tells of a series of experiences that can be seen as stages in the narrator's education. Each experience causes her to examine her attitudes and teaches her something about American ways and values. What does she learn at each stage? How do her encounters with the reality of American society change her idea of the American Dream?

3. How does her reading of American history enlighten Yezierska? How does she finally come to see herself in relation to America?

4. At the end of the story Yezierska offers, by implication, some advice about how America should treat immigrants. What do you think her advice is? How could America best encourage the hopes and talents of new immigrants?

JOE KLINE

The Good Life and Long Hours
of Nguyen Nguu

*Joe Kline is a writer who was born and raised in Rockaway Beach, New York.
He has written a book,* Payback, *about five Marines who returned from
Vietnam.*

KEY VOCABULARY

A **PANTHEON** is a temple dedicated to the gods.

A **TAOIST** is one who believes in the Chinese religious system of Tao ("The
Way") which is based on the teachings of Lao Tzu (sixth century B.C.). Tao-
ism is a mystical religion which holds that a world of the spirit which is beyond human understanding. In the centuries after Lao Tzu's death, it became
a folk religion, full of superstition and local gods.

Pensacola Bay was absolutely calm. The sun was sinking behind a   1
fringe of cattails, the air clear with a slight edge to it. A perfect evening—
for almost anything but shrimping. Shrimpers like it hot and dark and
rough. They love hurricanes.

Nguyen Nguu, a tiny thirty-six-year-old Vietnamese man, was alone
on the aft deck of his boat—the *Janice C*—darning his net. His hands
seemed much older than the rest of him, but they moved with the frantic
precision of a sewing machine. Nguu noticed my admiration; he smiled,
massaging the net. "Big fish make hole," he said. "I fix."

"Nice night," I said, to say something.

"Yeah, no good," he shrugged. He was sitting like a rag doll, legs
straight out, shoeless, the net a green nylon mesh over him. "No good fish.
Too cold."

Too cold . . . and yet, you never can tell. A month earlier, on a very   5
similar night—a little warmer, windier perhaps—Nguu had struck gold in
the bay. He and his wife, Phan Thang, were out alone (working harder than
the others, as always); there was no chatter on the CB, no blips on the radar,
no other boats out. It was about 10:00 P.M., a slow night—maybe a $200
night, little better than break-even—when he pulled in his tri-net and
found a hundred shrimp: big, fat ones. He put them in a pail and showed
Thang, who was up in the cabin steering. She turned the boat around, and

they trawled the stretch again. He set his timer for fifteen minutes, waited, then pulled in the tri-net once more. Another hundred or so plump, perfect shrimp. "It was cold," he would recall. "My wife wear four coats, but she not cold. She so excited." Through the night, they trawled back and forth over the same stretch. Every four hours they would haul in the big nets. What were all those shrimp *doing* out there on a cold December night? Nguu and Thang did not stop to talk, although they sometimes laughed as net after bulging net came in. They worked all night, and through most of the morning, sorting the catch, removing the heads from the larger shrimp to increase the price per pound. When it was done, they had more than seven hundred pounds, which they would sell for a near-miraculous $2,454.60.

This cool, perfect Friday in January would be nothing like that. The season was very much over now. There would be little serious shrimping till spring. Nguu was taking me out for a brief run, to show off his boat and his work; he swaggered about proudly in a blue baseball cap from Johnson's Diesel, Biloxi, Mississippi. Thang, a very attractive woman in civilian clothes, was distinctly Buddha-like in her layers of sweaters and coats and a Baltimore Orioles knitted cap pushed down over her eyebrows. She was busy in the galley, cooking a small feast—chicken, Chinese sausage, shrimp, tomatoes, noodles, and vegetables.

At dusk, Nguu started the engine. He and Thang pushed off, and we slid into the bay, coasting easily across the black glass surface. Just past the breakwater, Thang took the wheel and Nguu winched the two big nets— 22.5 feet long each, the legal limit—to the outriggers. For a moment, as Nguu lowered the rigs—prodigious wings, heavy with netting—on both sides aft, the boat seemed a great prehistoric bird skimming the bay; then the nets hit water and the boat slowed. When they submerged completely, the boat nearly stopped; the engine strained against the drag, the bay now molasses. We crawled toward deep water.

"Need more big engine," Nguu said. "This six cylinder. I like V-8. Here, this," handing me a pamphlet advertising an impressive piece of machinery. "Fifty-two thousand dollar," Nguu said. His English is fluent . . . when it comes to numbers; *words* are, obviously, less important. He can remember the price of every major item he has bought since coming to America five years ago and will recite each, given half a chance.

The latest acquisition—radar—is especially pleasing. "Only two other Vietnamese have," he said, turning on the screen, which glowed a luminous, high-tech green. "Very good. I can go work when foggy. See: big ship there, go to Gulf . . . Gulf there . . . shore there . . . four thousand dollar."

The attitude was somewhere between reverence and adoration. Nguu, 10 a **Taoist,** placed machinery in the same **pantheon** as did his ancestors—a gift from God. Machinery was the force that most differentiated America from his homeland. "No machine in Vietnam boat. Hard, hard work," he said. "America machine number one. Everything machine. I like that. America too easy."

"He caught all that $2,400 in one night?" said Allen Williams, who owns the wholesale fish house where Nguyen Nguu sells his shrimp. "Jeez, I thought it was a *week's* catch. Well, I can't say it surprises me. . . . *Nothing* that little guy does surprises me anymore. I sold him his first boat a few years ago, gave him two years to pay. He paid for it in one. Next thing I know, he's sold that boat and bought the one he has now, which is twice as big. . . . Next thing, he'll have a fleet. You can't work much harder than he does. He was out there for about a week after all the other boats came in at the end of the season. Of course, *none* of these people are exactly lazy."

"Do they work harder than the Anglos?" I asked.

"Well, I wouldn't want to say that. But . . . well, these Vietnamese are like your grandparents. They're like Americans used to be. They work like devils and pour it all back into the business. When the engine breaks, they fix it themselves. They make their own nets, and that keeps the overhead down—just gas, oil, and ice. The night Nguu brought in the $2,400, his overhead was probably only a hundred dollars or so. Of course, he won't have a night like that very often, but look here . . ."

Williams led me out to the docks. "See these boats over here on the left: snapper boats. Americans own them. Over there on the right: shrimpers," he said, pointing toward a picturesque tangle of nets and rigging. "Every last one of those boats is owned by a Vietnamese. In the past four years they've pretty much taken over shrimping on this bay."

Williams's rival, Sam Patti of the Joe Patti Seafood Company, goes even 15 further: "I'd say they revolutionized our business, and not too far down the road they're going to *control* the fishing industry on the Gulf Coast. They're going to own big steel-hull boats and wholesale houses. Why? 'Cause they believe in the old stuff: if you work hard enough, you can be anything in America. You should see some of these little guys shucking oysters—man, I've never seen anything like it. It's like Snow White and the Seven Dwarfs."

All of which hasn't gone down too easily with many *real* Americans who've been shrimping Pensacola Bay leisurely for generations. In the old days, a shrimper might go out four or five nights a week during the height of the season, stay out till midnight, then amble on home in time for last call. Often, shrimp boats were run as a sideline by people who had regular day jobs. The idea that you could actually make a full-time living at it seemed absurd. Why, you'd have to go out all night, seven days a week, for months on end. . . . Who'd ever want to work that hard, anyway?

When the first Vietnamese arrived in the mid-1970s, the Anglos were outraged. Rumors swept Pensacola Bay: The Vietnamese used mile-long nets, sometimes strung from boat to boat. They traveled in packs, picked bays clean. Vacuum cleaners, dredging barges, *anything* seemed possible. The Anglos threatened to bring in the Klan. A grand jury convened to investigate Vietnamese fishing practices. It was discovered that they were guilty of rampant industriousness.

In response to the threats and rumors, the Vietnamese stayed cool and blended in. Their presence had surprisingly little impact on Pensacola. There was no quaint, colorful Vietnamese neighborhood to provide a ready target for frustrated patriots. There was no social club, or hangout, or church: when the newcomers opened restaurants, they tended to camouflage them as "Oriental." They weren't exactly *hiding,* just trying not to make waves. "We've tried to blend in," said Mike Nguyen, who works for the Catholic Social Services refugee program. "The idea was: stay quiet, work hard, and there won't be any trouble." The only places where the Vietnamese seemed to congregate were the Williams and Patti fish houses, and out on the bay, where they kept each other awake in the deep night, chatting back and forth over their CBs.

By the time Nguyen Nguu arrived in Pensacola in 1981, the controversy had ebbed some. Nguu bought his first boat—a little thirty-four-footer—from Allen Williams a year later, after doing his best to avoid fishing for a time. He'd had enough of *that* in Vietnam; America was supposed to be different. He dreamed of becoming a diesel repairman. He had some of the skills but lacked the language to learn more. "I too old learn good English," he said. He didn't have to learn many words to fish, though—just numbers.

Nguu comes from a long line of fishermen in Da Nang. His family 20 owned a hundred-foot boat—a good boat, but certainly not equipped for the trip he would make in 1979 with his family and a dozen or so relatives across the South China Sea to the Philippines. Nguu is reluctant to talk about the circumstances that made the trip necessary: politics is not his favorite topic. During the war he served—not very enthusiastically—in the South Vietnamese army. "I cannot express my feelings about the war," he said, through an interpreter. "But *many* people were happy when it was over. They wanted only peace and did not know anything about the Communists. But soon these people realized that peace was not as they had expected."

Peace, for a fisherman in Da Nang, turned out to be rules and regulations and quotas and gas rationing, and a preponderance of their catch—at times, as much as 90 percent—had to be turned over to the government. Nguu heard that many fishermen in the south were leaving; he decided to try it himself, even though his wife was pregnant with their fifth child. The crossing didn't look to be particularly difficult if the weather held—a week, at most. "But on the third day there was a terrible storm and we lost most of our food and all our water," he recalled. "I thought then that very few of us would survive—certainly none of the children. But we came upon a large ship, which gave us food and water, and we made it."

Sponsored by Church World Service, they came to New York, where Phan Thang's brother—a former pilot in the South Vietnamese air force— was working as an electrician and living in a small apartment on Forty-second Street, just two blocks west of Times Square. Nguu and Thang were perplexed by the size of the buildings and by the weather . . . and by the other things they saw. "It was a very sinful place," Nguu recalled. "And very cold. My children had nosebleeds from the cold. We look on the map for someplace warm, and there is Pensacola."

Catholic Social Services was running an aggressive refugee resettlement program in north Florida; Vietnamese who had found places such as Chicago and Minneapolis and New York too cold were flocking south; some had been fishermen in Vietnam, but most not. The large fish wholesalers like Williams and Patti, in need of cheap, industrious labor, were happy to sponsor families. The women were given jobs in the fish houses, shucking oysters and heading shrimp; the men went out on the boats. "When they could scrape together the down payment for a little boat," said Allen Williams, "we'd give them a low-interest, sometimes a *no*-interest, loan. We gave them dock space free. In return, they agreed to sell us their catch."

Nguu avoided the bay for as long as he could. He searched for a diesel-repair training program. Meanwhile, Thang worked as a waitress and the family received welfare. Soon, though, Nguu began to sign on as a deckhand for other shrimpers—watching, learning (he had never shrimped in Vietnam). After a year, he borrowed $6,000 from his brother-in-law for a down payment on a boat; Allen Williams loaned him the rest of the $21,000 purchase price, interest free.

Nguu still keeps the purchase agreement for that first boat with his other important papers in a small, zippered plastic pencil case. "Mr. Williams trust me," he said. "He American father to me."

"What," I asked, "do you do for fun?"

Nguu laughed. It was a Saturday morning in January. Most of his six children were huddled around the Sony, lost in cartoons. The living and dining rooms were covered with the nets; Nguu spends the off-season cutting and sewing for other fishermen. Although it sometimes takes as long as a week to put one together, he charges only a hundred dollars per net—which pays the utility bills and is better than doing nothing. Nguu could not imagine doing nothing.

"Do you go out to the movies?" I pursued. "Do you go to restaurants? Is there some sort of Vietnamese social club?"

Nguu laughed. His oldest son, Binh, who is fourteen and speaks perfect English, explained: "My parents don't go out very much. Sometimes they may visit friends, but usually there just isn't time. Most days, during the season, they leave here about four in the afternoon, stay out on the bay all night, spend the morning sorting the catch, having it weighed, and cleaning the boat. They get home by noon."

"They get only four hours' sleep?"   30

"Well, sometimes you can take turns sleeping on the boat, getting an hour here or there."

Binh said that he takes charge of the younger children while his parents fish. He cooks dinner and puts them to sleep. Sometimes, during the summer, his mother will stay home and he'll go out on the boat with his father. "I don't like it very much," he said. "It's too hard. I want to be a doctor."

"Do you ever go on vacations?" I asked the father, who had been straining to keep up with what his son was saying, nodding with pride at the word *doctor.*

"Oh, no," Nguu said. "No time."

Still, it wouldn't be quite accurate to say that Nguyen Nguu never en- 35
joys himself. Evidence of his pleasure is all about the modest, rented, five-room brick house. There is an elaborate stereo system ("One hundred dollar, I got from friend," Nguu said) and a videocassette recorder ("My brother-in-law, he give"); out front, in the yard, is a nearly new Ford Econoline van with plush interior, CB radio, and stereo system ("Thirty-eight hundred dollar") and a shiny black Ford pickup truck ("Not mine," Nguu said unconvincingly, "friend's"). Nguu, it seemed, is as much an equipment junkie on land as he is on the bay. Food is cheap. Clothes are unimportant (he and his wife still wear sweaters and jackets the Baptists gave them five years ago). Machinery is all.

He dreams of larger, better boats; he is dizzy with the contraptions that could be bought. A V-8 engine, perhaps a whole new boat with a steel hull . . . with a steel hull, he'd no longer be imprisoned in Pensacola Bay . . . he could go out and fish the Gulf. He could buy the hull for $70,000, the V-8 engine for $52,000. He could do the rest of the work—the carpentry and electronics—himself. Alone on the bay in lonely morning hours, he dreams of these things; it is how he stays awake.

"I also make nets to not sleep," he said, standing on the bridge the night he took me fishing. "I never sit down. I sit, I sleep. Sometime, I sleep like this. . . ." He slumped over the wheel. "But I wake up quick. You like this work?"

"It seems hard," I said. "Do you make much money?"

Nguu shrugged. "Thirty thousand dollar, more or less," he said, artfully inexact.

We'd been out on the bay for little more than an hour. Nguu pulled in 40 the small seven-foot tri-net several times and gauged the catch. The results weren't very encouraging: a dozen or so shrimp, which looked like chubby grasshoppers with startling Day-Glo eyes; assorted squid and crabs, the crabs doing their antic sideways shuffle across the deck; lots of useless baby croakers and other small fish; a can of Diet 7-Up. "See," Nguu said. "No good. We go home now."

He stopped the boat just outside the breakwater and hauled in the big nets. Suspended above the aft deck, the catch looked like two giant green beach balls. Nguu loosed the ropes at the base of the nets, and the haul spilled onto the deck in a silverine cascade. Immediately, Thang was squatting over it with a metal hand rake, culling the shrimp and squid from the baby croakers and other fish. "Too many fish," Nguu said. "Not many shrimp. Twenty-five pounds, maybe. We stay out all night, maybe $200. You see?"

Thang was working furiously now, picking out shrimp, putting them into a plastic laundry basket, sweeping useless fish aside. She looked up at us and smiled, ineffably exotic in her Baltimore Orioles cap.

"My wife work good, yes?" Nguu asked.

"Does she like it?"

"I don't know," he replied. The question was superfluous, irrelevant. 45 "But lots of shrimp, she very happy. She like make money."

QUESTIONS FOR DISCUSSION

1. What does becoming "Americanized" mean to the Vietnamese people described in Klein's article? Would you say they have been Americanized?

2. What traditional "American values" do the Vietnamese hold?

3. What is "the good life" to Nguyen Nguu? Is he a success? If so, how would you account for his success? How did he achieve it?

4. How would you describe Nguu's idea of the American Dream?

5. How would you compare Nguyen Nguu's experience as an immigrant with Yezierska's, described in "America and I"? In what ways are their ideas of the American Dream similar? In what ways are they different?

✑ PETER H. SCHUCK

Latest Wave of Immigrants Raises Concerns over Whether Lady Liberty Still Opens Arms

Peter H. Schuck is a professor of law at Yale Law School. He has co-authored the book Citizenship Without Consent. *This article appeared in the* Tacoma News Tribune *on June 16, 1991.*

KEY VOCABULARY

AEGIS was originally the shield of the Greek god Zeus. In a general sense, "under the aegis" means "under the protection or sponsorship of a person or institution."

AFFIRMATIVE ACTION PROGRAMS are organized efforts by institutions to hire minority employees.

E PLURIBUS UNUM is Latin for "One out of Many."

GERRYMANDERING is the practice of dividing a state, county, or city into voting districts that give an unfair advantage to one of the parties in an election.

A **METAPHOR** is a figure of speech that says one thing is like something else. For example, to say that America is a melting pot suggests a comparison of the two things based on common characteristics.

PAROCHIAL LOYALTIES are feelings of allegiance to local groups rather than to national ones.

THE POLITICIZATION OF ETHNICITY means that ethnic groups have become politically active on their own behalf.

THE UNDOCUMENTED are foreign workers who have no papers allowing them to live and work in the United States.

Has the melting pot gone the way of Joe DiMaggio and other images 1 of a happier but irretrievably lost America?

Some people believe that a truer **metaphor** is a laboratory beaker brimming over with explosive chemicals in a high-stakes experiment that threatens to go awry. **E pluribus unum,** they fear, is being tragically reversed.

Hardly a week goes by without another outbreak of ethnic conflict making the national news. Yet there is ample reason to believe that from many groups, we can still forge one politically viable nation.

Ethnic conflict has always been with Americans, but lately it has become more noticeable, largely because of growth in the number of immigrants, their geographic concentration and diversity, the **politicization of ethnicity,** and heightened competition among low-income groups.
In the 1980s the United States admitted about 8.5 million people, in- 5
cluding 2.3 million under the 1986 amnesty law. The trend, moreover, was moving upward as the decade ended. That is almost double the total for the 1970s and close to the 8.8 million who came in the first decade of this century when immigration was essentially unrestricted.

The new immigrants are especially visible because they are concentrated in a small number of metropolitan areas. About 80 percent of the legal ones plan to live in six states; 37 percent plan to live in seven metropolitan areas in California. The **undocumented,** who depend more on informal job and protection networks, cluster even more than that; 42 percent of the amnesty applicants plan to live in those seven California communities. In cities like Miami, Houston, Los Angeles, and New York, recent immigrants are already important forces in the local economy, culture, and political system.

The newcomers are ethnically and linguistically distinct from most of the native population. In 1989 the top 10 source countries for legal (and amnestied) admissions were Mexico, El Salvador, Philippines, Vietnam, Korea, China, India, the Dominican Republic, Jamaica, and Iran. Although many are highly educated, on average they possess fewer skills than either the native population or the immigrants who came during the 1950s.

This remarkable diversity has two major causes: the 1965 amendments to the immigration law and the social chaos caused by the wars in Vietnam and Central America. The 1965 changes jettisoned longstanding national-origins quotas, which had favored immigrants from Europe and had permitted little or no legal immigration from Asia, the Pacific, Latin America, and Africa.

Meanwhile, the stakes in exclusive group identity have been rising. Ethnic politics assumed new significance during the 1970s and '80s—**affirmative-action programs** in employment, school admissions, and public services transformed ethnicity's social meaning.

Ethnic self-assertion gained greater political weight through the coer- 10
cive, symbolic force of law. Under the **aegis** of the Voting Rights Act, the Department of Justice and the courts countenanced, and even required, **gerrymandering** of legislative districts in pursuit of racially and ethnically defined conceptions of political equality. "Official English" policies were adopted by a number of states, and bilingual education became a fiercely contested public issue.

Finally, the continuing decline of central cities and lower-class family structures casts a long, dark shadow over the searing process of group competition. Many blacks and Puerto Ricans mired in decaying ghettos resent the upward mobility of more recently arrived Asians, Cubans, and Mexicans, who experience less residential segregation even at similar income levels. Competitive anxieties are driving deep wedges between those groups, as exemplified by their split over employer sanctions on the immigration laws.

Ethnic conflicts must be understood in the larger context of America's unique political culture. This culture is remarkably individualistic and competitive, nourishing a level of group loyalty and social fragmentation that other societies would find intolerable. Being a Frenchman, Briton, or German is both more confining and demanding than being an American. Unlike them, we do not subscribe to a common religious or racial heritage; instead, our cultural ideals are inclusionary: They accommodate everyone who will share the commitment to democracy, toleration, mobility, and the rule of law.

U.S. citizenship is easy to acquire, hard to lose and imposes few civic duties. Assimilation, always difficult, is probably easier here than anywhere else: The political culture applauds **parochial loyalties:** the main pressure to assimilate is economic, not legal, and most Americans celebrate their own immigrant roots.

Without exception, although at distressingly uneven rates, each new group has advanced far beyond its point of origin in the United States. Intermarriage among ethnic and racial groups continues to increase; although black-white intermarriage occurs at a much lower rate, it too has risen dramatically.

All public-opinion evidence indicates that Americans have grown 15 steadily more tolerant of minorities. The political power of the new groups is growing. Upward mobility may take a generation but for most groups it continues to occur. Latinos born in the United States or who have been here for at least 10 years have already matched the national averages in occupation, education, income, and language proficiency. A 1988 report by the Civil Rights Commission finds that Asian immigrants generally have higher family and per capita incomes than non-Latino whites, although Vietnamese, Filipino, and Indian immigrants still lag behind.

America's performance in integrating ethnic and racial minorities into the mainstream also compares quite favorably with that of other countries, most notably Western Europe. The rise of nativist, often racist movements seeking to bar foreigners is an ugly feature of French, German, and British politics, and their support will probably increase as conditions in Eastern Europe deteriorate. Of the significant immigrant-receiving countries, only Canada has arguably done as well as the United States in welcoming immigrants, but it is also much more selective in deciding which ones it will accept.

America's immigrant-welcoming tradition is not merely a thing of the past. Only a few months ago, Americans dramatically strengthened this commitment with the Immigration Act of 1990. Among other things, the new law further expands the number of legal immigrants; establishes a safe haven policy for Salvadorans and others who do not satisfy the technical definition of refugee; facilitates naturalization, and creates a new "diversity" category of immigration for people from countries (some in Europe) that have not recently sent many immigrants here.

I believe that the new law reflects America's attitude toward immigration far better than the media reports of ethnic strife. Both are true, but Americans evidently recognize that in the increasingly multicultural, interdependent, mobile world of the future, our openness to change and diversity will confer an immense advantage on us—economically, morally, culturally, and politically.

QUESTIONS FOR DISCUSSION

1. What is the thesis of Schuck's article?
2. In what ways are recent immigrants different from those who came before 1965?
3. What are the causes of the diversity of recent immigrants?
4. What evidence does Schuck give to support his point that Americans still demonstrate openness in their attitudes and policies toward immigrants? Does your own experience confirm or contradict Schuck's claim?

✍ RICHARD RODRIGUEZ
Gains and Losses

Richard Rodriguez, the son of Mexican immigrants, grew up in Sacramento, California. He attended Stanford and Columbia universities, finally earning a doctorate at the University of California, Berkeley. Rodriguez is a journalist by profession and has published two books, Hunger of Memory: The Education of Richard Rodriguez *(1982), from which this essay is taken, and* Days of Obligation: An Argument with My Father *(1992).*

KEY VOCABULARY

BEMUSED means bewildered, confused.

DIFFIDENT means lacking in self-confidence; shy.

INTRINSICAL means built-in, essential to the nature of the thing itself.

OVER-ANGLICIZING, the way it is used in this essay, means that Spanish-speaking people exaggerate American pronunciation of words, speaking them with a stronger American accent than Americans do.

Supporters of bilingual education today imply that students like me 1 miss a great deal by not being taught in their family's language. What they seem not to recognize is that, as a socially disadvantaged child, I considered Spanish to be a private language. What I needed to learn in school was that I had the right—and the obligation—to speak the public language of *los gringos.* The odd truth is that my first-grade classmates could have become bilingual, in the conventional sense of that word, more easily than I. Had they been taught (as upper-middle-class children are often taught early) a second language like Spanish or French, they could have regarded it simply as that: another public language. In my case such bilingualism could not have been so quickly achieved. What I did not believe was that I could speak a single public language.

Without question, it would have pleased me to hear my teachers address me in Spanish when I entered the classroom. I would have felt much less afraid. I would have trusted them and responded with ease. But I would have delayed—for how long postponed?—having to learn the language of public society. I would have evaded—and for how long could I have afforded to delay?—learning the great lesson of school, that I had a public identity.

Fortunately, my teachers were unsentimental about their responsibility. What they understood was that I needed to speak a public language. So their voices would search me out, asking me questions. Each time I'd hear them, I'd look up in surprise to see a nun's face frowning at me. I'd mumble, not really meaning to answer. The nun would persist, 'Richard, stand up. Don't look at the floor. Speak up. Speak to the entire class, not just to me!' But I couldn't believe that the English language was mine to use. (In part, I did not want to believe it.) I continued to mumble. I resisted the teacher's demands. (Did I somehow suspect that once I learned public language my pleasing family life would be changed?) Silent, waiting for the bell to sound, I remained dazed, **diffident,** afraid.

Because I wrongly imagined that English was **intrinsically** a public language and Spanish an **intrinsically** private one, I easily noted the difference between classroom language and the language of home. At school, words were directed to a general audience of listeners. ('Boys and girls.') Words were meaningfully ordered. And the point was not self-expression alone but to make oneself understood by many others. The teacher quizzed: 'Boys and girls, why do we use that word in this sentence? Could we think of a better word to use there? Would the sentence change its meaning if the words were differently arranged? And wasn't there a better way of saying much the same thing?' (I couldn't say. I wouldn't try to say.)

Three months. Five. Half a year passed. Unsmiling, ever watchful, my 5 teachers noted my silence. They began to connect my behavior with the difficult progress my older sister and brother were making. Until one Saturday morning three nuns arrived at the house to talk to our parents. Stiffly, they sat on the blue living room sofa. From the doorway of another room, spying the visitors, I noted the incongruity—the clash of two worlds, the faces and voices of school intruding upon the familiar setting of home. I overheard one voice gently wondering, 'Do your children speak only Spanish at home, Mrs. Rodriguez?' While another voice added, 'That Richard especially seems so timid and shy.'

That Rich-heard!

With great tact the visitors continued, 'Is it possible for you and your husband to encourage your children to practice their English when they are home?' Of course, my parents complied. What would they not do for their children's well-being? And how could they have questioned the Church's authority which those women represented? In an instant, they agreed to give up the language (the sounds) that had revealed and accentuated our family's closeness. The moment after the visitors left, the change was observed. '*Ahora,* speak to us *en inglés,*' my father and mother united to tell us.

At first, it seemed a kind of game. After dinner each night, the family gathered to practice 'our' English. (It was still then *inglés,* a language foreign to us, so we felt drawn as strangers to it.) Laughing, we would try to define words we could not pronounce. We played with strange English sounds, often **over-anglicizing** our pronunciations. And we filled the smiling gaps of our sentences with familiar Spanish sounds. But that was cheating, somebody shouted. Everyone laughed. In school, meanwhile, like my brother and sister, I was required to attend a daily tutoring session. I needed a full year of special attention. I also needed my teachers to keep my attention from straying in class by calling out, *Rich-heard*—their English voices slowly prying loose my ties to my other name, its three notes, *Ri-car-do.* Most of all I needed to hear my mother and father speak to me in a moment of seriousness in broken—suddenly heartbreaking—English. The scene was inevitable: One Saturday morning I entered the kitchen where my parents were talking in Spanish. I did not realize that they were talking in Spanish however until, at the moment they saw me, I heard their voices change to speak English. Those *gringo* sounds they uttered startled me. Pushed me away. In that moment of trivial misunderstanding and profound insight, I felt my throat twisted by unsounded grief. I turned quickly and left the room. But I had no place to escape to with Spanish. (The spell was broken.) My brother and sisters were speaking English in another part of the house.

Again and again in the days following, increasingly angry, I was obliged to hear my mother and father: 'Speak to us *en inglés.*' (*Speak.*) Only then did I determine to learn classroom English. Weeks after, it happened: One day in school I raised my hand to volunteer an answer. I spoke out in a loud voice. And I did not think it remarkable when the entire class understood. That day, I moved very far from the disadvantaged child I had been only days earlier. The belief, the calming assurance that I belonged in public, had at last taken hold.

Shortly after, I stopped hearing the high and loud sounds of *los gringos.* 10 A more and more confident speaker of English, I didn't trouble to listen to *how* strangers sounded, speaking to me. And there simply were too many English-speaking people in my day for me to hear American accents anymore. Conversations quickened. Listening to persons who sounded eccentrically pitched voices, I usually noted their sounds for an initial few seconds before I concentrated on *what* they were saying. Conversations became content-full. Transparent. Hearing someone's *tone* of voice—angry or questioning or sarcastic or happy or sad—I didn't distinguish it from the words it expressed. Sound and word were thus tightly wedded. At the end of a day, I was often **bemused,** always relieved, to realize how 'silent,' though crowded with words, my day in public had been. (This public silence measured and quickened the change in my life.)

At last, seven years old, I came to believe what had been technically true since my birth: I was an American citizen. But the special feeling of closeness at home was diminished by then. Gone was the desperate, urgent, intense feeling of being at home; rare was the experience of feeling myself individualized by family intimates. We remained a loving family, but one greatly changed. No longer so close; no longer bound tight by the pleasing and troubling knowledge of our public separateness. Neither my older brother nor sister rushed home after school anymore. Nor did I. When I arrived home there would often be neighborhood kids in the house. Or the house would be empty of sounds.

Following the dramatic Americanization of their children, even my parents grew more publicly confident. Especially my mother. She learned the names of all the people on our block. And she decided we needed to have a telephone installed in the house. My father continued to use the word *gringo*. But it was no longer charged with the old bitterness or distrust. (Stripped of any emotional content, the word simply became a name for those Americans not of Hispanic descent.) Hearing him, sometimes I wasn't sure if he was pronouncing the Spanish word *gringo* or saying gringo in English.

Matching the silence I started hearing in public was a new quiet at home. The family's quiet was partly due to the fact that, as we children learned more and more English, we shared fewer and fewer words with our parents. Sentences needed to be spoken slowly when a child addressed his mother or father. (Often the parent wouldn't understand.) The child would need to repeat himself. (Still the parent misunderstood.) The young voice, frustrated, would end up saying, 'Never mind'—the subject was closed. Dinners would be noisy with the clinking of knives and forks against dishes. My mother would smile softly between her remarks; my father at the other end of the table would chew and chew at his food, while he stared over the heads of his children.

My *mother!* My *father!* After English became my primary language, I   15
no longer knew what words to use in addressing my parents. The old Spanish words (those tender accents of sound) I had used earlier—*mamá* and *papá*— I couldn't use anymore. They would have been too painful reminders of how much had changed in my life. On the other hand, the words I heard neighborhood kids call *their* parents seemed equally unsatisfactory. *Mother* and *Father; Ma, Papa, Pa, Dad, Pop* (how I hated the all-American sound of that last word especially)—all these terms I felt were unsuitable, not really terms of address for *my* parents. As a result, I never used them at home. Whenever I'd speak to my parents, I would try to get their attention with eye contact alone. In public conversations, I'd refer to 'my parents' or 'my mother and father.'

My mother and father, for their part, responded differently, as their children spoke to them less. She grew restless, seemed troubled and anxious at the scarcity of words exchanged in the house. It was she who would question me about my day when I came home from school. She smiled at small talk. She pried at the edges of my sentences to get me to say something more. (What?) She'd join conversations she overheard, but her intrusions often stopped her children's talking. By contrast, my father seemed reconciled to the new quiet. Though his English improved somewhat, he retired into silence. At dinner he spoke very little. One night his children and even his wife helplessly giggled at his garbled English pronunciation of the Catholic Grace before Meals. Thereafter he made his wife recite the prayer at the start of each meal, even on formal occasions, when there were guests in the house. Hers became the public voice of the family. On official business, it was she, not my father, one would usually hear on the phone or in stores, talking to strangers. His children grew so accustomed to his silence that, years later, they would speak routinely of his shyness. (My mother would often try to explain: Both his parents died when he was eight. He was raised by an uncle who treated him like little more than a menial servant. He was never encouraged to speak. He grew up alone. A man of few words.) But my father was not shy, I realized, when I'd watch him speaking Spanish with relatives. Using Spanish, he was quickly effusive. Especially when talking with other men, his voice would spark, flicker, flare alive with sounds. In Spanish, he expressed ideas and feelings he rarely revealed in English. With firm Spanish sounds, he conveyed confidence and authority English would never allow him.

The silence at home, however, was finally more than a literal silence. Fewer words passed between parent and child, but more profound was the silence that resulted from my inattention to sounds. At about the time I no longer bothered to listen with care to the sounds of English in public, I grew careless about listening to the sounds family members made when they spoke. Most of the time I heard someone speaking at home and didn't distinguish his sounds from the words people uttered in public. I didn't even pay much attention to my parents' accented and ungrammatical speech. At least not at home. Only when I was with them in public would I grow alert to their accents. Though, even then, their sounds caused me less and less concern. For I was increasingly confident of my own public identity.

I would have been happier about my public success had I not sometimes recalled what it had been like earlier, when my family had conveyed its intimacy through a set of conveniently private sounds. Sometimes in public, hearing a stranger, I'd hark back to my past. A Mexican farmworker approached me downtown to ask directions to somewhere. '¿Hijito . . . ?' he said. And his voice summoned deep longing. Another time, standing beside my mother in the visiting room of a Carmelite convent, before the dense screen which rendered the nuns shadowy figures, I heard several Spanish-speaking nuns—their busy, singsong overlapping voices—assure us that yes, yes, we were remembered, all our family was remembered in their prayers. (Their voices echoed faraway family sounds.) Another day, a dark-faced old woman—her hand light on my shoulder—steadied herself against me as she boarded a bus. She murmured something I couldn't quite comprehend. Her Spanish voice came near, like the face of a never-before-seen relative in the instant before I was kissed. Her voice, like so many of the Spanish voices I'd hear in public, recalled the golden age of my youth. Hearing Spanish then, I continued to be a careful, if sad, listener to sounds. Hearing a Spanish-speaking family walking behind me, I turned to look. I smiled for an instant, before my glance found the Hispanic-looking faces of strangers in the crowd going by.

QUESTIONS FOR DISCUSSION

1. At the beginning of his essay, Rodriguez talks about the importance of learning a *public* language—English. Why is it so important to him to become proficient in English?

2. Discuss the title of the essay. What does Rodriguez gain and what does he lose in the process of learning English?

3. There is much talk of the *sound* of language in this essay. What feelings do the sounds of each of his languages evoke in Rodriguez? How does his sensitivity to sounds change in the course of his education?

4. How can this essay be seen as an argument against bilingual education? What reasons for his position can you gather from Rodriguez's story?

The following paper was written in response to question 9. The student chose to explain why she thinks a mosaic is a better metaphor for the U.S. than a melting pot. Notice in particular the way she analyzes the specific elements of the mosaic, as well as the relation between the parts and the whole, and compares them to the corresponding characteristics of the American people.

✍ STUDENT ESSAY:

America, the Cultural Mosaic

When I think of America, I think more of a cultural mosaic than a melting pot. For decades, many ethnic groups in this country have been struggling to keep their own identities. They don't want to be melted down. They have tried to smother the flame that would make them melted-down Americans. To these people, the image of the melting pot is not as positive as it sounds. In the steel industry, a melting pot is a large container into which different types of ore are thrown to make a certain type of alloy—one that is usually stronger than any of the individual metals used to make it. The melting pot was a useful metaphor at a time in American history when most immigrants were Europeans who wished to transform themselves into a new breed. It expressed the ideals of the new nation. But now the melting pot theory no longer applies. We are too many, too diverse, to ever hope that we could become one homogeneous people. What I believe we have become is a cultural mosaic.

A mosaic is made up of different colored tiles grouped together in such a way that a picture is formed. Each tile can stand on its own and can be cut in different shapes to fit into the picture. But one tile can never melt into another. The American people are that way. They can fit into the American picture, but they can never be made to fit entirely into a common mold. They stand on their own.

It is interesting to note that in a mosaic, a missing tile, or group of tiles, can detract from the overall quality of the picture. The same is true for the history of our country. For years, groups of ethnic people have been left out of the American picture, and we are finally starting to ask, "What's wrong with this picture?" Another interesting characteristic of a mosaic is that the cement in which the individual tiles are embedded is absolutely essential to the overall quality of the picture. It is the element that binds all of the tiles together. Without the cement, the mosaic is useless. The American people are bound together by one basic cement—the dream of being whatever they want. It is that dream which still brings people to these shores.

TOPICS FOR WRITING

1. In his *Letters from an American Farmer,* Crèvecoeur defines an American this way: "He is an American, who, leaving behind him all his ancient prejudices and manners, receives new ones from the new mode of life he has embraced, the new government he obeys, and new rank he holds. He becomes an American by being received in the broad lap of our great *Alma Mater.* Here individuals of all nations are melted into a new race of men. . . ."

   Keeping in mind the various views presented in this chapter, how accurate do you think this definition of an American is? Drawing on the sources in this chapter, develop an alternative definition of an American.

2. Imagine that you are writing a letter to Crèvecoeur explaining how American life today is different from life in the 18th century. Review the main features of American life he describes in his letter, then contrast them with the way that you see America today.

3. Using examples from the reading, as well as your own observations and experience, either confirm or argue against Jamake Highwater's claim that "The greatest distance between people is not space but culture." Include in your paper a summary of Highwater's justification for his claim.

4. In "Latest Wave of Immigrants Raises Concerns over Whether Lady Liberty Still Opens Arms," Peter Schuck discusses the effects of a new wave of immigration on American society. It has been projected that by the year 2000, white Americans will be a minority in this country.

   Do you think this is cause for concern or celebration? Do you agree or disagree with those who worry that "E Pluribus Unum" will be "tragically reversed"? In your introduction, summarize the main points of Schuck's article, then state your own opinion. In the body of the paper, develop your opinion with reasons and examples.

5. Most of the reading selections in this chapter deal with American life as seen from the perspective of people who are outside the mainstream. How have these readings changed your view of what life in America is like for minorities? Choose a few of the readings to use as examples, and include short summaries of important points from them as part of your own paper.

6. In what ways were the immigrant experiences of Anzia Yezierska and Nguyen Ngu similar? In what ways are the two authors different? Which one would you say is more "Americanized"?

7. To what extent do you think Nguyen Nguu fits Crèvecoeur's idea of how immigrants change when they come to America? What examples can you find in Joe Klein's essay to support your claim? Include in your introduction a short summary of Crèvecoeur's views on how immigrants should change.

8. Pick any two of the readings and discuss similarities and differences in their views of the idea of the "melting pot."

9. In recent years, several suggestions have been made to replace "the melting pot" with another metaphor that better reflects American society. Some well-known examples are the salad bar, the stew, the mosaic, and the patchwork quilt.

   Choose one of these, or invent a metaphor of your own, that you think gives a more accurate representation of America than the melting pot does. Develop your metaphor in detail to show in what specific ways the parts of the metaphor stand for specific features of American society.

10. To what extent do you think Jamake Highwater and Richard Rodriguez would agree or disagree about the importance of retaining one's native language? Briefly summarize both of their views on this subject, then explain why you think they would agree or disagree.

11. If you are a member of a minority group, describe a feature of your native country or culture that you think is important to keep. Consider customs, language, food, celebrations, family connections, community. Use your description to help the reader understand why the feature you've chosen is important.

12. Describe a feature of a minority culture from which you think mainstream Americans can learn something.

Calamity Jane (ca. 1852–1903), a legend-ary figure of the American West.

8 Rugged Individuals

> I would rather sit on a pumpkin, and have it all to myself, than to
> be crowded on a velvet cushion.
>
> –HENRY DAVID THOREAU

Since the early days of European settlement, America has been
seen as the place where enterprising individuals, freed from the restrictions
and class structure of the Old World, could go as far as their abilities and
capacity for hard work would take them. The accent is on the individual.
In Thomas Jefferson's familiar words from the *Declaration of Independence,*
"We hold these truths to be self-evident, that all men are created equal, that
they are endowed by their Creator with certain unalienable Rights, that
among these are Life, Liberty and the pursuit of Happiness."

Reverence for the individual runs deep in the American character. In
the late 19th century, this philosophy of individualism took shape in a type
of national hero that became known as "The Rugged Individual." The
Rugged Individual is the man (women were not included) who succeeds
through his own efforts, separating himself from the crowd by virtue of his
self-reliance, self-discipline, nerves of steel, hard work, native shrewdness,
"can-do" spirit, and, usually, a dash of luck. Although in reality The Rugged Individual seldom lived up to his image, his enduring popularity in the
public imagination reflects the esteem in which Americans hold "the self-
made man," the man who "does it his way," the "true competitor."

How did this American accent on the individual develop? To what
extent does the myth of The Rugged Individual reflect reality? What is the
place of individualism in American life? These are the kinds of questions
that the readings in this chapter attempt to answer.

✎ CHARLES BEARD

Individualism

Charles Beard, an influential American historian, received his Ph.D. from Columbia University in 1904. He taught at Columbia until 1917. He resigned when two of his colleagues were dismissed for opposing the United States' entry into World War I. In 1919, Beard helped to found The New School for Social Research and became a leader of the progressive movement. He wrote many books, most notably, with his wife Mary, The Rise of American Civilization. *The selection here comes from* The American Spirit.

KEY VOCABULARY

BIOLOGICAL DETERMINISM is one of the ideas derived from Darwinism. According to this idea, all creatures, including human beings, are what they are strictly as a result of their physical and chemical makeup.

CHATTEL is an item of personal property; more specifically, a slave.

DARWINISM is the theory that species evolve through natural selection and the struggle for survival. Charles Darwin published his controversial book *The Origin of Species* in 1859. His principles of biological evolution were later applied to society and developed into a parallel theory called "Social Darwinism." The Social Darwinists simplified Darwin's ideas and used them to justify a philosophy of economic freedom. This philosophy held that it was in the best interests of society for government not to regulate business, but to allow the principle of "survival of the fittest" to operate freely. These ideas are present in Andrew Carnegie's *Gospel of Wealth.*

INDOLENCE is laziness.

INEBRIETY means drunkenness.

IMPROVIDENCE is lack of caution, or concern for the future.

VESTED RIGHTS are, in law, those rights that are absolute, that cannot be taken away.

The word *individualism,* though stemming from the same root as individuality, branched off from it fundamentally in accent and content. Individualism was a newcomer in the American vocabulary. Apparently it did not attain a general circulation until near the middle of the nineteenth century. In origins, it seems to have been French or British, not American. The first use of the word cited in the *Oxford English Dictionary* was in 1835, in the translation of Tocqueville's *Démocratie en Amérique* by Henry Reeve. In Tocqueville's treatise the word meant to cut one's self off from one's family, friends, and society—a kind of self-chosen anarchy or outlawry.

The spirit of this arbitrary act of denying one's debts and obligations to family, friends, and society, of declaring one's complete independence from all social relations, entered into the idea of individualism as it was developed, especially in relation to economic activities and **vested rights.** When it reached a full formulation the idea embraced several very concrete affirmations, such as the following: Society is merely an aggregation of individuals struggling for existence competitively. The qualities or talents of the individual which prepare him or her for that struggle are to be attributed solely to personal merits and efforts; the individual is "self-made." In unrestrained competition, victory goes to the strong, the ambitious, the ingenious, the industrious, the "fittest to survive," and their rewards as victors are proportioned to the contributions of their labors to the total product, as justice requires; they get what they deserve, in short. In the strife among competing individuals, the production of wealth is increased while its distribution runs according to merits. Poverty is due to the **indolence,** lack of initiative, **improvidence,** dearth of ambition, the **inebriety,** or the restlessness of the poor themselves.

This world-view of human beings was reinforced by the rise and spread of **Darwinism**—the world-view of **biological determinism** for the activities of all living things, from the lowest to the highest ranges of the vegetable and animal kingdoms. According to that theory the evolution of all life had been and is through the struggle for existence, natural selection, and the survival of the fittest, the victors, in that competition. It is true that the cautious Darwin did not reduce his theory to this single formula, but the ultimate simplifiers did it and popularized it as such. When the apparent force of all nature was joined to the special interests of the men and women who survived and prospered in the prevailing economic regime, the doctrine of individualism seemed invincible to them. The idea of civilization was limited to humanity, but individualism assimilated mankind to the whole order of living things under one iron law.

Terrific momentum was given to the idea of individualism by its utility to the most powerful private interests in the country, now that the planting interests had lost their base in **chattel** slavery. Capitalists eager to rush forward in the business of making money and owners of property content with their possessions, or desirous of more, snapped up the doctrine as a "scientific" justification for their activities and accumulations. Energetic individuals without property, but bent on acquiring it, also heard the word and pronounced it good. All could resort to it as a shield against government intervention or as warrant for favors asked and received from government according to their personal interests.

QUESTIONS FOR DISCUSSION

1. What are the main elements of Beard's definition of individualism?
2. In what ways does Darwin's theory support individualism?
3. What elements of Darwin's theory of evolution spread to theories of society?
4. According to Beard, how is justice served by allowing individuals free reign in the struggle for existence?
5. Sometimes a writer's attitude toward his subject is *implied* rather than directly stated, so you, the reader, must interpret his meaning. Reread the last two paragraphs of the selection from Beard. What does Beard think of the "powerful private interests" that took up the doctrine of individualism? What were their motives? Did they adopt the doctrine just because they believed it was scientifically valid, or did they have other reasons?
   What words does Beard use that tip you off to his attitude?

✑ ANDREW CARNEGIE

From *The Gospel of Wealth*

*Andrew Carnegie immigrated to the United States from Scotland in 1848
and rose from bobbin boy in a cotton factory to become one of the wealthiest
men in the nation. He made his money in steel. Carnegie began publishing
articles in magazines in 1883 and published his first book,* The Triumph
of Democracy *in 1886.* The Gospel of Wealth, *from which this selection
was taken, came out in 1889. Carnegie became a spokesman for laissez faire
capitalism—the idea that the government should intervene as little as possible
in economic affairs. In this excerpt, Carnegie presents his arguments for this
belief.*

KEY VOCABULARY

CASTES are generally social classes, separated from others by distinction of
birth, rank, income, profession, or the like.

MÆCENAS was the name of a Roman statesman of the first century B.C.,
Gaius Maecenas. He was a patron of the Roman poets Horace and Virgil.
The term is usually used to mean a patron, especially one generous to artists.

SALUTARY denotes something which brings about improvement, benefit.

SWEDENBORG (Emanuel Swedenborg, 1688–1772) was a Swedish scientist
and theologian whose followers founded a religion in his name. They believed Christ was the God and that people could communicate directly with
the spiritual realm.

The problem of our age is the proper administration of wealth, that the   1
ties of brotherhood may still bind together the rich and poor in harmonious
relationship. The conditions of human life have not only been changed,
but revolutionized, within the past few hundred years. In former days there
was little difference between the dwelling, dress, food, and environment of
the chief and those of his retainers. The Indians are to-day where civilized
man then was. When visiting the Sioux, I was led to the wigwam of the
chief. It was like the others in external appearance, and even within the
difference was trifling between it and those of the poorest of his braves.
The contrast between the palace of the millionaire and the cottage of the
laborer with us to-day measures the change which has come with civilization. This change, however, is not to be deplored, but welcomed as highly

beneficial. It is well, nay, essential, for the progress of the race that the houses of some should be homes for all that is highest and best in literature and the arts, and for all the refinements of civilization, rather than that none should be so. Much better this great irregularity than universal squalor. Without wealth there can be no **Mæcenas.** The "good old times" were not good old times. Neither master nor servant was as well situated then as to-day. A relapse to old conditions would be disastrous to both—not the least so to him who serves—and would sweep away civilization with it. But whether the change be for good or ill, it is upon us, beyond our power to alter, and, therefore, to be accepted and made the best of. It is a waste of time to criticize the inevitable.

It is easy to see how the change has come. One illustration will serve for almost every phase of the cause. In the manufacture of products we have the whole story. It applies to all combinations of human industry, as stimulated and enlarged by the inventions of this scientific age. Formerly, articles were manufactured at the domestic hearth, or in small shops which formed part of the household. The master and his apprentices worked side by side, the latter living with the master, and therefore subject to the same conditions. When these apprentices rose to be masters, there was little or no change in their mode of life, and they, in turn, educated succeeding apprentices in the same routine. There was, substantially, social equality, and even political equality, for those engaged in industrial pursuits had then little or no voice in the State.

The inevitable result of such a mode of manufacture was crude articles at high prices. To-day the world obtains commodities of excellent quality at prices which even the preceding generation would have deemed incredible. In the commercial world similar causes have produced similar results, and the race is benefited thereby. The poor enjoy what the rich could not before afford. What were the luxuries have become the necessaries of life. The laborer has now more comforts than the farmer had a few generations ago. The farmer has more luxuries than the landlord had, and is more richly clad and better housed. The landlord has books and pictures rarer and appointments more artistic than the king could then obtain.

The price we pay for this **salutary** change is, no doubt, great. We assemble thousands of operatives in the factory, and in the mine, of whom the employer can know little or nothing, and to whom he is little better than a myth. All intercourse between them is at an end. Rigid **castes** are formed, and, as usual, mutual ignorance breeds mutual distrust. Each **caste** is without sympathy with the other, and ready to credit anything disparaging in regard to it. Under the law of competition, the employer of thousands is forced into the strictest economies, among which the rates paid to labor figure prominently, and often there is friction between the employer and the employed, between capital and labor, between rich and poor. Human society loses homogeneity.

The price which society pays for the law of competition, like the price 5 it pays for cheap comforts and luxuries, is also great; but the advantages of this law are also greater still than its cost—for it is to this law that we owe our wonderful material development, which brings improved conditions in its train. But, whether the law be benign or not, we must say of it, as we say of the change in the conditions of men to which we have referred: It is here; we cannot evade it; no substitutes for it have been found; and while the law may be sometimes hard for the individual, it is best for the race, because it insures the survival of the fittest in every department. We accept and welcome, therefore, as conditions to which we must accommodate ourselves, great inequality of environment; the concentration of business, industrial and commercial, in the hands of a few; and the law of competition between these, as being not only beneficial, but essential to the future progress of the race. Having accepted these, it follows that there must be great scope for the exercise of special ability in the merchant and in the manufacturer who has to conduct affairs upon a great scale. That this talent for organization and management is rare among men is proved by the fact that it invariably secures enormous rewards for its possessor, no matter where or under what laws or conditions. The experienced in affairs always rate the MAN whose services can be obtained as a partner as not only the first consideration, but such as render the question of his capital scarcely worth considering: for able men soon create capital; in the hands of those without the special talent required, capital soon takes wings. Such men become interested in firms or corporations using millions; and, estimating only simple interest to be made upon the capital invested, it is inevitable that their income must exceed their expenditure and that they must, therefore, accumulate wealth. Nor is there any middle ground which such men can occupy, because the great manufacturing or commercial concern which does not earn at least interest upon its capital soon becomes bankrupt. It must either go forward or fall behind; to stand still is impossible. It is a condition essential to its successful operation that it should be thus far profitable, and even that, in addition to interest on capital, it should make profit. It is a law, as certain as any of the others named, that men possessed of this peculiar talent for affairs, under the free play of economic forces must, of necessity, soon be in receipt of more revenue than can be judiciously expended upon themselves; and this law is as beneficial for the race as the others.

Objections to the foundations upon which society is based are not in order, because the condition of the race is better with these than it has been with any other which has been tried. Of the effect of any new substitutes proposed we cannot be sure. The Socialist or Anarchist who seeks to overturn present conditions is to be regarded as attacking the foundation upon which civilization itself rests, for civilization took its start from the day when the capable, industrious workman said to his incompetent and lazy fellow, "If thou dost not sow, thou shalt not reap," and thus ended primitive Communism by separating the drones from the bees. One who studies this subject will soon be brought face to face with the conclusion that upon the sacredness of property civilization itself depends—the right of the laborer to his hundred dollars in the savings-bank, and equally the legal right of the millionaire to his millions. Every man must be allowed "to sit under his own vine and fig-tree, with none to make afraid," if human society is to advance, or even to remain so far advanced as it is. To those who propose to substitute Communism for this intense Individualism, the answer therefore is: The race has tried that. All progress from that barbarous day to the present time has resulted from its displacement. Not evil, but good, has come to the race from the accumulation of wealth by those who have had the ability and energy to produce it. But even if we admit for a moment that it might be better for the race to discard its present foundation, Individualism,—that it is a nobler ideal that man should labor, not for himself alone, but in and for a brotherhood of his fellows, and share with them all in common, realizing **Swedenborg's** idea of heaven, where, as he says, the angels derive their happiness, not from laboring for self, but for each other,—even admit all this, and a sufficient answer is, This is not evolution, but revolution. It necessitates the changing of human nature itself—a work of eons, even if it were good to change it, which we cannot know.

It is not practicable in our day or in our age. Even if desirable theoretically, it belongs to another and long-succeeding sociological stratum. Our duty is with what is practicable now—with the next step possible in our day and generation. It is criminal to waste our energies in endeavoring to uproot, when all we can profitably accomplish is to bend the universal tree of humanity a little in the direction most favorable to the production of good fruit under existing circumstances. We might as well urge the destruction of the highest existing type of man because he failed to reach our ideal as to favor the destruction of Individualism, Private Property, the Law of Accumulation of Wealth, and the Law of Competition; for these are the highest result of human experience, the soil in which society, so far, has produced the best fruit. Unequally or unjustly, perhaps, as these laws sometimes operate, and imperfect as they appear to the Idealist, they are, nevertheless, like the highest type of man, the best and most valuable of all that humanity has yet accomplished.

QUESTIONS FOR DISCUSSION

1. In his first sentence, Carnegie talks about establishing a "harmonious relationship" between rich and poor. What do you think the nature of that relationship would be?

2. According to Carnegie, what caused the change from primitive society to modern civilization?

3. Why does Carnegie think that a great difference between rich and poor would be a good thing?

4. What, for Carnegie, is the measure of a civilization?

5. What is the price we must pay for civilization?

6. What elements of Darwinism do you find in Carnegie's writing?

7. What kind of men are, according to Carnegie, the "fittest" to survive?

8. Why does Carnegie think that laboring for "a brotherhood of his fellows" is not a practical idea? What, to him, is the difference between "evolution" and "revolution"?

✑ PATRICK GERSTER AND NICHOLAS CORDS

The Myth of Individualism

Both Patrick Gerster and Nicholas Cords have taught in the history department at Lakewood State Community College in White Bear Lake, Minnesota.

KEY VOCABULARY

PSEUDO-AMERICA is "false" America. *Pseudo-* is a prefix meaning "false."

The great attraction of America has always been individual freedom. In   1
turn, to most Americans individualism is the key factor assuring freedom as
well as the fundamental concept binding their national identity. It is with
this concept, in fact, that Americans appear to define their national consciousness; it serves as their central symbol of identification. Historians and
sociologists have noted that America is a "land where individualism is the
national faith," and that "of all peoples it was we who have led in the public
worship of individualism."

Some Americans, however, have of late come to question the depth of
the American commitment to individualism. But even for those willing to
admit that mass conformity of contemporary society makes it increasingly
difficult to practice individualism in modern America, the argument often
still prevails that in some fabled portion of the nation's historic past men
and women were able to achieve a great measure of personal freedom. This
golden moment is usually thought to have been the period of America's
nineteenth-century frontier development. It was supposedly the kind of
exhilarating personal freedom, for example, that Mark Twain wrote about
in *Huckleberry Finn* (1884). It was the kind of social and political individualism the historian Frederick Jackson Turner described in his famous paper,
"The Significance of the Frontier in American History" (1893). Writers
since Twain, however, have often remarked on the reluctance of Americans
to follow Huck's lead "to light out for the territory," and historians since
Turner have demonstrated that the overriding tendency of frontiersmen
was to imitate older and time-tested political models. Walter Prescott
Webb, combining good literature and history, for example, argued decades
ago that the men, women, and children of the Great Plains frontier seized

certain technological innovations to improve their lot, but showed little capacity for independence. "The status of the frontiersman as an independent thinker is questionable indeed," says Webb. Perhaps it is unfair even to expect that the frontiersman should have been an independent thinker. Nonconformity implies the possibility of varied reactions to the same situation, and "the frontier, with its rigorous conditions of life, was too exacting in its demands to allow of such choice for the frontiersman in the mode of his reaction." In recent years, then, the alleged individualism of America's frontier past has been judged to be largely mythical. Scholars increasingly have come to see that the supposed individualism of the "out country" was more a condition of hardiness and stamina than of intellectual independence and personal self-expression. Contrary to its mythology, and judging from the experience of its hardy pioneers, the American heritage seems as much one of conformity as freedom. At the same time, and to an increasing number of observers, the equation of individualism with Americanism—whether past or present—is more myth than reality. Despite the preciously mythical notion that America has been a breeding ground for individualism, it seems more certain that conformity and a lack of real variety in American life has often been the case in the land of the free.

The idea that America is a nation of individualists is not only false when applied to mythologized Puritans, frontiersmen, and legendary Huckleberry Finns and Horatio Algers, but also certainly lacks justification in its application to the average contemporary middle-class American. The nation of "individualists"—today represented by the **pseudo-America** of *TV Guide,* Monday Night Football, shopping malls, Dial-a-Prayer, "Let's Make a Deal," TV dinners, and Miss America Pageants—seems rather a country of mass conformity. Indeed, at various times social critics have warned of the dangers of mass culture and the "sphere of public opinion" while others have fundamentally questioned the tastes of mass society and what has been called "the herd mentality." All of this, however, has seemingly had little effect on a contemporary America which continues strenuously to proclaim its individualism. It seemingly continues to believe fervently in what the novelist Henry Miller has pointedly called the "air-conditioned nightmare"—the often plastic world of conformity that somehow passes for freedom.

True to their history, modern Americans continue to mouth the rhetoric of individualism while at the same time practicing mass consumption and receiving their values from the mass media. But even though it is proper to sharply criticize American society for its pretensions about individualism, it seems equally clear that undue emphasis has at times been given the by-now familiar picture of American middle-class uniformity. A particularly well-etched mythology, related to the questions of individualism and conformity, for example, has arisen concerning American suburbia.

QUESTIONS FOR DISCUSSION

1. Why do scholars now believe that the individualism of the 19th century frontiersmen was actually more a matter of stamina than of intellectual independence?

2. How do the examples from contemporary American society (paragraph 3) make a case for mass conformity rather than for individualism?

3. Give a few examples from our nation's history or popular culture that reflect the pervasive nature of the myth of individualism.

4. The authors caution in paragraph 4 that "undue emphasis has at times been given the by-now familiar picture of American middle-class uniformity." How can this be as misleading as the over-emphasis on individualism?

✍ GRETEL EHRLICH

About Men

Gretel Ehrlich, born in Santa Barbara in 1946, is a professional writer.
She has written numerous magazine articles, and her essays have been
collected in The Solace of Empty Spaces *(1985) and* Islands, Universe,
Home *(1988). She has also written* Wyoming Stories *(a collection of short*
stories), two volumes of poetry, and a novel, Heart Mountain. *Ms. Ehrlich*
lives on a ranch in Wyoming.

KEY VOCABULARY

ANDROGYNOUS refers to something that has both male and female
characteristics.

DISESTEEMED refers to something for which there is little regard, little favor.

JEKYLL AND HYDE refers to a character in Robert Louis Stevenson's story
The Strange Case of Dr. Jekyll and Mr. Hyde, who was alternately good and
evil. The term is used informally to mean a person with alternating pleasant
and unpleasant behavior.

MATERNALISM is the habit of treating people in a motherly way.

ROMANTICIZING means giving preference to feelings over reason, but it also
suggests seeing something as better than it really is (or was).

STOICISM is an attitude of endurance or bravery, an indifference to pain.

When I'm in New York but feeling lonely for Wyoming I look for the   1
Marlboro ads in the subway. What I'm aching to see is horseflesh, the glint
of a spur, a line of distant mountains, brimming creeks, and a reminder of
the ranchers and cowboys I've ridden with for the last eight years. But the
men I see in those posters with their stern, humorless looks remind me of
no one I know here. In our hellbent earnestness to **romanticize** the cowboy we've ironically **disesteemed** his true character. If he's "strong and
silent" it's because there's probably no one to talk to. If he "rides away into
the sunset" it's because he's been on horseback since four in the morning
moving cattle and he's trying, fifteen hours later, to get home to his family.
If he's "a rugged individualist" he's also part of a team: Ranch work is team-
work and even the glorified open-range cowboys of the 1880s rode up and
down the Chisholm Trail in the company of twenty or thirty other riders.
Instead of the macho, trigger-happy man our culture has perversely wanted

him to be, the cowboy is more apt to be convivial, quirky, and softhearted. To be "tough" on a ranch has nothing to do with conquests and displays of power. More often than not, circumstances—like the colt he's riding or an unexpected blizzard—are overpowering him. It's not toughness but "toughing it out" that counts. In other words, this macho, cultural artifact the cowboy has become is simply a man who possesses resilience, patience, and an instinct for survival. "Cowboys are just like a pile of rocks—everything happens to them. They get climbed on, kicked, rained and snowed on, scuffed up by wind. Their job is 'just to take it,' " one old-timer told me.

A cowboy is someone who loves his work. Since the hours are long—ten to fifteen hours a day—and the pay is $30 he has to. What's required of him is an odd mixture of physical vigor and **maternalism.** His part of the beef-raising industry is to birth and nurture calves and take care of their mothers. For the most part his work is done on horseback and in a lifetime he sees and comes to know more animals than people. The iconic myth surrounding him is built on American notions of heroism: the index of a man's value as measured in physical courage. Such ideas have perverted manliness into a self-absorbed race for cheap thrills. In a rancher's world, courage has less to do with facing danger than with acting spontaneously—usually on behalf of an animal or another rider. If a cow is stuck in a bog-hole he throws a loop around her neck, takes his dally (a half hitch around the saddle horn), and pulls her out with horsepower. If a calf is born sick, he may take her home, warm her in front of the kitchen fire, and massage her legs until dawn. One friend, whose favorite horse was trying to swim a lake with hobbles on, dove under water and cut her legs loose with a knife, then swam her to shore, his arm around her neck lifeguard-style, and saved her from drowning. Because these incidents are usually linked to someone or something outside himself, the westerner's courage is selfless, a form of compassion.

The physical punishment that goes with cowboying is greatly under-played. Once fear is dispensed with, the threshold of pain rises to meet the demands of the job. When Jane Fonda asked Robert Redford (in the film *Electric Horseman*) if he was sick as he struggled to his feet one morning, he replied, "No, just bent." For once the movies had it right. The cowboys I was sitting with laughed in agreement. Cowboys are rarely complainers; they show their **stoicism** by laughing at themselves.

If a rancher or cowboy has been thought of as a "man's man"—laconic, hard-drinking, inscrutable—there's almost no place in which the balancing act between male and female, manliness and femininity, can be more natural. If he's gruff, handsome, and physically fit on the outside, he's **androgynous** at the core. Ranchers are midwives, hunters, nurturers, providers, and conservationists all at once. What we've interpreted as toughness—weathered skin, calloused hands, a squint in the eye and a growl in the voice—only masks the tenderness inside. "Now don't go telling me these lambs are cute," one rancher warned me the first day I walked into the football-field-sized lambing sheds. The next thing I knew he was holding a black lamb. "Ain't this little rat good-lookin'?"

So many of the men who came to the West were southerners—men looking for work and a new life after the Civil War—that chivalrousness and strict codes of honor were soon thought of as western traits. There were very few women in Wyoming during territorial days, so when they did arrive (some as mail-order brides from places like Philadelphia) there was a standoffishness between the sexes and a formality that persists now. Ranchers still tip their hats and say, "Howdy, ma'am" instead of shaking hands with me.

Even young cowboys are often evasive with women. It's not that they're **Jekyll and Hyde** creatures—gentle with animals and rough on women—but rather, that they don't know how to bring their tenderness into the house and lack the vocabulary to express the complexity of what they feel. Dancing wildly all night becomes a metaphor for the explosive emotions pent up inside, and when these are, on occasion, released, they're so battery-charged and potent that one caress of the face or one "I love you" will peal for a long while.

The geographical vastness and the social isolation here make emotional evolution seem impossible. Those contradictions of the heart between respectability, logic, and convention on the one hand, and impulse, passion, and intuition on the other, played out wordlessly against the paradisical beauty of the West, give cowboys a wide-eyed but drawn look. Their lips pucker up, not with kisses but with immutability. They may want to break out, staying up all night with a lover just to talk, but they don't know how and can't imagine what the consequences will be. Those rare occasions when they do bare themselves result in confusion. "I feel as if I'd sprained my heart," one friend told me a month after such a meeting.

My friend Ted Hoagland wrote, "No one is as fragile as a woman but no one is as fragile as a man." For all the women here who use "fragileness" to avoid work or as a sexual ploy, there are men who try to hide theirs, all the while clinging to an adolescent dependency on women to cook their meals, wash their clothes, and keep the ranch house warm in winter. But there is true vulnerability in evidence here. Because these men work with animals, not machines or numbers, because they live outside in landscapes of torrential beauty, because they are confined to a place and a routine embellished with awesome variables, because calves die in the arms that pulled others into life, because they go to the mountains as if on a pilgrimage to find out what makes a herd of elk tick, their strength is also a softness, their toughness, a rare delicacy.

QUESTIONS FOR DISCUSSION

1. According to the first paragraph, what are some of the basic differences between the romanticized cowboy and the real cowboy? Are there any such differences between other cultural symbols and their counterparts in reality? Give some examples and explain.

2. What is the real relationship between work and physical courage in a cowboy's life?

3. Explain the discrepancies between the perceived outer emotional toughness of cowboys and their actual inner tenderness.

4. What is the role of geographical realities in the shaping of a cowboy's character and way of life?

5. According to Ehrlich, which of the cowboy's qualities make him a rugged individual, and which ones belie this image?

6. Why do shyness and formality best define the relationships between the sexes in the traditional world of ranching?

7. Define the expression "a man's man" and explain why the cowboy has been stereotyped as the embodiment of it. Does this expression truly reflect the cowboy's qualities? Explain.

✍ BARBARA CAWTHORNE CRAFTON

Men Are Very Delicate

Barbara Cawthorne Crafton is an Episcopal priest who lives in New York City. Her work has taken her from Trinity Church on Wall Street to the New York waterfront. She is now on the staff of Seamen's Church Institute, serving merchant sailors. Crafton has published essays in magazines and newspapers, including New Woman, Family Circle, *and the "Hers" column of* The New York Times Magazine.

KEY VOCABULARY

AMBIDEXTROUSNESS is the ability to use both hands with equal ease.

To **COLLUDE** is to act together secretly to achieve a goal.

A **DETRACTOR** is a person who tries to decrease the importance or value of something or someone.

To **EMASCULATE** means, literally, to castrate; more generally, it means to deprive someone of strength and vigor.

REFLEXIVE means, here, automatic.

I think I have to fire a man. I have tried warnings and changes in the job description and other changes in the work location and God knows what else. But it has become clear that he has no intention of working at the level of excellence of which he is capable and which his colleagues maintain, that he may be less than candid in his reporting of the work he does do, and that his fellow employees see all this and are wondering how long it's going to go on. So do my superiors, who also, then, wonder about *me*.

He has had **detractors** for years. People have been telling on this guy ever since I became his supervisor. I have suspected that some of the snitching is racist, and I still think that. I have suspected that some of the misgivings I myself have had about his work may be racist, too, the impatience of a WASP who hits the ground running with a person of another, more leisurely culture, one that was producing masterpieces of literature and sculpture when my ancestors were sitting around a campfire painting themselves blue. But dammit, I say to myself, *I* didn't paint myself blue, and he didn't write those poems. We're just trying to do a job here, and I don't think he's trying very hard. I have kept him on too long for the good of the group already.

He has a wife and two children. Can I put a father out of his job? When should I do it? Before Christmas so his unemployment can start the first of January? Or should I let him get through the holidays in innocence? What if he argues with me? What if he begs me to keep him on? What if he hates me? What if he drew my name for the office Christmas party?

I have known for a long time that one of my biggest enemies is my own desire to make men feel good. I threw spelling bees so that boys could win them. I remember one that I did not throw, and I am *still* cut by the hate in the glance Patrick Reeves shot me thirty years ago as I spelled "foreign" correctly and won. I have felt responsible for men's inadequacies all my life, it seems, and have expended a fair amount of energy shoring them up, patching them together so well that the stitches barely show. I have felt responsible for helping them to conceal the areas in which they fall short, creating distractions from these unpleasantnesses by serving as a loud cheerleader for the smallest of their virtues.

This makes me a very kind boss. I love everything they do. If I don't 5 love it, I feel it's somehow my fault. In a way that I now think **emasculating,** I have wanted to pick up after them, cleaning up their messes, following them with an invisible whisk broom and dust pan into which I sweep their mistakes so that nobody else will see them. In doing this, I deny them the opportunity to learn from the consequences of their errors, the painful but educational road people have to travel to advance. I have to fight myself—hard—to avoid showing these hurtful kindnesses.

I am not alone in this. Generations of women have made sure men looked smart and strong. And have made sure *they* didn't appear too smart and strong in the presence of the Other Kind. The male ego, we were told, simply couldn't tolerate the threat. It was only recently that we gave ourselves political permission to stop doing this. At last, we said, we can be what we are. What shocked me—continues to shock me—is how **reflexive** a thing it is for me, still, to try and smooth their paths. I still feel an obligation to support men in their work.

I type for a colleague when something has to get finished and all the secretaries are up to their ears. I made my living as a secretary once upon a time, and I'm fast. He uses a slow hunt-and-peck. I offer to help, and am proud of my speed. I love him. And I feel happy to have helped him meet his deadline. But I am also aware that what I have just done is a very stereotypical thing. I've put aside my work to help him finish his. I'll get mine done somehow. I always do.

Why aren't there more famous women composers and rocket scientists? One reason is that men are usually the ones who decide who's going to be famous. The other one is that men can usually find women to help arrange their worlds so they can do their work. Nobody does that for us.

Men are encouraged from childhood to be singleminded about their work, not to allow any distractions. And women are encouraged from childhood to set things up for them so that they don't have any. Don't make so much noise; your father is working. And when do we do *our* work? Late at night, when everyone is sleeping. Or early in the morning, before anyone else is up.

As a result of being spared like this, men have a low threshold for distraction. They are *delicate*. They are made nervous by having to do more than one thing at a time. They feel frazzled and angry if they have to answer three phone calls, and have a hard time settling back to work after the trauma. Women, on the other hand, develop the skill of doing many things at once. They tuck the phone in between their shoulders and their ears, hold a baby on one hip, stir a pot on the stove, all the while thinking about an idea for a story. They don't think it's unfair to have to do this. They think it's normal.

Women are just more complex than men about work. We've learned   10 how to be that way. We've learned to love our **ambidextrousness,** our snatches of solitary time, and to make the most of them. For years I got up at five so I could write with no kids around. The kids are grown up now, but I still do that. It has become my most creative time. I wouldn't give it up for anything. It's not particularly fair that it was necessary, but there you are. Men do their jobs brilliantly when they have little else to do. I should think they would. If they contended with the additional jobs many women have, they'd measure success differently. And they'd be stronger.

The goddess Kali, friend of Hindu women, is depicted with nine arms. That's about how many you need. She's not as affirming to men as we tend to be; she rains down death and destruction on those who treat women unjustly, and she doesn't care who they are. I don't know about *that*. There's got to be a middle ground between our **colluding** in men's privileging themselves and wanting to kill them. Marrying later may help—more brides today go into marriage with established careers and work habits than used to be the case. They have negotiating skills that ought to help them get a fair shake. Their husbands carry their babies around in canvas slings and shop at the same time. That's progress. But even now, even with babies in slings, the burden of home and child care is not equitably distributed in most marriages.

But it's an imperfect world. Things usually *aren't* equitable. Somebody usually has to give. It's usually the woman, and it usually makes her mad if she has time to think about it, and then she usually gets over being mad and makes the best of it. And grows in complexity as a result. Life is short, and most people don't want to fight their way through it. So couples point out to each other from time to time that things aren't fair, and a fairness that fits is found. It may be a little lopsided, and it's irritating when people pretend it's perfectly symmetrical. It's not. But it fits. That's the important thing.

QUESTIONS FOR DISCUSSION

1. According to Crafton, how do men and women approach work differently?

2. Why does the author feel guilty about the firing of her employee? Give as many reasons as you can find in the text.

3. What does Crafton mean when she says that women are in collusion with men in maintaining the status quo?

4. Do you agree that men are more delicate than women, as explained by this author? What examples could you give to support your view?

5. The author seems unsure whether perfect equality between genders is attainable, or even desirable. What do you think?

6. What specific human qualities would Crafton include in a definition of "ruggedness"? Give some examples from the text.

Interview with Bill Moyers

Anne Wortham is a sociologist at Washington and Lee University and a
continuing visiting scholar at the Hoover Institute. The following interview
with Bill Moyers was broadcast on PBS (Public Broadcasting Service) as part
of Moyers' "World of Ideas" series.

MOYERS: Your writings have made you a controversial figure, one who 1
criticizes the Civil Rights movement and its leaders for promoting reverse racism and the welfare state. How would you describe yourself to
a stranger who genuinely wanted to know what you stand for?

WORTHAM: I like to say that I'm an individualist. I believe that life is a
very important adventure that has to be carried out by individuals—in
cooperation with other individuals, yes, but always lived by individuals.
I take full responsibility for myself and for the kind of life I create and
the relationships I have with other people. I believe very strongly in
individual freedom, both internal freedom and external freedom.

MOYERS: Internal freedom being the power to make choices and external
freedom being freedom from the restraint of society, of others.

WORTHAM: Freedom from the restraint of society and within that context, therefore, freedom to realize my highest potential but to take responsibility for any failures or lack of knowledge that I have.

MOYERS: Well, that doesn't sound very controversial. 5

WORTHAM: I think most people would say that they do.

MOYERS: Why, then, are you so controversial?

WORTHAM: The controversy emerges when we begin to ask the question,
"But what do you mean by being an individualist? What do you mean
by freedom? What do you mean by liberty?"

I read a series of articles recently on the effect of television on
the American family and the American character. Throughout these
articles there is a bashing of individualism on the grounds that individualism is irresponsible, narcissistic, self-centered. It is, in fact, self-
centeredness that is being criticized as "individualism." But this is an
incorrect understanding of individualism. The kind of individualism
that I espouse is self-responsible. Self-responsibility can never be transformed into self-centeredness.

MOYERS: You said one of the reasons you looked forward to teaching at 10
Washington and Lee is that they still practice good manners there—

good manners is not a self-centered characteristic, it is an expression of living in society.

WORTHAM: Yes, and it is a statement of self-respect and respect for other human beings. It is a device for maintaining civility in human relations. The reason one would have allegiance to good manners and etiquette is because one values being human. And because one values being human, one values oneself and others. You would not want to give to another person more or less respect than you would yourself as a human being.

MOYERS: So individualism does not mean, "I have the right to do whatever I want to do, whenever I want to do it"?

WORTHAM: One has only the right to be oneself—within the boundaries of respect for others. There is a boundary between you and others. That's why we have etiquette. Behind the walls of etiquette and decorum is the autonomy of the individual. The reason etiquette was developed in the first place was to maintain individual freedom.

MOYERS: Here we sit under a sign that says "No Smoking"—and you don't because—

WORTHAM: —because there is a sign which is a statement addressed to 15 me and to everyone else which says that we, the administrators of the institution, prefer not to have smoking in this setting.

MOYERS: And you go along with that even though, individually, you believe you have the right to smoke.

WORTHAM: Yes, but I don't have the right to abuse an institutional rule, and by doing so, to contradict my unsigned, tacit agreement with the institution that by being a part of it, by accepting its invitation to work here, I shall honor certain rules. One doesn't sign anything—it is just understood in a civilized society.

MOYERS: "Civilized society"—what do you mean by that?

WORTHAM: A civilized society is one whose members expect that each will address at all times, as far as possible, the rational in man; that even when I may want to bash you over the head, I will be checked by my awareness of you as a rational entity, and I will not resort to force as an expression of my disagreement with you or even my feeling that you have been unjust to me; that in my disagreements with you, I will rely on the power of persuasion.

MOYERS: So that even if I act irrationally toward you, you're going to treat 20 me as a rational person.

WORTHAM: I remind myself that this is an irrational person who is betraying rationality and therefore himself.

MOYERS: So what happens inside when we all betray rationality?

WORTHAM: Well, we are very clever beings, you see. Rationality has the capacity for betraying itself. Rational men have the capacity to be irrational and to institutionalize irrationality. We've seen that in Nazi Germany.

QUESTIONS FOR DISCUSSION

1. What does Wortham mean by "internal freedom"?
2. How is Wortham's definition of individualism different from what she calls "an incorrect understanding of individualism"?
3. What is the role of good manners and etiquette in an individualistic society?
4. What does Wortham mean by "a civilized society"? What is the role of reason in such a society?
5. Why would Wortham's views be controversial?

✍ JOHN CAWELTI

The Meaning of the Self-Made Man

*John Cawelti, born in 1929, has taught English and humanities at the
University of Chicago since 1957. He has written several books on American
culture, including* The Six-Gun Mystique, Why Pop? *and* Apostles of
the Self-Made Man, *the book in which the following selection appeared.*

KEY VOCABULARY

NOUVEAU RICHE is a French term denoting a person who has only lately become rich. It is usually used disparagingly.

PARVENU is a French term for a person who has suddenly risen above his or
her social and economic class without the background and qualifications for
this new status.

THOMAS CARLYLE, JOHN RUSKIN, AND MATTHEW ARNOLD were well-
known 19th century British writers.

If you tell an American that he has no more chance to get ahead than a 1
Frenchman, he will probably not believe you, for Americans are fiercely
proud of the opportunities which they believe their uniquely open society
offers the average man. Every American boy has the chance to become
President of the United States, or at least a wealthy businessman. This
theme is, or at least used to be, a commonplace in newspaper, sermon,
political speech, and fiction. When he becomes successful, the American
self-made man likes to boast of his achievement, to exaggerate the obscurity
of his origin, and to point out the "Horatio Alger" quality of his career. In
Europe, where class traditions are stronger, the successful man often prefers
to forget his origins if they are in a lower class. Even the words which different countries have created to describe the "mobile man" indicate significant differences in attitude. Americans coined the term "self-made man."
The French expressions *parvenu* and *nouveau riche* point to the newness of
the individual's rise and not to the fact that he has succeeded by his own
exertions; in addition they carry a tone of condescension which is absent
from the American term.

Many social and geographical circumstances shaped American enthusiasm for the self-made man. The manifest opportunities of a large and relatively empty continent and the openness of a rapidly growing and changing

society impressed the idea of self-improvement on the public imagination. Immigration, too, helped make America a country of devotees of success by sending to her shores men who believed in their right and their need to better their condition. The ideal of rising in society was never subjected to the continual and devastating criticism of exponents of a traditional ideal of culture as it was in England, where, in spite of influential propagandists like Samuel Smiles, the self-made man was one of the prime targets of such big guns as **Carlyle, Ruskin,** and **Arnold.** The contrast between nineteenth-century English and American attitudes toward self-improvement appeared often in the comments of English travelers in America. Mrs. Trollope, who visited America in the 1830's, was stupefied by the pride that leading Americans took in the fact that they were self-taught and self-made, which, as she acidly remarked, meant to her only that they were badly taught and badly made.

QUESTIONS FOR DISCUSSION

1. Compare American and French attitudes toward opportunities of economic and social advancement.
2. What is the role of "social and geographical circumstances" in the shaping of "American enthusiasm for the self-made man"?
3. How has immigration also influenced these attitudes?
4. Do English attitudes toward the idea of the "self-made man" most resemble American attitudes or French ones? Explain.
5. Take a specific position, for American attitudes or for European ones, and defend it, offering reasons and examples to justify your choice.

In his essay on frontier life, an older student, who returned to college after many years away, takes issue with Gerster and Cords' "The Myth of Individualism." To support his case, this student offers both his own experience and evidence from Gretel Ehrlich's "About Men." His essay is a response to question 6, from the list included at the end of this chapter.

✍ STUDENT ESSAY:
It Is No Myth

In "The Myth of Individualism," Gerster and Cords would have you believe that life on the frontier was a way of dropping out, more of "a condition of hardiness and stamina than intellectual independence." They claim that the "individualism of America's frontier past has been judged to be largely mythical." Furthermore, they imply that people lived on the frontier because they lacked the intelligence or independence to make it anywhere else. Neither Mr. Gerster nor Mr. Cords, nor the scholars they quote, seem to write from experience. The myth of the rugged individual on the frontier might have been exaggerated over the years, but I believe there is still a kernel of truth in it.

My understanding of frontier life comes from close association with the people who were bred from the frontier and from my own interest in it as personal history. I am descended from people who settled the land, none having the desire to succumb to the "cut-throat" life of the city. Yes, mother nature was hard on them. But at least she was honest. They knew the risks and were willing to take them.

The people of the frontier had to be rugged. They faced many hardships. But out of necessity, they also had to come together and, I might add, with honest vigor and genuine helpfulness. These traits are not contradictory. To work together for a common goal or good cannot legitimately be twisted into a real or imagined lack of individualism or intelligence. Raising a barn, harvesting a large crop, or moving cattle to market were jobs much too large for one person to do alone. People working until their hands bled, neighbor working with neighbor, built both a sense of rugged individualism and community.

Gretel Ehrlich's view of the frontier, in "About Men," is at least authenticated with some experience. She chose to live in much the same way as the pioneers did. As a result, she possesses considerable insight into the "makin's" of the men who have descended from the pioneer. Throughout her article, she demonstrates that it is no myth that these people are intelligent, resourceful, and independent. True, Ehrlich softens the traditional image of the "macho, trigger-happy" cowboy. She gives him the qualities of tenderness and compassion. But this doesn't take anything away from him; he is still a man of toughness and courage.

Gerster and Cords imply that individualism consists of "intellectual independence and personal self-expression." I'm not sure that this is the whole story. It seems to me that the ability to survive on your own wits should be in there somewhere. And this doesn't mean that you can't team up with other people to get a job done. It takes just as much intelligence and probably more individualism to survive against nature than it does to close a business deal on Wall Street. The difference is that if you lose on Wall Street you may be financially broke, but if you lose against nature, you may be dead. Believe me, there is nothing mythical about that.

TOPICS FOR WRITING

1. Pick one writer from this chapter whose ideas make the most sense to you. Summarize the writer's main ideas, then write a paragraph explaining which ones you agree with and why you agree with them.

2. Re-read Charles Beard's "Individualism" and write an explanation of the importance of Darwinism to the shaping of the idea of individualism.

3. Write a brief essay showing that Andrew Carnegie is a firm believer in the idea of the "self-made man" as outlined in John Cawelti's "The Meaning of the Self-Made Man." First, summarize the main features of the self-made man in Cawelti's piece; then, using examples from *The Gospel of Wealth,* show why Carnegie belongs in this category.

4. Summarize the two ways of manufacturing products discussed by Andrew Carnegie, and explain which one he favors and why. Then evaluate Carnegie's position and explain why you agree or disagree with him.

5. Summarize Carnegie's attitude toward wealth, and then argue for or against his position, by using observations and examples from your own experience or contemporary American life.

6. Summarize the reasons that Gerster and Cords, in "The Myth of Individualism," think that the image of the frontier individualist is false. Then evaluate the strength of their argument. What standard do they use to define "individualism"? Is it a fair standard? Do you think the evidence they give is sufficient to make a convincing case? Which are the strongest arguments? Which are the weakest?

7. Compare the "self-made man" described by John Cawelti and the actual cowboy figure described by Gretel Ehrlich. To what extent does the cowboy fit Cawelti's definition? Use some short summaries of the readings to help develop your thesis.

8. Choose a main cowboy character from a "Western" film you have watched recently, outline important facts and events which would paint a clear picture of this character, and write a brief comparison between this Hollywood cowboy and Gretel Ehrlich's cowboy. In how many ways does the Hollywood image differ from the real thing?

9. How does Anne Wortham's definition of individualism differ from the one that Charles Beard describes? First, summarize Beard's definition, then show how Wortham's departs from it.

10. Write an essay explaining why Anne Wortham's views on individualism could be controversial.

11. Would Anne Wortham and Andrew Carnegie be more likely to agree or disagree about individualism? Explain on which particular points they might find common ground, and on which points they would be likely to argue.

12. Choose a current social issue or concern, describe it briefly, and explain how it reveals various American attitudes toward individualism. Consider such things as gun control, abortion rights, speed limits, prayer in schools, environmental regulations, anti-trust laws, bans on smoking in public buildings.

13. The readings in this chapter support the point that words often have different meanings for different people. Look at the different standards by which the writers included in this chapter define the quality of "ruggedness" (or toughness, or strength, or individualism). Using these definitions as examples, write a paper showing how words can be defined differently, depending on the "definer's" point of view.

14. In what ways would Gretel Ehrlich and Barbara Cawthorne Crafton agree or disagree in their views about men? Do the types of men they are writing about make a difference in the way the authors see the male character?

15. Suppose you are in complete agreement with Barbara Cawthorne Crafton's opinion that men are delicate. Write her a letter in which you give her advice about how to fire the man she speaks of in the beginning of her essay. Be sure to give reasons and details to justify the strategies you advise her to use. Imagine yourself as trying to persuade her that you are suggesting the best course of action for everyone concerned.

Thomas Hart Benton, The Changing West.

9 Working

Diligence is the mother of good luck, and God gives all things to industry. Then plough deep while sluggards sleep, and you shall have corn to sell and to keep.

–BENJAMIN FRANKLIN
From *Poor Richard's Almanac* (1732–57)

The "work ethic" holds that labor is good in itself; that a man or woman becomes a better person by virtue of the act of working. America's competitive spirit, the "work ethic" of this people, is alive and well on Labor Day, 1971.

–RICHARD M. NIXON

Belief in the value and rightness of work runs deep in the American character. This belief crossed the Atlantic with the Mayflower pilgrims in 1620 and migrated west with the pioneers, spreading and then taking root in their farms and villages and towns. Of course, people had to work hard to build a life in the American wilderness; but dedication to work was more than simple necessity—it was also a moral matter. We still hear of something called "The Puritan work ethic," and although some people say it is now in its death throes, few Americans grow up without someone, at some time, preaching to them the gospel of work in words much like Richard Nixon's Labor Day address.

Most of us have to work for a living; some of us even live to work. The kind of work we do and the importance we attach to it constitute a large— perhaps the largest—part of our lives. The question "What do you do?" is still one of the first we ask of a new acquaintance. In the eyes of others we are largely defined, our place in society determined, by what we do for a living. And our sense of our own worth is often tightly bound to the value of our work. The words "I work for a living" are worn as a badge of pride (as much as we would secretly like to strike oil or find gold or win the lottery).

In this chapter we will examine a variety of attitudes toward work—beginning with the Puritan one. The link between Puritan religious beliefs and Puritan attitudes toward work, thrift, and moderation is the subject of the first two selections in this chapter.

The other readings present the views of several modern writers on the subject of work—how they think and feel about it, and how it shapes their lives.

HENRY F. BEDFORD AND TREVOR COLBOURNE
From *The Americans: A Brief History*

Henry F. Bedford teaches history at Phillips Exeter Academy; Trevor Colbourne teaches at the University of New Hampshire. The reading selection that follows is from their book The Americans: A Brief History.

KEY VOCABULARY

An **ICONOCLAST** is a destroyer of sacred images; generally, one who attacks traditional ideas and institutions.

An **INDENTURED SERVANT** is a person bound into the service of another for a specific length of time.

A **MAGNATE** is a powerful and influential person, especially in business or industry.

Being **OMNIPOTENT** means having unlimited power and authority.

Being **OMNISCIENT** means having total knowledge.

PREDESTINATION is the doctrine that God has predetermined the "destiny" of all things.

THE PURITANS were a branch of the Protestant faith that had broken away from the Catholic Church during the Reformation in sixteenth-century Europe. In England the Puritans had belonged to the Anglican Church (The Church of England), which was Protestant, but in the eyes of the Puritans not "pure" enough because it retained some of the doctrines and practices of Catholicism, as well as the Catholic hierarchy of priests and bishops. The Puritans believed that each person could read the Bible without needing priests to interpret it.

A **SQUIRE** is a young nobleman ranked below a knight; generally, an English country gentleman.

SYLVAN means of the forest, a wooded place.

A **UTOPIA** is an imaginary perfect society.

A **YEOMAN** is, generally, an independent farmer; originally, it meant an Englishman who owned a small farm.

Hard work, thrift, and perseverance, or else damnation—the **Puri-** 1
tan's ethic was that of most of his countrymen of whatever religious persuasion, and it was an eminently sensible creed for an undeveloped country. Generations of Americans who had never heard of **predestination** learned early in life that leisure was an evil temptation, that thrift was the surest

route to wealth, and that success came to those who kept trying. In that form, Puritanism persists.

Experience on the farm reinforced the message from the **Puritan** pulpit. Sloth and gluttony were not only sinful but also self-defeating, because hard work and temperance were required to produce and preserve the harvest. Life on the farm was the godly life; the independent farmer, who with God's help brought wealth from the earth, personified virtue. The family farm has provided the example for the family business, and agrarian aspirations, values, and habits have outlasted the farms themselves. Americans still go to school by the agricultural calendar, protect farmers from a competitive market, and subsidize them through crop supports and in a host of more subtle ways. The nation's agrarian past has provided a model of virtue and a vision of **utopia.**

The city, by contrast, has seemed to be a center of sin, where thieves, gamblers, "slickers," and whores have waited impatiently to corrupt unwary countryfolk. This image of the city as the tempting serpent belies the urban roots of the republic. The first settlers lived in towns as well as on self-sufficient farms. A few mavericks sought the woods; most colonists preferred to cut them down. The frontier was something to be endured, not a **sylvan utopia.** Most settlers wanted to move with other people; they preferred an inhabited frontier. Neither the Pilgrims, nor the **Puritans** of Massachusetts Bay, nor the first families of Virginia were backwoods hicks.

Yet the dream of Americans, since the beginning, has been a dream of land. Open land lured Europeans across the Atlantic and their grandchildren across the Alleghenies. A man and his wife raised their family on the land, produced their bread and made their fortune from the land, and buried their dead in it. The dream lingers in the longing of urban Americans for that house in the country, for a suburban lawn and garden, and for the preservation of parks and open space.

Property in America has been the measure of accomplishment and the reward for effort. The accumulation of property, whether land or money, has always been a proper goal of life. America has been the land of opportunity, and Americans have come to think of economic growth as a permanent condition. We have assumed wealth to be unlimited, and that those who obtain it do so, not at the expense of others, but from the earth or from some other natural source of riches. Thus, any addition to one person's fortune was a net gain for the whole society. Economic individualism—or, less tactfully, greed—was supposed to produce social progress as well as a personal fortune. Whether the example be the **indentured servant** who accumulated a sizeable estate, the immigrant who rose from bobbin boy to industrial **magnate,** or the personable businessman of Irish parentage who made a fortune in the stock market, Americans have been proud, not resentful, of those who succeeded. The first immigrants, like those who came later, were simple people with simple tastes. Dukes, after all, do not usually emigrate, and paupers can rarely afford to. Most of the first arrivals were English **yeoman**—sturdy, hard-working farmers of the English countryside, whose agricultural skills and frugal habits were proverbial. The more prosperous settlers were gentry, men who in England had operated farms or occasionally businesses of moderate size, which brought them enough income for comfort but not enough for indolence. Although the companies and proprietors that established early settlements found their investments disappointing, the colonists themselves, whose expectations were more modest, discovered economic opportunity in land. And of land there was plenty. To own land in America became much more common than in England and carried fewer privileges. But the American landowner was as jealous of the rights of property as was the English **squire.**

The essential elements of what Americans call free-enterprise capitalism came with the earliest settlers. The terms are not precise, but Americans have always believed they knew what "free market," "fair competition," "individual enterprise," and "equal opportunity" meant. And they have been equally sure that monopoly, socialism, and special privilege were beyond the bounds of acceptable economic behavior. The **Puritans** knew what was proper; central to their code of conduct was the notion that hard work was morally uplifting. Other Puritan virtues, such as thrift, perseverance, honesty, sobriety, punctuality, and initiative, conveniently brought profits as well as clean consciences. Anyone can develop these virtues; capacity, aptitude, and genes are less important than character, which alone limits a person's horizon.

To be sure, Americans have not always practiced the economic theory they have preached. A monopoly, for example, even if unfair, has been enviously regarded as "good business." But while the economy has evolved from agricultural simplicity to the complexity of modern industry, the old economic vocabulary and many of the Puritan attitudes have endured.

Behavior depends in part upon laws and the size of one's bank balance. The way Americans behave, however, also results from the expectations of other Americans. The opinion of family, neighborhood, school, church, and clique can counteract the force of law and overcome financial handicaps. The assumptions and rituals that govern social contact, together with the natural impulse to associate with others, form cultural axioms, which serve as the base for probing American history.

One set of axioms derives from Protestant Christianity, especially in   10
the form loosely called Puritanism. Usage has robbed the term of precision,
and **Puritans,** in consequence, have been blamed for creating social trau-
mas they did not cause and for encouraging traits they did not esteem. Both
critics and admirers of the piety of the first settlers have attributed too much
to the people and their faith. The Puritan ethic and Protestant Christianity
are responsible neither for every virtue that ornamented American life after
1620 nor for every sin that stained it.

The **Puritan,** so the stereotype goes, was a gloomy, ascetic sort who
felt guilty if music, sex, art, games, color, or alcohol made his life interesting. His fatalistic belief in **predestination** led to obsession with the state of
his soul. He burned witches. His ministers preached of damnation in such
vivid terms that congregations felt the flames and smelled the brimstone.
Dour, driven, humorless, pious, penny-pinching, fanatical, and probably
neurotic, the **Puritan** was plagued, as one **iconoclast** has written, by his
"haunting fear that someone, somewhere, may be happy."

The picture will not do. The **Puritan** was less concerned with his soul
than some of his descendants are with their psyches. His life was no bleak
succession of prayer meetings unrelieved by beauty or pleasure. Sobriety
did not preclude the moderate use of spirits; a ban on music within the
meeting house did not forbid it outside; Puritan pewter was gracefully designed to please the eye.

If not entirely humorless, the **Puritan** was serious. He believed his task
on earth was to secure salvation; when he contemplated the magnitude of
that undertaking, he was not likely to be much amused. For, Puritans held,
humanity was sinful and could be redeemed only through the sovereign
grace of God. That God was eternal, **omnipotent,** and **omniscient,** so of
course He knew who would be saved and who condemned. Yet **predestination** was not unjust, for man could not define justice for God. And,
after all, life was full of inequities: as some were saved and some condemned,
so some were rich and others poor, some fortunate and others not; the grace
of God was beyond human understanding. Whatever his predestined fate,
the **Puritan** worked. Even if the Lord failed to reward diligence, at least
the effort could attract respect in one's community, which might in turn be
a sign of God's pleasure with His servant.

QUESTIONS FOR DISCUSSION

1. What "essential elements" of free market capitalism came to America
   with the earliest settlers?

2. What is the connection between the Puritan work ethic and Puritan beliefs about the purpose of human life?

3. In this essay, Bedford and Colbourne set out to correct the common stereotype of the Puritan. In what ways do they think the stereotype is false? In what ways is it accurate?

4. How did the Puritan farm provide a "model of virtue and a vision of Utopia"?

5. What specific values or virtues are associated with the "Puritan work ethic"?

6. Some Americans think the Puritan work ethic is dying out. Do you think this is true? Do people today consider hard work to be a moral matter, as former president Nixon claimed in the quotation presented at the beginning of this chapter?

✍ COTTON MATHER

From *Two Brief Discourses Directing a Christian in His Calling*

Cotton Mather, who was born in 1663 and died in 1728, was an American clergyman, theologian, and writer. He is regarded by many as the epitome of Puritan extremism. His best-known works are The Wonders of the Invisible World *(1693) and* The Christian Philosopher *(1721).*

KEY VOCABULARY

To be **HUMANE** is to have the good qualities of a human being, such as kindness, mercy, and compassion.

JACOB was a Hebrew patriarch, the father of twelve sons who became the ancestors of the twelve tribes of Israel.

PHARAOH is a title of the kings of ancient Egypt.

What is your Occupation? Genesis, XLVII. 3.   1

'Tis taken for granted then that they had One. It was the Question that **Pharaoh** put unto the Sons of **Jacob.** And it implies that every true Israelite should be able to give a good Answer unto such a Question. The Question which we are now to Discourse upon is, How a Christian may come to give a Good Answer unto that Question? or, How a Christian may come to give a Good Account of his Occupation and of his Behaviour in it?

There are Two Callings to be minded by All Christians. Every Christian hath a General Calling, Which is to Serve the Lord Jesus Christ and Save his own Soul in the Services of Religion that are incumbent on all the Children of men. God hath called us to Believe on His son, and Repent of our Sin, and observe the Sacred Means of our Communion with Himself, and bear our Testimony to His Truths and Wayes in the World: and every man in the world should herein conform to the Calls of that God, who hath called us with this Holy Calling. But then, every Christian hath also a Personal Calling; or, a certain Particular Employment by which his Usefulness in his Neighbourhood is distinguished, God hath made man a Sociable Creature. We expect Benefits from **Humane** Society. It is but equal, that **Humane** Society should Receive Benefits from Us. We are Beneficial to **Humane** Society by the Works of that Special Occupation in which we are to be employ'd according to the Order of God.

A Christian, at his Two Callings, is a man in a Boat, Rowing for Heaven, the House which our Heavenly Father hath intended for us. If he mind but one of his Callings, be it which it will, he pulls the Oar but on one side of the Boat, and will make but a poor dispatch to the Shoar of Eternal Blessedness. . . .

Would a man Rise by his Business? I say, then let him Rise to his 5 Business. It was foretold. Prov. 22:29, "Seest thou a man Diligint . . . in his Business? He shall stand before Kings"; He shall come to preferment. And it was instanced by him who foretold it; I Kings 11:28. "Solomon, seeing that the young man was industrious, he made him a Ruler." I tell you, with Diligence a man may do marvellous . . . things. Young man, work hard while you are Young; You'l Reap the effects of it when you are Old. Yea, How can you Ordinarily enjoy any Rest at Night, if you have not been well at work in the Day? Let your Business engross the most of your time. . . . Let every man have the Discretion to be well instructed in, and well acquainted with, all the mysteries of his Occupation. Be a master of your trade; count it a disgrace to be no workman. . . .

Acknowledge thy Dependence on the glorious God, for thy Thriving in the World. It is what we are minded of; Deut. VIII. 18. "Thou shalt remember the Lord thy God; for it is He that gives thee Power to get wealth." Be sensible of this; Riches come not always to them who are sharpest at inventing the most probable Methods of coming at it. Be sensible of this; The way to succeed in our Enterprizes, O Lord, I know the way of man is not in himself! Be sensible of this; In our Occupation we spread our Nets; but it is God who brings unto our Nets all that comes into them. . . .

QUESTIONS FOR DISCUSSION

1. According to Mather, what are the two callings of a Christian?
2. What arguments does Mather give to support his contention that hard work and rising in business are good?
3. According to Mather, who or what is responsible for any person's success?
4. Mather refers to what we would probably call a "job" as a "calling." What do you think is the difference between a calling and a job?
5. In the last paragraph, what is Mather warning his listeners against?

To Be of Use

Marge Piercy is a poet, essayist, and novelist. She has written eight novels, including Going Down Fast *and* Fly Away Home, *and her poems have been included in numerous anthologies. She has also co-authored a play,* The Last White Class.

KEY VOCABULARY

An **AMPHORA** is a jar having two handles and a narrow neck, used by the ancient Greeks and Romans to carry oil or wine.

BOTCHED means ruined through clumsiness.

The people I love the best   1
jump into work head first
without dallying in the shallows
and swim off with sure strokes almost out of sight.
They seem to become natives of that element,   5
the black sleek heads of seals
bouncing like half-submerged balls.

I love people who harness themselves, an ox to a heavy cart,
who pull like water buffalo, with massive patience,
who strain in the mud and the muck to move things forward,   10
who do what has to be done, again and again.

I want to be with people who submerge
in the task, who go into the fields to harvest
and work in a row and pass the bags along,
who stand in the line and haul in their places,   15
who are not parlor generals and field deserters
but move in a common rhythm
when the food must come in or the fire be put out.

The work of the world is common as mud.
Botched, it smears the hands, crumbles to dust.   20
But the thing worth doing well done
has a shape that satisfies, clean and evident.
Greek **amphoras** for wine or oil,

Hopi vases that held corn, are put in museums
but you know they were made to be used.   25
The pitcher cries for water to carry
and a person for work that is real.

QUESTIONS FOR DISCUSSION

1. According to the poem, what kinds of work are real?

2. What is the relationship between beauty and function in such objects as Greek amphoras and Hopi vases?

3. The line about people "who do what has to be done, again and again" would suggest tedium to some, yet Marge Piercy is full of admiration for these people. What is your reaction? Explain.

4. The words "parlor generals and field deserters" suggest a derisive attitude. Why do you think Piercy feels this way?

5. How many examples of *metaphor* and *simile* can you find in this poem? Considering the theme of the poem, why are these metaphors effective?

✍ WENDELL BERRY

The Joy of Work

Wendell Berry lives and writes on his farm in Kentucky and teaches English at the University of Kentucky. He works his farm with animals, rather than machinery, and has written extensively on topics having to do with responsible agriculture. Berry is also a novelist and poet and has published over two dozen books, including Home Economics *(1987),* Sex Economy and Freedom *(1993), and* Collected Poems: 1957–1982.

KEY VOCABULARY

CHAFF is the husk of grain that remains after separation from the seed. The husk and the grain are separated during threshing.

A **FUTURIST** is a person interested in the way patterns of contemporary life will develop in the future.

The university intellectuals are increasingly preoccupied with the fu- 1 ture. They are not especially interested in *preparing* for the future—which is something that people do by behaving considerately, moderately, con-servingly, and decently in the present—but in *predicting* the future, saying now what will happen then.

The most recent vision of the future I have seen is the work of 11 engineering professors at Purdue University. This one proposes what American life will be like at the beginning of the 21st century, and I venture to say that nobody has ever pipe-dreamed a more dismal "logical projec-tion," as the academic **futurists** call their work. The account offers a glimpse of the daily life in 2001 of "the fictitious Niray family, living in the imaginary Midland City, U.S.A." A few samples of the text will be enough to show what a perfect "world of the future" this is—for machines.

The hero of this fiction, Dave Niray, breakfasted on a "cylinder of Nutri-Juice"; in 2001 nobody cooks at home but a few eccentrics: gour-mets and old-fashioned people.

After drinking his breakfast, Dave began work. "Dave was an editor and feature writer for Trans Com News Service, one of the world's largest electronic news organizations. Although he routinely worked on stories of national and international events, he seldom left the apartment. His video screen gave him access to all of Trans Com's files. He could interview al-

most anyone in the world—from prime minister to Eskimo trader—via
Vision-Phone."

By Vision-Phone, Dave interviewed "the minister of agriculture in   5
Buenos Aires," composed his article, and then "activated the house moni-
tor computer system" which reminded him "that Rent-A-Robot would be
coming in to clean."

Ava, Dave's wife, worked in a factory. She did her work in a "control
room" before "an enormous array of keyboards, video screens, and ranks
and files of tiny lights." Her work was "kept track of" by a "central computer" known as "the front office." The members of "Ava's crew . . . were,
of course, machines." "Although she was called a supervisor, she really did
no supervision."

In the evening, the Nirays and their son, Billy, played electronic games
on their video screens.

This is a remarkable world in several respects. These people are apparently able to live an entire day without fulfilling directly any necessity of
their lives. They do not take pleasure in physical contact with anything or
anybody. It is not recorded that they ever touch or speak to each other. Nor
apparently, do they ever think a thought. Their entire mental life is devoted
to acquiring things, getting promoted, and being electronically amused.

This society is built exclusively on the twin principles of "convenience" and "control"—built, that is, on the dread of any kind of physical
activity remotely classifiable as work.

This future is so dismal, I think, because it is so nearly lifeless. The only   10
living creatures, or the only ones on view, are humans, and humans are
rigidly isolated from one another. They make no direct connections. They
deal with each other, as they deal with the material world, only through
technology. They live by remote control.

And so the first question raised by the work of these fanciful engineers
is: Where does satisfaction come from? They apparently think it comes
from living in a state of absolute control and perfect convenience, in which
one would never touch anything except push buttons.

The fact is, however, that a great many people have gladly turned off
the road that leads to Midland City, U.S.A. They are the home gardeners,
the homesteaders, the city people who have returned to farming, the people
of all kinds who have learned to do pleasing and necessary work with their
hands, the people who have undertaken to raise their own children. They
have willingly given up considerable amounts of convenience—and considerable amounts of control, too—and have made their lives more risky
and difficult than before.

Why? For satisfaction, I think. And where does satisfaction come
from? I think it comes from contact with the materials and lives of this

world, from the mutual dependence of creatures upon one another, from fellow feeling. But you cannot talk about satisfaction in abstract terms. There is no abstract satisfaction. Let me give an example.

Last summer we put up our second cutting of alfalfa on an extremely hot, humid afternoon. Our neighbors came in to help, and together we settled into what could pretty fairly be described as suffering. The hay field lies in a narrow river bottom, a hill on one side and tall trees along the river on the other. There was no breeze at all. The hot, bright, moist air seemed to wrap around us and stick to us while we loaded the wagons.

It was worse in the barn, where the tin roof raised the temperature and 15 held the air even closer. We worked more quietly than we usually do, not having the breath for talk. It was miserable, no doubt about it. And there was not a push button anywhere in reach.

But we stayed there and did the work, were even glad to do it, and experienced no futurological fits. When we were done, we told stories and laughed and talked a long time, sitting on a post pile in the shade of a big elm. It was a pleasing day.

Why was it pleasing? Nobody will ever figure that out by "logical pro-jection." The matter is too complex and too profound for logic. It was pleasing, for one thing, because we got done. That does not make logic, but it makes sense. For another thing, it was good hay, and we got it up in good shape. For another, we like each other and we work together because we want to.

And yet you cannot fully explain satisfaction in terms of just one day. Satisfaction rises out of the flow of time. When I was a boy I used to dread the hay harvest. It seemed an awful drudgery: the lifting was heavy and continuous; the weather was hot; the work was dusty; the **chaff** stuck to your skin and itched. And then one winter I stayed home and I fed out the hay we had put up the summer before. I learned the other half of the story then, and after that I never minded. The hay that goes up in the heat comes down into the mangers in the cold. That is when its meaning is clearest, and when the satisfaction is completed.

And so, six months after we shed all that sweat, there comes a bitter January evening when I go up to the horse barn to feed. It is nearly nightfall, and snowing hard. The north wind is driving the snow through the cracks in the barn wall. I bed the stalls, put corn in the troughs, climb into the loft and drop the rations of fragrant hay into the mangers. I go to the back door and open it; the horses come in and file along the driveway to their stalls, the snow piled white on their backs. The barn fills with the sounds of their eating. It is time to go home. I have my comfort ahead of me: talk, supper, fire in the stove, something to read. But I know too that all my animals are well fed and comfortable, and my comfort is enlarged in theirs. On such a night you do not feed out of necessity or duty. You never think of the money value of the animals. You feed and care for them out of fellow feeling, because you want to. And when I go out and shut the door, I am satisfied.

QUESTIONS FOR DISCUSSION

1. Why does Berry object to the vision of the future described in the first part of the essay?

2. How does Berry's defense of the value of work differ from the Puritan ethic? Would you say that Berry has a "work ethic"?

3. Berry says that the day spent putting up hay was "pleasing." That it was pleasing, he says, "does not make logic, but it makes sense." What do you think he means by this?

4. Do you think Berry has achieved success in his life? Why?

5. For Berry, what is the source of satisfaction?

✍ FRED MOODY

When Work Becomes an Obsession

Fred Moody is a freelance writer who lives on Bainbridge Island, Washington. He holds a degree in library science from the University of Michigan but has never worked as a librarian. He has worked as a janitor, Forest Service sawyer, editor, and sportswriter. Since 1983 he has covered the Seattle Seahawks football team for the Seattle Weekly, *and in 1989 he published the book* Fighting Chance: An NFL Season with the Seattle Seahawks.

KEY VOCABULARY

CALVINISM is the religious doctrine of John Calvin (1509–1564) which emphasized such things as the supremacy of scripture, the sinfulness of man, and a strict moral code.

A **DICTUM** is an authoritative pronouncement; also, a law or a popular saying.

JOIE DE TRAVAILLER is a French phrase meaning "joy of work."

The **RENAISSANCE** (meaning rebirth, revival) was a historical period that began in Italy in the fourteenth century and spread through Europe. The Renaissance saw a return of the learning, art, and literature of classical Greece and Rome to Europe, after the Middle Ages.

While recovering from his dramatic suicide attempt last year, Reagan's 1 former National Security Advisor Robert McFarlane made a poignant revelation to the *New York Times.* He had allowed his work "to become almost the exclusive measure of my worth."

McFarlane went on to describe his childhood, dominated by his stern father, who taught his son, by both **dictum** and example, to hide his emotions and to place the highest possible premium on success and accomplishment. Thus molded, McFarlane grew up to be a classic workaholic— an emotionally withdrawn person for whom success in the workplace is the sole reason for being. When he failed—as inevitably happens to all perfectionists—McFarlane fell into a suicidal depression.

It says something that McFarlane could be perceived throughout his career as a successful, admirable model rather than as a self-destructive overworker in need of help. As with the distinction between the energetic social drinker and the alcoholic, the difference between the devoted worker and the work addict is vague. The social climate of work and the esteem in and the work addict is vague. The social climate of work and the esteem in which the current generation holds work make workaholism seem far more of a virtue than a vice.

Work now pervades our non-working lives in unprecedented, widely accepted ways: cellular phones, answering machines, personal and portable computers. The career, for many people, has taken precedence over such time-honored human endeavors as building a strong family or seeking spiritual and philosophical truths. The person who works right up to the point of self-destruction is often accorded far more esteem than the person who seeks to lead a balanced life. Overworking is an American trait, much commented on by European observers; and it has become the hallmark of strenuous yuppies, whose chief complaint about life is "I don't have enough time."

It has gotten to the point where many fear that this widespread pres- 5 sure to work—at the expense of our physical health and the health of our relationships—has reached alarming dimensions. "I don't like to put in 80-hour weeks," says one engineer who often does, "but a lot of people do. And those are the people who get the projects and promotions."

To be sure, it is a simple fact of life that only the most ambitious among us can hope to excel. This is particularly true for baby boomers, who face unusual competition for the most interesting jobs. Many work hard, very hard. When does workaholism start to define a certain breed of worker whose *joie de travailler* sets him or her unmistakably apart from other ambitious co-workers? Both may work the same number of hours, but the workaholic works them to death, becoming as dependent on work as the addict is on his drug. A high level of psychological investment sets the workaholic apart. While appearing on the surface to be just as dedicated to company goals and success as the next worker, the work-obsessed employee is actually hard at work on a secret assignment: unconscious self-destruction.

No one has pinpointed workaholism, but many feel it now afflicts unprecedented numbers of workers. "I think that in the whole corporate work force in the last four or five years there's been a great inclination of people of all ages to work harder and longer," says Dr. Richard Thain, dean of external affairs at the University of Chicago Graduate School of Business. "People have almost a fear-of-God attitude toward work. They're ferocious."

Much of this new focus on work, Thain continues, is due to pressures in the marketplace brought on by America's change from an industrial to a service economy and by the heightened competition for jobs brought on by escalating numbers of business failures, mergers, and takeovers. There is also something deeper. "There's this new workaholic concentration that's taken over," Thain says. "These people think nothing of a 60-hour work week." Thain has labeled this unprecedented determination the "New **Calvinism.**" It is characterized by "this extremely single-minded devotion to hard work. They're after a kind of fulfillment, as if really hard work and success are God-given and they're ordained to succeed. I think it's crept up on people who don't realize it's going on."

Thain remembers the days not long ago when businesspeople lamented the loss of this country's traditional work ethic among America's young. "Back in the '60s," he says, "kids were just sitting around in parks, strumming guitars and trying to find themselves."

Twenty years later, having fled to the workplace as if they didn't like 10 what they found, they have caught their elders by surprise. "I often think that the very people who wanted this to happen are now very worried that the young guys are pushing them out. These newer people are the hardest-driving little devils. They're like the Puritans of old. And they take an almost masochistic delight in talking about how hard they work."

Thain sees more danger than benefit in the trend. "This is a swing of the pendulum back from the attitudes of the '60s," he says, "but it's swung back even farther than it was. I'm concerned about it. People may become so devoted to work that they will lose many of the civilized values that are supposed to be part of their education. We should be producing people who can give us sort of a **renaissance,** culturally and psychologically as well."

In addition, Thain views the new, heightened desire for work as something ultimately insatiable, a drive having less to do with money and status than with some mysterious urge to self-destruct. "These people are more motivated than anyone I've ever seen, and I haven't found that their drive is very easily satisfied. The few that I see who make all kinds of money and could quit, don't. Most of them will probably die young."

Psychiatrist Wayne Katon, a specialist in depression who frequently treats alcoholics, feels that workaholism is like any other form of addiction, with origins generally found in childhood.

Katon believes that work is the particular temptation of adults who as children were pressured too much to achieve. "A lot of high achievers I've worked with in therapy have been hard workers who put in 12-hour days," he says. "They were often sensitive kids who picked up very early that their parents needed them to be stars to boost the parents' low self-esteem. Their sense in growing up was that no one would care for them for who they really were. The only way they could get attention was by being the perfect person, the straight-A student.

"Unconsciously, the grown-up workaholic thinks his spouse won't like 15 him for what he is—she'll only like him for what he produces. By working long hours, he's saying, 'Hey, I'm okay—look at what I can do.' Often-times, he will feel a sense of loneliness, and whenever he slows down he feels depressed."

The adult's workaholic symptoms—which Katon believes are particu-larly widespread among America's baby boomers—are in this fashion psy-chologically predestined. The adult emotional life of many workaholics thus becomes a continuing, unconscious search for the emotional com-pleteness that eluded them in childhood. Psychoanalyst Alice Miller writes in *The Drama of the Gifted Child* that such people often suffer from depres-sion or its psychiatric flip side, grandiosity.

"The person who is grandiose," she writes, "is admired everywhere and needs this admiration; indeed, he cannot live without it. . . . Others are there to admire him, and he himself is constantly occupied, body and soul, with gaining that admiration. This is how his torturing dependence shows itself. The childhood trauma is repeated: He is always the child whom his [parent] admires, but at the same time he senses that so long as it is his qualities that are being admired, he is not loved for the person he really is at any given time. . . . In his compulsion to repeat he seeks insa-tiably for admiration, of which he never gets enough because admiration is not the same thing as love."

"Workaholism is pro-social as opposed to anti-social," says Katon. "The culture sort of shapes ways in which people deal with self-esteem deficits and problems with intimacy. In some cultures you might use drugs. In some, alcohol. In some you might fall into the workaholic pattern. In our culture now, if you're a workaholic, people think you're great. Our culture tends to feed type-A personality patterns, which are hard-driving, com-petitive, marked by an inability to relax. And I think nowadays that worka-holism is such a prominent thing. It's part of the yuppie era. People are very competitive. Everybody's talking about having their kids in six different lessons and having them in private school and so on. It's almost like the whole society is tuned into the workaholism ethic. And so for a lot of people it's very reinforcing. Money and power are ways of replacing feeling powerless inside."

On the cultural level, a workaholic is a victim of the American Dream— bequeathed to 20th century Americans by 16th century **Calvinists.**

"I think of our parents' generation as in a sense pushing their kids to 20 do what they never could," Katon says. "The father would work very hard at a job he didn't like, but his sons would damn well have a job they loved, and make a lot of money. So he . . . felt bad about what he was doing. On the other hand, he put all his eggs in the my-son-will-do-well basket." Now, Katon believes, the children of that father are not only trying to com-pensate their parents, but are passing on the insidious upward-mobility neurosis to their children. "It seems like our generation is more competitive. There's tremendous pressure on kids nowadays. People are making them read at younger ages, and there isn't enough focus on just letting them be kids and, for God's sake, not driving them so hard at such a young age."

Talk to a workaholic about his addiction, and you have the story of a conscious struggle against the invisible chains of unconscious compulsion. While outwardly their ambition and dedication is admirable and in many ways matched by co-workers who are not workaholic, there is an intensity about their work habits that sets them apart.

They are driven not by simple ambition or by the demands of their psychological longing. They are compelled to overwork not from without, but from within. They differ from healthy, genuinely achievement-oriented workers in the same way that compulsion differs from ambition. Where simply ambitious people work and achieve by choice, workaholics are unable to alter the self-destructive course of their lives.

At the cost of their own lives, workaholics seek to satisfy cravings they know to be insatiable. And they are impelled, as Robert McFarlane was, toward a critical encounter with the enduring demons of childhood.

QUESTIONS FOR DISCUSSION

1. Moody claims in paragraph 3, "It says something that McFarlane could be perceived throughout his career as a successful, admirable model rather than as a self-destructive overworker in need of help." What *does* it say?

2. Why does Richard Thain call the modern devotion to work "the New Calvinism"? How is it similar to or different from the Puritan work ethic?

3. What causes does Moody suggest are responsible for the recent increase in workaholism?

4. In what sense are workaholics "victims" of the American Dream? What version of the American Dream underlies this contention?

5. What are the defining characteristics of the workaholic? Consider the similarities between workaholism and other kinds of addiction, as well as the differences between workaholics and people who are simply ambitious.

✍ BARBARA EHRENREICH
Farewell to Work

Barbara Ehrenreich, born in 1941, is a journalist and author of several books. She is known as one of America's leading writers on women's issues. Her books include For Her Own Good: 150 Years of the Experts' Advice to Women *(1979),* Re-Making Love: The Feminization of Sex *(1986), and* The Worst Years of Our Lives *(1991).*

KEY VOCABULARY

A **CONSTELLATION** is a group of stars which is said to resemble a mythological character or animal. The term also refers to any related grouping of objects or ideas.

THE INDUSTRIAL REVOLUTION was brought about by the extensive use of machines in manufacturing. It began in England in the mid-eighteenth century and created widespread social and economic changes, particularly the shift from home manufacturing to large-scale factory production.

A **PROPAGANDIST** is a person who systematically spreads information or ideas in service of a cause. In popular usage, propaganda is often thought to be false or biased.

THE ROBBER BARONS were a group of late ninteenth-century American industrialists and financiers who became wealthy by unethical means, such as exploitation of labor, political manipulation, or shady stock market dealings.

I realize how important the work ethic is. I understand it occupies the position in the American **constellation** of values once held by motherhood and Girl Scout cookies. 1

Personally, I have nothing against work, particularly when performed quietly and unobtrusively by someone else. I just don't happen to think it's an appropriate subject for an "ethic." As a general rule, when something gets elevated to apple-pie status in the hierarchy of American values, you have to suspect that its actual monetary value is skidding toward zero. Take motherhood. Nobody ever thought of putting it on a moral pedestal until some brash feminists pointed out, about a century ago, that the pay is lousy and the career ladder nonexistent. Same thing about work. Would we all be so reverent about the "work ethic" if it weren't for the fact that the average working stiff's hourly pay is shrinking, year by year, toward the price of a local phone call?

Let us set the record straight: The work ethic is not a "traditional value." It is a johnny-come-lately value, along with thin thighs and non-smoking hotel rooms. In ancient times, work was considered a disgrace inflicted upon those who had failed to amass a nest egg through imperial conquest or other forms of organized looting. Only serfs, slaves, and women worked.

The work ethic came along a couple of millennia later, in the form of Puritanism—the idea that the amount of self-denial you endured in this life was a good measure of the amount of fun awaiting you in the next. But the work ethic only got off the ground with the **Industrial Revolution** and the arrival of the factory system. This was—let us be honest about it— simply a scheme for extending the benefits of the slave system into the age of emancipation.

Under the new system (a.k.a. capitalism, in this part of the world), huge 5 numbers of people had to be convinced to work extra hard, at pitifully low wages, so that the employing class would not have to work at all. Overnight, with the help of a great number of preachers and other well-rested **propagandists,** work was upgraded from an indignity to an "ethic."

But there was a catch. The aptly named *working* class came to resent the *resting* class. There followed riots, revolutions, graffiti. Quickly the word went out from the **robber barons** to the swelling leisure class of lawyers, financial consultants, plant managers, and other forerunners of the yuppie: Look busy! Don't go home until the proles have punched out! Make 'em think *we're* doing the work and that they're lucky to be able to hang around and help out!

The yuppies, when they came along a century or so later, had to look more righteously busy than anyone, for the simple reason that they did nothing at all. They did not sow, neither did they reap, but rather sat around pushing money through their modems in games known as "corporate take-over" and "international currency speculation."

One of the reasons they only lived for three years (1984–1987) was that they *never* rested, never took the time to chew between bites or gaze soulfully past their computer screens. What's worse, the mere rumor that someone—anyone—was not holding up his or her end of the work ethic was enough to send them into tantrums. They blamed lazy workers for The Decline of Productivity. They blamed lazy welfare mothers for The Budget Deficit. Their idea of utopia (as once laid out in that journal of higher yup thought, *The New Republic*) was the "Work Ethic State": no free lunches, no handouts, and too bad for all the miscreants and losers who refuse to fight their way up to the poverty level by working 80 hours a week at Wendy's.

Hence their rage at anyone who actually works—the "unproductive" American worker, or the woman attempting to raise a family on welfare benefits set below the average yuppie's monthly spa fee.

So let us replace their cruel and empty slogan—"Go for it!"—with the   10 cry that lies deep in every true worker's heart: "Gimme a break!" What this nation needs is not the work ethic, but a *job* ethic. If a job needs doing— highways repaired, babies changed, fields plowed—let's get it done. Otherwise, take five. Listen to some music, have a serious conversation with a three-year-old, write a poem, look at the sky. Let the yuppies Rest In Peace. The rest of us deserve a break.

QUESTIONS FOR DISCUSSION

1. Why does Barbara Ehrenreich think that work is not an appropriate subject for an ethic?

2. According to Ehrenreich, what is the origin of the work ethic?

3. Who are the Yuppies? What qualities characterize them?

4. How does Ehrenreich account for the importance of work to the Yuppies?

5. In the last paragraph, Ehrenreich says, "What this nation needs is not a work ethic, but a *job* ethic." What do you think she means by this?

✐ PAUL GOODMAN

Jobs

Paul Goodman, who died in 1972, was best-known as a social critic and philosopher of the New Left. He taught at several major universities and wrote for a number of periodicals, including Commentary, *the* Kenyon Review, *and the* Partisan Review. *A Ph.D. graduate of Columbia University, Goodman became an expert in community planning and also practiced psychotherapy. With Fritz Perls, he was co-founder of the Gestalt Therapy Institute. His books of social criticism, particularly* Growing Up Absurd *(from which the following selection was taken) and* Utopian Essays, *had a powerful influence on the generation of the 1960s and 1970s. In addition to this work, Goodman also found time to write novels, plays, and poems.*

KEY VOCABULARY

EXURBAN refers to a residential area situated farther from a city than the suburbs.

HUCKSTERS are people who sell things on the street or through the media. The word usually suggests the use of a "hard sell" or unscrupulous methods.

INGENUOUS means innocent, unsophisticated.

A **SURFEIT** is an oversupply of something, an excessive amount.

It's hard to grow up when there isn't enough man's work. There is 1 "nearly full employment" (with highly significant exceptions), but there get to be fewer jobs that are necessary or unquestionably useful; that require energy and draw on some of one's best capacities; and that can be done keeping one's honor and dignity. In explaining the widespread troubles of adolescents and young men, this simple objective factor is not much mentioned. Let us here insist on it.

By "man's work" I mean a very simple idea, so simple that it is clearer to **ingenuous** boys than to most adults. To produce necessary food and shelter is man's work. During most of economic history most men have done this drudging work, secure that it was justified and worthy of a man to do it, though often feeling that the social conditions under which they did it were *not* worthy of a man, thinking, "It's better to die than to live so hard"—but they worked on. When the environment is forbidding, as in the Swiss Alps or the Aran Islands, we regard such work with poetic awe. In emergencies it is heroic, as when the bakers of Paris maintained the supply of bread during the French Revolution, or the milkman did not miss a day's delivery when the bombs tore up London.

At present there is little such subsistence work. In *Communitas* my brother and I guess that one-tenth of our economy is devoted to it; it is more likely one-twentieth. Production of food is actively discouraged. Farmers are not wanted and the young men go elsewhere. (The farm population is now less than 15 percent of the total population.) Building, on the contrary, is immensely needed. New York City needs 65,000 new units a year, and is getting, net, 16,000. One would think that ambitious boys would flock to this work. But here we find that building, too, is discouraged. In a great city, for the last twenty years hundreds of thousands have been ill housed, yet we do not see science, industry, and labor enthusiastically enlisted in finding the quick solution to a definite problem. The promoters are interested in long-term investments, the real estate men in speculation, the city planners in votes and graft. The building craftsmen cannily see to it that their own numbers remain few, their methods antiquated, and their rewards high. None of these people is much interested in providing shelter, and nobody is at all interested in providing new manly jobs.

Once we turn away from the absolutely necessary subsistence jobs, however, we find that an enormous proportion of our production is not even unquestionably useful. Everybody knows and also feels this, and there has recently been a flood of books about our **surfeit** of honey, our insolent chariots, the follies of **exurban** ranch houses, our **hucksters,** and our synthetic demand. Many acute things are said about this useless production and advertising, but not much about the workmen producing it and their frame of mind; and nothing at all, so far as I have noticed, about the plight of a young fellow looking for a manly occupation. The eloquent critics of the American way of life have themselves been so seduced by it that they think only in terms of selling commodities and point out that the goods are valueless; but they fail to see that people are being wasted and their skills insulted. (To give an analogy, in the many gleeful onslaughts on the Popular Culture that have appeared in recent years, there has been little thought of the plight of the honest artist cut off from his audience and sometimes, in public arts such as theater and architecture, from his medium.)

What is strange about it? American society has tried so hard and so ably 5 to defend the practice and theory of production for profit and not primarily for use that now it has succeeded in making its jobs and products profitable and useless.

QUESTIONS FOR DISCUSSION

1. What does Goodman mean by "man's work"?
2. Why does Goodman think that building is discouraged in modern society?
3. How does "production for profit" affect the availability of "manly" jobs?
4. How would you describe the author's attitude (the tone) of this piece? Is he objective, calm, angry, sarcastic? Give examples to support your answer.
5. What is the difference between production for profit and production for use? To what kinds of products would each of these categories apply?

Responding to the second topic from this chapter's list, in "The Rewards of the Harvest," the writer contrasts the Puritan work ethic with Wendell Berry's attitude, expressed in "The Joy of Work." Short summaries and quotations are well-used to make the point. Notice also how in paragraph 3 the writer connects his discussion of Berry's views with his earlier discussion of the Puritans. Transitional phrases like "Unlike the Puritans . . ." remind the reader of the points being contrasted.

✍ STUDENT ESSAY:

The Rewards of the Harvest

Wendell Berry's approach to the value of work differs greatly from that of the Puritans. Berry worked hard because it brought him great personal satisfaction; the Puritans worked hard because of their religious beliefs. Although the two are at opposite ends of the spectrum when it comes to the reasons for work, they find common ground in the rewards that hard work can bring.

The Puritans were a religious group that believed they were on the earth to secure their salvation. To do this they needed to live a life of thrift, perseverance, and hard work. They believed that sloth and gluttony were not only sinful, but also self-defeating: hard work and temperance were required to produce and preserve the harvest. To the Puritans, life on the farm was the "Godly life" and was morally uplifting. They felt that with God's blessing and with hard work, they could both meet their daily needs and bring great wealth from the land.

Unlike the Puritans, Wendell Berry's reason for work was for the personal satisfaction it brought him. In "The Joy of Work," Berry writes that this satisfaction comes from contact with the "materials and lives of this world," from the "mutual dependence of creatures upon one another," and from the "fellow feeling" he received. Like the Puritans, Berry works hard on his farm. He tells of the effort that goes into planting and harvesting hay. Harvesting, he says, "could fairly be described as suffering. . . . The hot, bright, moist air seemed to wrap around us and stick to us while we loaded the wagons." Although the work is hard, Berry differs from the Puritans by emphasizing the *joy* of work. Work is pleasing, he says. The pleasure comes from a job well-done and from working with people who like each other and work together because they want to. But it is not just the harvest that gives satisfaction. Berry says that his satisfaction is completed in winter, when snow is on the ground and all the animals in the barn are eating the fruits of his labor.

Both the Puritans and Wendell Berry found that there is no room for sloth or gluttony in life if you want to produce a good harvest. It takes hard work and diligence to reap a reward from the land. For the Puritans, this hard work provided not only the necessities of life, but a sense of moral righteousness as well—the "work ethic." But they must have also felt, as they labored together to bring the harvest in, some of the same satisfaction Berry feels as he sits under the shade of an elm at the end of the day, relaxing and exchanging stories with his friends.

TOPICS FOR WRITING

1. Using information from *The Americans*, write an extended definition of the term "Puritan values."

2. How does Wendell Berry's defense of the value of work differ from the Puritan work ethic?

3. What similarities and differences in attitudes about work do you see in *The Americans* and Marge Piercy's "To Be of Use"?

4. Barbara Ehrenreich says that we don't need a *work* ethic, we need a *job* ethic. She doesn't explain exactly what a job ethic is, but she hints at it. What do you think she means by a "job ethic," and how is it different from a "work ethic"?

5. Using some of your own examples, develop further Cotton Mathers' distinction between a job and a calling, presented in "Two Callings."

6. It is likely that at least one of the selections in this chapter comes close to your own attitude toward work. It is also likely that none of them expresses exactly the same view as yours. Pick the one that you feel best expresses your ideas, then show how your view *differs* from it in some details.

7. In "When Work Becomes an Obsession" we read that Dr. Richard Thain has labeled the modern concentration on work "the new Calvinism." Though workaholics may share some characteristics with the Puritans, the two are clearly not the same. In what ways are they similar and in what ways different? (Think about *why* each of these groups puts such a high premium on work.)

8. In the manner of Wendell Berry's "The Joy of Work," describe a job you have held, showing why that job gives satisfaction.

9. Using material from Fred Moody's "When Work Becomes an Obsession" (and, if possible, your own experience), analyze the causes of the recent increase in workaholism.

10. In "When Work Becomes an Obsession" Fred Moody writes, "On a cultural level, the workaholic is a victim of the American Dream." Considering what you know about the American Dream, write an essay defending or opposing this statement.

11. Paul Goodman's essay "Jobs" is a defense of production for *use*. Take the opposite point of view and, using his essay as a model, write a defense of production for *profit*.

12. To what extent is the attitude toward work expressed in the poem "To Be of Use" the same as Paul Goodman's idea of "man's work"?

13. Using Paul Goodman's "Jobs" as a model, write an essay explaining your view of "women's work."

14. Using Barbara Ehrenreich's "Farewell to Work" as a starting point, write an extended definition of the term "Yuppie."

15. Some people say that young Americans no longer hold the values of the Puritan work ethic. If you agree with this assessment, explain *why* you think the work ethic has lost its force. What has caused its decline?

16. In "The Joy of Work" Wendell Berry argues against the automated world of the future he describes at the beginning. If you disagree with his appraisal, write a defense of this future world, arguing *for* its positive aspects.

17. In the quotation on the cover page of this chapter, Richard Nixon claims that "a man or woman becomes a better person by virtue of the act of working." With this in mind, write an essay speculating about the effects of work on a person's character. In what ways does work make people better (or worse)?

Jack Delano, "At the Bus Station."

10 A Dream Deferred

> "We can never be satisfied as long as our children are stripped of their selfhood and robbed of their dignity by signs stating 'For Whites Only.' "
>
> –MARTIN LUTHER KING, JR.

"I have a dream," said Martin Luther King, Jr., in his famous speech, giving voice to the frustrated hopes of black Americans.

The black American experience is unique; unlike others who came to America, blacks had no choice. They were carted like cattle across the Atlantic and sold on auction blocks like so much meat. Their history has been a story of struggle to claim their humanity and their place in the American Dream. It still goes on.

The following poem by Langston Hughes, a black poet and writer of the early twentieth century, expresses in graphic metaphors the consequences of excluding people from full participation in the dream.

.

ℒ Dream Deferred

What happens to a dream deferred?

Does it dry up
like a raisin in the sun?

Or fester like a sore—
And then run?

Does it stink like rotten meat?
Or crust and sugar over—
like a syrupy sweet?

Maybe it just sags
like a heavy load.
Or does it explode?

In the readings in this chapter, black American writers wrestle with the problems of their own special circumstances.

✎ JAMES BALDWIN

My Dungeon Shook

James Baldwin was an African American novelist, short story writer, and essayist. His first novel, Go Tell It on the Mountain *(1953), a story of the religious awakening of a fourteen-year-old boy in Harlem, established his reputation as a major writer. In a later novel,* Another Country *(1961), he dealt with personal relationships among blacks and whites. Baldwin's nonfiction books include* Notes of a Native Son *(1955),* Nobody Knows My Name: More Notes of a Native Son *(1961), and* The Fire Next Time *(1963). For many years Baldwin lived in self-exile in Paris.*

KEY VOCABULARY

THE EMANCIPATION PROCLAMATION was issued by President Lincoln, effective January 1, 1863, and declared the freedom of all slaves in territories still at war with the Union.

HOMER was an ancient Greek poet. There is disagreement among scholars about the authorship of works attributed to him, but Homer is traditionally recognized as the author of two epic poems, *The Iliad* and *The Odyssey*.

TRUCULENT means fierce, scathing, defiant.

UNASSAILABLE means undeniable, unquestionable.

Letter to my nephew on the one hundredth anniversary of the **Emancipation**

Dear James:

I have begun this letter five times and torn it up five times. I keep seeing your face, which is also the face of your father and my brother. Like him, you are tough, dark, vulnerable, moody—with a very definite tendency to sound **truculent** because you want no one to think you are soft. You may be like your grandfather in this, I don't know, but certainly both you and your father resemble him very much physically. Well, he is dead, he never saw you, and he had a terrible life; he was defeated long before he died because, at the bottom of his heart, he really believed what white people said about him. This is one of the reasons that he became so holy. I am sure that your father has told you something about all that. Neither you nor your father exhibit any tendency towards holiness: you really are of another era, part of what happened when the Negro left the land and came into what the late E. Franklin Frazier called "the cities of destruction." You can only

267

be destroyed by believing that you really are what the white world calls a *nigger*. I tell you this because I love you, and please don't you ever forget it.

I have known both of you all your lives, have carried your Daddy in my arms and on my shoulders, kissed and spanked him and watched him learn to walk. I don't know if you've known anybody from that far back; if you've loved anybody that long, first as an infant, then as a child, then as a man, you gain a strange perspective on time and human pain and effort. Other people cannot see what I see whenever I look into your father's face, for behind your father's face as it is today are all those other faces which were his. Let him laugh and I see a cellar your father does not remember and a house he does not remember and I hear in his present laughter his laughter as a child. Let him curse and I remember him falling down the cellar steps, and howling, and I remember, with pain, his tears, which my hand or your grandmother's so easily wiped away. But no one's hand can wipe away those tears he sheds invisibly today, which one hears in his laughter and in his speech and in his songs. I know what the world has done to my brother and how narrowly he has survived it. And I know, which is much worse, and this is the crime of which I accuse my country and my countrymen, and for which neither I nor time nor history will ever forgive them, that they have destroyed and are destroying hundreds of thousands of lives and do not know it and do not want to know it. One can be, indeed one must strive to become, tough and philosophical concerning destruction and death, for this is what most of mankind has been best at since we have heard of man. (But remember: *most* of mankind is not *all* of mankind.) But it is not permissible that the authors of devastation should also be innocent. It is the innocence which constitutes the crime.

Now, my dear namesake, these innocent and well-meaning people, your countrymen, have caused you to be born under conditions not very far removed from those described for us by Charles Dickens in the London of more than a hundred years ago. (I hear the chorus of the innocents screaming, "No! This is not true! How *bitter* you are!"—but I am writing this letter to *you,* to try to tell you something about how to handle *them,* for most of them do not yet really know that you exist. I *know* the conditions under which you were born, for I was there. Your countrymen were *not* there, and haven't made it yet. Your grandmother was also there, and no one has ever accused her of being bitter. I suggest that the innocents check with her. She isn't hard to find. Your countrymen don't know that *she* exists, either, though she has been working for them all their lives.)

Well, you were born, here you came, something like fourteen years ago; and though your father and mother and grandmother, looking about the streets through which they were carrying you, staring at the walls into which they brought you, had every reason to be heavyhearted, yet they were not. For here you were, Big James, named for me—you were a big baby, I was not—here you were: to be loved. To be loved, baby, hard, at once, and forever, to strengthen you against the loveless world. Remember that: I know how black it looks today, for you. It looked bad that day, too, yes, we were trembling. We have not stopped trembling yet, but if we had not loved each other none of us would have survived. And now you must survive because we love you, and for the sake of your children and your children's children.

This innocent country set you down in a ghetto in which, in fact, it 5 intended that you should perish. Let me spell out precisely what I mean by that, for the heart of the matter is here, and the root of my dispute with my country. You were born where you were born and faced the future that you faced because you were black and *for no other reason*. The limits of your ambition were, thus, expected to be set forever. You were born into a society which spelled out with brutal clarity, and in as many ways as possible, that you were a worthless human being. You were not expected to aspire to excellence: you were expected to make peace with mediocrity. Wherever you have turned, James, in your short time on this earth, you have been told where you could go and what you could do (and *how* you could do it) and where you could live and whom you could marry. I know your countrymen do not agree with me about this, and I hear them saying, "You exaggerate." They do not know Harlem, and I do. So do you. Take no one's word for anything, including mine—but trust your experience. Know whence you came. If you know whence you came, there is really no limit to where you can go. The details and symbols of your life have been deliberately constructed to make you believe what white people say about you. Please try to remember that what they believe, as well as what they do and cause you to endure, does not testify to your inferiority but to their inhumanity and fear. Please try to be clear, dear James, through the storm which rages about your youthful head today, about the reality which lies behind the words *acceptance* and *integration*. There is no reason for you to try to become like white people and there is no basis whatever for their impertinent assumption that *they* must accept *you*. The really terrible thing, old buddy, is that *you* must accept them. And I mean that very seriously. You must accept them and accept them with love. For these innocent people have no other hope. They are, in effect, still trapped in a history which they do not understand; and until they understand it, they cannot be released from it. They have had to believe for many years, and for innumerable reasons, that black men are inferior to white men. Many of them, indeed, know better, but, as you will discover, people find it difficult to act on what they know. To act is to be committed, and to be committed is to be in danger. In this case, the danger, in the minds of most white Americans, is the loss of their identity. Try to imagine how you would feel if you woke up one morning to find the sun shining and all the stars aflame. You would be frightened because it is out of the order of nature. Any upheaval in the universe is terrifying because it so profoundly attacks one's sense of one's own reality. Well, the black man has functioned in the white man's world as a fixed star, as an immovable pillar: and as he moves out of his place, heaven and earth are shaken to their foundations. You, don't be afraid. I said that it was intended that you should perish in the ghetto, perish by never being allowed to go behind the white man's definitions, by never being allowed to spell your proper name. You have, and many of us have, defeated this intention; and, by a terrible law, a terrible paradox, those innocents who believed that your imprisonment made them safe are losing their grasp of reality. But these men are your brothers—your lost, younger brothers. And if the word *integration* means anything, this is what it means: that we, with love, shall force our brothers to see themselves as they are, to cease fleeing from reality and begin to change it. For this is your home, my friend, do not be driven from it; great men have done great things here, and will again, and we can make America what America must become. It will be hard, James, but you come from sturdy, peasant stock, men who picked cotton and dammed rivers and built railroads, and, in the teeth of the most terrifying odds, achieved an **unassailable** and monumental dignity. You come from a long line of great poets, some of the greatest poets since **Homer**. One of them said, *The very time I thought I was lost, My dungeon shook and my chains fell off.*

You know, and I know, that the country is celebrating one hundred years of freedom one hundred years too soon. We cannot be free until they are free. God bless you, James, and Godspeed.

Your uncle,
James

QUESTIONS FOR DISCUSSION

1. Why does Baldwin say of whites, "It is the innocence which constitutes the crime"?
2. What is the root of Baldwin's dispute with his country?
3. According to Baldwin, what expectations do white Americans have of blacks?
4. Baldwin reverses the common misunderstanding about the words *acceptance* and *integration*. What is the logic of his claim that his nephew must accept white people, rather than the other way around?
5. "My Dungeon Shook" is a personal letter from Baldwin to his 14-year-old nephew. Yet it also marks a public occasion—the 100th anniversary of the emancipation of the slaves. In what ways is Baldwin's voice personal and in what ways public?

❧ MARTIN LUTHER KING, JR.

Three Ways of Responding to Oppression

*The Reverend Martin Luther King, Jr. is one of the best-known figures in
recent American history. He led the movement for civil rights for African
Americans in the 1950s and 1960s, and his writings and speeches gave
eloquent voice to the struggles and aspirations of African American people.
King advocated a strong but non-violent resistance to oppression. He was
assassinated on April 4, 1968, in Memphis, Tennessee.*

KEY VOCABULARY

HEGELIAN PHILOSOPHY was developed by the German philosopher Georg
Wilhelm Friedrich Hegel (1770–1831). Hegel saw history as a dynamic process governed by a law called the *Dialectical Law*. According to the Dialectical
Law, the forward progress of history is produced by the conflicting interests
and impulses of people. Hegel claimed that any idea (thesis) contains seeds of
its opposite (antithesis). The conflict between the two results in a resolution
(synthesis), which in turn produces another antithesis. And the process goes
on toward a greater realization of reason and freedom.

IMPERATIVE means, here, mandatory; something that must be done.

SUBLIME means grand, majestic, of high spiritual, moral, or intellectual
worth.

Oppressed people deal with their oppression in three characteristic 1
ways. One way is acquiescence: the oppressed resign themselves to their
doom. They tacitly adjust themselves to oppression, and thereby become
conditioned to it. In every movement toward freedom some of the oppressed prefer to remain oppressed. Almost 2,800 years ago Moses set out
to lead the children of Israel from the slavery of Egypt to the freedom of
the promised land. He soon discovered that slaves do not always welcome
their deliverers. They become accustomed to being slaves. They would
rather bear those ills they have, as Shakespeare pointed out, than flee to
others that they know not of. They prefer the "fleshpots of Egypt" to the
ordeals of emancipation.

There is such a thing as the freedom of exhaustion. Some people are
so worn down by the yoke of oppression that they give up. A few years ago
in the slum areas of Atlanta, a Negro guitarist used to sing almost daily:

"Been down so long that down don't bother me." This is the type of negative freedom and resignation that often engulfs the life of the oppressed.

But this is not the way out. To accept passively an unjust system is to coöperate with that system; thereby the oppressed become as evil as the oppressor. Noncoöperation with evil is as much a moral obligation as is coöperation with good. The oppressed must never allow the conscience of the oppressor to slumber. Religion reminds every man that he is his brother's keeper. To accept injustice or segregation passively is to say to the oppressor that his actions are morally right. It is a way of allowing his conscience to fall asleep. At this moment the oppressed fails to be his brother's keeper. So acquiescence—while often the easier way—is not the moral way. It is the way of the coward. The Negro cannot win the respect of his oppressor by acquiescing; he merely increases the oppressor's arrogance and contempt. Acquiescence is interpreted as proof of the Negro's inferiority. The Negro cannot win the respect of the white people of the South or the peoples of the world if he is willing to sell the future of his children for his personal and immediate comfort and safety.

A second way that oppressed people sometimes deal with oppression is to resort to physical violence and corroding hatred. Violence often brings about momentary results. Nations have frequently won their independence in battle. But in spite of temporary victories, violence never brings permanent peace. It solves no social problem; it merely creates new and more complicated ones.

Violence as a way of achieving racial justice is both impractical and 5 immoral. It is impractical because it is a descending spiral ending in destruction for all. The old law of an eye for an eye leaves everybody blind. It is immoral because it seeks to humiliate the opponent rather than win his understanding; it seeks to annihilate rather than to convert. Violence is immoral because it thrives on hatred rather than love. It destroys community and makes brotherhood impossible. It leaves society in monologue rather than dialogue. Violence ends by defeating itself. It creates bitterness in the survivors and brutality in the destroyers. A voice echoes through time saying to every potential Peter, "Put up your sword." History is cluttered with the wreckage of nations that failed to follow this command.

If the American Negro and other victims of oppression succumb to the temptation of using violence in the struggle for freedom, future generations will be the recipients of a desolate night of bitterness, and our chief legacy to them will be an endless reign of meaningless chaos. Violence is not the way.

The third way open to oppressed people in their quest for freedom is the way of nonviolent resistance. Like the synthesis in **Hegelian philosophy,** the principle of nonviolent resistance seeks to reconcile the truths of two opposites—acquiescence and violence—while avoiding the extremes and immoralities of both. The nonviolent resister agrees with the person who acquiesces that one should not be physically aggressive toward his opponent; but he balances the equation by agreeing with the person of violence that evil must be resisted. He avoids the nonresistance of the former and the violent resistance of the latter. With nonviolent resistance, no individual or group need submit to any wrong, nor need anyone resort to violence in order to right a wrong.

It seems to me that this is the method that must guide the actions of the Negro in the present crisis in race relations. Through nonviolent resistance the Negro will be able to rise to the noble height of opposing the unjust system while loving the perpetrators of the system. The Negro must work passionately and unrelentingly for full stature as a citizen, but he must not use inferior methods to gain it. He must never come to terms with falsehood, malice, hate, or destruction.

Nonviolent resistance makes it possible for the Negro to remain in the South and struggle for his rights. The Negro's problem will not be solved by running away. He cannot listen to the glib suggestion of those who would urge him to migrate en masse to other sections of the country. By grasping his great opportunity in the South he can make a lasting contribution to the moral strength of the nation and set a **sublime** example of courage for generations yet unborn.

By nonviolent resistance, the Negro can also enlist all men of good will in his struggle for equality. The problem is not a purely racial one, with Negroes set against whites. In the end, it is not a struggle between people at all, but a tension between justice and injustice. Nonviolent resistance is not aimed against oppressors but against oppression. Under its banner consciences, not racial groups, are enlisted.

If the Negro is to achieve the goal of integration, he must organize himself into a militant and nonviolent mass movement. All three elements are indispensable. The movement for equality and justice can only be a success if it has both a mass and militant character; the barriers to be overcome require both. Nonviolence is an **imperative** in order to bring about ultimate community.

A mass movement of a militant quality that is not at the same time committed to nonviolence tends to generate conflict, which in turn breeds anarchy. The support of the participants and the sympathy of the uncommitted are both inhibited by the threat that bloodshed will engulf the community. This reaction in turn encourages the opposition to threaten and resort to force. When, however, the mass movement repudiates violence while moving resolutely toward its goal, its opponents are revealed as the instigators and practitioners of violence if it occurs. Then public support is magnetically attracted to the advocates of nonviolence, while those who employ violence are literally disarmed by overwhelming sentiment against their stand.

QUESTIONS FOR DISCUSSION

1. According to King, how do some slaves react to slavery? Why?
2. Why is acquiescence detrimental to the moral standing of blacks?
3. Why does King think that violence is ultimately unproductive?
4. King uses a number of Biblical references and quotations in developing his essay. Considering the reasons he gives for his conclusions, why are these references especially appropriate?
5. King argues that violence is immoral. What would you say *are* the elements of King's moral code?

✍ ZORA NEALE HURSTON

How It Feels to Be Colored Me

Zora Neale Hurston was a student of anthropology and a writer. She attended Howard University, Barnard College, and Columbia University. According to the contemporary novelist Alice Walker, Hurston studied anthropology in order to learn "the ways of her own people, and what ancient rituals, customs, and beliefs had made them unique." Hurston is best known for her novel Their Eyes Were Watching God *(1937) and her autobiography* Dust Tracks on a Road *(1937). A collection of her works (edited by Alice Walker),* I Love Myself When I Am Laughing, *was published in 1979.*

KEY VOCABULARY

An **ASSEGAI** is a light spear used by southern African tribesmen.

BOULE MICH refers to Saint Michel boulevard, the main artery of the Latin Quarter in Paris, where many students and artists live.

CIRCUMLOCUTION is the process of talking around a subject, not getting to the point.

A **GALLERY SEAT** is a cheaper theater seat, located in an upper floor of the theater and projecting over the rear part of the main floor.

The **HEGIRA** was, originally, the flight of Mohammed from Mecca to Medina in 622 A.D., when he was expelled from Mecca by the magistrates. Generally, the term can mean any flight from danger.

OLEANDERS are poisonous evergreen shrubs that grow in warm climates. They have fragrant flowers of white, rose, or purple.

A **PROSCENIUM** is, in the modern theater, the area located between the curtain and the orchestra.

I am colored but I offer nothing in the way of extenuating circum- 1 stances except the fact that I am the only Negro in the United States whose grandfather on the mother's side was *not* an Indian chief.

I remember the very day that I became colored. Up to my thirteenth year I lived in the little Negro town of Eatonville, Florida. It is exclusively a colored town. The only white people I knew passed through the town going to or coming from Orlando. The native whites rode dusty horses, the Northern tourists chugged down the sandy village road in automobiles. The town knew the Southerners and never stopped cane chewing when they passed. But the Northerners were something else again. They were peered at cautiously from behind curtains by the timid. The more venture-some would come out on the porch to watch them go past and got just as much pleasure out of the tourists as the tourists got out of the village. The front porch might seem a daring place for the rest of the town, but it was a **gallery seat** to me. My favorite place was atop the gate-post. **Proscenium** box for a born first-nighter. Not only did I enjoy the show, but I didn't mind the actors knowing that I liked it. I usually spoke to them in passing. I'd wave at them and when they returned my salute, I would say something like this: "Howdy-do-well-I-thank-you-where-you-goin'?" Usually the automobile or the horse paused at this, and after a queer exchange of compliments, I would probably "go a piece of the way" with them, as we say in farthest Florida. If one of my family happened to come to the front in time to see me, of course negotiations would be rudely broken off. But even so, it is clear that I was the first "welcome-to-our-state" Floridian and I hope the Miami Chamber of Commerce will please take notice.

During this period, white people differed from colored to me only in that they rode through town and never lived there. They liked to hear me "speak pieces" and sing and wanted to see me dance the parse-me-la, and gave me generously of their small silver for doing these things, which seemed strange to me for I wanted to do them so much that I needed bribing to stop. Only they didn't know it. The colored people gave no dimes. They deplored any joyful tendencies in me, but I was their Zora nevertheless. I belonged to them, to the nearby hotels, to the county—everybody's Zora.

But changes came in the family when I was thirteen, and I was sent to   5 school in Jacksonville. I left Eatonville, the town of the **oleanders,** as Zora. When I disembarked from the river-boat at Jacksonville, she was no more. It seemed that I had suffered a sea change. I was not Zora of Orange County any more, I was now a little colored girl. I found it out in certain ways. In my heart as well as in the mirror, I became a fast brown—warranted not to rub nor run.

But I am not tragically colored. There is no great sorrow dammed up in my soul, nor lurking behind my eyes. I do not mind at all. I do not belong to the sobbing school of Negrohood who hold that nature some-how has given them a lowdown dirty deal and whose feelings are all hurt about it. Even in the helter-skelter skirmish that is my life, I have seen that the world is to the strong regardless of a little pigmentation more or less. No, I do not weep at the world—I am too busy sharpening my oyster knife.

Someone is always at my elbow reminding me that I am the grand-daughter of slaves. It fails to register depression with me. Slavery is sixty years in the past. The operation was successful and the patient is doing well, thank you. The terrible struggle that made me an American out of a potential slave said "On the line!" The Reconstruction said "Get set!"; and the generation before said "Go!" I am off to a flying start and I must not halt in the stretch to look behind and weep. Slavery is the price I paid for civilization, and the choice was not with me. It is a bully adventure and worth all that I have paid through my ancestors for it. No one on earth ever had a greater chance for glory. The world to be won and nothing to be lost. It is thrilling to think—to know that for any act of mine, I shall get twice as much praise or twice as much blame. It is quite exciting to hold the center of the national stage, with the spectators not knowing whether to laugh or to weep.

The position of my white neighbor is much more difficult. No brown specter pulls up a chair beside me when I sit down to eat. No dark ghost thrusts its leg against mine in bed. The game of keeping what one has is never so exciting as the game of getting.

I do not always feel colored. Even now I often achieve the unconscious Zora of Eatonville before the **Hegira.** I feel most colored when I am thrown against a sharp white background.

For instance at Barnard. "Beside the waters of the Hudson" I feel my 10 race. Among the thousand white persons, I am a dark rock surged upon, overswept by a creamy sea. I am surged upon and overswept, but through it all, I remain myself. When covered by the waters, I am; and the ebb but reveals me again.

Sometimes it is the other way around. A white person is set down in our midst, but the contrast is just as sharp for me. For instance, when I sit in the drafty basement that is The New World Cabaret with a white person, my color comes. We enter chatting about any little nothing that we have in common and are seated by the jazz waiters. In the abrupt way that jazz orchestras have, this one plunges into a number. It loses no time in **circumlocutions,** but gets right down to business. It constricts the thorax and splits the heart with its tempo and narcotic harmonies. This orchestra grows rambunctious, rears on its hind legs and attacks the tonal veil with primitive fury, rending it, clawing it until it breaks through to the jungle beyond. I follow those heathen—follow them exultingly. I dance wildly inside myself; I yell within, I whoop; I shake my **assegai** above my head, I hurl it true to the mark *yeeeeoouw!* I am in the jungle and living in the jungle way. My face is painted red and yellow and my body is painted blue. My pulse is throbbing like a war drum. I want to slaughter something—give pain, give death to what, I do not know. But the piece ends. The men of the orchestra wipe their lips and rest their fingers. I creep back slowly to the veneer we call civilization with the last tone and find the white friend sitting motionless in his seat, smoking calmly.

"Good music they have here," he remarks, drumming the table with his fingertips.

Music! The great blobs of purple and red emotion have not touched him. He has only heard what I felt. He is far away and I see him but dimly across the ocean and the continent that have fallen between us. He is so pale with his whiteness then and I am *so* colored.

At certain times I have no race, I am *me*. When I set my hat at a certain angle and saunter down Seventh Avenue, Harlem City, feeling as snooty as the lions in front of the Forty-Second Street Library, for instance. So far as my feelings are concerned, Peggy Hopkins Joyce on the **Boule Mich** with her gorgeous raiment, stately carriage, knees knocking together in a most aristocratic manner, has nothing on me. The cosmic Zora emerges. I belong to no race nor time. I am the eternal feminine with its string of beads.

I have no separate feeling about being an American citizen and colored.   15
I am merely a fragment of the Great Soul that surges within boundaries. My country, right or wrong.

Sometimes I feel discriminated against, but it does not make me angry. It merely astonishes me. How *can* any deny themselves the pleasure of my company! It's beyond me.

But in the main, I feel like a brown bag of miscellany propped against a wall. Against a wall in company with other bags, white, red, and yellow. Pour out the contents, and there is discovered a jumble of small things priceless and worthless. A first-water diamond, an empty spool, bits of broken glass, lengths of string, a key to a door long since crumbled away, a rusty knife-blade, old shoes saved for a road that never was and never will be, a nail bent under the weight of things too heavy for any nail, a dried flower or two, still a little fragrant. In your hand is the brown bag. On the ground before you is the jumble it held—so much like the jumble in the bags, could they be emptied, that all might be dumped in a single heap and the bags refilled without altering the content of any greatly. A bit of colored glass more or less would not matter. Perhaps that is how the Great Stuffer of Bags filled them in the first place—who knows?

QUESTIONS FOR DISCUSSION

1. What are the author's expressed and implied attitudes toward being "colored"?

2. Do you think that Hurston's attitudes about race are determined mainly by personal experiences or by historical events and context? Give some examples from the text to support your view.

3. What does the example of the New World Cabaret reveal about Hurston's self-image? What does it reveal about her attitudes toward whites?

4. What do you think the author means by the "Great Soul"? Offer a possible definition for it.

5. Would you describe the author's childhood as happy or sad? Explain with examples.

MAYA ANGELOU

My Name Is Margaret

Maya Angelou is a woman of many talents: she is a novelist, poet, playwright, actress, composer, singer, and civil rights activist. She has written a series of autobiographical novels, beginning with I Know Why the Caged Bird Sings *(1970), which was followed by* Gather Together in My Name *(1974),* Singin' and Swingin' and Gettin' Merry Like Christmas *(1976),* The Heart of a Woman *(1981), and* All God's Children Got Travelling Shoes *(1986). In January 1993, President Clinton invited her to write an original poem, "On the Pulse of Morning," to be recited at his inauguration. The selection below comes from* I Know Why the Caged Bird Sings.

KEY VOCABULARY

THE CHESHIRE CAT, from *Alice's Adventures in Wonderland* by Lewis Carroll, is a grinning cat that gradually disappears until only its grin remains visible.

A **DEBUTANTE** is a young woman, as a rule from a prominent family, who is officially entering society, usually at a special party or ball.

IMPUDENT means disrespectful, rude.

Recently a white woman from Texas, who would quickly describe 1 herself as a liberal, asked me about my hometown. When I told her that in Stamps my grandmother had owned the only Negro general merchandise store since the turn of the century, she exclaimed, "Why, you were a **debutante.**" Ridiculous and even ludicrous. But Negro girls in small Southern towns, whether poverty-stricken or just munching along on a few of life's necessities, were given as extensive and irrelevant preparations for adulthood as rich white girls shown in magazines. Admittedly the training was not the same. While white girls learned to waltz and sit gracefully with a tea cup balanced on their knees, we were lagging behind, learning the mid-Victorian values with very little money to indulge them. (Come and see Edna Lomax spending the money she made picking cotton on five balls of ecru tatting thread. Her fingers are bound to snag the work and she'll have to repeat the stitches time and time again. But she knows that when she buys the thread.)

We were required to embroider and I had trunkfuls of colorful dish-towels, pillowcases, runners, and handkerchiefs to my credit. I mastered the art of crocheting and tatting, and there was a lifetime's supply of dainty doilies that would never be used in sacheted dresser drawers. It went without saying that all girls could iron and wash, but the finer touches around the home, like setting a table with real silver, baking roasts, and cooking vegetables without meat, had to be learned elsewhere. Usually at the source of those habits. During my tenth year, a white woman's kitchen became my finishing school.

Mrs. Viola Cullinan was a plump woman who lived in a three-bedroom house somewhere behind the post office. She was singularly unattractive until she smiled, and then the lines around her eyes and mouth which made her look perpetually dirty disappeared, and her face looked like the mask of an impish elf. She usually rested her smile until late afternoon when her women friends dropped in and Miss Glory, the cook, served them cold drinks on the closed-in porch.

The exactness of her house was inhuman. This glass went here and only here. That cup had its place and it was an act of **impudent** rebellion to place it anywhere else. At twelve o'clock the table was set. At 12:15 Mrs. Cullinan sat down to dinner (whether her husband had arrived or not). At 12:16 Miss Glory brought out the food.

It took me a week to learn the difference between a salad plate, a bread 5 plate, and a dessert plate.

Mrs. Cullinan kept up the tradition of her wealthy parents. She was from Virginia. Miss Glory, who was a descendant of slaves that had worked for the Cullinans, told me her history. She had married beneath her (according to Miss Glory). Her husband's family hadn't had their money very long and what they had "didn't 'mount to much."

As ugly as she was, I thought privately, she was lucky to get a husband above or beneath her station. But Miss Glory wouldn't let me say a thing against her mistress. She was very patient with me, however, over the housework. She explained the dishware, silverware, and servants' bells. The large round bowl in which soup was served wasn't a soup bowl, it was a tureen. There were goblets, sherbet glasses, ice-cream glasses, wine glasses, green glass coffee cups with matching saucers, and water glasses. I had a glass to drink from, and it sat with Miss Glory's on a separate shelf from the others. Soup spoons, gravy boat, butter knives, salad forks, and carving platter were additions to my vocabulary and in fact almost represented a new language. I was fascinated with the novelty, with the fluttering Mrs. Cullinan and her Alice-in-Wonderland house.

Her husband remains, in my memory, undefined. I lumped him with all the other white men that I had ever seen and tried not to see.

On our way home one evening, Miss Glory told me that Mrs. Cullinan couldn't have children. She said that she was too delicate-boned. It was hard

to imagine bones at all under those layers of fat. Miss Glory went on to say
that the doctor had taken out all her lady organs. I reasoned that a pig's
organs included the lungs, heart, and liver, so if Mrs. Cullinan was walking
around without those essentials, it explained why she drank alcohol out of
unmarked bottles. She was keeping herself embalmed.

When I spoke to Bailey about it, he agreed that I was right, but he also   10
informed me that Mr. Cullinan had two daughters by a colored lady and
that I knew them very well. He added that the girls were the spitting image
of their father. I was unable to remember what he looked like, although I
had just left him a few hours before, but I thought of the Coleman girls.
They were very light-skinned and certainly didn't look very much like their
mother (no one ever mentioned Mr. Coleman).

My pity for Mrs. Cullinan preceded me the next morning like the
Cheshire cat's smile. Those girls, who could have been her daughters,
were beautiful. They didn't have to straighten their hair. Even when they
were caught in the rain, their braids still hung down straight like tamed
snakes. Their mouths were pouty little cupid's bows. Mrs. Cullinan didn't
know what she missed. Or maybe she did. Poor Mrs. Cullinan.

For weeks after, I arrived early, left late, and tried very hard to make up
for her barrenness. If she had had her own children, she wouldn't have had
to ask me to run a thousand errands from her back door to the back door
of her friends. Poor old Mrs. Cullinan.

Then one evening Miss Glory told me to serve the ladies on the porch.
After I set the tray down and turned toward the kitchen, one of the women
asked, "What's your name, girl?" It was the speckled-faced one. Mrs. Cullinan said, "She doesn't talk much. Her name's Margaret."

"Is she dumb?"

"No. As I understand it, she can talk when she wants to but she's usu-   15
ally quiet as a little mouse. Aren't you, Margaret?"

I smiled at her. Poor thing. No organs and couldn't even pronounce
my name correctly.

"She's a sweet little thing, though."

"Well, that may be, but the name's too long. I'd never bother myself.
I'd call her Mary if I was you."

I fumed into the kitchen. That horrible woman would never have the
chance to call me Mary because if I was starving I'd never work for her. I
decided I wouldn't pee on her if her heart was on fire. Giggles drifted in off
the porch and into Miss Glory's pots. I wondered what they could be laughing about.

Whitefolks were so strange. Could they be talking about me? Every-   20
body knew that they stuck together better than the Negroes did. It was
possible that Mrs. Cullinan had friends in St. Louis who heard about a girl

from Stamps being in court and wrote to tell her. Maybe she knew about Mr. Freeman.

My lunch was in my mouth a second time and I went outside and relieved myself on the bed of four-o'clocks. Miss Glory thought I might be coming down with something and told me to go on home, that Momma would give me some herb tea, and she'd explain to her mistress.

I realized how foolish I was being before I reached the pond. Of course Mrs. Cullinan didn't know. Otherwise she wouldn't have given me the two nice dresses that Momma cut down, and she certainly wouldn't have called me a "sweet little thing." My stomach felt fine, and I didn't mention anything to Momma.

That evening I decided to write a poem on being white, fat, old, and without children. It was going to be a tragic ballad. I would have to watch her carefully to capture the essence of her loneliness and pain.

The very next day, she called me by the wrong name. Miss Glory and I were washing up the lunch dishes when Mrs. Cullinan came to the doorway. "Mary?"

Miss Glory asked, "Who?"   25

Mrs. Cullinan, sagging a little, knew and I knew. "I want Mary to go down to Mrs. Randall's and take her some soup. She's not been feeling well for a few days."

Miss Glory's face was a wonder to see. "You mean Margaret, ma'am. Her name's Margaret."

"That's too long. She's Mary from now on. Heat that soup from last night and put it in the china tureen and, Mary, I want you to carry it carefully."

Every person I knew had a hellish horror of being "called out of his name." It was a dangerous practice to call a Negro anything that could be loosely construed as insulting because of the centuries of their having been called niggers, jigs, dinges, blackbirds, crows, boots, and spooks.

Miss Glory had a fleeting second of feeling sorry for me. Than as she 30 handed me the hot tureen she said, "Don't mind, don't pay that no mind. Sticks and stones may break your bones, but words . . . You know, I been working for her for twenty years."

She held the back door open for me. "Twenty years. I wasn't much older than you. My name used to be Hallelujah. That's what Ma named me, but my mistress give me 'Glory,' and it stuck. I likes it better too."

I was in the little path that ran behind the houses when Miss Glory shouted, "It's shorter too."

For a few seconds it was a tossup over whether I would laugh (imagine being named Hallelujah) or cry (imagine letting some white woman rename you for her convenience). My anger saved me from either outburst. I had to quit the job, but the problem was going to be how to do it. Momma wouldn't allow me to quit for just any reason.

"She's a peach. That woman is a real peach." Mrs. Randall's maid was talking as she took the soup from me, and I wondered what her name used to be and what she answered to now.

For a week I looked into Mrs. Cullinan's face as she called me Mary.   35 She ignored my coming late and leaving early. Miss Glory was a little annoyed because I had begun to leave egg yolk on the dishes and wasn't putting much heart in polishing the silver. I hoped that she would complain to our boss, but she didn't.

Then Bailey solved my dilemma. He had me describe the contents of the cupboard and the particular plates she liked best. Her favorite piece was a casserole shaped like a fish and the green glass coffee cups. I kept his instructions in mind, so on the next day when Miss Glory was hanging out clothes and I had again been told to serve the old biddies on the porch, I dropped the empty serving tray. When I heard Mrs. Cullinan scream, "Mary!" I picked up the casserole and two of the green glass cups in readiness. As she rounded the kitchen door I let them fall on the tiled floor.

I could never absolutely describe to Bailey what happened next, because each time I got to the part where she fell on the floor and screwed up her ugly face to cry, we burst out laughing. She actually wobbled around on the floor and picked up shards of the cups and cried, "Oh, Momma. Oh, dear Gawd. It's Momma's china from Virginia. Oh, Momma, I sorry."

Miss Glory came running in from the yard and the women from the porch crowded around. Miss Glory was almost as broken up as her mistress. "You mean to say she broke our Virginia dishes? What we gone do?"

Mrs. Cullinan cried louder, "That clumsy nigger. Clumsy little black nigger."

Old speckled-face leaned down and asked, "Who did it, Viola? Was it   40 Mary? Who did it?"

Everything was happening so fast I can't remember whether her action preceded her words, but I know that Mrs. Cullinan said, "Her name's Margaret, goddamn it, her name's Margaret." And she threw a wedge of the broken plate at me. It could have been the hysteria which put her aim off, but the flying crockery caught Miss Glory right over her ear and she started screaming.

I left the front door wide open so all the neighbors could hear.

Mrs. Cullinan was right about one thing. My name wasn't Mary.

QUESTIONS FOR DISCUSSION

1. Why does Maya Angelou find the white woman's suggestion that she was a debutante "ridiculous and even ludicrous"?

2. How is Mrs. Cullinan's kitchen a "finishing school" for Margaret?

3. What do you think is the relationship between Margaret and Bailey? Explain your views.

4. Do you think Margaret admires Glory or looks down on her?

5. Trace Margaret's changes in attitude toward Mrs. Cullinan.

6. Why does Margaret leave "the front door open so all the neighbors could hear"?

7. Discuss all the details about names in this story which reinforce the main idea about the importance of names.

✍ BRENT STAPLES

Black Men and Public Space

Brent Staples is a journalist, a member of the editorial board of The New York Times, *and author of* Parallel Times: A Memoir *(1991). He holds a Ph.D. in psychology from the University of Chicago.*

KEY VOCABULARY

AD HOC is a Latin term meaning "for a specific purpose, case, or situation."
CONGENIAL means agreeable, sympathetic.
A **CONSTITUTIONAL** is a walk taken to benefit one's health.
ERRANT means straying from the proper course or standards; wrong.
LABYRINTHINE means "like a labyrinth," or maze—an intricate or confusing network of pathways.
SOLACE is comfort in time of sorrow or misfortune.

My first victim was a woman—white, well dressed, probably in her 1 late twenties. I came upon her late one evening on a deserted street in Hyde Park, a relatively affluent neighborhood in an otherwise mean, impoverished section of Chicago. As I swung onto the avenue behind her, there seemed to be a discreet, uninflammatory distance between us. Not so. She cast back a worried glance. To her, the youngish black man—a broad six feet two inches with a beard and billowing hair, both hands shoved into the pockets of a bulky military jacket—seemed menacingly close. After a few more quick glimpses, she picked up her pace and was soon running in earnest. Within seconds she disappeared into a cross street.

That was more than a decade ago. I was twenty-two years old, a graduate student newly arrived at the University of Chicago. It was in the echo of that terrified woman's footfalls that I first began to know the unwieldy inheritance I'd come into—the ability to alter public space in ugly ways. It was clear that she thought herself the quarry of a mugger, a rapist, or worse. Suffering a bout of insomnia, however, I was stalking sleep, not defenseless wayfarers. As a softy who is scarcely able to take a knife to a raw chicken— let alone hold one to a person's throat—I was surprised, embarrassed, and dismayed all at once. Her flight made me feel like an accomplice in tyranny. It also made it clear that I was indistinguishable from the muggers who occasionally seeped into the area from the surrounding ghetto. That first encounter, and those that followed, signified that a vast, unnerving gulf lay between nighttime pedestrians—particularly women—and me. And I soon gathered that being perceived as dangerous is a hazard in itself. I only needed to turn a corner into a dicey situation, or crowd some frightened, armed person in a foyer somewhere, or make an errant move after being pulled over by a policeman. Where fear and weapons meet—and they often do in urban America—there is always the possibility of death.

In that first year, my first away from my hometown, I was to become thoroughly familiar with the language of fear. At dark, shadowy intersections, I could cross in front of a car stopped at a traffic light and elicit the *thunk, thunk, thunk, thunk* of the driver—black, white, male, or female—hammering down the door locks. On less traveled streets after dark, I grew accustomed to but never comfortable with people crossing to the other side of the street rather than pass me. Then there were the standard unpleasantries with policemen, doormen, bouncers, cabdrivers, and others whose business it is to screen out troublesome individuals *before* there is any nastiness.

I moved to New York nearly two years ago and I have remained an avid night walker. In central Manhattan, the near-constant crowd cover minimizes tense one-on-one street encounters. Elsewhere—in SoHo, for example, where sidewalks are narrow and tightly spaced buildings shut out the sky—things can get very taut indeed.

After dark, on the warrenlike streets of Brooklyn where I live, I often 5 see women who fear the worst from me. They seem to have set their faces on neutral, and with their purse straps strung across their chests bandolier-style, they forge ahead as though bracing themselves against being tackled. I understand, of course, that the danger they perceive is not a hallucination. Women are particularly vulnerable to street violence, and young black males are drastically overrepresented among the perpetrators of that violence. Yet these truths are no **solace** against the kind of alienation that comes of being ever the suspect, a fearsome entity with whom pedestrians avoid making eye contact.

It is not altogether clear to me how I reached the ripe old age of twenty-two without being conscious of the lethality nighttime pedestrians attributed to me. Perhaps it was because in Chester, Pennsylvania, the small, angry industrial town where I came of age in the 1960s, I was scarcely noticeable against a backdrop of gang warfare, street knifings, and murders. I grew up one of the good boys, had perhaps a half-dozen fistfights. In retrospect, my shyness of combat has clear sources.

As a boy, I saw countless tough guys locked away; I have since buried several, too. They were babies, really—a teenage cousin, a brother of twenty-two, a childhood friend in his mid-twenties—all gone down in episodes of bravado played out in the streets. I came to doubt the virtues of intimidation early on. I chose, perhaps unconsciously, to remain a shadow—timid, but a survivor.

The fearsomeness mistakenly attributed to me in public places often has a perilous flavor. The most frightening of these confusions occurred in the late 1970s and early 1980s, when I worked as a journalist in Chicago. One day, rushing into the office of a magazine I was writing for with a deadline story in hand, I was mistaken for a burglar. The office manager called security and, with an **ad hoc** posse, pursued me through the **labyrinthine** halls, nearly to my editor's door. I had no way of proving who I was. I could only move briskly toward the company of someone who knew me.

Another time I was on assignment for a local paper and killing time before an interview. I entered a jewelry store on the city's affluent Near North Side. The proprietor excused herself and returned with an enormous red Doberman pinscher straining at the end of a leash. She stood, the dog extended toward me, silent to my questions, her eyes bulging nearly out of her head. I took a cursory look around, nodded, and bade her good night.

Relatively speaking, however, I never fared as badly as another black [10] male journalist. He went to nearby Waukegan, Illinois, a couple of summers ago to work on a story about a murderer who was born there. Mistaking the reporter for the killer, police officers hauled him from his car at gunpoint and but for his press credentials would probably have tried to book him. Such episodes are not uncommon. Black men trade tales like this all the time.

Over the years, I learned to smother the rage I felt at so often being taken for a criminal. Not to do so would surely have led to madness. I now take precautions to make myself less threatening. I move about with care, particularly late in the evening. I give a wide berth to nervous people on subway platforms during the wee hours, particularly when I have exchanged business clothes for jeans. If I happen to be entering a building behind some people who appear skittish, I may walk by, letting them clear the lobby before I return, so as not to seem to be following them. I have been calm and extremely **congenial** on those rare occasions when I've been pulled over by the police.

And on late-evening **constitutionals** I employ what has proved to be an excellent tension-reducing measure: I whistle melodies from Beethoven and Vivaldi and the more popular classical composers. Even steely New Yorkers hunching toward nighttime destinations seem to relax, and occasionally they even join in the tune. Virtually everybody seems to sense that a mugger wouldn't be warbling bright, sunny selections from Vivaldi's *Four*

Seasons. It is my equivalent of the cowbell that hikers wear when they know they are in bear country.

QUESTIONS FOR DISCUSSION

1. Staples' first statement in this essay is "My first victim was a woman." What, exactly, does the author mean here? Explain.

2. What are some examples of "the language of fear"? Does such a language exist, or is it only in the author's mind?

3. What are Staples' feelings about his childhood? Use details from the essay to support your answer.

4. How much of the described women's reactions is based on prejudice? How much is based on common sense?

5. Staples whistles "melodies from Beethoven and Vivaldi" to reduce tension in the pedestrians he encounters. Can you think of any other tension-reducing strategies for late-night encounters with strangers?

The following essay, responding to the first topic from the list included at the end of the chapter, contrasts Brent Staples' way of dealing with racial discrimination with Zora Neale Hurston's way. The paper is organized "point-by-point"—Hurston first, then Staples. But notice how the writer uses comparisons within the paragraphs to connect the two.

✍ STUDENT ESSAY:

Two Ways of Responding to Racism

Two African American writers describe very different ways of dealing with racism. In his essay "Black Men and Public Space," Brent Staples tells how he, a black man, inspires fear in white people when he encounters them in public places, particularly at night. Because he is black, people assume he is a dangerous character. Women cross the street to avoid him, and people in the subway move away. Staples deals with these situations by trying to portray himself as a harmless person. His way of handling racial prejudice is to change his behavior. The second writer, Zora Neale Hurston, shows us another way of dealing with racism. In "How It Feels to Be Colored Me," she describes how she faces racism directly through the strength of her own personality. Where Staples changes his behavior to avoid racial tension, Hurston doesn't change herself for anyone.

Whenever she encounters racial prejudice, Hurston remains self-assured. She accepts racism as a fact but tries her best to overcome it. Unlike Staples, who has learned to "smother" his rage, Hurston feels no anger. She writes, "Sometimes I feel discriminated against, but it does not make me angry. It merely astonishes me. How *can* any deny themselves the pleasure of my company! It's beyond me." Hurston obviously sees herself as a strong, confident woman. She believes that "the world is to the strong regardless of a little pigmentation more or less." Furthermore, Hurston feels that in some cases her race gives her an advantage. She describes a visit with a white friend to a club called The New World Cabaret. After hearing an overwhelming, rambunctious performance by a jazz orchestra, she feels excited and wild inside: "I dance wildly inside myself; I yell within, I whoop." Her white friend, on the other hand, remained almost motionless. The emotion of the music has not touched him. Hurston writes, "He is so pale with his whiteness then and I am *so* colored."

While Hurston seems to soar above discrimination, Staples is depressed and dismayed by it. He chooses to change himself to adapt to the hostile white society. He feels hopeless to overcome discrimination. He would rather "choose to remain a shadow—timid, but a survivor." Unlike Hurston's aggressive courage in facing or ignoring racial conflicts, he decides to avoid them by changing his behavior. Once he realizes that he has "the ability to alter public space in ugly ways," he feels surprised and angry. Then he tries to "smother the rage" and yield to the whites "with care" in order to alleviate tension.

There are probably many reasons for these differences between the two writers. For one thing, Staples is a man; Hurston is a woman. Staples recognizes that "Women are particularly vulnerable to street violence, and young black males are drastically overrepresented among the perpetrators of that violence." Simply because he is a black male, Staples is seen as more dangerous, particularly in large, crime-filled cities like New York and Chicago. Moreover, Hurston was raised in a small Florida town where people were relatively friendly toward each other. Staples, who is from Chester, Pennsylvania, grew up "against a backdrop of gang warfare, street knifings, and murders." He learned to keep a low profile and stay out of fights. He says that his "shyness of combat has clear sources." Hurston describes herself as an outgoing, joyful child. She sat on the gatepost of her porch, waving and singing to people passing by. She felt that she belonged in her town. Staples never gives the feeling that he belonged anywhere. Hurston seems to belong wherever she goes. Staples is always a stranger.

TOPICS FOR WRITING

1. Compare and contrast the writers' attitudes in two of the essays in this chapter. In your paper show how the writers are similar and how they are different in the way they respond to living as African Americans in a white society.

2. Using Brent Staples' essay as a guide, describe an encounter you have had with racial prejudice. Tell what happened and how you responded to it.

3. Choose the essay from this chapter that you think offers the best way of dealing with prejudice or oppression. Explain why you think the essay you have chosen presents the best solution.

4. Explain in detail what you think Maya Angelou means when she says "a white woman's kitchen was my finishing school." (The term "finishing school" is an interesting one for her to use here. It traditionally refers to high-class private schools where rich young ladies are sent to give them the polish that is expected of them.)

5. Discuss what you think James Baldwin means when he says of whites, "It is the innocence which constitutes the crime."

6. In the wake of the Los Angeles riots, there was much discussion of violent versus non-violent protest. Martin Luther King, Jr.'s idea of non-violent resistance has been a strong theme in the civil rights movement since the 1960s, but there is also the counter-argument that only violence will bring about any real changes in society. What do you think about this issue? Given King's arguments, do you think there is any justification for what happened in Los Angeles?

7. Why do you think James Baldwin, in "My Dungeon Shook," says to his nephew, "You must accept them [whites] and accept them with love"? Explain the reasoning that leads Baldwin to give this advice.

8. Explain precisely what Zora Neale Hurston means when she says, "I became colored." Discuss also what caused her to come to this realization.

9. In "Black Men and Public Space," Brent Staples says that early in life he "chose, perhaps unconsciously, to remain a shadow—timid, but a survivor." Do you think this is an accurate characterization of the way in which Staples deals with problems that arise from his being black? Or could you suggest a better term than "timid" to describe his behavior?

10. Using the readings in the chapter, write a paper that classifies the ways in which the writers have dealt with problems that arise from living in

a white society. You will need to create and define several categories based on the writers' approaches to the problems.

11. Using Martin Luther King, Jr.'s essay as a model, write an essay of your own discussing three ways of dealing with a contemporary social issue. Like King, you might want to use your essay to argue that one of the ways is better than the others.

12. In what ways are the young Zora Neale Hurston and Margaret, the central character of Angelou's "My Name Is Margaret," similar and in what ways are they different?

13. Using James Baldwin's "My Dungeon Shook" as a model, write a letter to one of your young relatives or friends attempting to persuade him or her to grow and mature in a certain direction.

11 Self and Society

> "Few things are more calculated to rob the individual of his defenses than the idea that his interests and those of society can be wholly compatible. The good society is the one in which they are most compatible, but they never can be completely so, and one who lets The Organization be the judge ultimately sacrifices himself."
>
> –WILLIAM H. WHYTE

In his essay "Self-Reliance," the American writer and philosopher Ralph Waldo Emerson proclaimed, "Society everywhere is in conspiracy against the manhood of every one of its members. . . . Whoso would be a man must be a nonconformist."

Emerson's words go to the heart of the American cult of individualism: The individual and society are adversaries, opponents in the battle for the self.

However, human beings seem to be social creatures. Aside from the occasional hermit hunched in his cave gnawing on roots and berries, we prefer the company of others. We desire a sense of community, of belonging to something larger than ourselves.

It is not easy for these two impulses to co-exist in harmony. Communities apply pressure on their members to adopt certain standards of thought, speech, dress, behavior. Who hasn't felt, at some time or another, the pressure to fall in line, to do what everyone else is doing, whether it's wearing the right clothes, driving the right car, or holding the right opinions? At the same time, we may want to be recognized as different, unique individuals, not little clones stamped out of a mold.

As we are social beings, our identities are to some extent (some would say *entirely*) formed by the communities in which we live. In large part we learn from those around us how to behave, how to think, and what to value. Though the law may protect individual liberties, society has other ways of influencing us. Most people want to be accepted by some kind of a group, and acceptance usually hinges on a certain degree of conformity. These needs for community and acceptance often run counter to the full expression of individualism. In addition to this conflict, particularly in an age dominated by huge bureaucracies and corporations, by mass production and mass communications, the rugged individual seems to be giving way to the company man, the face in the crowd, the pale bureaucrat who seems little more than a soft cog in a giant machine. Many observers in modern times have expressed the fear that the age of mass everything is also producing mass human beings—faceless, molded by a few trend setters and image makers.

The readings in this chapter reflect on several issues having to do with the relationship between the individual and society. These issues revolve around a number of related themes: self-reliance, community, conformity, equality, competition, and cooperation. As you read, look for these themes, and mark and annotate the text as you find them.

.⸎ᵥ Henry Steele Commager

The Standardized American

Henry Steele Commager, one of America's leading historians, has been a professor of American history at New York University, Columbia University, and Amherst University. He has also served as a visiting professor at numerous universities in the United States and abroad. Commager has written, co-authored, and edited dozens of books. Best known are The Growth of the American Republic *(1931) and* The American Mind *(1950), the book from which the following selection was taken.*

KEY VOCABULARY

CYNICISM was originally an ancient Greek philosophical school founded by Anthisthenes of Athens. Its members believed that virtue is the only good and self-control is the only means of achieving virtue. More recently, cynicism is the belief that all people are motivated by selfishness.

A **GENEALOGY** is a record of the descent of a family or an individual from an ancestor; a family tree.

Although still persuaded that his was the best of all countries, the American of the mid-twentieth century was by no means so sure that his was the best of all times, and after he entered the atomic age he could not rid himself of the fear that his world might end not with a whimper but with a bang. His optimism, which persisted, was instinctive rather than rationalized, and he was no longer prepared to insist that the good fortune which he enjoyed, in a war-stricken world, was the reward of virtue rather than of mere geographical isolation. He knew that if there was indeed any such thing as progress it would continue to be illustrated by America, but he was less confident of the validity of the concept than at any previous time in his history.

As he was less zealous for the future, he became more concerned with the past: small families and the cultivation of **genealogy** seemed to go together. He seemed more conscious of his own history than at any time since the Civil War and, after a brief interval of **cynicism** and disillusionment in the decade of the twenties, found more satisfaction in its contemplation. In everything but manners and morals he was more inclined to let the past set his standards than had been customary. While it would be an exaggeration to say that he regarded America as a finished product, it was demonstrable that he did not welcome change with his earlier enthusiasm or regard the future as a romantic adventure.

The tendency to trust the past rather than the future and the familiar rather than the original reflected an instinct for conformity that revealed itself in countless ways. Businessmen were expected to conform in matters of dress as well as in matters of thought, and the business suit became almost a uniform, while women, who yearned to look different, came to seem turned out almost by machine process, each with the same make-up, the same accessories, and the same patter. A thousand books on etiquette, a thousand courses in manners and speech and parlor acquirements, proclaimed the universal fear of being different. Slang, which represented an effort to get away from conventional language, became as conventional as the speech which Victorian novelists ascribed to their characters. As society put a premium on conformity, individualism declined and eccentricity all but disappeared. Standardization, induced by the press, the moving pictures, the radio, schools, business, urban life, and a hundred other agencies and intangibles, permeated American life. From Maine to Florida, from Delaware to California, almost all country clubs were alike, and with the spread of the chain store, the filling station, motion-picture palaces, and beauty parlors, towns and cities all over the country came to take on a standardized appearance. With advertisements dictating styles and manners, conversation and amusements, the habits of eating and drinking, the conventions of friendship and of business, and the techniques of love and marriage, nature conformed to commercial art.

QUESTIONS FOR DISCUSSION

1. Why does Commager say that American optimism at mid-century was instinctive rather than rationalized?

2. Do you agree that, in general, as people are less confident about the future, they become more concerned with the past?

3. Paraphrase the main idea of the last paragraph.

✍ W. H. AUDEN

The Unknown Citizen

W. H. Auden, English poet and dramatist, was one of a British group of writers who, during the 1930s, believed that socialism might solve the economic and political problems of the time. Later, during World War II, Auden became more interested in Christianity than socialism, particularly in the saving power of love. The title of his long poem The Age of Anxiety *(1947) has stuck as a descriptive label for the twenthieth century.*

KEY VOCABULARY

A **EUGENIST** is an advocate of, or specialist in, improving the human race through genetic control.

A **SCAB,** here, is a worker who goes to work in spite of a strike by a labor union.

To JS/07/M/378
This Marble Monument Is Erected by the State

He was found by the Bureau of Statistics to be   1
One against whom there was no official complaint,
And all the reports on his conduct agree
That, in the modern sense of an old-fashioned word, he was a saint,
For in everything he did he served the Greater Community.   5
Except for the War till the day he retired
He worked in a factory and never got fired,
But satisfied his employers, Fudge Motors Inc.
Yet he wasn't a **scab** or odd in his views,
For his Union reports that he paid his dues,   10
(Our report on his Union shows it was sound)
And our Social Psychology workers found
That he was popular with his mates and liked a drink.
The Press are convinced that he bought a paper every day
And that his reactions to advertisements were normal in every way.   15
Policies taken out in his name prove that he was fully insured,
And his Health-card shows he was once in hospital but left it cured.
Both Producers Research and High-Grade Living declare
He was fully sensible to the advantages of the Installment Plan

And had everything necessary to the Modern Man,   20
A gramophone, a radio, a car and a frigidaire.
Our researchers into Public Opinion are content
That he held the proper opinions for the time of year;
When there was peace, he was for peace; when there was war, he went.
He was married and added five children to the population,   25
Which our **Eugenist** says was the right number for a parent of his
    generation,
And our teachers report that he never interfered with their education.
Was he free? Was he happy? The question is absurd:
Had anything been wrong, we should certainly have heard.

QUESTIONS FOR DISCUSSION

1. What does "serving the Greater Community" mean in this poem?
2. In what ways do you think the Unknown Citizen's reactions to advertisements were "normal"? What does "normal" mean?
3. How do you think this man behaved in school?
4. Does the author of the poem think the Unknown Citizen was free and
   happy? What words and images in the poem give a clue about the
   author's attitude?
5. In the last line, who is "we"?
6. Why is the poem titled "The Unknown Citizen"?

ℒ ELLEN GOODMAN

The Company Man

*Ellen Goodman was born in Massachusetts in 1941 and graduated from
Radcliff College. She writes a syndicated column, "At Large," for the
Boston Globe. Goodman's books include four collections of essays:* Close
to Home *(1979),* At Large *(1981),* Keeping in Touch *(1985), and*
Value Judgments *(1993). She has also published a collection of interviews,*
Turning Points *(1979).*

KEY VOCABULARY

THROMBOSIS is the formation of a blood clot which obstructs a blood vessel
or heart cavity.

A **TYPE A** personality is one composed of a cluster of traits that include competitiveness, aggressiveness, hostility, and impatience.

He worked himself to death, finally and precisely, at 3:00 A.M. Sunday   1
morning.

The obituary didn't say that, of course. It said that he died of a coronary
thrombosis—I think that was it—but everyone among his friends and
acquaintances knew it instantly. He was a perfect **Type A,** a workaholic, a
classic, they said to each other and shook their heads—and thought for five
or ten minutes about the way they lived.

This man who worked himself to death finally and precisely at 3:00
A.M. Sunday morning—on his day off—was fifty-one years old and a vice-
president. He was, however, one of six vice-presidents, and one of three
who might conceivably—if the president died or retired soon enough—
have moved to the top spot. Phil knew that.

He worked six days a week, five of them until eight or nine at night,
during a time when his own company had begun the four-day week for
everyone but the executives. He worked like the Important People. He had
no outside "extracurricular interests," unless, of course, you think about a
monthly golf game that way. To Phil, it was work. He always ate egg salad
sandwiches at his desk. He was, of course, overweight, by 20 or 25 pounds.
He thought it was okay, though, because he didn't smoke.

On Saturdays, Phil wore a sports jacket to the office instead of a suit,   5
because it was the weekend.

He had a lot of people working for him, maybe sixty, and most of them liked him most of the time. Three of them will be seriously considered for his job. The obituary didn't mention that.

But it did list his "survivors" quite accurately. He is survived by his wife, Helen, forty-eight years old, a good woman of no particular marketable skills, who worked in an office before marrying and mothering. She had, according to her daughter, given up trying to compete with his work years ago, when the children were small. A company friend said, "I know how much you will miss him." And she answered, "I already have."

"Missing him all these years," she must have given up part of herself which had cared too much for the man. She would be "well taken care of."

His "dearly beloved" eldest of the "dearly beloved" children is a hard-working executive in a manufacturing firm down South. In the day and a half before the funeral, he went around the neighborhood researching his father, asking the neighbors what he was like. They were embarrassed.

His second child is a girl, who is twenty-four and newly married. She 10 lives near her mother and they are close, but whenever she was alone with her father, in a car driving somewhere, they had nothing to say to each other.

The youngest is twenty, a boy, a high-school graduate who has spent the last couple of years, like a lot of his friends, doing enough odd jobs to stay in grass and food. He was the one who tried to grab at his father, and tried to mean enough to him to keep the man at home. He was his father's favorite. Over the last two years, Phil stayed up nights worrying about the boy.

The boy once said, "My father and I only board here."

At the funeral, the sixty-year-old company president told the forty-eight-year-old widow that the fifty-one-year-old deceased had meant much to the company and would be missed and would be hard to replace. The widow didn't look him in the eye. She was afraid he would read her bitterness and, after all, she would need him to straighten out the finances—the stock options and all that.

Phil was overweight and nervous and worked too hard. If he wasn't at the office, he was worried about it. Phil was a Type A, a heart-attack natural. You could have picked him out in a minute from a lineup.

So when he finally worked himself to death, at precisely 3:00 A.M. 15 Sunday morning, no one was really surprised.

By 5:00 P.M. the afternoon of the funeral, the company president had begun, discreetly of course, with care and taste, to make inquiries about his replacement. One of three men. He asked around: "Who's been working the hardest?"

QUESTIONS FOR DISCUSSION

1. Did the company man work himself to death willingly? How so?
2. Briefly summarize the company man's relationship with his family.
3. Does the article present the company in a favorable or unfavorable light? Explain.
4. What common characteristics can you find between the company man and the unknown citizen? How about the company man and the standardized American? Use details from the readings to support your answer.

ℐ❥ ANNIE DILLARD

From *An American Childhood*

Annie Dillard was born in 1945 in Pittsburgh, Pennsylvania, and received her B.A. and M.A. degrees from Hollins College. Her first book, Pilgrim at Tinker Creek *(1974), won her the Pulitzer Prize for nonfiction. She has also written a collection of poems,* Tickets for a Prayer Wheel, *and several other nonfiction books:* Teaching a Stone to Talk *(1882),* An American Childhood *(1987), and* A Writing Life *(1989). Annie Dillard now lives in Washington State.*

In the following excerpt from An American Childhood, *Dillard writes about her mother, a woman who insisted that her children become independent.*

KEY VOCABULARY

To **CAPITALIZE,** in business, means to supply the capital—money—needed for an enterprise.

COWING means intimidating, or frightening with threats.

The **MCCARTHY HEARINGS** were Congressional hearings held in the early 1950s by then–Chairman of the Senate Permanent Investigating Subcommittee Joseph McCarthy of Wisconsin. McCarthy investigated communist subversion in the U.S. government and army. McCarthy was condemned by the Senate for making unfounded accusations and using questionable investigative methods.

OSTRACISM is banishment from society.

SAMSON, in the Bible, was an Israelite known for his great strength. He was betrayed by his Philistine mistress, Delilah, who discovered that his great strength lay in his hair. She cut off his hair in his sleep, so he was easily captured by the Philistines, who were at that time an enemy of Israel.

TOOLING UP means building the equipment needed to produce a product.

TORPID means dull or sluggish, lacking in vitality.

Mother's energy and intelligence suited her for a greater role in a larger   1
arena—mayor of New York, say—than the one she had. She followed American politics closely; she had been known to vote for Democrats. She saw how things should be run, but she had nothing to run but our household. Even there, small minds bugged her; she was smarter than the people who designed the things she had to use all day for the length of her life.

"Look," she said. "Whoever designed this corkscrew never used one.

Why would anyone sell it without trying it out?" So she invented a better one. She showed me a drawing of it. The spirit of American enterprise never faded in Mother. If **capitalizing** and **tooling up** had been as interesting as theorizing and thinking up, she would have fired up a new factory every week, and chaired several hundred corporations.

"It grieves me," she would say, "it grieves my heart," that the company that made one superior product packaged it poorly, or took the wrong tack in its advertising. She knew, as she held the thing mournfully in her two hands, that she'd never find another. She was right. We children wholly sympathized, and so did Father; what could she do, what could anyone do, about it? She was **Samson** in chains. She paced.

She didn't like the taste of stamps so she didn't lick stamps; she licked the corner of the envelope instead. She glued sandpaper to the sides of kitchen drawers, and under kitchen cabinets, so she always had a handy place to strike a match. She designed, and hounded workmen to build against all norms, doubly wide kitchen counters and elevated bathroom sinks. To splint a finger, she stuck it in a lightweight cigar tube. Conversely, to protect a pack of cigarettes, she carried it in a Band-Aid box. She drew plans for an over-the-finger toothbrush for babies, an oven rack that slid up and down, and—the family favorite—Lendalarm. Lendalarm was a beeper you attached to books (or tools) you loaned friends. After ten days, the beeper sounded. Only the rightful owner could silence it.

She repeatedly reminded us of P. T. Barnum's dictum: You could sell   5 anything to anybody if you marketed it right. The adman who thought of making Americans believe they needed underarm deodorant was a visionary. So, too, was the hero who made a success of a new product, Ivory soap. The executives were horrified, Mother told me, that a cake of this stuff floated. Soap wasn't supposed to float. Anyone would be able to tell it was mostly whipped-up air. Then some inspired adman made a leap: Advertise that it floats. Flaunt it. The rest is history.

She respected the rare few who broke through to new ways. "Look," she'd say, "here's an intelligent apron." She called upon us to admire intelligent control knobs and intelligent pan handles, intelligent andirons and picture frames and knife sharpeners. She questioned everything, every pair of scissors, every knitting needle, gardening glove, tape dispenser. Hers was a restless mental vigor that just about ignited the dumb household objects with its force.

Torpid conformity was a kind of sin; it was stupidity itself, the mighty stream against which Mother would never cease to struggle. If you held no minority opinions, or if you failed to risk total **ostracism** for them daily, the world would be a better place without you.

Always I heard Mother's emotional voice asking Amy and me the same few questions: "Is that your own idea? Or somebody else's?" "*Giant* is a good movie," I pronounced to the family at dinner. "Oh, really?" Mother warmed to these occasions. She all but rolled up her sleeves. She knew I hadn't seen it. "Is that your considered opinion?"

She herself held many unpopular, even fantastic, positions. She was scathingly sarcastic about the **McCarthy hearings** while they took place, right on our living-room television; she frantically opposed Father's wait-and-see calm. "We don't know enough about it," he said. "I do," she said. "I know all I need to know."

She asserted, against all opposition, that people who lived in trailer 10 parks were not bad but simply poor, and had as much right to settle on beautiful land, such as rural Ligonier, Pennsylvania, as did the oldest of families in the finest of hidden houses. Therefore, the people who owned trailer parks, and sought zoning changes to permit trailer parks, needed our help. Her profound belief that the country-club pool sweeper was a person, and that the department-store saleslady, the bus driver, telephone operator, and house-painter were people, and even in groups the steelworkers who carried pickets and the Christmas shoppers who clogged intersections were people—this was a conviction common enough in democratic Pittsburgh, but not altogether common among our friends' parents, or even, perhaps, among our parents' friends.

Opposition emboldened Mother, and she would take on anybody on any issue—the chairman of the board, at a cocktail party, on the current strike; she would fly at him in a flurry of passion, as a songbird selflessly attacks a big hawk.

"Eisenhower's going to win," I announced after school. She lowered her magazine and looked me in the eyes: "How do you know?" I was doomed. It was fatal to say, "Everyone says so." We all knew well what happened. "Do you consult this Everyone before you make your decisions? What if Everyone decided to round up all the Jews?" Mother knew there was no danger of **cowing** me. She simply tried to keep us all awake. And in fact it was always clear to Amy and me, and to Molly when she grew old enough to listen, that if our classmates came to cruelty, just as much as if the neighborhood or the nation came to madness, we were expected to take, and would be each separately capable of taking, a stand.

QUESTIONS FOR DISCUSSION

1. Why does Dillard call her mother "Samson in chains"?
2. What is her mother's attitude toward intelligence? Toward conformity? Give examples from the text.

3. What is her mother's relationship with members of her own social class?

4. How do Dillard's mother's qualities compare with what people think of as the traditional mother?

5. Was her mother a good role model for her daughters? What kind of expectations for her daughters did she have? What kind of women do you think the girls probably grew up to be?

6. What characteristics of "individualism" does Dillard's mother possess?

✍ ELENA ASTURIAS

Growing Up in the U.S.:
A First Generation Look

Elena Asturias, born in San Francisco in 1963, grew up in the United States and in Guatemala. She has law degrees from McGeorge Law School of the University of the Pacific and from Georgetown University. Asturias is vice-president of the Latino Lawyers of San Francisco, an organization concerned with the way laws and public policy affect the Latin American community; she is currently an attorney practicing business law in San Francisco.

KEY VOCABULARY

An **ADAGE** is a short saying, a proverb or maxim.

FEASIBLE denotes something that is possible to do.

MONOLINGUAL means speaking only one language.

To **REITERATE** means to repeat, to say over again.

UTILITARIAN means useful, practical.

When I was three, the name I learned to print was Elena María del 1
Pilar Asturias Texidor. It would be shortened in school to Elena Asturias
and, on occasion, altered by **monolingual** nuns to Helen.

Growing up in the United States as a first generation Hispana has had
its advantages and disadvantages. Assimilating an awareness of two cultures
adds breadth to one's perspective. Among the most **utilitarian** benefits for
society at large is the ability to share different traditions, cultures, and perspectives with others. The constant arrival of new immigrants nourishes this
diversity, recharging society and inspiring those already here.

However, I do not consider myself a typical Hispana, but rather just
one example of a Latin American raised in the U.S. My parents are both
educators. My father, a retired university professor, is from Quezaltenango,
Guatemala, and my mother, a community college administrator, was born
in Fajardo, Puerto Rico. Although both cultures share common themes,
there are tremendous differences in their respective traditions and attitudes.
In our family, we often joked that theirs was an "inter-racial marriage."

Summers were spent in Guatemala, and we occasionally vacationed on
La Perla del Caribe, renting a home on the beach. The time spent visiting

our parents' homelands bound us to their cultures and nurtured an appreciation for the roots they had sown in us.

My sister and I were educated in the American school system and the Latin American social system. We learned to behave properly at home, which included sitting and conversing with adults rather than entrenching ourselves in a world all our own. Our parents instilled in us the importance of caring for elderly and ill family members with constancy and patience. The traditional strength of the Latin family helped us as we developed a bicultural existence in the United States.

Preserving the language of their homelands was also of great importance to my parents. We spoke only Spanish at home, though both my parents speak flawless English. Help with school work was the only exception to this rule; it was generously given in English. We read *Don Quixote* as well as *Cinderella*. Our childrens' songs were those of CriCri, not the U.S. equivalent. Raised to respect our families, along with a healthy dose of fear lest we bring shame upon those we loved, we were motivated to study, learn, and serve our community.

Our parents' firm commitment to community service is perhaps the most unique heirloom handed down to us as children. They took us on peace marches in the 60s and 70s even before we were able to walk. I vividly recall the view, perched atop my father's shoulders, of a massive swell of humanity marching for peace.

My parents also taught us about our family history: how our grandfather was jailed and had to flee Guatemala because of his involvement in land reform; how he received the Orden del Quetzal, the highest medal given to a civilian, for his work in vaccinating an entire region of Guatemala. These and other similar stories gave us a special sense of pride in our heritage and obligation to our community.

As teenagers, my mother enlisted our help in the political campaigns she supported. We distributed leaflets, made phone calls, canvassed to get the vote out and were accustomed to attending and helping organize fundraisers and other political events. This involvement in the U.S. political process helped us see that individuals can make a difference and that opportunities to do so are there for achievement.

What we learned and lived at home set us up for very real confrontations with the world outside our four walls. The early curfews, the chaperons, the conservative manner we dressed—all contributed to the feeling that we were different. Our parents explained that these differences would add something extra to our characters. We were special, not different, and therefore more was expected of us. What made these "extra" requirements **feasible** was our parents' ability to balance our strict upbringing with the love and attention we needed.

Although some advantages of growing up in the U.S. are harder to measure, I gained a type of personal strength, self-reliance and independence I may not have found if I'd been raised in the more sheltered home life of the traditional Latin American household. However, there are trade-offs—the security and stability, the sense of belonging, of knowing one's roots fostered in a strong Latin home are often sacrificed to the risktaking needed to maximize one's potential in the U.S.

The more I visited my Latin American cousins and relatives, the more I began to notice a growing distance in our attitudes over politics, social issues, and familial questions. Our educations were shaping us into citizens of our respective countries with correspondent attitudes and concerns. Although we retained similar cultural values and traditions, the older we got the less we agreed on the international scale.

We celebrated Christmas on December 24th as well as the Three Kings Day, preparing for the arrival of the giftbearers with cereal for the camels and wine for the weary travelers. Mornings of January 6th meant awakening early and rushing downstairs to check shoes left by the door for our unwrapped gifts and the remains of the goodies we'd left. Special occasions were celebrated with tamales, *paches* (Guatemala) and *pasteles* (Puerto Rico) and *Las Mañanitas* was recited on our birthdays. The outward manifestations of Latin American culture were not only for our enjoyment, but for the enjoyment of our non-Latin friends who were always included in these celebrations.

Perhaps the most poignant loss on a personal level is the inability to express myself as well in Spanish as in English. It's difficult when you're educated in one language to theorize in another or to write on topics as fluidly. My hope lies in the **adage** "practice makes perfect!"

If our upbringing taught us anything it is that as Hispanas transplanted 15 as such in the U.S., we have a responsibility to educate society in the depth and beauty of our Latin American heritage and the immense contribution we can make to this country. By helping new arrivals and those less fortunate, we ensure the survival of our identity and the reinforcement of our values. To **reiterate** an appropriate verse of Jose Martí, recently quoted in Los Angeles at the National Network of Hispanic Women's Round-table, " . . . *No hay caminos, los caminos se forman al hacer—no para nosotros pero para los por venir*" ("There are no established roads; roads are built by doing, not for ourselves, but for those to come").

QUESTIONS FOR DISCUSSION

1. In Asturias' view, how is the Latin American sense of community different from the North American one?

2. In what ways did Elena Asturias' education distance her from her Latin American relatives? Give examples.

3. Does the author consider herself and her upbringing typical of Latinos? Explain.

4. Which aspects of her upbringing does Asturias value the most? Explain.

5. For what purpose does Asturias compare Latin and U.S. societies? What point is she trying to make?

✐ LYDIA MINATOYA

From *Talking to High Monks in the Snow*

Lydia Minatoya was born in Albany, New York. She received her Ph.D. from the University of Maryland in 1981, and began teaching counseling psychology. From 1983 to 1985 she taught and travelled in Asia. In 1991 she received a PEN/Jerard Fund Award for Talking to High Monks in the Snow: An Asian American Odyssey. *The following selection is from this book, her first. Minatoya now lives in Seattle, Washington, and works as a community college counselor and teacher.*

KEY VOCABULARY

ALLITERATION is a poetic term which refers to two or more words that have the same beginning sound: for example, "Peter Piper picked a peck of pickled peppers."

ASSONANTAL RHYME is a kind of rhyme in which the vowel sounds of words rhyme but the consonants don't; for example, *brave* and *vain*.

A **FOIL** is a person who, by contrast, highlights the distinctive characteristics of another person.

RELOCATION, here, refers to the imprisonment of Japanese Americans in camps during World War II.

SOPORIFIC refers to something that makes one sleepy.

STOIC, here, means the quality of seeming indifference to either joy, grief, pleasure, or pain.

A **SYLPH** was originally a soulless being thought to inhabit the air. The word now denotes a slim, graceful woman.

Perhaps it begins with my naming. During her pregnancy, my mother 1 was reading Dr. Spock. "Children need to belong," he cautioned. "An unusual name can make them the subject of ridicule." My father frowned when he heard this. He stole a worried glance at my sister. Burdened by her Japanese name, Misa played unsuspectingly on the kitchen floor.

The Japanese know full well the dangers of conspicuousness. "The nail that sticks out gets pounded down," cautions an old maxim. In America, **Relocation** was all the proof they needed.

And so it was, with great earnestness, my parents searched for a conventional name. They wanted me to have the full true promise of America.

"I will ask my colleague Froilan," said my father. "He is the smartest man I know."

"And he has poetic soul," said my mother, who cared about such things.

In due course, Father consulted Froilan. He gave Froilan his conditions for suitability.

"First, if possible, the full name should be alliterative," said my father. "Like Misa Minatoya." He closed his eyes and sang my sister's name. "Second, if not an **alliteration,** at least the name should have **assonantal rhyme.**"

Call it adaptive behavior. Coming from a land swept by savage typhoons, ravaged by earthquakes and volcanoes, the Japanese have evolved a view of the world: a cooperative, **stoic,** almost magical way of thinking. Get along, work hard, and never quite see the things that can bring you pain. Against the tyranny of nature, of feudal lords, of wartime hysteria, the charm works equally well.

And so my parents gave me an American name and hoped that I could pass. They nourished me with the American dream: Opportunity, Will, Transformation.

When I was four and my sister was eight, Misa regularly used me as a comic **foil.** She would bring her playmates home from school and query me as I sat amidst the milk bottles on the front steps.

"What do you want to be when you grow up?" she would say. She would nudge her audience into attentiveness.

"A mother kitty cat!" I would enthuse. Our cat had just delivered her first litter of kittens and I was enchanted by the rasping tongue and soft meowings of motherhood.

"And what makes you think you can become a cat?" Misa would prompt, gesturing to her howling friends—wait for this; it gets better yet.

"This is America," I stoutly would declare. "I can grow up to be anything that I want!"

My faith was unshakable. I believed. Opportunity. Will. Transformation.

When we lived in Albany, I always was the teachers' pet. "So tiny, so precocious, so prettily dressed!" They thought I was a living doll and this was fine with me.

My father knew that the effusive praise would die. He had been through this with my sister. After five years of being a perfect darling, Misa had reached the age where students were tracked by ability. Then, the anger started. Misa had tested into the advanced track. It was impossible, the community declared. Misa was forbidden entry into advanced classes as long as there were white children being placed below her. In her defense, before an angry rabble, my father made a presentation to the Board of Education.

But I was too young to know of this. I knew only that my teachers praised and petted me. They took me to other classes as an example. "Watch now, as Lydia demonstrates attentive behavior," they would croon as I was led to an empty desk at the head of the class. I had a routine. I would sit carefully, spreading my petticoated skirt neatly beneath me. I would pull my chair close to the desk, crossing my swinging legs at my snowy white anklets. I would fold my hands carefully on the desk before me and stare pensively at the blackboard.

This routine won me few friends. The sixth-grade boys threw rocks at me. They danced around me in a tight circle, pulling at the corners of their eyes. "Ching Chong Chinaman," they chanted. But teachers loved me. When I was in first grade, a third-grade teacher went weeping to the principal. She begged to have me skipped. She was leaving to get married and wanted her turn with the dolly.

When we moved, the greatest shock was the knowledge that I had lost 20 my charm. From the first, my teacher failed to notice me. But to me, it did not matter. I was in love. I watched her moods, her needs, her small vanities. I was determined to ingratiate.

Miss Hempstead was a shimmering vision with a small upturned nose and eyes that were kewpie-doll blue. Slender as a **sylph**, she tripped around the classroom, all saucy in her high-heeled shoes. Whenever I looked at Miss Hempstead, I pitied the Albany teachers whom, formerly, I had adored. Poor old Miss Rosenberg. With a shiver of distaste, I recalled her loose fleshy arms, her mottled hands, the scent of lavender as she crushed me to her heavy breasts.

Miss Hempstead had a pet of her own. Her name was Linda Sherlock. I watched Linda closely and plotted Miss Hempstead's courtship. The key was the piano. Miss Hempstead played the piano. She fancied herself a musical star. She sang songs from Broadway revues and shaped her students' reactions. "Getting to know you," she would sing. We would smile at her in a staged manner and position ourselves obediently at her feet.

Miss Hempstead was famous for her ability to soothe. Each day at rest time, she played the piano and sang **soporific** songs. Linda Sherlock was the only child who succumbed. Routinely, Linda's head would bend and nod until she crumpled gracefully onto her folded arms. A tousled strand of blond hair would fall across her forehead. Miss Hempstead would end her song, would gently lower the keyboard cover. She would turn toward the restive eyes of the class. "Isn't she sweetness itself!" Miss Hempstead would declare. It made me want to vomit.

I was growing weary. My studiousness, my attentiveness, my fastidious grooming and pert poise: all were failing me. I changed my tactics. I became a problem. Miss Hempstead sent me home with nasty notes in sealed envelopes: Lydia is a slow child, a noisy child, her presence is disruptive. My mother looked at me with surprise, "*Nani desu ka?* Are you having problems with your teacher?" But I was tenacious. I pushed harder and harder, firmly caught in the obsessive need of the scorned.

One day I snapped. As Miss Hempstead began to sing her wretched lullabies, my head dropped to the desk with a powerful CRACK! It lolled there, briefly, then rolled toward the edge with a momentum that sent my entire body catapulting to the floor. Miss Hempstead's spine stretched slightly, like a cat that senses danger. Otherwise, she paid no heed. The linoleum floor was smooth and cool. It emitted a faint pleasant odor: a mixture of chalk dust and wax.

I began to snore heavily. The class sat electrified. There would be no drowsing today. The music went on and on. Finally, one boy could not stand it. "Miss Hempstead," he probed plaintively, "Lydia has fallen asleep on the floor!" Miss Hempstead did not turn. Her playing grew slightly strident but she did not falter.

I lay on the floor through rest time. I lay on the floor through math drill. I lay on the floor while my classmates scraped around me, pushing their sturdy little wooden desks into the configuration for reading circle. It was not until penmanship practice that I finally stretched and stirred. I rose like Sleeping Beauty and slipped back to my seat. I smiled enigmatically. A spell had been broken. I never again had a crush on a teacher.

QUESTIONS FOR DISCUSSION

1. How does Minatoya's naming foretell her childhood transformation?
2. List some of the differences between older generation Japanese Americans and their children, as implied in this selection.
3. What does the author mean when she says, "Misa regularly used me as a comic foil"?
4. What qualities make Lydia the teacher's pet in Albany?
5. Which of Miss Hempstead's qualities attract Lydia?
6. In what ways does Lydia change her behavior in response to social pressures? What does she do in order to "fit in"?
7. What spell is broken when Lydia rises from the floor and slips back to her seat?

✍ KURT VONNEGUT, JR.

Harrison Bergeron

Born in Indianapolis, Indiana, in 1922, Kurt Vonnegut, Jr. began his career as a reporter and public relations man. He began writing for science fiction magazines and has been a freelance writer since 1950. Novels such as Cat's Cradle *(1963) and* Slaughterhouse Five *(1969) won him widespread popularity during the 1960s and 1970s, particularly among college students. Vonnegut is regarded as a humorist and satirist of the dark side of life.*

KEY VOCABULARY

A **BALL PEEN** hammer is a hammer with one rounded end.

A **GRACKLE** is a type of blackbird, or myna.

SASHWEIGHTS are weights placed inside the frame of a window, attached to the window with a rope and pulley, for the purpose of making the window easier to open.

The year was 2081, and everybody was finally equal. They weren't only 1
equal before God and the law. They were equal every which way. Nobody was smarter than anybody else. Nobody was better looking than anybody else. Nobody was stronger or quicker than anybody else. All this equality was due to the 211th, 212th, and 213th Amendments to the Constitution, and to the unceasing vigilance of agents of the United States Handicapper General.

Some things about living still weren't quite right, though. April, for instance, still drove people crazy by not being springtime. And it was in that clammy month that the H-G men took George and Hazel Bergeron's fourteen-year-old son, Harrison, away.

It was tragic, all right, but George and Hazel couldn't think about it very hard. Hazel had a perfectly average intelligence, which meant she couldn't think about anything except in short bursts. And George, while his intelligence was way above normal, had a little mental handicap radio in his ear. He was required by law to wear it at all times. It was tuned to a government transmitter. Every twenty seconds or so, the transmitter would send out some sharp noise to keep people like George from taking unfair advantage of their brains.

George and Hazel were watching television. There were tears on

Hazel's cheeks, but she'd forgotten for the moment what they were about. On the television screen were ballerinas.   5
A buzzer sounded in George's head. His thoughts fled in panic, like bandits from a burglar alarm.

"That was a real pretty dance, that dance they just did," said Hazel.

"Huh?" said George.

"That dance—it was nice," said Hazel.

"Yup," said George. He tried to think a little about the ballerinas. They   10
weren't really very good—no better than anybody else would have been, anyway. They were burdened with **sashweights** and bags of birdshot, and their faces were masked, so that no one, seeing a free and graceful gesture or a pretty face, would feel like something the cat drug in. George was toying with the vague notion that maybe dancers shouldn't be handicapped. But he didn't get very far with it before another noise in his ear radio scattered his thoughts.

George winced. So did two out of the eight ballerinas.

Hazel saw him wince. Having no mental handicap herself, she had to ask George what the latest sound had been.

"Sounded like somebody hitting a milk bottle with a **ball peen** hammer," said George.

"I'd think it would be real interesting, hearing all the different sounds," said Hazel, a little envious. "All the things they think up."

"Um," said George.   15

"Only, if I was Handicapper General, you know what I would do?" said Hazel. Hazel, as a matter of fact, bore a strong resemblance to the Handicapper General, a woman named Diana Moon Glampers. "If I was Diana Moon Glampers," said Hazel, "I'd have chimes on Sunday—just chimes. Kind of in honor of religion."

"I could think, if it was just chimes," said George.

"Well—maybe make 'em real loud," said Hazel. "I think I'd make a good Handicapper General."

"Good as anybody else," said George.

"Who knows better'n I do what normal is?" said Hazel.   20

"Right," said George. He began to think glimmeringly about his abnormal son who was now in jail, about Harrison, but a twenty-one-gun salute in his head stopped that.

"Boy!" said Hazel, "that was a doozy, wasn't it?"

It was such a doozy that George was white and trembling, and tears stood on the rims of his red eyes. Two of the eight ballerinas had collapsed to the studio floor, were holding their temples.

"All of a sudden you look so tired," said Hazel. "Why don't you stretch out on the sofa, so's you can rest your handicap bag on the pillows, honeybunch." She was referring to the forty-seven pounds of birdshot in a canvas bag, which was padlocked around George's neck. "Go on and rest the bag for a little while," she said. "I don't care if you're not equal to me for a while."

George weighed the bag with his hands. "I don't mind it," he said. "I   25 don't notice it any more. It's just a part of me."

"You been so tired lately—kind of wore out," said Hazel. "If there was just some way we could make a little hole in the bottom of the bag, and just take out a few of them lead balls. Just a few."

"Two years in prison and two thousand dollars fine for every ball I took out," said George. "I don't call that a bargain."

"If you could just take a few out when you came home from work," said Hazel. "I mean—you don't compete with anybody around here. You just set around."

"If I tried to get away with it," said George, "then other people'd get away with it—and pretty soon we'd be right back to the dark ages again, with everybody competing against everybody else. You wouldn't like that, would you?"

"I'd hate it," said Hazel.   30

"There you are," said George. "The minute people start cheating on laws, what do you think happens to society?"

If Hazel hadn't been able to come up with an answer to this question, George couldn't have supplied one. A siren was going off in his head.

"Reckon it'd fall all apart," said Hazel.

"What would?" said George blankly.

"Society," said Hazel uncertainly. "Wasn't that what you just said?"   35

"Who knows?" said George.

The television program was suddenly interrupted for a news bulletin. It wasn't clear at first as to what the bulletin was about, since the announcer, like all announcers, had a serious speech impediment. For about half a minute, and in a state of high excitement, the announcer tried to say, "Ladies and gentlemen—"

He finally gave up, handed the bulletin to a ballerina to read.

"That's all right—" Hazel said of the announcer, "he tried. That's the big thing. He tried to do the best he could with what God gave him. He should get a nice raise for trying so hard."

"Ladies and gentlemen—" said the ballerina, reading the bulletin. She   40 must have been extraordinarily beautiful, because the mask she wore was hideous. And it was easy to see that she was the strongest and most graceful of all the dancers, for her handicap bags were as big as those worn by two-hundred-pound men.

And she had to apologize at once for her voice, which was a very unfair voice for a woman to use. Her voice was a warm, luminous, timeless melody. "Excuse me—" she said, and she began again, making her voice absolutely uncompetitive.

"Harrison Bergeron, age fourteen," she said in a **grackle** squawk, "has just escaped from jail, where he was held on suspicion of plotting to over-throw the government. He is a genius and an athlete, is under-handicapped, and should be regarded as extremely dangerous."

A police photograph of Harrison Bergeron was flashed on the screen—upside down, then sideways, upside down again, then right side up. The picture showed the full length of Harrison against a background calibrated in feet and inches. He was exactly seven feet tall.

The rest of Harrison's appearance was Halloween and hardware. Nobody had ever born heavier handicaps. He had outgrown hindrances faster than the H-G men could think them up. Instead of a little ear radio for a mental handicap, he wore a tremendous pair of earphones, and spectacles with thick wavy lenses. The spectacles were intended to make him not only half blind, but to give him whanging headaches besides.

Scrap metal was hung all over him. Ordinarily, there was a certain sym- 45 metry, a military neatness to the handicaps issued to strong people, but Harrison looked like a walking junkyard. In the race of life, Harrison car-ried three hundred pounds.

And to offset his good looks, the H-G men required that he wear at all times a red rubber ball for a nose, keep his eyebrows shaved off, and cover his even white teeth with black caps at snaggle-tooth random.

"If you see this boy," said the ballerina, "do not—I repeat, do not—try to reason with him."

There was the shriek of a door being torn from its hinges.

Screams and barking cries of consternation came from the television set. The photograph of Harrison Bergeron on the screen jumped again and again, as though dancing to the tune of an earthquake.

George Bergeron correctly identified the earthquake, and well he 50 might have—for many was the time his own home had danced to the same crashing tune. "My God—" said George, "that must be Harrison!"

The realization was blasted from his mind instantly by the sound of an automobile collision in his head.

When George could open his eyes again, the photograph of Harrison was gone. A living, breathing Harrison filled the screen.

Clanking, clownish, and huge, Harrison stood in the center of the stu-dio. The knob of the uprooted studio door was still in his hand. Ballerinas, technicians, musicians, and announcers cowered on their knees before him, expecting to die.

"I am the Emperor!" cried Harrison. "Do you hear? I am the Emperor! Everybody must do what I say at once!" He stamped his foot and the studio shook.

"Even as I stand here—" he bellowed, "crippled, hobbled, sickened— 55 I am a greater ruler than any man who ever lived! Now watch me become what I *can* become!"

Harrison tore the straps of his handicap harness like wet tissue paper, tore straps guaranteed to support five thousand pounds.

Harrison's scrap-iron handicaps crashed to the floor.

Harrison thrust his thumbs under the bar of the padlock that secured his head harness. The bar snapped like celery. Harrison smashed his headphones and spectacles against the wall.

He flung away his rubber-ball nose, revealed a man that would have awed Thor, the god of thunder.

"I shall now select my Empress!" he said, looking down on the cow- 60 ering people. "Let the first woman who dares rise to her feet claim her mate and her throne!"

A moment passed, and then a ballerina arose, swaying like a willow.

Harrison plucked the mental handicap from her ear, snapped off her physical handicaps with marvellous delicacy. Last of all, he removed her mask.

She was blindingly beautiful.

"Now—" said Harrison, taking her hand, "shall we show the people the meaning of the word dance? Music!" he commanded.

The musicians scrambled back into their chairs, and Harrison stripped 65 them of their handicaps, too. "Play your best," he told them, "and I'll make you barons and dukes and earls."

The music began. It was normal at first—cheap, silly, false. But Harrison snatched two musicians from their chairs, waved them like batons as he sang the music as he wanted it played. He slammed them back into their chairs.

The music began again and was much improved.

Harrison and his Empress merely listened to the music for a while— listened gravely, as though synchronizing their heartbeats with it.

They shifted their weights to their toes.

Harrison placed his big hands on the girl's tiny waist, letting her sense 70 the weightlessness that would soon be hers.

And then, in an explosion of joy and grace, into the air they sprang!

Not only were the laws of the land abandoned, but the law of gravity and the laws of motion as well.

They reeled, whirled, swiveled, flounced, capered, gamboled, and spun.

They leaped like deer on the moon.

The studio ceiling was thirty feet high, but each leap brought the 75 dancers nearer to it.

It became their obvious intention to kiss the ceiling.

They kissed it.

And then, neutralizing gravity with love and pure will, they remained suspended in air inches below the ceiling, and they kissed each other for a long, long time.

It was then that Diana Moon Glampers, the Handicapper General, came into the studio with a double-barreled ten-gauge shotgun. She fired twice, and the Emperor and the Empress were dead before they hit the floor.

Diana Moon Glampers loaded the gun again. She aimed it at the mu- 80
sicians and told them they had ten seconds to get their handicaps back on.

It was then that the Bergerons' television tube burned out.

Hazel turned to comment about the blackout to George. But George had gone out into the kitchen for a can of beer.

George came back in with the beer, paused while a handicap signal shook him up. And then he sat down again. "You been crying?" he said to Hazel.

"Yup," she said.

"What about?" he said.   85

"I forget," she said. "Something real sad on television."

"What was it?" he said.

"It's all kind of mixed up in my mind," said Hazel.

"Forget sad things," said George.

"I always do," said Hazel.   90

"That's my girl," said George. He winced. There was the sound of a rivetting gun in his head.

"Gee—I could tell that one was a doozy," said Hazel.

"You can say that again," said George.

"Gee—" said Hazel, "I could tell that one was a doozy."

QUESTIONS FOR DISCUSSION

1. How would you characterize the attitude about equality implied in this story?

2. As implied by this story, what are the characteristics of a typical "average" person?

3. In what ways could this story be called a *satire* (a work that ridicules vices, stupidities, etc.)? What is Vonnegut satirizing?

4. In what ways does this story use stereotypical qualities of certain types of people to make its point? Give examples.

5. What parallels do you see between this story and the poem "The Unknown Citizen"?

In the following essay, the writer describes the requirements for being part of a high-school clique called "homies." He identifies three main requirements of the group and devotes a paragraph to each one. Notice how the opening sentence of each paragraph both provides a transition from the previous paragraph and introduces the next one. While this paper is a response to the theme of the chapter, the writer's material is drawn entirely from his own experience.

✍ STUDENT ESSAY:

How to Become a Homie

In high school, there was great pressure to belong to some kind of group. If you didn't belong, you were considered strange, an outcast. My high school had a clique for almost everyone: the rockers, the grunge/alternative, the nerds and geeks, the jocks, and the one I'm most familiar with, the "homies." Each group had its own style, and its members could easily be identified by the way they dressed, their behavior, even their language. Anyone who wanted to belong to one of these groups had to first adopt its style. This didn't guarantee that you would be part of the group, but it was the necessary first step. To be considered for membership, the "wannabe" homie had to meet several strict requirements.

Since members of any group are recognized first by the way they dress, the first requirement to become a homie is the wardrobe. The homie's general appearance is one of "bagginess." Everything on him looks about six sizes too large. The crotch of his pants is down around his knees, and the shoulders of his shirt and jacket come down around his elbows. An optional accessory to this outfit is a hat—preferably a baseball hat from a college or professional sports team, worn backwards.

The next requirement to become a homie is to learn the language. To an outsider, the way homies talk to each other sounds like a foreign language. Greetings are shortened to "what up," "wus goin' on," "ay yo G," or just a simple "YO!" In the vocabulary of the homie there may be missing consonants, vowels, conjunctions, and articles. But the homie is also likely to create words that seem to have no meaning, except to other homies. The "wannabe" homie must master such words and phrases as "whack," "dope," "phat," "yo," "I got props," and "dis', da hood." No respectable homie would be caught saying things like "Good morning," or "How do you do."

The last thing that identifies a true homie is his car. It doesn't really matter what kind of car it is; it's what is in the car that counts. A homie's car might be covered with rust and enveloped in a cloud of blue smoke, but it will be decked out with hundreds of dollars worth of stereo equipment, consisting of numerous subwoofers and amplifiers, which put out as many decibels as possible. The idea is that the bass can be heard before the car is seen, and the bass must rock the car when it is stopped.

In his life, a homie is mainly concerned with being a homie. Nothing else matters. A homie could care less if he offends other people. In fact, being offensive is part of being a homie. Nothing pleases a homie more than pulling up beside a nice, family wagon at a stoplight and cranking up the bass until the windows rattle and the other driver glances over with a mixture of disgust and fear. That's living.

TOPICS FOR WRITING

1. Using information from any of the readings in this chapter, elaborate on the tension between individualism and conformity that is mentioned in the Introduction to this chapter. Approach this problem as if you are writing to someone from a foreign country who knows little about the culture of the United States.

2. From information in "The Standardized American" and "The Unknown Citizen," what conclusions can you draw about the causes of widespread conformity in American society?

3. Suppose that, rather than dying, Harrison Bergeron succeeds in becoming the "Emperor" and organizing life and society in a manner to his own liking. How do you think the story would end? Try rewriting the ending. Make it consistent with what you know about Harrison from the story.

4. Using W. H. Auden's poem "The Unknown Citizen" as a model, write a poem portraying another "statistical human" such as "The Unknown Student," "The Unknown Soldier," "The Unknown Senior Citizen," etc.

5. Re-read "The Company Man" and consider the following scenario: his widow and daughter, who had severed emotional ties to him long before his death, continue their lives relatively unchanged; his two sons, however, are greatly affected by his untimely death, for reasons revealed in the text, and make drastic changes in their lives. Write a narrative about the turn their lives might take from this point on, describing the changes and the reasons for them.

6. Explain the ways in which the mother in the excerpt from Annie Dillard's An American Childhood has resisted conformity. Give examples from the text to support your conclusions.

7. In the excerpt from Lydia Minatoya's Talking to High Monks in the Snow," what did her Japanese-American parents want for their children: individualism, assimilation, or both? Use examples from the reading to support your view.

8. In Elena Asturias' "Growing Up in the U.S.," which beneficial aspects of growing up are described as being fostered by U.S. life and society, and which ones are presented as better nurtured in Latin societies? Include examples of both social and family interaction in these cultures.

9. Choose three social forces (i.e. family, religion, peer group, education, etc.) and analyze their influence on the person you are today. Were

these institutions a positive or a negative force? Did they foster your development, or hinder it?

10. How would you classify yourself in terms of the categories discussed in this chapter? Are you an individualist or a conformist? Are you a rebel or an unknown citizen? Give examples to support your view.

11. The readings in this chapter point to two major kinds of forces at work on shaping the individual self: the larger forces of society, and the more subtle, but more immediate, forces of the family. As you think about these readings, which of the two forces seems to have the stronger influence as we grow up? Write an essay explaining why you think one or the other is the more influential.

The world's tallest sandcastle.

12 The Pursuit of Happiness

Everyone speaks of it;
few know it.

–MME. JEANNE P. ROLAND

It is guaranteed to every American. The Declaration of Independence says so: "We hold these truths to be self-evident. . . ."

It is not happiness itself, but the *pursuit* of happiness that is guaranteed, and judging by the enormous number of self-help books on the market, the pursuit is proceeding at a frenzied pace.

To our Puritan forebears, happiness was not the issue; salvation was. Indulging personal desires was thought to be sinful, the road to hell. But times have changed. As professor William Lazer of Florida Atlantic University says, "Now people are more willing to break out of the mold and seek self-fulfillment, both physically and psychologically."

Throughout the ages, thoughtful men and women have wrestled with the question of happiness: What is it? How is it achieved? It was the central question that occupied Socrates, that tireless inquisitor: What is the good life, and how can one live it? Some writers, including some in this chapter, have even raised doubts about the whole idea of the pursuit of happiness. Is happiness something that can be pursued directly? Or is it simply the by-product of a life well-lived? Although these writers might disagree about the nature and pursuit of happiness, they agree that there is probably more to happiness than a warm puppy.

✑ LOUIS HARRIS
A Sometimes Thing Called Happiness

Louis Harris, born in 1921, is one of America's leading public opinion pollsters. He has also been a columnist for The Washington Post, Newsweek, and The Chicago Tribune. *Harris has authored a number of books, among them* The Negro Revolution in America *(1964),* Black-Jewish Relations in New York City: The Anguish of Change *(1973), and* Inside America *(1987),* the book from which the selection below was taken.

KEY VOCABULARY

A **BOOSTER** is an active promoter of something, such as a cause, a place, or an idea.

A **MODICUM** is a small amount of something.

How Many Say Life Is Really Satisfying?

1

At first glance, the fact that 63% of the American people say they are "very satisfied" with their life might be taken to mean that America in the late 1980s is one happy land, as U.S. **boosters,** many politicians, advertising people, chambers of commerce, and others would have you believe. On second thought, though, the fact that 35% report that they are something less than really satisfied with their lives means that fully 62 million adults feel that life is not entirely fulfilling.

Who's Happy and Who's Not

Satisfaction with life varies widely with a host of factors:

- By age, the older a person gets, the more satisfied he or she is with life. Only 53% of young people 18 to 24 express satisfaction. This rises to 59% among those 25 to 34 years of age, 62% among those 35 to 39, to 73% among those 50 to 64, and levels out at 72% among those 65 and older. Clearly, the older people get, the more likely they are to have come to terms with themselves and their lives. Put another way, with age, a number of fulfillments take place along with a lowering of

329

expectations. In turn, this leads to greater adjustment and satisfaction with one's lot.

• By sex, 66% of all men say they are satisfied with their lives, compared with a lower 61% of all women. A lower 57% of employed mothers express satisfaction with their lives. The pressures of coping with work, a home, and raising children at the same time are not wholly conducive to a sense of high personal satisfaction, even though American society obviously is committed to that goal.

• By income, there is little doubt that the more money you make, the 5 more likely you are to feel satisfied with your lot. Only 47% of those earning $7,500 or under express satisfaction with their lives, compared with 66% in the $25,000–$35,000 income bracket, and a big 73% among those earning $50,000 and over. The saying that money can't buy happiness may be at best only a half-truth.

• Whites (64%) are more pleased with their lives than blacks, only 58% of whom express satisfaction.

When people are asked to choose what they feel is the greatest single source of happiness—"great wealth," "good health," or "personal satisfaction from accomplishment," good health wins with 46%, followed closely by (44%) satisfaction from personal achievement. Great wealth trails far in the rear at 6%, though, as just seen, not having enough money can quickly unravel a sense of satisfaction with one's condition. Those who put a high premium on good health are the elderly, single people, homeowners, and women. Getting happiness more from their accomplishments are young people, particularly Yuppies, the college-educated, and people with children.

For all of the sustained and continuing good times in America in recent years and the much-reported upbeat feelings from the revival of patriotism, there is solid evidence that, compared with the 1970s, satisfaction with key aspects of personal life is declining:

• Those pleased with their friendships have declined over the same period from 70% to 65%.

• The number satisfied with their health and physical condition has 10 dropped from 61% to 55%.

• Those happy about their nonwork, leisure-time activities have dropped from 56% to 52%.

• Finally, the number pleased with the city or the place where they live has declined from 48% to 43%.

Observation

It is abundantly clear that what starts out as an upbeat report about happiness in the U.S. during the latter part of the 1980s turns out *not* to be entirely the case upon closer inspection. Indeed, when asked bluntly if their happiness has been going up over the past 5 years, 55% say it has, while fully 44% say it has not. Those with higher incomes, the better-educated, whites, those with jobs, people with kids and bigger families all report being more happy. Older people, working women, the less well educated, single people, those without children, and lower-income people all say they are less happy now.

Indeed, as in so many other ways, the privileged tend to get more satisfaction out of life than those who are not privileged. A **modicum** of affluence appears to be a necessary precondition for a reasonably happy life in the U.S. in the late 1980s.

But as the decade of the 1980s has unfolded, affluence has grown apace   15 during the long and sustained good times. Why, then, should all the signs point to a decline in personal satisfaction across the land?

The answer is found dramatically in the fact that satisfaction with one's life varies more sharply with how much stress people live under than any other single factor. Among those who experience low stress, 74% report being really satisfied with their lives. Among those with moderate stress as a regular diet, 55% are pleased with their lot. Among those with high stress, a lowly 32% express satisfaction with life.

The great irony, of course, is that, as reported elsewhere in this book, the most affluent are the most stress-ridden in America in the late 1980s. It is a fact that higher-income people are more satisfied with life than lower-income types. But many of the privileged are robbed of real satisfaction with life because they are also plagued by excessive stress, a price many pay to achieve affluence.

Obviously, the happiest people in America, then, should be people of means who live under little stress. Unfortunately, such a breed appears to be diminishing from the land—and at a fairly rapid rate.

QUESTIONS FOR DISCUSSION

1. As a pollster, Louis Harris naturally makes use of statistics to support his argument. What is your own attitude toward statistics as a means of proving one's point?
2. According to this piece, what is the relationship between affluence and happiness in our society?

3. How does stress affect the relationship between affluence and happiness?

4. Which statistical group do you belong to? Do the findings for that group fit your own situation? Explain.

5. The last paragraph says that the "happiest people in America . . . [appear] to be diminishing from the land." What is the reason for this?

✍ ALEXIS DE TOCQUEVILLE

Equality and Materialism

Alexis de Tocqueville, a French aristocrat, was born in Paris on July 29, 1805. In May 1831, at the age of 25, he visited America to examine democracy first-hand. Aware that democracy was a growing force in his own country and in other parts of the world, de Tocqueville came to study the strengths and weaknesses of American democracy. As he put it, "It is not, then, merely to satisfy a legitimate curiosity that I have examined America; my wish has been to find there instruction by which we may ourselves profit. . . ." De Tocqueville left the United States in February 1832, after a stay of only nine months. Yet his book Democracy in America, *from which the following excerpt was taken, remains one of the most penetrating studies ever written of the effects of democracy on government, society, and character.*

KEY VOCABULARY

BOOTLESS means useless, futile, having no benefit.

To **CIRCUMSCRIBE** means to confine within certain boundaries; to define.

ENERVATED means weakened, drained of strength.

To **LET,** here, means to rent or lease.

VICISSITUDE means a change or variation in something; changeability, particularly in a person's affairs or fortune.

A **VORTEX** is a whirlwind or whirlpool.

. . . In America I saw the freest and most enlightened men placed in the happiest circumstances that the world affords: it seemed to me as if a cloud habitually hung upon their brow, and I thought them serious and almost sad even in their pleasures. . . . It is strange to see with what feverish ardour the Americans pursue their own welfare; and to watch the vague dread that constantly torments them lest they should not have chosen the shortest path which may lead to it. A native of the United States clings to this world's goods as if he were certain never to die; and he is so hasty in grasping at all within his reach that one would suppose he was constantly afraid of not living long enough to enjoy them. He clutches everything, he holds nothing fast, but soon loosens his grasp to pursue fresh gratifications.

In the United States a man builds a house to spend his latter years in it, and he sells it before the roof is on: he plants a garden, and **lets** it just as the trees are coming into bearing: he brings a field into tillage, and leaves other men to gather the crops: he embraces a profession, and gives it up: he settles in a place, which he soon afterward leaves, to carry his changeable longings elsewhere. If his private affairs leave him any leisure, he instantly plunges into the **vortex** of politics; and if at the end of a year of unremitting labour he finds he has a few days' vacation, his eager curiosity whirls him over the vast extent of the United States, and he will travel fifteen hundred miles in a few days to shake off his happiness. Death at length overtakes him, but it is before he is weary of his **bootless** chase of that complete felicity which is forever on the wing.

At first sight there is something surprising in this strange unrest of so many happy men, restless in the midst of abundance. The spectacle itself is, however, as old as the world; the novelty is to see a whole people furnish an exemplification of it. Their taste for physical gratifications must be regarded as the original source of that secret inquietude that the actions of the Americans betray, and of that inconstancy of which they afford fresh examples every day. He who has set his heart exclusively upon the pursuit of worldly welfare is always in a hurry, for he has but a limited time at his disposal to reach it, to grasp it, and to enjoy it. The recollection of the brevity of life is a constant spur to him. Besides the good things which he possesses, he every instant fancies a thousand others which death will prevent him from trying if he does not try them soon. This thought fills him with anxiety, fear, and regret, and keeps his mind in ceaseless trepidation, which leads him perpetually to change his plans and his abode. If in addition to the taste for physical well-being a social condition be superadded, in which the laws and customs make no condition permanent, here is a great additional stimulant to this restlessness of temper. Men will then be seen continually to change their track, for fear of missing the shortest cut to happiness. It may readily be conceived that if men, passionately bent upon physical gratifications, desire eagerly, they are also easily discouraged: as their ultimate object is to enjoy, the means to reach that object must be prompt and easy, or the trouble of acquiring the gratification would be greater than the gratification itself. Their prevailing frame of mind, then, is at once ardent and relaxed, violent and **enervated.** Death is often less dreaded than perseverance in continuous efforts to one end.

The equality of conditions leads by a still straighter road to several of the effects which I have here described. When all the privileges of birth and fortune are abolished, when all professions are accessible to all, and a man's own energies may place him at the top of any one of them, an easy and unbounded career seems open to his ambition, and he will readily persuade himself that he is born to no vulgar destinies. But this is an erroneous notion, which is corrected by daily experience. The same equality which allows every citizen to conceive these lofty hopes renders all the citizens less able to realize them: it **circumscribes** their powers on every side, while it gives freer scope to their desires. Not only are they themselves powerless, but they are met at every step by immense obstacles, which they did not at first perceive. They have swept away the privileges of some of their fellow-creatures which stood in their way, but they have opened the door to universal competition: the barrier has changed its shape rather than its position. When men are nearly alike, and all follow the same track, it is very difficult for any one individual to walk quick and cleave a way through the dense throng which surrounds and presses him. This constant strife between the propensities springing from the equality of conditions and the means it supplies to satisfy them harasses and wearies the mind.

It is possible to conceive men arrived at a degree of freedom which 5 should completely content them; they would then enjoy their independence without anxiety and without impatience. But men will never establish any equality with which they can be contented. Whatever efforts a people may make, they will never succeed in reducing all the conditions of society to a perfect level; and even if they unhappily attained that absolute and complete depression, the inequality of minds would still remain, which, coming directly from the hand of God, will forever escape the laws of man. However democratic, then, the social state and the political constitution of a people may be, it is certain that every member of the community will always find out several points about him that command his own position; and we may foresee that his looks will be doggedly fixed in that direction. When inequality of conditions is the common law of society, the most marked inequalities do not strike the eye: when everything is nearly on the same level, the slightest are marked enough to hurt it. Hence the desire of equality always becomes more insatiable in proportion as equality is more complete.

Among democratic nations men easily attain a certain equality of conditions: they can never attain the equality they desire. It perpetually retires from before them, yet without hiding itself from their sight, and in retiring draws them on. At every moment they think they are about to grasp it; it escapes at every moment from their hold. They are near enough to see its charms, but too far off to enjoy them; and before they have fully tasted its delights they die. To these causes must be attributed that strange melancholy that oftentimes will haunt the inhabitants of democratic countries in the midst of their abundance, and that disgust at life that sometimes seizes upon them in the midst of calm and easy circumstances. . . .

. . . Among aristocratic nations every man is pretty nearly stationary in his own sphere; but men are astonishingly unlike each other—their passions, their notions, their habits, and their tastes are essentially different: nothing changes, but everything differs. In democracies, on the contrary, all men are alike and do things pretty nearly alike. It is true that they are subject to great and frequent **vicissitudes;** but as the same events of good or adverse fortune are continually recurring, the name of the actors only is changed, the piece is always the same. The aspect of American society is animated, because men and things are always changing, but it is monotonous, because all these changes are alike.

Men living in democratic ages have many passions, but most of their passions either end in the love of riches or proceed from it. The cause of this is, not that their souls are narrower, but that the importance of money is really greater at such times. When all the members of a community are independent of or indifferent to each other, the co-operation of each of them can only be obtained by paying for it: this infinitely multiplies the purposes to which wealth may be applied, and increases its value. When the reverence that belonged to what is old has vanished, birth, condition, and profession no longer distinguish men, or scarcely distinguish them at all: hardly anything but money remains to create strongly marked differences between them, and to raise some of them above the common level. The distinction originating in wealth is increased by the disappearance and diminution of all other distinctions. Among aristocratic nations money only reaches to a few points on the vast circle of man's desires—in democracies it seems to lead to all. The love of wealth is therefore to be traced, either as a principal or an accessory motive, at the bottom of all that the Americans do: this gives to all their passions a sort of family likeness, and soon renders the survey of them exceedingly wearisome. This perpetual recurrence of the same passion is monotonous; the peculiar methods by which this passion seeks its own gratification are no less so.

In an orderly and constituted democracy like the United States, where men can not enrich themselves by war, by public office, or by political confiscation, the love of wealth mainly drives them into business and manufactures. Although these pursuits often bring about great commotions and disasters, they can not prosper without strictly regular habits and a long routine of petty uniform acts. The stronger the passion is, the more regular are these habits, and the more uniform are these acts. It may be said that it is the vehemence of their desires which makes the Americans so methodical; it perturbs their minds, but it disciplines their lives.

The remark I here apply to America may indeed be addressed to almost 10 all our contemporaries. Variety is disappearing from the human race; the same ways of acting, thinking, and feeling are to be met with all over the world. This is not only because nations work more upon each other, and are more faithful in their mutual imitation; but as the men of each country relinquish more and more the peculiar opinions and feelings of a caste, a profession, or a family, they simultaneously arrive at something nearer to the constitution of man, which is everywhere the same. Thus they become more alike, even without having imitated each other. Like travellers scattered about some large wood, which is intersected by paths converging to one point, if all of them keep their eyes fixed upon that point and advance toward it, they insensibly draw nearer together—though they seek not, though they see not, though they know not each other; and they will be surprised at length to find themselves all collected on the same spot. . . .

QUESTIONS FOR DISCUSSION

1. Given de Tocqueville's background, do you find his attitude toward democracy predictable? Explain.

2. In de Tocqueville's view, what is the relationship between happiness and materialism?

3. Although de Tocqueville's observations about American society were made in the 1830's, do they still apply today? Explain.

4. What are the difficulties and obstacles that citizens of an equalitarian society must overcome, as opposed to those facing citizens in a class-bound society?

5. Which parts of de Tocqueville's argument do you agree with? Which ones do you disagree with?

⚘ JOHN CIARDI

Is Everybody Happy?

John Ciardi, the only son of an Italian immigrant family, served as English professor, director of the Bread Loaf Writers Conference, host of the CBS magazine show "Accent," and poetry editor for Saturday Review *magazine. A noted poet and essayist, Ciardi died on Easter Sunday 1986.*

KEY VOCABULARY

ASCETICISM is the belief in a life of self-discipline, without the comforts of society.

CATATONIC means immobile, in a stupor.

A **KNAVE,** in early English, was a male servant. Today, the word denotes an unprincipled and crafty man.

ORTHOPEDICS is the branch of medicine that deals with the treatment of bone disorders.

A **PHARMACOPOEIA** is a book containing an official list of medicinal drugs, along with instructions for their preparation and use.

THOREAU, HENRY DAVID (1817–1862) was an American writer best known for his book *Walden,* an account of two years he spent living in a cabin on Walden Pond, Massachusetts. Thoreau wrote on the importance of living simply in order to achieve happiness and contentment.

1. The right to pursue happiness is issued to Americans with their birth certificates, but no one seems quite sure which way it ran. It may be we are issued a hunting license but offered no game. Jonathan Swift seemed to think so when he attacked the idea of happiness as "the possession of being well-deceived," the felicity of being "a fool among **knaves.**" For Swift saw society as Vanity Fair, the land of false goals.

2. It is, of course, un-American to think in terms of fools and **knaves.** We do, however, seem to be dedicated to the idea of buying our way to happiness. We shall all have made it to Heaven when we possess enough.

3. And at the same time the forces of American commercialism are hugely dedicated to making us deliberately unhappy. Advertising is one of our major industries, and advertising exists not to satisfy desires but to create them—and to create them faster than any man's budget can satisfy

them. For that matter, our whole economy is based on a dedicated insatiability. We are taught that to possess is to be happy, and then we are made to want. We are even told it is our duty to want. It was only a few years ago, to cite a single example, that car dealers across the country were flying banners that read "You Auto Buy Now." They were calling upon Americans, as an act approaching patriotism, to buy at once, with money they did not have, automobiles they did not really need, and which they would be required to grow tired of by the time next year's models were released.

4. Or look at any of the women's magazines. There, as Bernard DeVoto once pointed out, advertising begins as poetry in the front pages and ends as **pharmacopoeia** and therapy in the back pages. The poetry of the front matter is the dream of perfect beauty. This is the baby skin that must be hers. These, the flawless teeth. This, the perfumed breath she must exhale. This, the sixteen-year-old figure she must display at forty, at fifty, at sixty, and forever.

5. Once past the vaguely uplifting fiction and feature articles, the reader finds the other face of the dream in the back matter. This is the harness into which Mother must strap herself in order to display that perfect figure. These, the chin straps she must sleep in. This is the salve that restores all, this is her laxative, these are the tablets that melt away fat, these are the hormones of perpetual youth, these are the stockings that hide varicose veins.

6. Obviously no half-sane person can be completely persuaded either by such poetry or by such **pharmacopoeia** and **orthopedics.** Yet someone is obviously trying to buy the dream as offered and spending billions every year in the attempt. Clearly the happiness-market is not running out of customers, but what is it trying to buy?

7. The idea "happiness," to be sure, will not sit still for easy definition: the best one can do is to try to set some extremes to the idea and then work in toward the middle. To think of happiness as acquisitive and competitive will do to set the materialistic extreme. To think of it as the idea one senses in, say, a holy man of India will do to set the spiritual extreme. That holy man's idea of happiness is in needing nothing from outside himself. In wanting nothing, he lacks nothing. He sits immobile, rapt in contemplation, free even of his own body. Or nearly free of it. If devout admirers bring him food he eats it; if not, he starves indifferently. Why be concerned? What is physical is an illusion to him. Contemplation is his joy and he achieves it through a fantastically demanding discipline, the accomplishment of which is itself a joy within him.

8. Is he a happy man? Perhaps his happiness is only another sort of illusion. But who can take it from him? And who will dare say it is more illusory than happiness on the installment plan?

9. But, perhaps because I am Western, I doubt such **catatonic** happiness, as I doubt the dreams of the happiness-market. What is certain is that his way of happiness would be torture to almost any Western man. Yet these extremes will still serve to frame the area within which all of us must find some sort of balance. **Thoreau**—a creature of both Eastern and Western thought—had his own firm sense of that balance. His aim was to save on the low levels in order to spend on the high.

10. Possession for its own sake or in competition with the rest of the neighborhood would have been **Thoreau's** idea of the low levels. The active discipline of heightening one's perception of what is enduring in nature would have been his idea of the high. What he saved from the low was time and effort he could spend on the high. Thoreau certainly disapproved of starvation, but he would put into feeding himself only as much effort as would keep him functioning for more important efforts.

11. Effort is the gist of it. There is no happiness except as we take on life-engaging difficulties. Short of the impossible, as Yeats puts it, the satisfactions we get from a lifetime depend on how high we choose our difficulties. Robert Frost was thinking in something like the same terms when he spoke of "The pleasure of taking pains." The mortal flaw in the advertised version of happiness is in the fact that it purports to be effortless.

12. We demand difficulty even in our games. We demand it because without difficulty there can be no game. A game is a way of making something hard for the fun of it. The rules of the game are an arbitrary imposition of difficulty. When the spoilsport ruins the fun, he always does so by refusing to play by the rules. It is easier to win at chess if you are free, at your pleasure, to change the wholly arbitrary rules, but the fun is in winning within the rules. No difficulty, no fun.

13. The buyers and sellers at the happiness-market seem too often to have lost their sense of the pleasure of difficulty. Heaven knows what they are playing, but it seems a dull game. And the Indian holy man seems dull to us, I suppose, because he seems to be refusing to play anything at all. The Western weakness may be in the illusion that happiness can be bought. Perhaps the Eastern weakness is in the idea that there is such a thing as perfect (and therefore static) happiness.

14. Happiness is never more than partial. There are no pure states of mankind. Whatever else happiness may be, it is neither in having nor in being, but in becoming. What the Founding Fathers declared for us as an inherent right, we should do well to remember, was not happiness but the *pursuit* of happiness. What they might have underlined, could they have foreseen the happiness-market, it the cardinal fact that happiness is in the pursuit itself, in the meaningful pursuit of what is life-engaging and life-revealing, which is to say, in the idea of *becoming*. A nation is not measured by what it possesses or wants to possess, but by what it wants to become.

15. By all means let the happiness-market sell us minor satisfactions and even minor follies so long as we keep them in scale and buy them out of spiritual change. I am no customer for either puritanism or **asceticism.** But drop any real spiritual capital at those bazaars, and what you come home to will be your own poorhouse.

QUESTIONS FOR DISCUSSION

1. According to Ciardi, how does Western society reinforce the idea that money can buy happiness?
2. What is the Indian holy man's idea of happiness?
3. Does Ciardi endorse the Western or the Eastern view of happiness? Explain.
4. Can happiness ever be complete? Explain why or why not.

✍ ASHLEY MONTAGU

The Pursuit of Happiness

Born in London in 1905, Ashley Montagu came to the United States in 1927 and received his Ph.D. in anthropology from Columbia University in 1937. He served as a professor of anthropology at Rutgers University and as anthropology advisor to NBC. Through his writings and numerous television and radio appearances, Montagu became one of the best-known anthropologists in the world. He once said that his "major interest is the relation of cultural factors to the physical and behavioral evolution of man." Among Montagu's books are The Direction of Human Development: Biological and Social Bases *(1955, 1970),* A Handbook of Anthropology *(1960), and* The Elephant Man: A Study in Human Dignity *(1971).*

KEY VOCABULARY

An **ABODE** is a dwelling place, or home.

FRENETICALLY refers to something done in a frenzy, with quick, aimless motion.

LIBERTINISM is promiscuity. A "libertine" is someone who acts without moral restraint.

Happiness, in America, is a guarantee set out in the Declaration of 1 Independence. It is one of the unalienable rights, the other two being life and liberty. As that distinguished American philosopher the late Fred Allen once remarked, "You only live once. But if you live it right, once is enough." And most Americans are **frenetically** engaged in attempting to live it right.

Liberty is interpreted as the moral right to get away with as much as one can without being caught or, to put it in the higher English, economic **libertinism.** Happiness is the biggest business. American parents are dedicated to the proposition that unless their children are a mighty sight happier than they themselves were as children, they have failed as parents. And so, of course, everything must be made easy for the children, and their every need satisfied. Even the bandages with which their scratches are covered must be "ouchless." It is all very well meaning, but brainless, and it does a lot of harm. It is the myth of happiness that is at the root of the trouble, and it is, therefore, worth examining.

The pursuit of happiness in America is perhaps the most misconceived of human endeavors. Life and liberty are indeed necessities, but the pursuit of happiness is a fool's game, a will-o'-the-wisp that eludes all who believe that by making it a goal, they can, by the prescribed or some other means, achieve it. The truth is—and it is not a sad truth—that happiness cannot be pursued and caught like a butterfly in the collector's net. It defies pursuit, and all attempts to contain it are vain. Nor can it be purchased. It is one of the many things that money cannot buy.

Who was it who started this hare, and how long ago? At English dog races there is a mechanical hare that the dogs chase but are never supposed to catch—but sometimes they do make a catch in spite of the men working the machine. The god in the machine who presides over the races that men run sees to it that they seldom catch up with the hare. He knows that permitting them to catch the hare is no way to run a race, thereby exhibiting the wisdom we have a right to expect from an all-seeing and understanding god in possession of all his faculties. Competent gods possess horse sense; this is more than human beings do. And horse sense has been defined as that which enables a horse not to bet on human beings.

The truth is that it is not the purpose of life, of a human being's life, to be happy. Perhaps this is a shocking statement to those who have been conditioned to feel otherwise, but it is nonetheless true for all that. If true, then millions of human beings have misspent and are misspending their lives.

What is happiness? The answer to that question is not a matter of definition, but rather what most people mean by happiness. What is it that they desire for themselves and for others when they think of happiness? Apart from the obvious requirements of health, money, an attractive spouse, gratifying children, a beautiful **abode,** esteem, prestige, recognition, wit, wisdom, valor, love, and the attainment of whatever one has set one's heart on, what other ingredients should go into this cake? Possibly a good many others, but this will be according to each person's fancy.

My own view is that not one of these conditions is either a necessary or a sufficient condition of happiness, although one or all of them together may give some people for a time a feeling of whatever they consider happiness to be. But such a feeling soon loses its power to please as, in time, one returns to the steadying level of everyday life. I believe with Aristotle that the steadiest and most enduring states of which human beings are capable are states that are characterized by an absence of pain—physical pain and mental pain. Such states of the positive absence of pain are appreciated for the most part only when they are interrupted, as by the experience of illness or a bereavement. It is in the state when one is least conscious of oneself that one is likely to be at one's happiest. What folly it is to believe otherwise! To believe that those occasional peak experiences, those thrilling moments when the goal one has set oneself has been achieved, or it just feels good to be alive, or one receives an unexpected windfall, or one's work is highly praised, are likely to be numerous and prolonged is silly. Such occasions are indeed memorable, but the feelings of euphoria they generate do not endure, nor should they. How unpleasant it would be to be in a constant state of high spirits! Madmen are often so. The healthy-minded are content with occasional elevations of spirit. It is the sick and the depressed who seek to buoy their flagging spirits with drugs and "thrills" that will render them high.

There is a Kentucky hillbilly response to the greeting "How are you?" It is, "So's t' git along." It is enough—perhaps more than enough, but enough. As Lord Morley remarked many years ago, it is enough for a man to be, to do, and to depart gracefully. How ridiculous this cult of happiness is! "So's t' git along." That is what the majority of human beings who live at a subsistence level would be willing to settle for. To have enough to keep body and soul together, a bed to sleep on, a spouse, sexual satisfaction, and children. The rest is gravy. Those who live at a subsistence level are unconcerned with such trivial and unreal matters as happiness. It is only when the standard of living rises that the interest in happiness seems to develop—not, it would appear, because life has in other ways become happier, but largely because under the improved conditions of life the new problems that are created produce the pressures, the need, for their reduction. And one way of counterbalancing, it is thought, the weight of these new problems is the pursuit of happiness. It sounds silly put that way, but it is no less than the truth. And what is no less than the truth is that life will always be difficult. "Life," as E. M. Forster put it, "is a public performance on the violin, in which you must learn the instrument as you go along." It takes a lot of stress and strain to bring off such a performance, and if sometimes we manage a credible few bars, it is as pleasant as it is unexpected. And so it is. The moments of happiness we enjoy take us by surprise. It is not that we seize them, but that they seize us. Walking in a field on a lovely summer day, and suddenly stopping in one's tracks, filled with the beauty of it all, feeling how good it is to be alive—*this* is happiness.

But would the felon in the same field, pursued by his trackers, looking about him and perceiving the same beauty, glad that he was alive, say that at that moment he was happy? I think not. The sudden glory one experiences at such moments, if I interpret it aright, represents the expression, the culmination, the reward for something that has been earned—not by any means something that one has set out to earn, but a by-product of the dedication, the labor, that has been involved. Those who, looking back on their lives, have reflected most deeply on the matter, have independently arrived at the same conclusion—namely, that work is the most dependable of all sources of happiness. As Voltaire put it in *Candide*, "Labor preserves us from three great evils—weariness, vice, and want. . . . Let us work without disputing; it is the only way to render life tolerable." Baudelaire wrote, "How many years of fatigue and punishment it takes to learn the simple truth that work, that disagreeable thing, is the only way of not suffering in life, or at all events of suffering less." John Ruskin wrote, "When men are rightly occupied, their amusement grows out of their work, as the colour-petals out of a fruitful flower." Ask yourself whether you are happy, said John Stuart Mill, and you cease to be so. Seek happiness, and it will escape you. Happiness is a by-product of other things and comes by the way, chiefly as a by-product of work.

It is not so much the pursuit of happiness as the happiness of pursuit 10 that is most likely to yield the desired gratifications, and then only occasionally. It is work, work that one delights in, that is the surest guarantor of happiness. But even here it is a work that has to be earned by labor in one's earlier years. One should labor so hard in youth that everything one does subsequently is easy by comparison. In much of America we take the opposite view, and by trying to make things as easy as possible in childhood and youth, we most of the time succeed only in making them difficult later.

QUESTIONS FOR DISCUSSION

1. Why does Montagu say that "The pursuit of happiness in America is perhaps the most misconceived of human endeavors"?

2. What is happiness, according to Montagu? Do you agree? Explain.

3. According to this essay, what is the "surest guarantee of happiness"? Why?

4. Sometimes, people say that hardship builds character. Would Montagu agree with this? Give examples from the essay to support your answer.

5. Do Ciardi and Montagu agree about the role of work in the attainment of happiness? Give details.

6. When have you been happiest? Describe the occasion and explain how it compares with the author's view.

ℒ LEO GURKO

Flights from the Unavoidable Self

Born in 1914, Leo Gurko came to the United States with his family in 1917. He has worked as an editor, freelance writer, and professor of English. He has taught at Hunter College, New York, since 1957 and is now Professor Emeritus. His books include The Angry Decade *(1947),* Tom Paine: Freedom's Apostle *(1957), and* Heroes, Highbrows and the Popular Mind *(1953), the book from which the following selection was taken.*

KEY VOCABULARY

To **CONTRACT** means, here, to make smaller.
GREGARIOUS means sociable, liking to be with others.
JIVE is a slang term originally meaning jazz or swing music; generally, the term is used for deceptive or glib talk.

One of the roughest hurdles in the struggle for maturity is the accep- 1
tance of the self and its responsibilities. Not one's self as other people would
have it or as standardized pressures require, but the real self, expressing the
individual's special drives, qualities, and temperament, which make him
unique. This involves doing one's own thinking, making one's own decisions, assuming responsibility for one's own actions.

Since our real selves are necessarily imperfect and complex, we are
under constant pressure to substitute for them other selves, simpler, more
perfect, easier to live with. Our willingness to yield to these attractive substitute images and live according to their lights, rather than our own, pulls
us away from reality and in this way from our emotional growth. Yet in the
long run we can no more avoid our selves than we can escape our bodies
or minds.

The acceptance of the real, the unavoidable self, however difficult and
even painful, is a basic measurement of our advance to maturity.

The American can endure almost all states except solitude. At home in
the world of material objects and gadgets, eager for the company of others,
he is restless and uneasy in the company of himself. His society is crammed
to the bursting point with clubs, groups, associations, lodges, fraternities
and sororities, organizations of every description which he joins in great
numbers, less to be with his fellows than to get away from himself. He is an

Elk, Oddfellow, Shriner, Moose, Eagle, or American Legionnaire. He is a Rotarian, Kiwanian, Mason, or Knight of Columbus. He attends church for reasons more social than religious. He joins societies that seek to protect ownerless animals or aim at world government or rehearse the operettas of Gilbert and Sullivan. He attaches himself to the countless booster clubs that dot the civic landscape with posters advertising Belleville as the town of industrial opportunity, or Dead Lick as the biggest little city in the country. He attends innumerable conventions with unflagging enthusiasm. Bars, taverns, bowling alleys, poolrooms, gymnasiums, country clubs, are social centers that attract him in large clusters. When he is not in formal contact with others, he is listening to the radio, or sitting in front of a television set, or watching a movie, one in a dark crowd. He is never alone if he can help it.

From her listening post on the campus of Smith College, Mary Ellen 5 Chase reports, in *Woman's Day,* the same flight from solitude: "I am particularly impressed by the repeated aversion, which countless girls express, to being by themselves . . . I hear . . . every morning . . . frenzied appeals for company. 'Wait for me! I'm coming!' 'Don't go without me.' As we stream onward by scores across the campus, I overhear the same desolations repeated again and again: 'I had the most boring evening. Not a soul came to my room.' 'I can't possibly go alone. It would be just too awful.' 'I don't think there's another girl in this college from Idaho (or Dakota, or Montana). Whatever shall I do after Chicago, all that train ride alone?' 'If I only had a roommate, it might help some. At least I'd have someone to talk to at night.' 'She's nice, you know, but she must be a bit queer. She's forever going off all by herself!' "[1]

Moreover, solitude is associated with failure, a pattern traced by Karen Horney in her last book, *Neurosis and Human Growth:*

> . . . he must feel accepted by others. He needs such acceptance in whatever form it is available: attention, approval, gratitude, affection, sympathy, love, sex. To make it clear by comparison: just as in our civilization many people feel worth as much as the money they are "making," so the self-effacing type measures his value in the currency of love, using the word here as a comprehensive term for the various forms of acceptance. He is worth as much as he is liked, needed, wanted, or loved.
>
> Furthermore, he needs human contact and company because he cannot stand being alone for any length of time. He easily feels lost, as if he were cut off from life. . . .

---

[1] Mary Ellen Chase, "Are We Afraid To Be Alone?" *Woman's Day,* October 1949.

The need for company is all the greater since being alone means to him proof of being unwanted and unliked and is therefore a disgrace, to be kept secret. It is a disgrace to go alone to the movies or on a vacation and a disgrace to be alone over the week end when others are sociable. This is an illustration of the extent to which his self-confidence is dependent upon somebody's caring for him in some way. He also needs others to give meaning and zest to whatever his is doing.[2]

A key word in American life is popularity, the tense pursuit of which has crushed many a youthful spirit. Once source of Willy Loman's tragedy in *Death of a Salesman* was his anguished desire to be not only "liked," but "well-liked," and not just by some people but by everybody. Since popularity implies not being by oneself, it makes the exclusive company of that self difficult to bear with comfort and painful to contemplate. The process begins early. Babies who do not respond visibly to the hovering presence of strangers are less cooed over. Children who do not play readily with other children arouse the concern of parents and the pity of neighbors. Teenagers out of the high-school swim are supposed to be wretched. Young people without dates are either unattractive or queer. Men who are not one of the boys, women who keep to themselves, are treated as snobs or dismissed as failures. From the earliest age the American is taught to be **gregarious,** to function in high gear in the company of others, to seek his success through fraternities, lodges, and associations. Movies dealing with campus life have rescued any number of retiring students (male and female both, spotted instantly by their shell-rimmed glasses) from their shyness by teaching them **jive** or maneuvering them into a romance or discovering in them unsuspected athletic ability—that is to say, working them into one of the approved social activities on the campus and weaning them as fast as possible from an unhealthy attachment to their studies. Studiousness is regarded as the biggest possible drag on a young person's success at school. The same ideas are disseminated in magazine stories where the simple homebody never gets her man until she primps up a bit, displays a little sex appeal, and strikes out for herself. The solitude of study or laboratory may be all right for the occasional genius, though even he has rough going during his lifetime, but for most people it is one of the lowest and least satisfying forms of existence.

The quest for popularity carries the individual away from his own identity. He tends to cultivate not those qualities which are uniquely his, but those which he thinks will make him popular. If these qualities are alien to his nature, he will strive all the more desperately to assume them. The gap

---

[2]Karen Horney, *Neurosis and Human Growth* (New York: Norton, 1950), p. 227.

that thus grows up between his actual self and his "popular" one not only produces tensions that become more and more difficult to resolve but keeps him from growing into his full stature as a whole human being. The result is a society of people who are more and more collectively alike and less and less individually different—a society which, contrary to the democratic ideal, **contracts** rather than expands the area in which its members can assert their own unique potentialities.

QUESTIONS FOR DISCUSSION

1. How would you define the idea of "self" implied by this piece? Why does the author say that "real selves are necessarily imperfect and complex"?

2. Do you agree that solitude is unpleasant, or even frightening, to Americans?

3. The author mentions Willy Loman, the central character in Arthur Miller's play *Death of a Salesman,* as an embodiment of the American pursuit of popularity. Give some other examples of characters from theater, film, or television that you think also embody this pursuit.

4. Both de Tocqueville and Gurko agree that, in a strange way, the American obsession with individualism and equality "contracts rather than expands the area in which its members can assert their own unique potentialities." That is, the obsession with individualism creates *fewer* opportunities for a person to really be unique. Why is this so? Considering your own experience, do you agree with this assertion?

ℐ JOHN CHEEVER

The Enormous Radio

John Cheever was born in Quincy, Massachusetts. His first novel, The Wapshot Chronicle *(1958), won the National Book Award. He has written four novels and six collections of short stories. Cheever was a frequent contributor to* The New Yorker *magazine.*

KEY VOCABULARY

CAUCASIAN, here, refers to a mountainous region in the former Soviet Union, between the Black and Caspian Seas.

THE COROMANDEL COAST is the southeastern coast of India, extending from a point opposite the island of Ceylon (Sri Lanka) to the Kistna River.

FITCH is the fur of an Old World polecat, a species of which the skunk is a member.

FURTIVE means secretive, stealthy.

GUMWOOD is the wood of any tree that is a source of gum or rubber, such as the Eucalyptus or Nyssa.

MALEVOLENT means evil, malignant, spiteful.

SORDID means dirty, wretched, morally degraded.

TIMBRE is the distinctive tone of a musical instrument or voice.

Jim and Irene Westcott were the kind of people who seem to strike   1
that satisfactory average of income, endeavor, and respectability that is
reached by the statistical reports in college alumni bulletins. They were the
parents of two young children, they had been married nine years, they lived
on the twelfth floor of an apartment house near Sutton Place, they went to
the theatre on an average of 10.3 times a year, and they hoped someday to
live in Westchester. Irene Westcott was a pleasant, rather plain girl with soft
brown hair and a wide, fine forehead upon which nothing at all had been
written, and in the cold weather she wore a coat of **fitch** skins dyed to
resemble mink. You could not say that Jim Westcott looked younger than
he was, but you could at least say of him that he seemed to feel younger.
He wore his graying hair cut very short, he dressed in the kind of clothes
his class had worn at Andover, and his manner was earnest, vehement, and
intentionally naïve. The Westcotts differed from their friends, their classmates, and their neighbors only in an interest they shared in serious music.

They went to a great many concerts—although they seldom mentioned this to anyone—and they spent a good deal of time listening to music on the radio.

Their radio was an old instrument, sensitive, unpredictable, and beyond repair. Neither of them understood the mechanics of radio—or of any of the other appliances that surrounded them—and when the instrument faltered, Jim would strike the side of the cabinet with his hand. This sometimes helped. One Sunday afternoon, in the middle of a Schubert quartet, the music faded away altogether. Jim struck the cabinet repeatedly, but there was no response; the Schubert was lost to them forever. He promised to buy Irene a new radio, and on Monday when he came home from work he told her that he had got one. He refused to describe it, and said it would be a surprise for her when it came.

The radio was delivered at the kitchen door the following afternoon, and with the assistance of her maid and the handyman Irene uncrated it and brought it into the living room. She was struck at once with the physical ugliness of the large **gumwood** cabinet. Irene was proud of her living room, she had chosen its furnishings and colors as carefully as she chose her clothes, and now it seemed to her that the new radio stood among her intimate possessions like an aggressive intruder. She was confounded by the number of dials and switches on the instrument panel, and she studied them thoroughly before she put the plug into a wall socket and turned the radio on. The dials flooded with a **malevolent** green light, and in the distance she heard the music of a piano quintet. The quintet was in the distance for only an instant; it bore down upon her with a speed greater than light and filled the apartment with the noise of music amplified so mightily that it knocked a china ornament from a table to the floor. She rushed to the instrument and reduced the volume. The violent forces that were snared in the ugly **gumwood** cabinet made her uneasy. Her children came home from school then, and she took them to the Park. It was not until later in the afternoon that she was able to return to the radio.

The maid had given the children their suppers and was supervising their baths when Irene turned on the radio, reduced the volume, and sat down to listen to a Mozart quintet that she knew and enjoyed. The music came through clearly. The new instrument had a much purer tone, she thought, than the old one. She decided that tone was most important and that she could conceal the cabinet behind a sofa. But as soon as she had made her peace with the radio, the interference began. A crackling sound like the noise of a burning powder fuse began to accompany the singing of the strings. Beyond the music, there was a rustling that reminded Irene unpleasantly of the sea, and as the quintet progressed, these noises were joined by many others. She tried all the dials and switches but nothing dimmed the interference, and she sat down, disappointed and bewildered, and tried to trace the flight of the melody. The elevator shaft in her building ran beside the living-room wall, and it was the noise of the elevator that gave her a clue to the character of the static. The rattling of the elevator cables and the opening and closing of the elevator doors were reproduced in her loud-speaker, and, realizing that the radio was sensitive to electrical currents of all sorts, she began to discern through the Mozart the ringing of telephone bells, the dialing of phones, and the lamentation of a vacuum cleaner. By listening more carefully, she was able to distinguish doorbells, elevator bells, electric razors, and Waring mixers, whose sounds had been picked up from the apartments that surrounded hers and transmitted through her loud-speaker. The powerful and ugly instrument, with its mistaken sensitivity to discord, was more than she could hope to master, so she turned the thing off and went into the nursery to see her children.

When Jim Westcott came home that night, he went to the radio con-   5
fidently and worked the controls. He had the same sort of experience Irene had had. A man was speaking on the station Jim had chosen, and his voice swung instantly from the distance into a force so powerful that it shook the apartment. Jim turned the volume control and reduced the voice. Then, a minute or two later, the interference began. The ringing of telephones and doorbells set in, joined by the rasp of the elevator doors and the whir of cooking appliances. The character of the noise had changed since Irene had tried the radio earlier; the last of the electric razors was being unplugged, the vacuum cleaners had all been returned to their closets, and the static reflected that change in pace that overtakes the city after the sun goes down. He fiddled with the knobs but couldn't get rid of the noises, so he turned the radio off and told Irene that in the morning he'd call the people who had sold it to him and give them hell.

The following afternoon, when Irene returned to the apartment from a luncheon date, the maid told her that a man had come and fixed the radio. Irene went into the living room before she took off her hat or her furs and tried the instrument. From the loudspeaker came a recording of the "Mis-souri Waltz." It reminded her of the thin, scratchy music from an old-fashioned phonograph that she sometimes heard across the lake where she spent her summers. She waited until the waltz had finished, expecting an explanation of the recording, but there was none. The music was followed by silence, and then the plaintive and scratchy record was repeated. She turned the dial and got a satisfactory burst of **Caucasian** music—the thump of bare feet in the dust and the rattle of coin jewelry—but in the background she could hear the ringing of bells and a confusion of voices. Her children came home from school then, and she turned off the radio and went to the nursery.

When Jim came home that night, he was tired, and he took a bath and changed his clothes. Then he joined Irene in the living room. He had just turned on the radio when the maid announced dinner, so he left it on, and he and Irene went to the table.

Jim was too tired to make even a pretense of sociability, and there was nothing about the dinner to hold Irene's interest, so her attention wandered from the food to the deposits of silver polish on the candlesticks and from there to the music in the other room. She listened for a few minutes to a Chopin prelude and then was surprised to hear a man's voice break in. "For Christ's sake, Kathy," he said, "do you always have to play the piano when I get home?" The music stopped abruptly. "It's the only chance I have," a woman said. "I'm at the office all day." "So am I," the man said. He added something obscene about an upright piano, and slammed a door. The passionate and melancholy music began again.

"Did you hear that?" Irene asked.

"What?" Jim was eating his dessert.   10

"The radio. A man said something while the music was still going on—something dirty."

"It's probably a play."

"I don't think it *is* a play," Irene said.

They left the table and took their coffee into the living room. Irene asked Jim to try another station. He turned the knob. "Have you seen my garters?" a man asked. "Button me up," a woman said. "Have you seen my garters?" the man said again. "Just button me up and I'll find your garters," the woman said. Jim shifted to another station. "I wish you wouldn't leave apple cores in the ashtrays," a man said. "I hate the smell."

"This is strange," Jim said.   15

"Isn't it?" Irene said.

Jim turned the knob again. "'On the **coast of Coromandel** where the early pumpkins blow,'" a woman with a pronounced English accent said, "'in the middle of the woods lived the Yonghy-Bonghy-Bò. Two old chairs, and half a candle, one old jug without a handle . . .'"

"My God!" Irene cried. "That's the Sweeneys' nurse."

"'These were all his worldly goods,'" the British voice continued.

"Turn that thing off," Irene said. "Maybe they can hear *us.*" Jim   20 switched the radio off. "That was Miss Armstrong, the Sweeneys' nurse," Irene said. "She must be reading to the little girl. They live in 17-B. I've talked with Miss Armstrong in the Park. I know her voice very well. We must be getting other people's apartments."

"That's impossible," Jim said.

"Well, that was the Sweeneys' nurse," Irene said hotly. "I know her voice. I know it very well. I'm wondering if they can hear us."

Jim turned the switch. First from a distance and then nearer, nearer, as if borne on the wind, came the pure accents of the Sweeneys' nurse again: "'Lady Jingly! Lady Jungly!'" she said, "'sitting where the pumpkins blow, will you come and be my wife? said the Yonghy-Bonghy-Bò . . .'"

Jim went over to the radio and said "Hello" loudly into the speaker.

"'I am tired of living singly,'" the nurse went on, "'on this coast so wild and shingly, I'm a-weary of my life; if you'll come and be my wife, quite serene would be my life . . .'" 25

"I guess she can't hear us," Irene said. "Try something else."

Jim turned to another station, and the living room was filled with the uproar of a cocktail party that had overshot its mark. Someone was playing the piano and singing the "Whiffenpoof Song," and the voices that surrounded the piano were vehement and happy. "Eat some more sandwiches," a woman shrieked. There were screams of laughter and a dish of some sort crashed to the floor.

"Those must be the Fullers, in 11-E," Irene said. "I knew they were giving a party this afternoon. I saw her in the liquor store. Isn't this too divine? Try something else. See if you can get those people in 18-C."

The Westcotts overheard that evening a monologue on salmon fishing in Canada, a bridge game, running comments on home movies of what had apparently been a fortnight at Sea Island, and a bitter family quarrel about an overdraft at the bank. They turned off their radio at midnight and went to bed, weak with laughter. Sometime in the night, their son began to call for a glass of water and Irene got one and took it to his room. It was very early. All the lights in the neighborhood were extinguished, and from the boy's window she could see the empty street. She went into the living room and tried the radio. There was some faint coughing, a moan, and then a man spoke. "Are you all right, darling?" he asked. "Yes," a woman said wearily. "Yes, I'm all right, I guess," and then she added with great feeling, "But, you know, Charlie, I don't feel like myself any more. Sometimes there are about fifteen or twenty minutes in the week when I feel like myself. I don't like to go to another doctor, because the doctor's bills are so awful already, but I just don't feel like myself, Charlie. I just never feel like myself." They were not young, Irene thought. She guessed from the **timbre** of their voices that they were middle-aged. The restrained melancholy of the dialogue and the draft from the bedroom window made her shiver, and she went back to bed.

The following morning, Irene cooked breakfast for the family—the maid didn't come up from her room in the basement until ten—braided her daughter's hair, and waited at the door until her children and her husband had been carried away in the elevator. Then she went into the living 30 room and tried the radio. "I don't want to go to school," a child screamed. "I hate school. I won't go to school. I hate school." "You will go to school," an enraged woman said. "We paid eight hundred dollars to get you into that school and you'll go if it kills you." The next number on the dial produced the worn record of the "Missouri Waltz." Irene shifted the control and invaded the privacy of several breakfast tables. She overheard demonstrations of indigestion, carnal love, abysmal vanity, faith, and despair. Irene's life was nearly as simple and sheltered as it appeared to be, and the forthright and sometimes brutal language that came from the loudspeaker that morning astonished and troubled her. She continued to listen until her maid came in. Then she turned off the radio quickly, since this insight, she realized, was a **furtive** one.

Irene had a luncheon date with a friend that day, and she left her apartment at a little after twelve. There were a number of women in the elevator when it stopped at her floor. She stared at their handsome and impassive faces, their furs, and the cloth flowers in their hats. Which one of them had been to Sea Island? she wondered. Which one had overdrawn her bank account? The elevator stopped at the tenth floor and a woman with a pair of Skye terriers joined them. Her hair was rigged high on her head and she wore a mink cape. She was humming the "Missouri Waltz."

Irene had two Martinis at lunch, and she looked searchingly at her friend and wondered what her secrets were. They had intended to go shopping after lunch, but Irene excused herself and went home. She told the maid that she was not to be disturbed; then she went into the living room, closed the doors, and switched on the radio. She heard, in the course of the afternoon, the halting conversation of a woman entertaining her aunt, the hysterical conclusion of a luncheon party, and a hostess briefing her maid about some cocktail guests. "Don't give the best Scotch to anyone who hasn't white hair," the hostess said. "See if you can get rid of that liver paste before you pass those hot things, and could you lend me five dollars? I want to tip the elevator man."

As the afternoon waned, the conversations increased in intensity. From where Irene sat, she could see the open sky above the East River. There were hundreds of clouds in the sky, as though the south wind had broken the winter into pieces and were blowing it north, and on her radio she could hear the arrival of cocktail guests and the return of children and businessmen from their schools and offices. "I found a good-sized diamond on the bathroom floor this morning," a woman said. "It must have fallen out of that bracelet Mrs. Dunston was wearing last night." "We'll sell it," a man said. "Take it down to the jeweler on Madison Avenue and sell it. Mrs. Dunston won't know the difference, and we could use a couple of hundred bucks . . .'" "'Oranges and lemons, say the bells of St. Clement's,'" the Sweeneys' nurse sang. "'Halfpence and farthings, say the bells of St. Martin's. When will you pay me? say the bells at old Bailey . . .'" "It's not a hat," a woman cried, and at her back roared a cocktail party. "It's not a hat, it's a love affair. That's what Walter Florell said. He said it's not a hat, it's a love affair," and then, in a lower voice, the same woman added, "Talk to somebody, for Christ's sake, honey, talk to somebody. If she catches you standing here not talking to anybody, she'll take us off her invitation list, and I love these parties."

The Westcotts were going out for dinner that night, and when Jim came home, Irene was dressing. She seemed sad and vague, and he brought her a drink. They were dining with friends in the neighborhood, and they walked to where they were going. The sky was broad and filled with light. It was one of those splendid spring evenings that excite memory and desire, and the air that touched their hands and faces felt very soft. A Salvation Army band was on the corner playing "Jesus Is Sweeter." Irene drew on her husband's arm and held him there for a minute, to hear the music. "They're really such nice people, aren't they?" she said. "They have such nice faces. Actually, they're so much nicer than a lot of the people we know." She took a bill from her purse and walked over and dropped it into the tambourine. There was in her face, when she returned to her husband, a look of radiant melancholy that he was not familiar with. And her conduct at the dinner party that night seemed strange to him, too. She interrupted her hostess rudely and stared at the people across the table from her with an intensity for which she would have punished her children.

It was still mild when they walked home from the party, and Irene 35 looked up at the spring stars. "'How far that little candle throws its beams,'" she exclaimed. "'So shines a good deed in a naughty world.'" She waited that night until Jim had fallen asleep, and then went into the living room and turned on the radio.

Jim came home at about six the next night. Emma, the maid, let him in, and he had taken off his hat and was taking off his coat when Irene ran into the hall. Her face was shining with tears and her hair was disordered. "Go up to 16-C, Jim!" she screamed. "Don't take off your coat. Go up to 16-C. Mr. Osborn's beating his wife. They've been quarreling since four o'clock, and now he's hitting her. Go up there and stop him."

From the radio in the living room, Jim heard screams, obscenities, and thuds. "You know you don't have to listen to this sort of thing," he said. He strode into the living room and turned the switch. "It's indecent," he said. "It's like looking in windows. You know you don't have to listen to this sort of thing. You can turn if off."

"Oh, it's so horrible, it's so dreadful," Irene was sobbing. "I've been listening all day, and it's so depressing."

"Well, if it's so depressing, why do you listen to it? I bought this damned radio to give you some pleasure," he said. "I paid a great deal of money for it. I thought it might make you happy. I wanted to make you happy."

"Don't, don't, don't, don't quarrel with me," she moaned, and laid her 40 head on his shoulder. "All the others have been quarreling all day. Everybody's been quarreling. They're all worried about money. Mrs. Hutchinson's mother is dying of cancer in Florida and they don't have enough money to send her to the Mayo Clinic. At least, Mr. Hutchinson says they don't have enough money. And some woman in this building is having an affair with the handyman—with that hideous handyman. It's too disgusting. And Mrs. Melville has heart trouble and Mr. Hendricks is going to lose his job in April and Mrs. Hendricks is horrid about the whole thing and that girl who plays the 'Missouri Waltz' is a whore, a common whore, and the elevator man has tuberculosis and Mr. Osborn has been beating Mrs. Osborn." She wailed, she trembled with grief and checked the stream of tears down her face with the heel of her palm.

"Well, why do you have to listen?" Jim asked again. "Why do you have to listen to this stuff if it makes you so miserable?"

"Oh, don't, don't, don't," she cried. "Life is too terrible, too **sordid** and awful. But we've never been like that, have we, darling? Have we? I mean, we've always been good and decent and loving to one another, haven't we? And we have two children, two beautiful children. Our lives aren't **sordid,** are they, darling? Are they?" She flung her arms around his neck and drew his face down to hers. "We're happy, aren't we, darling? We are happy, aren't we?"

"Of course we're happy," he said tiredly. He began to surrender his resentment. "Of course we're happy. I'll have that damned radio fixed or taken away tomorrow." He stroked her soft hair. "My poor girl," he said.

"You love me, don't you?" she asked. "And we're not hypercritical or worried about money or dishonest, are we?"

"No, darling," he said. 45

A man came in the morning and fixed the radio. Irene turned it on cautiously and was happy to hear a California-wine commercial and a recording of Beethoven's Ninth Symphony, including Schiller's "Ode to Joy." She kept the radio on all day and nothing untoward came from the speaker.

A Spanish suite was being played when Jim came home. "Is everything all right?" he asked. His face was pale, she thought. They had some cocktails and went in to dinner to the "Anvil Chorus" from Il Trovatore. This was followed by Debussy's "La Mer."

"I paid the bill for the radio today," Jim said. "It cost four hundred dollars. I hope you'll get some enjoyment out of it."

"Oh, I'm sure I will," Irene said.

"Four hundred dollars is a good deal more than I can afford," he went 50
on. "I wanted to get something that you'd enjoy. It's the last extravagance
we'll be able to indulge in this year. I see that you haven't paid your clothing
bills yet. I saw them on your dressing table." He looked directly at her.
"Why did you tell me you'd paid them? Why did you lie to me?"

"I just didn't want you to worry, Jim," she said. She drank some water.
"I'll be able to pay my bills out of this month's allowance. There were the
slipcovers last month, and that party."

"You've got to learn to handle the money I give you a little more in-
telligently, Irene," he said. "You've got to understand that we won't have as
much money this year as we had last. I had a very sobering talk with Mitch-
ell today. No one is buying anything. We're spending all our time promoting new issues, and you know how long that takes. I'm not getting any
younger, you know. I'm thirty-seven. My hair will be gray next year. I
haven't done as well as I'd hoped to do. And I don't suppose things will get
any better."

"Yes, dear," she said.

"We've got to start cutting down," Jim said. "We've got to think of
the children. To be perfectly frank with you, I worry about money a great
deal. I'm not at all sure of the future. No one is. If anything should happen
to me, there's the insurance, but that wouldn't go very far today. I've
worked awfully hard to give you and the children a comfortable life," he
said bitterly. "I don't like to see all of my energies, all of my youth, wasted
in fur coats and radios and slipcovers and—"

"Please, Jim," she said. "Please. They'll hear us."   55

"*Who'll hear us?* Emma can't hear us."

"The radio."

"Oh, I'm sick!" he shouted. "I'm sick to death of your apprehensive-
ness. The radio can't hear us. Nobody can hear us. And what if they can
hear us? Who cares?"

Irene got up from the table and went into the living room. Jim went to
the door and shouted at her from there. "Why are you so Christly all of a
sudden? What's turned you overnight into a convent girl? You stole your
mother's jewelry before they probated her will. You never gave your sister
a cent of that money that was intended for her—not even when she needed
it. You made Grace Howland's life miserable, and where was all your piety
and your virtue when you went to that abortionist? I'll never forget how
cool you were. You packed your bag and went off to have that child murdered as if you were going to Nassau. If you'd had any reasons, if you'd had
any good reasons—"

Irene stood for a minute before the hideous cabinet, disgraced and 60 sickened, but she held her hand on the switch before she extinguished the music and the voices, hoping that the instrument might speak to her kindly, that she might hear the Sweeneys' nurse. Jim continued to shout at her from the door. The voice on the radio was suave and noncommittal. "An early-morning railroad disaster in Tokyo," the loudspeaker said, "killed twenty-nine people. A fire in a Catholic hospital near Buffalo for the care of blind children was extinguished early this morning by nuns. The temperature is forty-seven. The humidity is eighty-nine."

QUESTIONS FOR DISCUSSION

1. In the beginning of the story, are the Westcotts portrayed as a happy couple? Give some examples that show the family's contentment.

2. What role does music play in the couple's happiness?

3. Why do you think that it is Irene Westcott, and not Jim Westcott, who becomes obsessed with the radio?

4. Is Jim Westcott unaffected by the radio? Explain your answer and offer some details from the story to support your view.

5. Why do you think this had to be an *enormous* radio? Would a small, pocket-sized radio have worked just as well in the story?

6. Which ideas about the pursuit of happiness presented in the other readings in this chapter do you find also present in this story?

In the following essay, a student from Hong Kong tells why he agrees with John Ciardi's claim that happiness comes from taking on "life-engaging difficulties." He uses both the essay and his own observations to develop his idea, responding to topic 8 from the list that concludes this chapter.

✍ STUDENT ESSAY:

The Pursuit of Difficulty

In his essay "Is Everybody Happy?" John Ciardi writes that "There is no happiness except as we take on life-engaging difficulties." This might sound contradictory to many people who think of happiness as freedom from difficulty, people who enjoy themselves only on weekends. However, I find a lot of truth in Ciardi's words. For me, happiness is completely different from fun and pleasure. Happiness comes from achieving personal goals, and, more importantly, it comes after enduring pain.

It seems that many people can scarcely distinguish fun or pleasure from real happiness. People living extravagant, exciting lives are widely regarded as being incessantly happy. For example, Hollywood stars, who own fancy cars, beautiful clothes, and countless invitations to celebrity parties are admired by many people. However, they seem to be frequently obsessed by the problems of drug addiction, divorce, or family scandals. They try to avoid disclosure of their personal secrets in order for their images not to be destroyed. This fun-filled happiness turns out to be an illusion, vague and elusive. My late grandmother once told me that she never regretted anything about her whole life. She didn't achieve any enormous success during her life; she did what she needed to do as a housewife. A close-knit family and a few grown-up children made her happy. She might not describe raising children as "fun." She usually talked about how much trouble her children had given her. Nevertheless, there was a sparkle in her eyes, and I could see that successfully raising a family had made her very happy.

Like Ciardi, I believe that real happiness is built on pain and difficulty. I never trust painless satisfaction. It doesn't last. It seems that the more difficulties I endure on the road to success, the more durable is the happiness I gain. If I do well in an easy class, I don't feel the solid sense of satisfaction I feel when I do well in a difficult one. I am happier if I win a tennis match against a strong opponent than if I defeat a weak one. I have noticed also that most successful businessmen mention their painful pasts and emphasize the difficulties they had to overcome to get where they are. The happiness that comes after a hard struggle is more meaningful and real. As Ciardi says, "The right to pursue happiness is issued to Americans with their birth certificates." Can happiness be pursued? I don't think so. Both Ciardi and Ashley Montagu, in his essay entitled "The Pursuit of Happiness," agree that chasing after happiness is a vain pursuit. As Montagu says, happiness is "a by-product of the dedication, the labor, that has been involved." Perhaps it would be better if the Declaration of Independence had guaranteed "Life, liberty, and the freedom to choose our difficulties."

TOPICS FOR WRITING

1. Discuss the role of money in American attitudes toward happiness, and give examples from any of the essays in this chapter to illustrate your explanation.

2. Compare de Tocqueville and Gurko's views on the American obsession with individualism and equality. Where do they agree and where do they disagree?

3. Using your own examples, show that de Tocqueville's observations about American society, although made in the 1830s, still apply today.

4. Describe an instance when you have been happy, and explain which elements of this experience contributed to your happiness.

5. In "Flights from the Unavoidable Self," Gurko says, "One of the roughest hurdles in the struggle for maturity is the acceptance of the self and its responsibilities." If you agree with this statement, write an essay supporting the view that maturity is a necessary ingredient of happiness.

6. Discuss the two different views of happiness the Westcotts hold in "The Enormous Radio." Use details and examples from the story to support your assertions.

7. Using examples from "The Enormous Radio," describe Irene Westcott's change from a contented mother and wife to a disillusioned and deeply unhappy person.

8. Choose one of the quotations below and use it as a springboard for a definition of your own idea of happiness.

From Ashley Montagu, "The Pursuit of Happiness":

". . . everything must be made easy for the children, and their every need satisfied."

"The pursuit of happiness in America is the most misconceived of human endeavors."

"The truth is that it is not the purpose of life, of a human being's life, to be happy."

"It is in the state when one is least conscious of oneself that one is likely to be at one's happiest."

"Work is the most dependable of all sources of happiness."

From John Ciardi, "Is Everybody Happy?":

"We [Americans] do seem to be dedicated to the idea of buying our way to happiness."

"There is no happiness except as we take on life-engaging difficulties."
"The mortal flaw in the advertised version of happiness is in the fact that it purports to be effortless."
"Whatever happiness may be, it is neither in having nor in being, but in becoming."

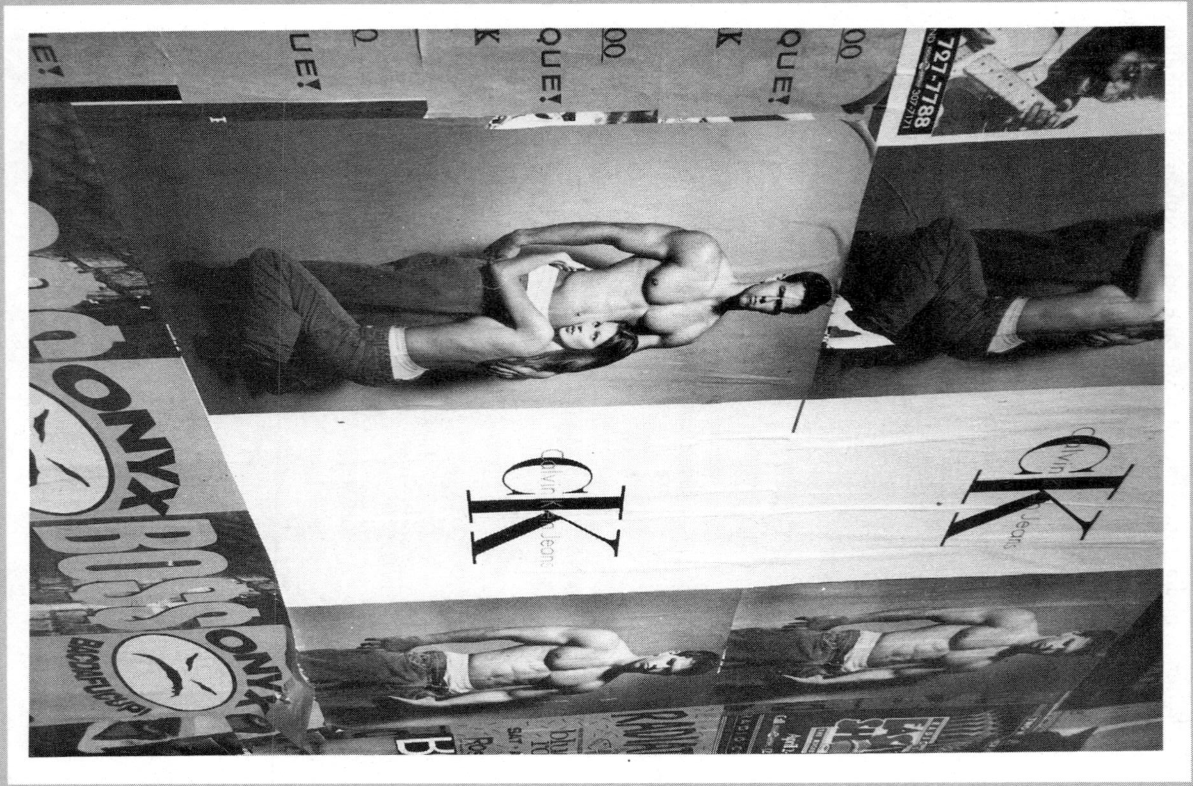
727-7788
ONYX
ONYX

13 Madison Avenue Dreams

"The consumer is to the manufacturer, the department stores and the advertising agencies, what the green frog is to the physiologist."

–JOHN WATSON
founder of behavioral psychology

In America, the pursuit of happiness often looks the same as the pursuit of things. In fact, John Locke, the British philosopher who furnished Thomas Jefferson with many of his ideas, defined the inalienable rights as "Life, liberty and the pursuit of *property*."

We pursue property, and the sellers of property pursue us. Advertising has grown from a simple act of announcing one's product or place of business to a multi-billion dollar operation that uses state-of-the-art techniques to get our attention and manipulate our behavior. Advertisers were among the first to put depth psychology to practical use, and they've done it with a vengeance.

Advertising is everywhere. It has been estimated that the average American is exposed to something like 1,400 ads every day: print ads, radio and TV ads, billboards, posters, flyers, shop signs. Such a policy of saturation must have some effect. Some analysts argue that the collective effect of all these ads is like a constant drumbeat, pounding out the message that all of life's problems can be solved by buying something.

How do ads work? Most often by association. Not many ads simply try to sell the product on its own merits. Instead they try to create a link between the product and some intangible benefit: you'll get the girl if only you'll brush your teeth with our stuff; life will be one happy beach party if only you'll drink plenty of cola. A common saying in the advertising industry is, "Don't sell the steak, sell the sizzle."

Advertisers are well aware that people have emotional needs and weaknesses. We need to feel powerful, we need to belong and to be accepted by others, we need to be successful, popular, beautiful. Whatever it is we want, advertisers will be sure to hitch a product to it.

The selections in this chapter probe the words and images beamed to us daily by Madison Avenue, New York's street of advertising agencies, the place where dreams are bought and sold.

P. T. BARNUM

From *Struggles and Triumphs*

Phineas Taylor (P. T.) Barnum was an American showman, best known for his partnership in the Barnum and Baily Circus— "The Greatest Show on Earth." As a young man, Barnum worked as a hat salesman, a grocery clerk, and proprietor of a boarding house. He entered show business when he acquired a run-down museum in New York City, stocked it with freaks and oddities, and called it "Barnum's American Museum." He joined with James Anthony Baily in 1881 to create the famous circus.

Barnum also served in the Connecticut legislature and as mayor of Bridgeport, Connecticut.

KEY VOCABULARY

MONOMANIA is an exaggerated or even pathological obsession with a single idea.

PALLIATION is the act of making something seem less serious, reducing pain or intensity.

I thoroughly understood the art of advertising, not merely by means of 1 printer's ink, which I have always used freely, and to which I confess myself so much indebted for my success, but by turning every possible circumstance to my account. It was my **monomania** to make the Museum the town wonder and town talk. I often seized upon an opportunity by instinct, even before I had a very definite conception as to how it should be used, and it seemed, somehow, to mature itself and serve my purpose. As an illustration, one morning a stout, hearty-looking man came into my ticket-office and begged some money. I asked him why he did not work and earn his living? He replied that he could get nothing to do, and that he would be glad of any job at a dollar a day. I handed him a quarter of a dollar, told him to go and get his breakfast and return, and I would employ him, at light labor, at a dollar and a half a day. When he returned I gave him five common bricks.

"Now," said I, "go and lay a brick on the sidewalk at the corner of Broadway and Ann street; another close by the Museum; a third diagonally across the way, at the corner of Broadway and Vesey street, by the Astor House; put down the fourth on the sidewalk, in front of St. Paul's Church, opposite; then, with the fifth brick in hand, take up a rapid march from one point to another, making the circuit, exchanging your brick at every point, and say nothing to any one.

"What is the object of this?" inquired the man.

"No matter," I replied; "all you need to know is that it brings you fifteen cents wages an hour. It is a bit of my fun, and to assist me properly you must seem to be as deaf as a post; wear a serious countenance; answer no questions; pay no attention to any one; but attend faithfully at the work, and at the end of every hour, by St. Paul's clock, show this ticket at the Museum door; enter, walking solemnly through every hall in the building; pass out, and resume your work."

With the remark that it was "all one to him, so long as he could earn   5 his living," the man placed his bricks, and began his round. Half an hour afterwards, at least five hundred people were watching his mysterious movements. He had assumed a military step and bearing, and, looking as sober as a judge, he made no response whatever to the constant inquiries as to the object of his singular conduct. At the end of the first hour, the sidewalks in the vicinity were packed with people, all anxious to solve the mystery. The man, as directed, then went into the Museum, devoting fifteen minutes to a solemn survey of the halls, and afterwards returning to his round. This was repeated every hour till sundown, and whenever the man went into the Museum a dozen or more persons would buy tickets and follow him, hoping to gratify their curiosity in regard to the purpose of his movements. This was continued for several days—the curious people who followed the man into the Museum considerably more than paying his wages—till finally the policeman, to whom I imparted my object, complained that the obstruction of the sidewalk by crowds had become so serious that I must call in my "brick man." This trivial incident excited considerable talk and amusement; it advertised me; and it materially advanced my purpose of making a lively corner near the Museum. . . .

I determined to make people talk about my Museum; to exclaim over its wonders; to have men and women all over the country say: "There is not another place in the United States where so much can be seen for twenty-five cents as in Barnum's American Museum." It was the best advertisement I could possible have, and one for which I could afford to pay. I knew, too, that it was an honorable advertisement, because it was as deserved as it was spontaneous. And so, in addition to the permanent collection and the ordinary attractions of the stage, I labored to keep the Museum well supplied with transient novelties; I exhibited such living curiosities as a rhinoceros, giraffes, grizzly bears, ourangoutangs, great serpents and whatever else of the kind money would buy or enterprise secure.

It was the world's way then, as it is now, to excite the community with flaming posters, promising almost everything for next to nothing. I confess that I took no pains to set my enterprising fellow-citizens a better example. I fell in with the world's way; and if my "puffing" was more persistent, my advertising more audacious, my posters more glaring, my pictures more exaggerated, my flags more patriotic and my transparencies more brilliant than they would have been under the management of my neighbors, it was not because I had less scruple than they, but more energy, far more ingenuity, and a better foundation for such promises. In all this, if I cannot be justified, I at least find **palliation** in the fact that I presented a wilderness of wonderful, instructive, and amusing realities of such evident and marked merit that I have yet to learn of a single instance where a visitor went away from the Museum complaining that he had been defrauded of his money. Surely this is an offset to any eccentricities to which I may have resorted to make my establishment widely known. . . .

QUESTIONS FOR DISCUSSION

1. Why is the work P. T. Barnum gives the beggar a nice example of "the art of advertising"? First, explain what Barnum means by "the art of advertising."

2. Would a museum be a good choice for "the town wonder and town talk"? Consider whether it would have been a good choice at the time Barnum was writing (late ninteenth century), as well as today.

3. Why is ingenuity an indispensable quality of the successful advertiser?

4. What does the townspeople's reaction to Barnum's scheme say about human nature?

✒ DAVID GUTERSON

Moneyball! On the Relentless Promotion of Pro Sports

David Guterson is a contributing editor of Harper's Magazine. *He is also the author of the recently published novel,* Snow Falling on Cedars.

KEY VOCABULARY

An ICON was, originally, a sacred image of a Christian personage, such as Christ or a saint; generally, the word refers to any symbol, like a flag or statue, that is held in high regard.

A TOTEM is an animal, plant, or other natural object that serves as an emblem of a tribe or clan in some primal societies.

Last June, as the New York Rangers and the New York Knicks stood 1 poised to win the Stanley Cup and the National Basketball Association championship, their owner, Viacom Inc., an $11 billion conglomerate, announced its unsentimental intention to sell the teams. The price for the Knicks, the experts predicted, might reach $200 million; for the Rangers, $100 million—and whatever pride Viacom might have taken in either team was as irrelevant to the deal as the muttering of hometown fans. Sports was business, not poetry, and any twelve- or sixty-year-old kid who thought otherwise had never bought a goalie or 100,000 gallons of beer.

At halftime of the seventh game of the NBA finals, which the Knicks lost to the Houston Rockets at Madison Square Garden, NBA commissioner David Stern told NBC sportscaster Bob Costas that the NBA's steering committee would ponder changing the placement of the three-point line in order to raise scores—and, by implication, TV ratings. The championship game itself flowed seamlessly into and out of commercials featuring products hawked by Shaquille O'Neal, Patrick Ewing, and Charles Barkley; ads for NBA-licensed videos of slam-dunking players; and promos for an odd, NBC-televised competition featuring Dream Team II, a squad composed of NBA stars. The unfolding of the game, it was clear to me, had become indivisible from the promotion of products, and I asked myself, while staring at the television, whether the game, its poetry and beauty, hadn't suffered deeply in the process. I wondered whether it was possible for sport to be commodified and still resemble itself. Could the poetry of sport survive?

Professional sport, it seems fair to say, is a primary expression of the American character at the end of the twentieth century. Like money, it is something we love, a first waking thought and a chronic passion, as well as a vast sector of the economy, a wellspring for contemporary myth and to-tem, and a media phenomenon of the highest order. Our sports can fend off the brute facts of existence, temporarily arrest the sadness of life, briefly shroud the inevitability of death, and provide the happy illusion of meaning through long, enchanted afternoons. The elation of games can hold us spellbound until finally we are forced to accept their endings, and then we are spent and returned to life, rendered hollow or exuberantly fulfilled, but always afterward cognizant of the real world, with its bits of peanut shell under our shoes and the dark hint of rain to the west. In short, nothing about our national life is quite so national as sport is. Sport is a language we all speak. Sport is a mirror. Sport is life. Through sport we might know ourselves.

But what is it that so commands our attention? On May 1 of this year, to pick a day at random—a sunlit Sunday in most parts of the country and an occasion in other times and places for dancing, flower gathering, or So-cialist parades—millions of American men and women sat in thrall to the games displayed for long hours on their televisions. It was in no way an unusual day in the annals of televised sport: on ABC, a National Hockey League play-off game, followed by the Shell Houston Open golf tourna-ment; on NBC, *The NBA Show,* followed by three NBA play-off games televised over the course of seven hours; the LPGA Sprint golf champion-ship, airing for two hours on CBS, followed by programs called *Eye on Sports, Golf Club,* and *Sports Folly;* a regular-season baseball game—the At-lanta Braves against the Pittsburgh Pirates—for three morning hours on TBS; another NBA play-off game—the Portland Trail Blazers against the Houston Rockets—for two and a half hours on TNT; and, of course, ESPN, the network devoted entirely to sport, which on this day aired the NASCAR Winston Select 500, the Las Vegas Senior Golf Classic, and the Boston Red Sox against the California Angels, all punctuated by constant scores and updates and by news-format shows like *Sports Report, Sports-Center,* and *SportsWeekly.* Meanwhile, on CNN Headline News, an eternal ticker tape of game scores ran silently beneath footage of the carnage in Bosnia, so that while contemplating the mud-stained face of a murdered Muslim, say, viewers were aware that in the second quarter the Blazers had just gone up by three after trailing the Rockets a minute earlier. Finally, there was ESPN2, the MTV of the sporting world—slam dunks coming one after the other, set to the latest hip-hop hits; athletes slashing and smashing and trash-talking, taunting, pointing, pumping their fists, dancing, cavorting, and stylishly posturing, generally playing to the camera. Across the spectrum of the thirty or more channels that make up American television, sport in all of its glory and diversity was a good deal more prevalent than anything else—which is, perhaps, just another way of saying that it was like outdated sitcoms, infomercials, and other forms of programming filler: safe, brainless, lucrative.

That day in May was another proof of what sports fans intuitively 5 know: that there is now no end to "major" sporting events and that these are sequenced in the calendar such that each may be watched by as large an audience as possible. New Year's Day, to begin at the beginning, is largely an occasion for ever-proliferating college football bowl games; three weeks later fans turn toward pro football's Super Bowl. In February this year came the Winter Olympics, followed in March by NCAA basketball's Final Four tournament and then in April by NBA play-off contests, which, together with the NHL play-offs and golf tournaments, held fan interest into mid-June. Sport's movers and shakers, distressed by the long, sweet lull of baseball's season, sought this July to sell soccer to Americans in the hope that the World Cup might supply, in future years, a spasm of interest through hot summers. This fall first the U.S. Open and then the World Series will command fans' attention, and then suddenly football and basketball will return, and the cycle will repeat itself. Sport's endless season binds fans upon a wheel where the end is always merely the beginning, one championship but a prelude to the next.

And that endless season is now overwhelmingly commercial. Arenas and the vast perimeters of stadiums are thoroughly festooned with advertisements and big-screen graphics that fans can neither ignore nor turn away from: the scoreboard, the game clock, the scorer's bench, the chairs where NBA players rest, the shirts and sweatpants worn by ball boys, the cups players drink from and the towels around their necks—even the shoes they wear on their feet—are chockablock with sales messages. Last year baseball's American League voted to allow its teams to install rotating electronic signs in their parks, and in some these signs are now placed above and behind first and third bases. (Home plate, the holiest spot on the field, was traditionally immune to advertising, yet in five major league stadiums the space behind home plate has been sold—including my hometown of Seattle, where when Ken Griffey Jr. steps up to the plate he is framed against an electronic sign advertising Starbucks Coffee, Ace Hardware, and Nintendo, among other companies.) Every nuance of a televised game is similarly freighted with logos and slogans: a power play, a fast break, or steal; a report on rebounds, assists, or blocks; an instant replay or twenty-second time-out—all have become occasions for celebrating the name of a paint manufacturer, telephone company, or overnight courier service. When I look at the slogans and **icons** of business now pasted everywhere across the fields and screens of play, I am more than just merely irritated. For me they mar the aesthetic of games, subvert the clean lines of the unfolding ice dance, draw my eye from the breaking curve of a pitch, and generally destroy most of my pleasure.

QUESTIONS FOR DISCUSSION

1. Why, according to the article, are sports events a year-round affair?

2. Is the author tolerant or critical of the relationship between sports and commercialism? Give examples.

3. Why is home plate considered "the holiest spot on the field"? How does this statement about home plate, as well as the use of words like *totem* and *icon,* imply the almost religious place of sports in American culture?

4. Explain your views about the role of money in sports.

✍ JEFFREY SCHRANK

Psychosell

Jeffrey Schrank is the editor of Media Mix Newsletters *and a contributing editor of* Media Methods. *He has written several books, among them* Teaching Human Beings: 101 Subversive Activities for the Classroom *and* Snap, Crackle, and Pop: The Illusion of Free Choice in America, *the book from which the following selection was taken.*

KEY VOCABULARY

ALDOUS HUXLEY (1894–1963) was an English novelist and essayist whose best-known book, *Brave New World,* expresses his concern over the dangers of scientific progress.

A **DOCTRINE** is a body of principles or ideas which are thought to be truthful and believable.

HERBERT GEORGE (H. G.) WELLS (1866–1946) was an English journalist and novelist. He wrote science fiction, historical novels, and popular accounts of history and science. He is best known for his novels *The Invisible Man, The Time Machine* and *The War of the Worlds.*

LEGION, here, means a large number, a multitude.

LUCRATIVE means profitable.

NEUROSIS can refer to several disorders of the mind or emotions that produce abnormal symptoms, such as anxiety or phobia (exaggerated fear of something).

PECUNIARY means monetary; related to money.

A **SEMANTICIST** is a specialist in meaning, especially the meaning of language. Generally, "semantics" is the study of signs and symbols and that which they represent.

Putting aside the blinding criticisms and feelings about advertising, we   1
can see ads as reflections of our national psychology. Ads often exploit holes
in the national personality. We can either condemn the exploitation or use
the ads to see the holes more clearly—or both.

Humans are symbol-makers and abstractionists who give meaning to
things. Advertisers are not responsible for this phenomenon; it exists in cultures where advertising does not. Primitive tribes have status symbols; a row
of pots on the roof of a hut can symbolize a successful provider just as clearly

as a Cadillac in the driveway. But advertisers do attach psychological labels to objects and present them as capable of filling certain personality holes. Coca-Cola promises the "real thing" not only to counter a Seven-Up "Uncola" campaign but also because phoniness and artificiality are so much a part of our culture. Pepsi "helps 'em come alive" only because there are so many people out of touch with themselves and feeling a deadness inside. Countless products from beer to boots promise masculinity (and define it as well) because there are so many males who have serious doubts about their sexual identity.

After viewing a thousand ads and commercials (equivalent to the number seen by an average person in three days), two basic personality holes might be quite evident—the lack of genuinely pleasurable experiences and the absence of self-acceptance. It is these holes that advertisers have found most **lucrative** and most exploitable.

Ads that illustrate and imply fun, excitement, adventure, and pleasure are among the most common precisely because these experiences are missing from so many lives. Just as the well person does not constantly ask himself how he feels, the society with a healthy amount of pleasurable experience would not respond to such advertising. A truly pleasure-loving society would be invulnerable to the illusory promises presented in ads for soft drinks, alcoholic beverages, franchise food, or hundreds of other products. There would be no room for a communications system to tell citizens that a cigarette will help them come "alive with pleasure" or a beer will enable them to "reach for all the gusto you can" or that a soft drink can "add life."

A national virtue of self-acceptance would send the ad world into tur- 5
moil. For ads that promise to provide a measure of indirect self-acceptance are **legion.** A most common kind of ad shows the owner or user of a product being accepted by others. This need for approval, acceptance, and even status is a sign of the lack of self-acceptance. A self-accepting individual will still use soap, wear clothes, and drive an automobile, but his or her use of these items is not prompted by the need to gain acceptance—there is no hole to fill. Advertising that associates approval by neighbors and friends, members of the opposite sex and society in general with products thrives only where self-acceptance is lacking.

Ads not only reflect the national psychology, they also educate. **H. G. Wells's** fictional advertising man, Dickon Clissold, had the right idea:

> "Advertising; what is it? Education. Modern Education, nothing more or less. The airs schoolmasters and college dons give themselves are extraordinary. They think they're the only people who teach. We teach ten times as much . . .

"The only use I've got for schools now is to fit people to read advertisements. After that, *we* take over. Yes, we—the advertisers."

From the seller's viewpoint advertising is persuasion; from the buyer's viewpoint it is education. No single group of people spends as much time or money per lesson to educate the masses as do the creators of ads.

Ads participate in a feedback loop. They reflect a society they have helped to educate, and part of the advertising reflection is the effect of the advertising itself. Every ad that exploits a personality hole educates the audience toward using a particular product to fill that hole. Just as drug ads teach a crude and sometimes dangerous form of self-medication, psychosell ads teach a form of self-analysis and cure for psychological problems.

An ad that stirs a hidden doubt, that causes a person to ask, "Why does no one love me?"; "Why don't I have more friends?"; "Why am I lonely?" invariably goes on to suggest a partial cure—use our product. If an announcer for Pepsi would appear on screen and say

"Are you lonely? Do you feel left out? Do you sometimes feel that everybody else has all the fun in life? Are you bored and isolated? Well, if you are, drink Pepsi and find yourself instantly a part of all those energetic, joyful, young-at-heart people who also drink Pepsi,"

such an ad would be greeted as either laughable or insulting by the viewing audience. Yet the old "Pepsi generation" campaign used pictures and a jingle to make exactly such a point.

The danger in psychosell techniques is not that people might switch 10 from Coke to Pepsi in soft-drink loyalties or abandon Scope for Listerine. The danger is that millions learn (especially if the message is repeated often enough, as ads are) that problems in self-acceptance and boredom can be alleviated by corporate products. Which brand to buy is secondary to ads as education; the primary lesson is that the product itself satisfies psychological needs.

This is a dangerous **doctrine,** for as long as masses of people believe that personality holes can be filled by items bought in stores it matters little which brands they buy. The failure of the gospel of advertising to solve problems merely leads people on to buy a reportedly more effective or prestigious brand (be it a car, house, or perfume) rather than to question their motives for the original purchase. Psychosell ads educate us to look "out there" for solutions instead of within. Advertising promotes and thrives on the **neurosis** that passes for normality. Ads teach that personal failures can be avoided by things almost as a witch doctor promises magic charms to cure illnesses. By so doing they contribute to mass **neurosis** and alienation as well as pseudo-choice. Our most effective means of education sell instant solutions instead of the motivation needed to gain psychological maturity. The danger of the "hidden persuaders" is not that they are seldom noticed, but that they help to keep ourself hidden.

If one pages through some old magazines rescued from the basement, a few psychosell techniques stand out. An ad for jeeps shows a lone man in a red jeep from a very low camera angle. The jeep seems almost to be flying against the backdrop of a blue sky with a few massive clouds. The ground looks more like a wheat field with a crew cut, and the picture is obviously an artist's drawing rather than a photograph. The headline pasted over the sky is "The Great Escape." The ad is typical, neither especially creative nor unusually perceptive.

The promise of a "great escape" would hardly be worth the thousands of dollars the magazine page costs unless there are a great many people who feel a need to escape. The ad appeals to those who feel imprisoned. Its headline probes that part of each of us that feels trapped—perhaps by work or family responsibilities or the problems of being human. The ad visually promises that a jeep will provide freedom.

The picture evokes the dream of wide-open space and the freedom of the frontier and a man alone on his trusted horse. The name of the jeep model, the copy tells us, is "Renegade," carrying further both the wild West theme and the escape from boredom—who ever heard of a bored renegade? The buyer of a jeep can share the dream of the early Americans to escape to the uncivilized lands of the wild West. The combination of a man and his machine facing the wide-open spaces is often used in ads for snowmobiles, autos, motorcycles, recreational vehicles, and boats. In many of the ads the machine is presented as a surrogate horse or woman (or both) and the promise of freedom and excitement is at least implied.

The copy in the jeep ad reads: 15

Comin' at you—the famous Jeep CJ-5, the ultimate get-up-an'-go machine. Get a hold of one of these babies, like this sporty Jeep Renegade, and you're in for the ride of your life.

She was born to run free far from the pavement. Built to take hard knocks in her stride, the Renegade boasts a brawny suspension, heavy duty axles and a tight 32.9 ft. turning diameter. Roll bar, fender tip extensions, and special aluminum wheels come with this spirited beauty.

. . . '74 Jeep Renegade for a really great escape.

It would be quite easy to dismiss the copy as embarrassing writing by a frustrated poet. But it would be more accurate to consider ad copy a form of poetry—call it **pecuniary** poetry. **Aldous Huxley** recognized that

"The advertisement is one of the most interesting and difficult of modern literary forms." **Semanticist** S. I. Hayakawa agrees that advertising is a form of poetry. Both use strict economy of language, paying careful attention to the slightest connotations and emotional effects of the words chosen. Both use intentional ambiguity to add meaning on multiple levels. Both advertising and poetry strive to give the objects of daily experience meanings beyond themselves. Ad writers, like poets, must invest things with significance since man is a maker and buyer of symbols more than things. The task of the copywriter is to poeticize consumer goods.

The jeep copy is intentionally ambiguous. Much of the copy can be applied not only to the product, but also to a woman. The jeep is "baby," "*she* was born," and is a "spirited beauty" who will give you the "ride of your life" if you are so lucky as to be able to "get a hold of one of these babies." And since the woman thus categorized would hardly be a feminist, the reader notes she is "built to take hard knocks in her stride." Of course, much of the copy could also be applied with some accuracy to a horse.

Considering the ad as education, we find it teaches that escape is equivalent to freedom. The jeep does not provide freedom, only its illusion. Freedom is not the possession of a machine that enables one to ride in fields on weekends. The ad teaches that freedom is the ability to afford occasional escape from whatever is preventing freedom. Ads, such as the psychosexual one for jeep, according to Erich Fromm in *Escape from Freedom,* "give . . . satisfaction by their daydreaming qualities just as the movies do, but at the same time they increase his feeling of smallness and powerlessness."

A few pages later in the magazine (which, by the way, contains more pages of advertising than editorial content) the same theme is repeated in a Yamaha ad with the headline "The great getaway machines." This ad shows romantic couples rather than a man alone but promises that the cycles will help the rider "leave behind the regimented week that was." The ad continues the theme of using a machine to rediscover the delights of Eden.

Lane furniture has a small ad showing a couple in a New York high 20 rise, standing at the bedroom door admiring each other or the Lane bedroom set. The headline asks, "Furniture or modern art?" and the copy answers, "It's both." The ad cautions potential buyers not to "be surprised if your friends view it as a work of art." The bedroom set is quite attractive but the illusion spun is that it has something to do with art. The furniture is mass produced and the woodlike carved surface is molded plastic. The pattern is given the out-West name of "Pueblo." The ad is a bit of art education (and where else can the casual reader obtain art education?) both denigrating the concept of art and strengthening the hold of kitsch.

The illusions that ads create are dangerous insofar as they are an education system that teaches us to look out there, into the marketplace, to solve problems and enhance our self-image. They are also dangerous because, as Alfred Korzybski, the founder of general **semantics,** points out, "Human beings are a symbolic class of life. Those who rule our symbols, rule us."

QUESTIONS FOR DISCUSSION

1. According to Schrank, what are the two personality "holes" revealed and exploited by advertising?
2. Can advertising be an educational tool? In what ways?
3. What is the "feedback loop" in which advertisements participate?
4. Name a few of the "psychosell" techniques mentioned in this text.
5. Why is ambiguity helpful to successful advertising?
6. Why does Schrank think that the illusions created by ads are dangerous?

♌ PATRICIA J. WILLIAMS

The Fiction of Truth in Advertising

*Patricia J. Williams, born in 1951, has a law degree from Harvard Law
School and is currently professor of law at Columbia Law School. She writes
primarily on civil rights issues and legal ethics. The selection below is from her
book* The Alchemy of Race and Rights *(1991).*

KEY VOCABULARY

AURAL means perceived by the ear; heard.

HUCKSTERISM is a derogatory term suggesting peddling—in the street or on
television alike—with no concern other than making money.

JUXTAPOSITION means the placing of two or more things side-by-side.

THE LANHAM ACT is a U.S. statute enacted in 1947 that revised trademark
laws.

A **LOGARITHM,** in this context, represents a difficult and tedious mathematical calculation.

NARCISSISTIC means having excessive admiration for oneself. In Greek mythology, Narcissus was a youth who rejected the love of another and then
pined away in love with his own image reflected in a pool. He was ultimately
transformed into the flower bearing his name.

When I first started teaching consumer protection a decade ago, the
mathematics of false advertising was simple. If the box or brochure said
"100% cotton," you merely took the item in question and subtracted it
from the words: Any difference was the measure of your legal remedy.
Sometimes you had to add in buyer's expertise or multiply the whole by
seller's bad faith, but generally the whole reason people even took a class in
consumer protection was that you didn't have to learn **logarithms.** Today,
however, advertisers almost never represent anything remotely related to
the reality of the product—or the politician—they are trying to sell; misrepresentation, the heart of false-advertising statutes, is very hard to prove.
Increasingly, television ads are characterized by scenarios that neither mention the product nor contain a description of any sort. What fills the sixty
seconds are "concepts" and diffuse images—images that used to be dis-
cursive, floating in the background, creating a mellow consumerist backdrop—which now dominate and direct content. Nothing is promised,
everything is evoked: warm fuzzy camera angles; "peak" experiences; happy

pictures, mood-shaping music; almost always a smarmy, soft-peddling over-voice purring "This magic moment has been brought to you by . . ."

An example, in the form of an anecdote: About a year ago, I was sitting at home, installed before the television set. I was preparing for a class in consumer protection. The next day's assignment was false advertising, and I was shopping for an advertisement whose structure I could use as a starting point for discussion. An ad for Georges Marciano clothing flashed on the screen and dragged me in, first with the music, South African music of haunting urgency, the echoing simultaneity of nonlinear music, the syncopation of quickening-heartbeat percussive music, dragging the ear. In the picture, a woman with long blond hair in sunglasses ran from a crowd of photographers and an admiring public. The film was black and white, a series of frames jaggedly succeeding each other, like a patchwork of secretly taken stills. Sliced into the sequence of her running away were shots of the blond and her manager/bodyguard/boyfriend packing. He packed the passports and the handgun, she packed the Georges Marciano jeans. The climax came when she burst into a room of exploding flashbulbs—a blazing bath of white light.

The effect of this particular visual and **aural juxtaposition** was the appearance of the music as being inside the woman's head or her heart. The music was primal, dangerous, desperate. The woman's crisis of adoration framed the burning necessity of this profound music, and the soaring universality of sound became white, female, privatized. The pulsing movement of the music elevated this event of **narcissistic** voyeurism to elemental importance. The music overflowed boundaries. Voices merged and surged; mood drifted and soared in the listening. African voices swelled and rose in the intricate music of knowledge, the wisdom of rhythm, the physics of echoing chasms bounded in intervals, the harmonic bells of voices striking each other in excitement and the wind, black African voices making music of the trees, of groundhogs, of whistling birds and pure chortling streams. It was generous shared music, open and eternal.

The pictures presented sought privacy. The chase was an invasion; the photographers pursued her private moments; she resisted even as her glamour consented. The viewer was drawn into desire to see her never-quite-revealed face, swept along by the urgency of her running to privacy, even as we never quite acknowledged her right to it. Thus the moment of climax, the flashing of cameras in her face (and ours, so completely have we identified with her), was one of release and relief. The music acted against the pictures. The mind resolved it queerly. The positive magnetic boundlessness of the music was turned into negative exposure. The run for privacy became an orgasmic peep show, the moment of negative exposure almost joyful.

In my lap, my textbook lay heavy, unattended pages drifting open to 5
the **Lanham Act:**

> *False designations of origin and false descriptions forbidden:*
> . . . any person who shall affix, apply, or annex, or use in
> connection with any goods or services . . . a false designation of
> origin, or any false description or representation, including words
> or other symbols tending falsely to describe or represent the same,
> and shall cause such goods or services to enter into commerce, and
> any person who shall with knowledge of the falsity of such . . .
> description or representation cause or procure the same to be
> transported or used in commerce . . . or used, shall be liable to a
> civil action . . . by any person who believes that he is or is likely
> to be damaged by the use of any such false description or
> representation.[1]

I have recounted this story at some length, not just for its illustrative
contrast between the sight and the sound of an advertisement, but also because the relationship between the music and the pictures can serve as a
metaphor for the tension between the political and marketplace dynamic
that is my larger subject. I think that the invisible corruption of one by the
other has consequences that are, ultimately, dehumanizing.

Ours is not the first generation to fall prey to false needs; but ours is
the first generation of admakers to realize the complete fulfillment of the
consumerist vision through the fine-tuning of sheer **hucksterism.** Surfaces, fantasies, appearances, and vague associations are the order of the day.
So completely have substance, reality, and utility been subverted that products are purified into mere wisps of labels, floating signifiers of their former
selves. "Coke" can as easily add life plastered on clothing as poured in a
cup. Calculating a remedy for this new-age consumptive pandering is prob-
lematic. If people like—and buy—the enigmatic emptiness used to push
products, then describing a harm becomes elusive. But it is elusive precisely
because the imagery and vocabulary of advertising have shifted the focus
from need to disguise. With this shift has come—either manipulated or
galloping gladly behind—a greater public appetite for illusion and disguise.
And in the wake of that has come an enormous shift of national industry,
national resources, and national consciousness.

QUESTIONS FOR DISCUSSION

1. What does Williams claim is the current relationship between TV advertisements and the products they represent?

---

[1] ¶ 243(a), Lanham Act, 15 U.S.C.S. ¶ 21125(a)(1988).

2. Explain how the advertising example in the text (the one for Georges Marciano clothing) is structured and why its two most important parts can be said to work against each other.

3. In what way does the example of the clothing advertisement evade the provisions of the Lanham Act?

4. According to Williams, how can advertising be "dehumanizing"?

5. With respect to the public's "appetite for illusion and disguise," what is the main difference between previous generations and the present one?

✍ HENRYK SKOLIMOWSKI

The Language of Advertising

Henryk Skolimowski has been an Assistant Professor of Philosophy at the University of Southern California and has published a book titled Polish Analytical Philosophy.

KEY VOCABULARY

An **AMULET** is an object worn, usually around the neck, to protect against evil or injury, or to bring good luck.

DISTORTION means, here, misrepresentation.

DOUBLETALK is language that is meaningless or that evades an issue by talking around it.

GEORGE ORWELL is the pen name of Eric Blair (1903–1950), the English novelist, essayist, and political satirist. His book *1984* is a satirical novel set in a totalitarian society of the future in which there is no place for truth, since historical records are destroyed and propaganda replaces information. Thought and love are punished, and privacy is impossible. The novel tells the story of a man and girl who rebel against this society.

A **LEXICOGRAPHER** is a person who writes or compiles a dictionary.

Communication is for humans. It is the mark of a rational man to grasp the content of a message irrespective of the form of its presentation—that is, irrespective of its linguistic expression. The nature of any communication in which the actual information conveyed is less significant than the manner of its presentation is, to say the least, illogical. The illogical man is what advertising is after. This is why advertising is so anti-rational; this is why it aims at uprooting not only the rationality of man but his common sense; this is why it indulges in exuberant but deplorable linguistic orgies.

Distortion of language, violation of logic, and corruption of values are about the most common devices through which advertising operates. This is particularly striking in endless perversions of the word FREE. Since this word has such a powerful impact on us, there is no limit to its abuse. In his novel *1984,* **George Orwell** showed that what is required for establishing a "perfect" dictatorship is perhaps no more than a systematic reform of language. The condition is, however, that the reform must be thorough and complete. "**Doubletalk**" as a possible reality has, since Orwell's novel, been viewed with horror, but not with incredulity. The question is whether

doubletalk has not already become part of our reality, has not already been diffused in our blood stream through means different from those Orwell conceived of. Isn't it true that advertising has become a perfect Orwellian institution?

Nowadays there is in operation a **doubletalk** concept of freedom according to which protecting the public from fraud and deceit and warning people about dangers to their health is but "an erosion of freedom." This concept of freedom is, needless to say, advocated and defended by advertising agencies. In the opinion of admen, "freedom" for people means protecting people from their common sense and ability to think. For many admen "freedom" means freedom to advertise in whatsoever manner is profitable, freedom to force you to buy, freedom to penetrate your subconscious, freedom to dupe you, to hook you, to make a sucker of you, freedom to take away your freedom. Anything else is for them but an "erosion of freedom." Hail Mr. Orwell! Hail **doubletalk!**

Now to turn to some concrete illustrations:

> "Mustang! A Car to Make Weak Men Strong,
> Strong Men Invincible."

Do not say that we do not believe such obvious blusterings. We do. It seems that the art of magicians—according to which some incantations evoke events, bring rain, heal wounds; some **amulets** bring good luck, prevent bad luck or illness—has been re-established by contemporary advertising. Motor cars in particular are the **amulets** of the atomic age. They possess all the miraculous qualities you wish them to possess—from being a substitute for a sweetheart (or mistress, if you prefer) to being a soothing balm to a crushed ego. Dictionaries usually define an automobile as a self-propelled vehicle for transportation of people or goods. The car industry and car dealers are of a quite different opinion. Perhaps **lexicographers** are outdated in their conception of "automobile."

Roughly speaking, motor cars are advertised to be **amulets** of two ⁵ kinds. The first casts spells on us and makes us happy, or builds up our personality, or adds to our strength, or makes us invincible if we are already strong; the second casts spells on others and, while we drive this magic vehicle, makes other people see us as more important, more influential, more irresistible. As yet, there are no cars which, being driven by us, would bring punishment upon our enemies. Perhaps one day this will come to pass. The question is how many of us can really resist the incantations of car dealers and remain impervious to the "magical" qualities allegedly embodied in the modern automobile. How many of us can remain uninfluenced by the continuous flow of messages, in spite of our ability to see the nonsense of each one individually?

QUESTIONS FOR DISCUSSION

1. Why is advertising specifically targeting "illogical man"?
2. What are the most common devices used by advertising?
3. Define the "doubletalk concept of freedom."
4. Why are cars "the amulets of the atomic age"?

This essay analyzes the effects of beauty ads in Good Housekeeping *magazine. The writer's tone is informal and conversational, humorous in places, but she also makes some serious points about how these ads might affect women. She is writing in response to the first topic from the list that concludes this chapter.*

✒ STUDENT ESSAY:

Superwife

On the surface, *Good Housekeeping* is a magazine full of helpful hints for the homemaker. The articles and advertisements feature beautifully decorated rooms, delicious (and healthy) recipes, beauty tips, ideas for crafts, advice on raising children, and ways of saving money. While there is some good, practical advice in this magazine, it also projects an image of women as desperately in need of acceptance—self-acceptance and the acceptance of husbands and children. But the magazine as a whole, and ads in particular, set an impossible standard. The ads for beauty products are especially guilty. They imply that the "complete" woman is not only a great homemaker, but also a beautiful, romantic partner—a "Superwife."

An ad for Revlon hair color, for example, shows a woman lying on her back, her thick, long hair cascading down beyond the borders of the page. The model is obviously young (not over twenty-one). Her makeup is perfect, and she oozes sensuality: eyes half-closed, lips slightly parted, fingers poised to run through her hair. She is wearing black and lying on a red background. The caption reads, "If nature didn't give you hair color this beautiful, Revlon will." Now, there is more to this than some hair dye. Like many ads, this one suggests that if you buy this stuff, you get the whole package—youth, beauty, elegance, romance. The frazzled homemaker sees herself at ease, awaiting hubby (of course, the house is spotless, the children are safely tucked away, dinner is bubbling on the stove, and a bottle of Dom Perignon is chilling on ice).

Another ad, this one for Maybelline's "Undetectable Creme Concealer," promises a "perfect skin day." Smear some of this on your face and, presto, you can look just like that beautiful young model in the black, low-cut, off-the-shoulder outfit. She's standing in the sunshine, her hands on her hips, directing a coy smile at some unknown person off-camera. Under the picture is the caption, "Maybe she's born with it. Maybe it's Maybelline." (Is it real, or is it Memorex?) This cream is supposed to hide wrinkles, but considering the age of the model (she looks about eighteen), I doubt that she's been within a mile of a wrinkle. Here is someone with nothing to conceal selling concealer, telling all the housewives out there that if they don't look like this, there's something wrong with them.

According to the message of *Good Housekeeping,* the modern woman should be able to keep a perfect house, cook like a French chef, raise wonderful children *and* remain young and beautiful. As I was thinking about these things, out of curiosity I glanced through my husband's *Bowhunter* magazine. This magazine is for "real men," the kind that get out in the woods with their red and black plaid shirts and shoot things with bows and arrows. There was nothing in the magazine that suggested a bowhunter, to be an effective man, needs to be young and attractive. More often than not, these men are creased and rugged-looking. Nothing in the magazine suggests that they need to do *anything* to please their wives. Maybe bringing home the meat is enough.

The more I look at *Good Housekeeping,* the more I see the load of guilt it places on women. To feel that we're accepted, we have to please everyone. We have to give our children "quality time" and healthy foods, our husbands the perfect house and the eighteen-year-old models they fantasize about. I remember reading Sylvia Rabiner's article "How the Superwoman Myth Puts Women Down." She says that constantly hearing stories of successful women only gave her an inferiority complex. The "Superwife" myth in the pages of *Good Housekeeping* does the same thing. It perpetuates an impossible dream of the woman who can do everything and remain eternally youthful. And the fact that it is an impossible dream keeps women from being happy with who they are, which keeps them coming back for more dyes and lotions and potions, which I'm sure keeps the people at Revlon and Maybelline *very* happy.

TOPICS FOR WRITING

1. Choose an advertisement—print media or television—and write an explanation of the advertisement's purpose and of the means it uses to achieve its purpose. Describe the ad clearly, well enough for the reader to visualize it, and consider the following questions in writing your explanation.

   Who is the advertiser?

   What is the *explicit* purpose of the ad? (What is it trying to sell?)

   What *implicit* appeals does it make to the assumed desires of the audience?

   What audience is the advertisement aimed toward?

   What assumptions does the advertiser make about the self-interests of the audience?

   What words and images tie the product or service being sold to the self-interests of the audience?

   Does the advertiser evoke any commonly accepted values and beliefs to relate the product to the audience?

2. P. T. Barnum devises an ingenious scheme to make his "museum the town wonder and town talk." Choose a specific issue or location from your community and devise a similarly ingenious scheme to bring it to the attention of the public. Describe and explain your scheme in an essay.

3. One of the debates regarding advertising revolves around whether advertisements fulfill a need for information or whether they actually cause a craving for otherwise unneeded products and services. Saturday morning children-targeted advertising, for example, is often cited on both sides of this debate.

   Using examples from the readings in this chapter and from your own observation, develop a case supporting one of the sides in this debate. Do advertisements have a useful purpose, or do they simply create desires for unnecessary things?

4. Using information from any of the readings in this chapter, discuss the ways in which advertising can be dangerous. Set up several categories that reflect different kinds of danger.

5. Using David Guterson's essay "Moneyball!" as a model, write an argument showing how a time-honored and beloved American institution has become overwhelmingly commercialized.

6. Choose two advertisements for the same type of product (for example cars), as advertised in magazines aimed at different audiences. Analyze how the ads differ in their appeals depending on the assumed interests of the intended audience.

7. Using information from Henryk Skolimowski's "The Language of Advertising" and Patricia J. Williams' "The Fiction of Truth in Advertising," explain how advertising has developed methods of using words, images, and sounds to create increasingly misleading messages.

8. Choose two print advertisements of the same type of product but from two different decades (for example the 1990s and the 1950s). What similarities and differences do you find in the assumptions the advertisers make about the audience's beliefs, attitudes, and values?

9. Choose an ad directed at a specific group of consumers (for example skateboarders) and explain how it reveals the knowledge and assumptions of the advertisers about the targeted group.

10. Using the information in Jeffrey Schrank's "Psychosell," write, in your own words, a definition of the term *psychosell*. Then find some examples of your own, either from television or print media, to illustrate your definition.

The Statue of Liberty undergoing repairs, 1984.

14 The Dream Revised

All things must change
To something new, to something strange.
   –HENRY WADSWORTH LONGFELLOW

In this chapter, Richard Rodriguez asks the central question: "Does America still exist?" We hear that young people today are the first generation in American history that cannot expect to be better off than their parents. We hear of diminishing opportunities and lower expectations. We hear that young Americans no longer hold the traditional values of hard work, thrift, self-reliance, and fair play. The Japanese have called American workers soft and lazy. America, they say, has lost its edge.

The American Dream was built on the assumption of endless growth, an upward march toward a better and better life—usually defined in economic terms. But the frontier closed in 1890, and there is no more free land. An ambitious youth can no longer start out sweeping the factory floor and rise to the top of the company without first taking a detour through Harvard Business School. And that most solid symbol of the American Dream realized, a home of one's own, is getting harder and harder to come by.

As Bob Dylan warbled thirty years ago, "The times, they are a-changin'. "

In this chapter, we take a final look at the notion of the American Dream as the twentieth century draws to a close. Is the idea still alive? And if it is, what form will it take to meet the conditions of life in these times? In short, what can we look forward to?

✍ WILLIAM HENRY III

Beyond the Melting Pot

William Henry III was an associate editor at Time *magazine from 1981 until his death in 1994. He graduated from Yale University and did graduate work at Boston University. Henry began his career with the* Boston Globe *in 1971, worked for the* New York Daily News *from 1980 to 1981, then joined the staff of* Time. *He reported on politics and education and worked as a columnist, an art and movie critic, and a television editor. He also served on the faculties of Tufts, Yale, and New York University.*

KEY VOCABULARY

MICROCOSM means literally "small world." A microcosm contains the essential features of a larger world.

Someday soon, surely much sooner than most people who filled out 1
their Census forms last week realize, white Americans will become a minority group. Long before that day arrives, the presumption that the "typical" U.S. citizen is someone who traces his or her descent in a direct line to Europe will be part of the past. By the time . . . elementary students at Brentwood Science Magnet School in Brentwood, Calif., reach midlife, their diverse ethnic experience in the classroom will be echoed in neighborhoods and workplaces throughout the U.S.

Already 1 American in 4 defines himself or herself as Hispanic or nonwhite. If current trends in immigration and birth rates persist, the Hispanic population will have further increased an estimated 21%, the Asian presence about 22%, blacks almost 12% and whites a little more than 2% when the 20th century ends. By 2020, a date no further into the future than John F. Kennedy's election is in the past, the number of U.S. residents who are Hispanic or nonwhite will have more than doubled, to nearly 115 million, while the white population will not be increasing at all. By 2056, when someone born today will be 66 years old, the "average" U.S. resident, as defined by Census statistics, will trace his or her descent to Africa, Asia, the Hispanic world, the Pacific Islands, Arabia—almost anywhere but white Europe.

While there may remain towns or outposts where even a black family will be something of an oddity, where English and Irish and German surnames will predominate, where a traditional (some will wistfully say "real") America will still be seen on almost every street corner, they will be only the vestiges of an earlier nation. The former majority will learn, as a normal part of everyday life, the meaning of the Latin slogan engraved on U.S. coins—E PLURIBUS UNUM, one formed from many.

Among the younger populations that go to school and provide new entrants to the work force, the change will happen sooner. In some places an America beyond the melting pot has already arrived. In New York State some 40% of elementary- and secondary-school children belong to an ethnic minority. Within a decade, the proportion is expected to approach 50%. In California white pupils are already a minority. Hispanics (who, regardless of their complexion, generally distinguish themselves from both blacks and whites) account for 31.4% of public school enrollment, blacks add 8.9%, and Asians and others amount to 11%—for a nonwhite total of 51.3%. This finding is not only a reflection of white flight from desegregated public schools. Whites of all ages account for just 58% of California's population. In San Jose bearers of the Vietnamese surname Nguyen outnumber the Joneses in the telephone directory 14 columns to eight.

Nor is the change confined to the coasts. Some 12,000 Hmong refu- 5 gees from Laos have settled in St. Paul. At some Atlanta low-rent apartment complexes that used to be virtually all black, social workers today need to speak Spanish. At the Sesame Hut restaurant in Houston, a Korean immigrant owner trains Hispanic immigrant workers to prepare Chinese-style food for a largely black clientele. The Detroit area has 200,000 people of Middle Eastern descent; some 1,500 small grocery and convenience stores in the vicinity are owned by a whole subculture of Chaldean Christians with roots in Iraq. "Once America was a **microcosm** of European nationalities," says Molefi Asante, chairman of the department of African-American studies at Temple University in Philadelphia. "Today America is a microcosm of the world."

History suggests that sustaining a truly multiracial society is difficult, or at least unusual. Only a handful of great powers of the distant past— Pharaonic Egypt and Imperial Rome, most notably—managed to maintain a distinct national identity while embracing, and being ruled by, an ethnic mélange. The most ethnically diverse contemporary power, the Soviet Union, is beset with secessionist demands and near tribal conflicts. But such comparisons are flawed, because those empires were launched by conquest and maintained through an aggressive military presence. The U.S. was created, and continues to be redefined, primarily by voluntary immigration. This process has been one of the country's great strengths, infusing it with talent and energy. The "browning of America" offers tremendous opportunity for capitalizing anew on the merits of many peoples from many lands. Yet this fundamental change in the ethnic makeup of the U.S. also poses risks. The American character is resilient and thrives on change. But past periods of rapid evolution have also, alas, brought out deeper, more fearful aspects of the national soul.

QUESTIONS FOR DISCUSSION

1. What do the statistics of the latest census reveal about demographic trends in the U.S.?

2. What does the title of this article imply about changes in the attitude of Americans toward their society?

3. What were the demographics in the grade school you attended?

4. Why is sustaining a multiracial society more difficult than sustaining a uniracial one?

✍ ANDREI CODRESCU

The Uses of American Space

Born in Transylvania, Romania, in 1946, Andrei Codrescu fled the communist regime in 1966 and emigrated to the United States. He is now a professor of English at Louisiana State University, Baton Rouge, and for the past ten years has been a commentator on National Public Radio's "All Things Considered." A collection of his radio commentaries, Zombification, was published in 1994. The selection below is one of these commentaries. Codrescu's other books include Road Scholar *(also a movie starring the author), and* The Muse Is Always Half Dressed in New Orleans. *Codrescu also edits a journal of books and ideas,* Exquisite Corpse.

KEY VOCABULARY

BRAVADO means false courage.

CUM (as in "TV-cum-candle") is a Latin term meaning "plus." As it is commonly used, it carries the sense of "as" (TV-*as*-candle).

A **DEMOGRAPHER** is an expert on the characteristics of human populations.

The **HMONG** are a hill tribe from Laos, many of whom have relocated in the United States since the end of the Vietnam War.

SILESIA is a region of central Europe, now chiefly within Southwestern Poland.

The Infinite Column by Constantin Brâncuşi is one of the most famous 1
sculptures in the world. Its spiraling thrust suggests infinity, universality, and
hope. Brâncuşi, the Romanian-French sculptor who created it at the beginning of our century, took its shape from a humble detail of a peasant
house in the mountains of Romania, a carved wooden porch support. The
humble origin of Brâncuşi's universal symbol is important. Romanians, like
other people under the merciless gun of history, have never put their faith
in big, official buildings where the power of the day resided. They preferred
instead to stay close to the earth and to make their own statements about
the purpose of space.

I have been thinking about Brâncuşi's column again after reading a
book called *The New Americans* by Al Santoli, a collection of interviews
with recent refugees and immigrants who are changing American space and
challenging its conventional uses.

By the middle of the next century Americans of European extraction will be a minority in the United States if the recent emigration trends continue. So say **demographers,** with a mixture of concern and **bravado.** The concern is that American cities will all look like the futuristic Los Angeles in *Blade Runner,* where racially mixed gangs roam the streets speaking a vaguely oriental mélange of martial Japanese and obscene Spanglish. On the other hand, recent immigrants are saving our decaying cities by transforming urban war zones into vibrant ethnic villages. The Vietnamese have created a "little Vietnam" in uptown Chicago; there is a Korean city in midtown Manhattan, and a "little Odessa" in Queens. There is even a **Hmong** tribe fishing village in Minnesota. These are fairly dramatic examples, but the big view tells only part of the story. There are also the humble details. Josef Patyna, a former Solidarity organizer from Poland interviewed in Santoli's book, lives in a "two story white house on a quiet tree-lined street . . ." in Providence, Rhode Island. "Their living room is graced with a bright painting of Pope John Paul II, which is reflected in a large mirror above the fireplace. On the mantel is a glass beer mug, inscribed with the Virgin Mary of the Passion, the logo of the **Silesian** coal miners' guild. A single red candle is set on top of the television."

One feels that all these details are important to the Patynas, but there is something about that red candle on top of the television that really gets me. It is as if the Patynas, who are about to be engulfed by America as it pours out of its TV mouthpiece, are trying to contain and resist its onslaught. They have joined the living light of their symbolic candle to the cold light of the electronic eye in order to make peace between the two worlds they know, between past and present, Poland and America. Like Brâncuşi's *Infinite Column,* the Patynas' TV-**cum**-candle is a humble detail with a universal echo. It is the first ripple from which wider circles of change transform American space.

QUESTIONS FOR DISCUSSION

1. What "American space" does this essay focus on?

2. How does the *Infinite Column* reflect the author's assertion that "Romanians, like other people under the merciless gun of history, have never put their faith in big, official buildings where the power of the day resided"?

3. What is the "mixture of concern and bravado" Codrescu speaks about?

4. What does the red candle symbolize? What sort of a "transformation of American space" does it stand for? How is it contrasted with the light of the television?

✍ RICHARD RODRIGUEZ

Does America Still Exist?

Richard Rodriguez, the son of Mexican immigrants, grew up in Sacramento, California. He attended Stanford and Columbia universities, and earned a doctorate at the University of California, Berkeley. Rodriguez is a journalist by profession and has published two books, Hunger of Memory: The Education of Richard Rodriguez *(1982), and* Days of Obligation: An Argument with My Mexican Father *(1992).*

KEY VOCABULARY

An **ATRIUM** is an open inner space in a building. Originally, an atrium was an open courtyard, but later also enclosed.

The **FEAST OF THE DEAD** is an annual Mexican holiday (November 1–2) that combines Catholic and Indian ritual. On this holiday, Mexicans remember and honor the dead by giving and trading candy skulls, which are gobbled up by flocks of children dressed as skeletons.

The **INDIAN VIRGIN** is the Virgin of Guadalupe, the patron saint of Mexico. Legend has it that the Virgin Mary appeared to an Indian peasant after the Spanish conquest, and that she had Indian features and spoke the Nahuatl language.

NATIVIST refers to a point of view that favors the interests of the native inhabitants of a country over those of immigrants.

An **OBBLIGATO** is a part of a piece of music that cannot be left out (from the Italian *obbligare,* to obligate).

PAULINE refers to Saint Paul, the Apostle of Christ and author of the New Testament book *Acts* and a number of epistles.

For the children of immigrant parents the knowledge comes easier. 1
America exists everywhere in the city—on billboards, frankly in the smell of French fries and popcorn. It exists in the pace: traffic lights, the assertions of neon, the mysterious bong-bong-bong through the **atriums** of department stores. America exists as the voice of the crowd, a menacing sound—the high nasal accent of American English.

When I was a boy in Sacramento (California, the fifties), people would ask me, "Where you from?" I was born in this country, but I knew the question meant to decipher my darkness, my looks.

My mother once instructed me to say, "I am an American of American descent." By the time I was nine or ten, I wanted to say, but dared not reply, "I am an American."

Immigrants come to America and, against hostility or mere loneliness, they recreate a homeland in the parlor, tacking up postcards or calendars of some impossible blue—lake or sea or sky. Children of immigrant parents are supposed to perch on a hyphen between two countries. Relatives assume the achievement as much as anyone. Relatives are, in any case, surprised when the child begins losing old ways. One day at the family picnic the boy wanders away from their spiced food and faceless stories to watch other boys play baseball in the distance.

There is sorrow in the American memory, guilty sorrow for having left 5 something behind—Portugal, China, Norway. The American story is the story of immigrant children and of their children—children no longer able to speak to grandparents. The memory of exile becomes inarticulate as it passes from generation to generation, along with wedding rings and pocket watches—like some mute stone in a wad of old lace. Europe. Asia. Eden.

But, it needs to be said, if this is a country where one stops being Vietnamese or Italian, this is a country where one begins to be an American. America exists as a culture and a grin, a faith and a shrug. It is clasped in a handshake, called by a first name.

As much as the country is joined in a common culture, however, Americans are reluctant to celebrate the process of assimilation. We pledge allegiance to diversity. America was born Protestant and bred Puritan, and the notion of community we share is derived from a seventeenth-century faith. Presidents and the pages of ninth-grade civics readers yet proclaim the orthodoxy: We are gathered together—but as individuals, with separate pasts, distinct destinies. Our society is as paradoxical as a Puritan congregation: We stand together, alone.

Americans have traditionally defined themselves by what they refused to include. As often, however, Americans have struggled, turned in good conscience at last to assert the great Protestant virtue of tolerance. Despite outbreaks of **nativist** frenzy, America has remained an immigrant country, open and true to itself.

Against pious emblems of rural America—soda fountain, Elks hall, Protestant church, and now shopping mall—stands the cold-hearted city, crowded with races and ambitions, curious laughter, much that is odd. Nevertheless, it is the city that has most truly represented America. In the city, however, the millions of singular lives have had no richer notion of wholeness to describe them than the idea of pluralism.

"Where you from?" the American asks the immigrant child. "Mexico," the 10 *boy learns to say.*

Mexico, the country of my blood ancestors, offers formal contrast to the American achievement. If the United States was formed by Protestant individualism, Mexico was shaped by a medieval Catholic dream of one world. The Spanish journeyed to Mexico to plunder, and they may have gone, in God's name, with an arrogance peculiar to those who intend to convert. But through the conversion, the Indian converted the Spaniard. A new race was born, the *mestizo,* wedding European to Indian. José Vasconcelos, the Mexican philosopher, has celebrated this New World creation, proclaiming it the "cosmic race."

Centuries later, in a San Francisco restaurant, a Mexican-American lawyer of my acquaintance says, in English, over *salade niçoise,* that he does not intend to assimilate into gringo society. His claim is echoed by a chorus of others (Italian-Americans, Greeks, Asians) in this era of ethnic pride. The melting pot has been retired, clanking, into the museum of quaint disgrace, alongside Aunt Jemima and the Katzenjammer Kids. But resistance to assimilation is characteristically American. It only makes clear how inevitable the process of assimilation actually is.

For generations, this has been the pattern. Immigrant parents have sent their children to school (simply, they thought) to acquire the "skills" to survive in the city. The child returned home with a voice his parents barely recognized or understood, couldn't trust, and didn't like.

In Eastern cities—Philadelphia, New York, Boston, Baltimore—class after class gathered immigrant children to women (usually women) who stood in front of rooms full of children, changing children. So also for me in the 1950s. Irish-Catholic nuns. California. The old story. The hyphen tipped to the right, away from Mexico and toward a confusing but true American identity.

I speak now in the chromium American accent of my grammar 15 school classmates—Billy Reckers, Mike Bradley, Carol Schmidt, Kathy O'Grady. . . . I believe I became like my classmates, became German, Polish, and (like my teachers) Irish. And because assimilation is always reciprocal, my classmates got something of me. (I mean sad eyes; belief in the **Indian Virgin;** a taste for sugar skulls on the **Feast of the Dead.**) In the blending, we became what our parents could never have been, and we carried America one revolution further.

"Does America still exist?" Americans have been asking the question for so long that to ask it again only proves our continuous link. But perhaps the question deserves to be asked with urgency—now. Since the black civil rights movement of the 1960s, our tenuous notion of a shared public life has deteriorated notably.

The struggle of black men and women did not eradicate racism, but it became the great moment in the life of America's conscience. Water hoses, bulldogs, blood—the images, rendered black, white, rectangular, passed into living rooms.

It is hard to look at a photograph of a crowd taken, say, in 1890 or in 1930 and not notice the absence of blacks. (It becomes an impertinence to wonder if America *still* exists.)

In the sixties, other groups of Americans learned to champion their rights by analogy to the black civil rights movement. But the heroic vision faded. Dr. Martin Luther King, Jr. had spoken with **Pauline** eloquence of a nation that would unite Christian and Jew, old and young, rich and poor. Within a decade, the struggles of the 1960s were reduced to a bureaucratic competition for little more than pieces of a representational pie. The quest for a portion of power became an end in itself. The metaphor for the American city of the 1970s was a committee: one black, one woman, one person under thirty. . . .

If the small town had sinned against America by too neatly defining who could be an American, the city's sin was a romantic secession. One noticed the romanticism in the antiwar movement—certain demonstrators who demonstrated a lack of tact or desire to persuade and seemed content to play secular protestants. One noticed the romanticism in the competition among members of "minority groups" to claim the status of Primary Victim. To Americans unconfident of their common identity, minority standing became a way of asserting individuality. Middle-class Americans—men and women clearly not the primary victims of social oppression—brandished their suffering with exuberance.

The dream of a single society probably died with *The Ed Sullivan Show.* The reality of America persists. Teenagers pass through big-city high schools banded in racial groups, their collars turned up to a uniform shrug. But then they graduate to jobs at the phone company or in banks, where they end up working alongside people unlike themselves. Typists and tellers walk out together at lunchtime.

It is easier for us as Americans to believe the obvious fact of our separateness—easier to imagine the black and white Americas prophesied by the Kerner report (broken glass, street fires)—than to recognize the reality of a city street at lunchtime. Americans are wedded by proximity to a common culture. The panhandler at one corner is related to the pamphleteer at the next who is related to the banker who is kin to the Chinese old man wearing an MIT sweatshirt. In any true national history, Thomas Jefferson begets Martin Luther King, Jr. who begets the Gray Panthers. It is because we lack a vision of ourselves entire—the city street is crowded and we are each preoccupied with finding our own way home—that we lack an appropriate hymn.

Under my window now passes a little white girl softly rehearsing to herself a Motown **obbligato.**

QUESTIONS FOR DISCUSSION

1. How do the children of immigrants inevitably begin "losing old ways"?
2. Why does Rodriguez say that Americans are "reluctant to celebrate the process of assimilation"?
3. Explain why it is that cities define America most closely.
4. Why is the Mexican-American lawyer unwilling to assimilate? How successful do you think he is?
5. What does the author mean by "romanticism"? What kind of social force is this romanticism?
6. Why does Rodriguez think the mestizo is an optimistic symbol of the cultural future of America?

⚮ ANGELO PELLEGRINI

Two American Dreams

Angelo Pellegrini was born in Italy and came to the United States in 1913. He was professor of English at the University of Washington from 1958 until his death in 1991. In addition to publications in professional journals, Pellegrini wrote several books about the immigrant experience: Immigrant's Return *(1951),* America by Choice *(1956), and* American Dream: An Immigrant's Quest *(1986), from which the following selection was taken. Pellegrini also wrote popular articles on a variety of subjects, including gardening, wine, and food.*

KEY VOCABULARY

CONGENIAL means suited to one's needs; agreeable.

CORNUCOPIA, originally from Latin, means literally "horn of plenty," a goat's horn overflowing with fruit, flowers, and corn, signifying prosperity. Generally, the word denotes abundance.

LATENT refers to something that is present, but not visible; concealed.

What is the American dream? Is it to rise from log cabin origins to the White House? From a clerk to the president of a corporation? From poverty to wealth? From obscurity to professional distinction? Or is it a more modest dream—to have **congenial** employment, a happy family, and own one's own home? By the end of the recently celebrated bicentennial, many of these goals had been achieved by the millions who had come to America during the two preceding centuries. Since most had been drawn hither by the promise implicit in America's fabulous natural endowment, it was inevitable that they should conceive the American dream in economic terms. But economic gain has no more than marginal relevance to my vision of the dream.

Anyone who has more than an elementary knowledge of American history will agree that there are two American dreams: the collective and the individual. The collective dream was, initially, the enduring hope that the nation would progress in accordance with the "truths, ends, and purposes" set forth in the Declaration of Independence and the Constitution, especially its preamble and the Bill of Rights. I shall have something to say later on how this dream has fared.

As for the individual dream: its content—that which one dreams of and seeks to gain—is highly personal; the right to the dream, with the realistic hope of gaining what one seeks, is the supreme heritage, transmitted from generation to generation, of every American citizen. This legacy is structured in our democracy. When Jefferson, in writing the Declaration of Independence, substituted "the pursuit of happiness" for Locke's word "property" in listing a person's inalienable rights, the right to the dream became a part of the fundamental law.

During the first two centuries after the founding fathers had established the new nation, the dream, as one of economic gain, was realized with relative ease by those who were shrewd, aggressive, and richly endowed with the acquisitive instinct; and it was during these decades that the nation's endowment—land—was up for grabs. Thereafter, when what was left of the total natural endowment was largely in the domain of private enterprise and when the growth of monopolies had reduced the effectiveness of competition and the plenitude of general opportunities, there was a tendency, for the first time in our history, to become skeptical about the American dream as one of economic gain. It was no longer possible, for example, to do what Rockefeller had done. At sixteen years of age he began work as a clerk. At age twenty-four he invested three thousand dollars in an oil refinery; and at age forty he owned ninety percent of the nation's oil refineries. This was symbolic of what could be dreamed of and achieved during that period in our economic history when so much was available to anyone whose talent and temperament were **congenial** to that sort of quest.

Similarly, about six decades later, when my generation graduated from college in the middle twenties, opportunities for employment or for venturing into one's own enterprise were virtually unlimited. When the agents of higher education had come to urge our high school senior class to go to college, they sought to persuade us by a single argument: the more education you have, the greater will be your income. Commencement speakers made the same promise, along with certain pieties that no one took seriously. The sequel proved them prophetic. For while we worked toward a college degree, we had the assurance that our studies were an apprenticeship in the real life course we would follow thereafter. Nor were we disappointed; when we graduated, and had had a much needed rest after years of laborious study, each one of us proceeded to the workplace that the logic of the times had made available to us. Those who had chosen to continue their studies in graduate school were welcomed by the dean with no questions asked—an undergraduate degree was the only requirement. Not so today.

Forty years later, when my son graduated from the university, employment opportunities were severely limited. He, with a degree in romance languages, and one of his friends, with a degree in philosophy, could find no employment, so they did what had probably never been done before. Using their backgrounds in humanistic studies to lure salmon into their nets, they earned their bread as commercial fishermen in Bristol Bay. It was rumored that their extraordinary success prompted others in the fishing fleet seeking to increase their catch to return to school and earn a degree in liberal arts.

What, then, of the dream in our and future generations? Is it myth or reality? Such dreams as Rockefeller indulged in are now out of the question. Considering the continuing depletion of the planet's major resource systems, wisdom requires us to dream of ways of conserving rather than exploiting what remains of our natural endowment. This is not only a matter of declared national policy, but it ought also to be the concern of every individual. One who, in his personal design for living, avoids waste, extravagance, conspicuous consumption—quite independently of what the community may require—is a true conservationist. One who owns a plot of ground, adds to its natural fertility, and keeps it productive, helps to maintain, even by ever so little, the nation's **cornucopia**. One who plants a tree of a rare variety, or who gathers seeds of certain flora and provides for their germination and development is reducing the number of species that are in danger of extinction. These are dreams that increase self-respect because they embody what is right and proper and, though they require little of the dreamer, they add enormously to the general welfare.

There is current evidence, for those whose goal it is to rise from the log cabin (that is, from humble origins) to political or other eminence, that such opportunities are still a reality. The governors of our two most populous states, several senators, a score or more congressmen, and hundreds of others who have achieved eminence in business and the professions are children of immigrants who had little or no education and who began life as common laborers. Their gift to the new land was the talent and intelligence lodged in their genes, and those who were capable of dreaming, and who lived long enough, would see the dream realized in their children. Imagine, for example, the felicity that must grace the golden years of the parents of Mario Cuomo, governor of New York.

As I said above, economic gain is of no more than marginal relevance to my conception of the dream. The opportunity to earn one's bread, yes. That is a condition precedent to all else. Beyond that, the American Dream, properly conceived, is the inalienable right to seek happiness in self-realization. A just society, the overall goal of which is to promote the general welfare, says, in effect, to each of its members: Know thyself. Discover as early as possible your talent, your highest potential, and within the framework of that self-knowledge, set a course, pursue it with vigor and imagination so that you may realize what was **latent** in your inborn physical and spiritual endowments. Where you need legitimate aid in your quest, society will provide it. And always remember that in your design for living the welfare of others is no less important than your own.

Bearing this in mind, I suggest that we forget about economic gain and 10 concentrate on becoming something—the best that is **latent** in us. The dream, thus conceived, is and always has been a reality. The more we insist on the dream as an inalienable right and pursue it with determination, the more likely it will be to remain a live option available to all. For ultimately it derives from us, the people, and, as a community working together and intent on the same ends, we are, at any moment in our history, more likely to be what we had intended to become than to be something else. With that vision always in focus, every advance we make may very well lead to another and every realization of the dream will engender another.

QUESTIONS FOR DISCUSSION

1. What are the main characteristics of the two American dreams described by Pellegrini?

2. What are the differences in economic opportunity between the time of Rockefeller and the time of Pellegrini's son's college graduation?

3. What does the author mean by "self-realization"?

4. Do you agree with the essay's optimistic ending? Explain your view.

✍ CELESTE MACLEOD

From *Horatio Alger Farewell!*
The End of the American Dream

Celeste MacLeod has written for a number of magazines, including The
Nation, Library Journal, *and* California Living. *She has also served as
chair of Berkeley Support Services, a resource-referral center for transient
youth. The selection below is from her book* Horatio Alger, Farewell!

KEY VOCABULARY

To **EXHORT** is to persuade or urge using strong argument.

GOAD is, literally, a pointed stick used for prodding animals. Generally, it
means anything used to encourage action.

INHERENT refers to a natural and inseparable characteristic of someone or
something; inborn.

RETRENCHMENT means cutting down, economizing. It was originally a
military term for a fortification behind the main wall of a town, to which
troops could retreat if necessary.

TOTALITARIAN means a way of governing by authority, which attempts to
control every aspect of one's life.

To **WEND** means to make one's way, usually along a winding route.

Upward mobility was the essence of the American dream. In the new 1
land of democracy and freedom, everyone who tried hard enough could
rise and become rich—according to the dream. Individual initiative and
persistence were automatic stairsteps to financial success. Horatio Alger, a
nineteenth-century American minister, wrote more than 100 novels for
boys that illustrated the dream in action: Alger's heroes invariably went
from rags to riches through hard work and virtue.

Two interlocking premises supported the American dream—unlimited
opportunity and an endless frontier to provide that opportunity. Without
the frontier, the dream could not have survived.

The dream of riches for everybody originated in the United States, but
it has become one of our most popular exports. The idea that everyone
who works hard enough can become wealthy, regardless of social class or
advantages (and irrespective of the economic and political situation in one's
country), has universal appeal. It is a modern-day fairy tale wherein effort

is the magic wand and every person turns into his or her own fairy god-mother. The **inherent** justice of such a tale, its suitability as an inspirational piece for children, makes the story an unbeatable favorite. The American dream has helped raise expectations across the globe.

Belief in the dream has a special advantage for those who embrace its tenets: It serves as a screen that shuts out the real world, at least temporarily. The reality is that opportunity is shrinking, in the United States and else-where. When the frontiers ended, so did the basis of the dream.

Although a highly visible minority of individuals in the United States 5 and other Western countries are better off financially than ever before, the common experience is that jobs are increasingly difficult to find. How to earn a living is becoming a dilemma instead of a choice for more and more people entering adulthood. Vast numbers of young people—ranging from unskilled laborers who quit school at sixteen through holders of doctoral degrees from prestigious universities—cannot find jobs. Their problem is not lack of effort or individual initiative; it is a lack of jobs. More people are looking for work than there are jobs available for them to fill. Automa-tion has been a primary factor in eroding the dream's promise of jobs for everybody; technological innovations have caused great numbers of un-skilled and semiskilled workers to be replaced by machines.

In the past, migration was the trump card of the poor. If all else failed, you could leave home and seek opportunity in some other place. You could emigrate (leave your native land and enter another nation as an immigrant), or you could migrate (move within your own country, often from farm to city after the coming of the Industrial Revolution).

Today emigration is closing as an option for the poor. The countries that used to absorb large numbers of immigrants regularly (i.e., United States, Canada, Australia) are experiencing high rates of unemployment themselves, so they no longer want or need the poor and unskilled as im-migrants. To the contrary, it is the rich and the highly skilled technicians who are welcome as immigrants these days.

Migration within one's own country is still open, and it remains a popular option. Whenever unemployment increases, so does migration, even though the areas people move to in search of work often have higher rates of unemployment than the communities they left behind. But the dream says that opportunity awaits them someplace, and so people keep moving, hoping to find it in the next town. . . .

Money is the key word to the history of the United States. Long before the colonies became an independent nation, the desire for wealth was al-ready a national obsession. "The only principle of life propagated among the young people is to get money, and men are only esteemed according to what they are worth—that is, the money they are possessed of," an observer in New York City reported in 1784.[1] A century later the French traveler Alexis de Tocqueville noted this same quality: "In America then everyone finds facilities, unknown elsewhere, for making or increasing his fortune. The spirit of gain is always on the stretch, and the human mind, constantly diverted from pleasures of imagination and the labours of the intellect, is there swayed by no impulse but the pursuit of wealth."[2]

Tocqueville viewed this scramble for wealth as a natural consequence 10 of freedom under democracy coupled with the fortuitous discovery of a rich continent. Newspaper editor Horace Greeley echoed these same sentiments when he told a group of young people in 1867: "There is in this land of ours larger opportunities, more just and well-grounded hopes, than any other land whereon the sun ever shone."[3]

Everyone could succeed in the United States, because there was plenty of space on the undeveloped frontier. (The fact that numerous tribes of Indians were already living on that frontier was conveniently overlooked. The Indians were pushed out of the way of progress or killed.) Success or failure depended on the individual; if you were rugged enough, hardworking, and persistent, you were bound to get rich. Or so went the legend of the self-made man. . . .

Now that there are no more frontiers or undiscovered continents for rugged individuals to conquer, we need a different dream. The challenge facing the United States and other Western nations in the coming century is whether they can end dire poverty, put limits on individual and corporate wealth, and usher in full employment without also inaugurating the **totalitarian** excesses that have so often accompanied attempts to effect such changes in communist nations. An equitable balance between the rights of the individual and the needs of the community and nation has yet to be worked out in most countries in either power bloc, but it is essential that we work toward this goal. . . .

The United States did attempt to eradicate poverty and lessen the income gap during the 1960s, but there was no corresponding drive to lessen the concentration of wealth. We assumed that there was plenty for all. Today, only those who bury their heads in the sand (or remain in executive suites far from the masses of population) can still believe that fairy tale.

---

[1] The observer was Cadwallader Colden. Quoted in Wyllie, p. 12. [Wyllie, Irvin G. *The Self-Made Man in America: The Myth of Rags to Riches.* New York: Macmillan, Free Press, 1966.]

[2] Tocqueville, p. 41. [*Democracy in America.* Introduction by John Stuart Mill. Vol. 2, 1840. New York: Schocken, 1961.]

[3] Quoted in Wyllie, p. 22.

Lowering Our Expectations

People at every income level, except the very bottom, need to lower their expectations. Now when a leader **exhorts** the people to lower their expectations for the common good, he speaks to those in the middle and lower income ranges, because they constitute the majority; he does not **exhort** those in the highest income brackets to buy one less luxury car or beachfront retreat. The wealthy are exempted from **retrenchment.** This has got to change.

People in the middle and lower income ranges will not be convinced 15 that they should tighten their own belts as long as others live in opulence. If we are to lower our expectations, then those in the top income brackets must also reduce their standard of living (and the number of their investments) and learn to find satisfactions in life that do not depend on having more money and power than other people. We can no longer afford to allow enormous holdings of personal and corporate wealth to accumulate and multiply.

Changing Our Perceptions of Success

Another significant change must occur before people in the nonaffluent society will relinquish the dream of riches—a change that strikes at the core of the dream. We must stop ranking people as failures if they do not make enough money to become affluent.

Labor specialist B. J. Widick summed up workers' grievances about this attitude of the affluent society in *Auto Work and Its Discontents:* "They [workers] do have a grievance against society, with its middle-class values, and that is the general contempt in which factory workers, in particular assembly-line workers, are held, making it doubly difficult for blue-collar workers to maintain a sense of personal pride and dignity."

Workers are placed in a double bind: They are regarded as inferior if they remain in the nonaffluent society; but when they try to climb up, as the dream encourages them to do, they find that the affluent society has no place for them.

. . . Far more people want professional jobs than the country can use in that capacity. Higher pay and greater intellectual stimulation motivate this aspiration in part, but the desire for status—the determination to be ranked as somebody in the community—is an equally strong **goad.**

It is time to stop preaching upward mobility as the only way to go, 20 time to give recognition to people who are satisfied (or at least willing) to stay where they are—and who perform much of the labor that keeps our society going. By pretending to be a classless society, we rob the working class of status and dignity. . . .

Meanwhile, the new migrants **wend** their way from city to city in search of opportunities that do not exist for them. Without help from their governments, and encouragement to lower their expectations, the new migrants will remain wanderers, part of a growing army of unemployed youths in Europe and the United States who have become surplus commodities in their own countries. Their presence mocks the Alger myth, and undermines their nations' priorities.

When countries with the capability of putting men on the moon and developing hydrogen bombs declare that it is impossible for them to devise methods of employing all their people who want to work, then something is clearly amiss with their systems and values. It is time for changes.

The end of the American dream may seem sad, even tragic, to some people. But it need not be a time for mourning. In the United States we have come through our childhood as a nation and lived through a stormy adolescence in the past two decades. Perhaps we are ready for a new dream, a mature dream that does not center on individual desires for grandiose wealth and the power to play God. It could be that in the century ahead, a different dream can serve us just as well or better.

QUESTIONS FOR DISCUSSION

1. Why does MacLeod say that the American Dream could not have survived without the frontier?

2. Would MacLeod and Pellegrini agree on a definition of the American Dream? Explain.

3. What are the primary causes of the recent scarcity of jobs at all skill levels?

4. Why does MacLeod believe that we must lower our expectations?

5. What is the "double bind" of the working class?

6. What different version of the American Dream does the author present at the close of the essay?

✍ PICO IYER

The Global Village Finally Arrives

Pico Iyer was born in Oxford, England, in 1957, and was educated at Eton, Oxford, and Harvard. He is an essayist for Time *magazine and has written three books about travel:* Video Night in Katmandu *(1988),* The Lady and the Monk: Four Seasons in Kyoto *(1991), and* Falling off the Map *(1993).*

KEY VOCABULARY

COSMOPOLITAN means common to the whole world, not just national or local; at home anywhere.

ECLECTICISM is the free selection of things from a number of different sources.

EXPATS is a shortened form of "expatriates," meaning people who have left their native country to live in another.

LINGUA FRANCA was, originally, a language spoken in the Mediterranean region, composed of elements of several other languages. Generally, the term refers to any language that is used in common by people of different nationalities.

MESTIZO means a person of mixed European and Native American ancestry.

A MONGREL is an animal or plant (especially a dog) that is of a mixed breed, or a person of mixed racial stock. The word is usually used to suggest something of lower quality.

POLYGLOT means made up of a mixture of several languages.

SOIGNÉ, a French word, means sophisticated, polished, elegant.

This is the typical day of a relatively typical soul in today's diversified 1 world. I wake up to the sound of my Japanese clock radio, put on a T shirt sent me by an uncle in Nigeria and walk out into the street, past German cars, to my office. Around me are English-language students from Korea, Switzerland, and Argentina—all on this Spanish-named road in this Mediterranean-style town. On TV, I find, the news is in Mandarin; today's baseball game is being broadcast in Korean. For lunch I can walk to a sushi bar, a tandoori palace, a Thai café, or the newest burrito joint (run by an old Japanese lady). Who am I, I sometimes wonder, the son of Indian parents and a British citizen who spends much of his time in Japan (and is therefore—what else?—an American permanent resident)? And where am I?

I am, as it happens, in Southern California, in a quiet, relatively unin-ternational town, but I could as easily be in Vancouver or Sydney or Lon-don or Hong Kong. All the world's a rainbow coalition, more and more; the whole planet, you might say, is going global. When I fly to Toronto, or Paris, or Singapore, I disembark in a world as hyphenated as the one I left. More and more of the globe looks like America, but an America that is itself looking more and more like the rest of the globe. Los Angeles fa-mously teaches 82 different languages in its schools. In this respect, the city seems only to bear out the old adage that what is in California today is in America tomorrow, and next week around the globe.

In ways that were hardly conceivable even a generation ago, the new world order is a version of the New World writ large: a wide-open frontier of **polyglot** terms and postnational trends. A common multiculturalism links us all—call it Planet Hollywood, Planet Reebok, or the United Col-ors of Benetton. *Taxi* and *hotel* and *disco* are universal terms now, but so too are *karaoke* and *yoga* and *pizza*. For the gourmet alone, there is *tiramisù* at the Burger King in Kyoto, echt angel-hair pasta in Saigon, and enchiladas on every menu in Nepal.

But deeper than mere goods, it is souls that are mingling. In Brussels, a center of the new "unified Europe," 1 new baby in every 4 is Arab. Whole parts of the Paraguayan capital of Asunción are largely Korean. And when the prostitutes of Melbourne distributed some pro-condom pamphlets, one of the languages they used was Macedonian. Even Japan, which prides itself on its centuries-old socially engineered uniculture, swarms with Iranian il-legals, Western executives, Pakistani laborers, and Filipina hostesses.

The global village is defined, as we know, by an international youth 5 culture that takes its cues from American pop culture. Kids in Perth and Prague and New Delhi are all tuning in to *Santa Barbara* on TV, and wrig-gling into 501 jeans, while singing along to Madonna's latest in English. CNN (which has grown 70-fold in 13 years) now reaches more than 140 countries; an American football championship pits London against Barce-lona. As fast as the world comes to America, America goes round the world—but it is an America that is itself multi-tongued and many hued, an America of Amy Tan and Janet Jackson and movies with dialogue in Lakota.

For far more than goods and artifacts, the one great influence being broadcast around the world in greater numbers and at greater speed than ever before is people. What were once clear divisions are now tangles of crossed lines: there are 40,000 "Canadians" resident in Hong Kong, many of whose first language is Cantonese. And with people come customs: while new immigrants from Taiwan and Vietnam and India—some of the so-called Asian Calvinists—import all-American values of hard work and family closeness and entrepreneurial energy to America, America is sending its values of upward mobility and individualism and melting-pot hopefulness to Taipei and Saigon and Bombay.

Values, in fact, travel at the speed of fax; by now, almost half the world's Mormons live outside the U.S. A diversity of one culture quickly becomes a diversity of many: the "typical American" who goes to Japan today may be a third-generation Japanese American, or the son of a Japanese woman married to a California serviceman, or the offspring of a Salvadoran father and an Italian mother from San Francisco. When he goes out with a Japanese woman, more than two cultures are brought into play.

None of this, of course, is new: Chinese silks were all the rage in Rome centuries ago, and Alexandria before the time of Christ was a paradigm of the modern universal city. Not even American **eclecticism** is new: many a small town has long known Chinese restaurants, Indian doctors, and Lebanese grocers. But now all these cultures are crossing at the speed of light. And the rising diversity of the planet is something more than mere **cosmopolitanism**: it is a fundamental recoloring of the very complexion of societies. Cities like Paris, or Hong Kong, have always had a **soigné,** international air and served as magnets for exiles and émigrés, but now smaller places are multinational too. Marseilles speaks French with a distinctly North African twang. Islamic fundamentalism has one of its strongholds in Bradford, England. It is the sleepy coastal towns of Queensland, Australia, that print their menus in Japanese.

The dangers this internationalism presents are evident: not for nothing did the Tower of Babel collapse. As national borders fall, tribal alliances, and new manmade divisions rise up, and the world learns every day terrible new meanings of the word Balkanization. And while some places are wired for international transmission, others (think of Iran or North Korea or Burma) remain as isolated as ever, widening the gap between the haves and the have-nots, or what Alvin Toffler has called the "fast" and the "slow" worlds. Tokyo has more telephones than the whole continent of Africa.

Nonetheless, whether we like it or not, the "transnational" future is 10 upon us: as Kenichi Ohmae, the international economist, suggests with his talk of a "borderless economy," capitalism's allegiances are to products, not places. "Capital is now global," Robert Reich, the Secretary of Labor, has said, pointing out that when an Iowan buys a Pontiac from General Motors, 60% of his money goes to South Korea, Japan, West Germany, Taiwan, Singapore, Britain, and Barbados. Culturally we are being re-formed daily by the cadences of world music and world fiction: where the great Canadian writers of an older generation had names like Frye and Davies and Laurence, now they are called Ondaatje and Mistry and Skvorecky.

As space shrinks, moreover, time accelerates. This hip-hop mishmash is spreading overnight. When my parents were in college, there were all of seven foreigners living in Tibet, a country the size of Western Europe, and in its entire history the country had seen fewer than 2,000 Westerners. Now a Danish student in Lhasa is scarcely more surprising than a Tibetan in Copenhagen. Already a city like Miami is beyond the wildest dreams of 1968; how much more so will its face in 2018 defy our predictions of today?

It would be easy, seeing all this, to say that the world is moving toward the *Raza Cósmica* (Cosmic Race), predicted by the Mexican thinker José Vasconcelos in the '20s—a glorious blend of **mongrels** and **mestizos.** It may be more relevant to suppose that more and more of the world may come to resemble Hong Kong, a stateless special economic zone full of **expats** and exiles linked by the **lingua franca** of English and the global marketplace. Some urbanists already see the world as a grid of 30 or so highly advanced city-regions, or technopoles, all plugged into the same international circuit.

The world will not become America. Anyone who has been to a baseball game in Osaka, or a Pizza Hut in Moscow, knows instantly that she is not in Kansas. But America may still, if only symbolically, be a model for the world. *E Pluribus Unum,* after all, is on the dollar bill. As Federico Mayor Zaragoza, the director-general of UNESCO, has said, "America's main role in the new world order is not as a military superpower, but as a multicultural superpower."

The traditional metaphor for this is that of a mosaic. But Richard Rodriguez, the Mexican-American essayist who is a psalmist for our new hybrid forms, points out that the interaction is more fluid than that, more human, subject to daily revision. "I am Chinese," he says, "because I live in San Francisco, a Chinese city. I became Irish in America. I became Portuguese in America." And even as he announces this new truth, Portuguese women are becoming American, and Irishmen are becoming Portuguese, and Sydney (or is it Toronto?) is thinking to compare itself with the "Chinese city" we know as San Francisco.

QUESTIONS FOR DISCUSSION

1. In the second paragraph, what is it about Southern California that suggests the future of America?

2. What does the author mean by the statement, "A common multiculturalism links us all"? Explain.

3. What is the role of American pop culture in "The Global Village"?

4. What role do mobility and technological change play in the formation of the global village?

5. What are the dangers of internationalism?

6. What do urbanists mean by "technopoles"?

7. Do you find any parallels between the views of Pico Iyer and those of Richard Rodriguez? Explain and give a few examples.

✑ CATHERINE LIM

Paper

Catherine Lim is one of the foremost writers of Singapore, which is the smallest country in Southeast Asia. She has published several collections of stories, including Stories of Singapore, *from which "Paper" was taken (1978),* Or Else, The Lightning God and Other Stories *(1980), and* The Shadow of a Shadow of a Dream—Love Stories of Singapore *(1981). The Singapore stock exchange (SES All-Singapore), which is the backdrop for "Paper," is known as one of the most unstable in the world.*

KEY VOCABULARY

An **AMALGAM** is a mixture made up of diverse elements.
BROKING HOUSES are companies that buy and sell stocks for their clients—stockbrokers.
CURRIES are spicy sauces or relishes made with curry powder.
WIZENED means dried up, shriveled, withered.

He wanted it, he dreamed of it, he hankered after it, as an addict after 1
his opiate. Once the notion of a big beautiful house had lodged itself in his imagination, Tay Soon nurtured it until it became the consuming passion of his life. A house. A dream house such as he had seen on his drives with his wife and children along the roads bordering the prestigious housing estates on the island, and in the glossy pages of *Homes* and *Modern Living*. Or rather, it was a house which was an **amalgam** of the best, the most beautiful aspects of the houses he had seen. He knew every detail of his dream house already, from the aluminium sliding doors to the actual shade of the dining room carpet to the shape of the swimming pool. Kidney. He rather liked the shape. He was not ashamed of the enthusiasm with which he spoke of the dream house, an enthusiasm that belonged to women only, he was told. Indeed, his enthusiasm was so great that it had infected his wife and even his children, small though they were. Soon his wife Yee Lian was describing to her sister Yee Yeng the dream house in all its perfection of shape and decor, and the children were telling their cousins and friends, "My daddy says that when our house is ready . . ."

They talked of the dream house endlessly. It had become a reality stronger than the reality of the small terrace house which they were sharing with Tay Soon's mother, to whom it belonged. Tay Soon's mother, whose little business of selling bottled **curries** and vegetable preserves which she made herself left her little time for dreams, clucked her tongue and shook her head and made sarcastic remarks about the ambitiousness of young people nowadays.

"What's wrong with this house we're staying in?" she asked petulantly. "Aren't we all comfortable in it?"

Not as long as you have your horrid ancestral altars all over the place, and your grotesque sense of colour—imagine painting the kitchen wall bright pink. But Yee Lian was tactful enough to keep the remarks to herself, or to make them only to her sister Yee Yeng, otherwise they were sure to reach the old lady, and there would be no end to her sharp tongue.

The house—the dream house—it would be a far cry from the little 5 terrace house in which they were all staying now, and Tay Soon and Yee Lian talked endlessly about it, and it grew magnificently in their imaginations, this dream house of theirs with its timbered ceiling and panelled walls and sunken circular sitting room which was to be carpeted in rich amber. It was no empty dream, for there was much money in the bank already. Forty thousand dollars had been saved. The house would cost many times that, but Tay Soon and Yee Lian with their good salaries would be able to manage very well. Once they took care of the down payment, they would be able to pay back monthly over a period of ten years—fifteen, twenty— what did it matter how long it took as long as the dream house was theirs? It had become the symbol of the peak of earthly achievement, and all of Tay Soon's energies and devotion were directed towards its realisation. His mother said, "You're a show-off; what's so grand about marble flooring and a swimming pool? Why don't you put your money to better use?" But the forty thousand grew steadily, and after Tay Soon and Yee Lian had put in every cent of their annual bonuses, it grew to forty eight thousand, and husband and wife smiled at the smooth way their plans were going.

It was a time of growing interest in the stock market. The quotations for stocks and shares were climbing the charts, and the crowds in the rooms of the **broking houses** were growing perceptibly. Might we not do something about this? Yee Lian said to her husband. Do you know that Dr. Soo bought Rustan Banking for four dollars and today the shares are worth seven dollars each? The temptation was great. The rewards were almost immediate. Thirty thousand dollars' worth of NBE became fifty-five thousand almost overnight. Tay Soon and Yee Lian whooped. They put their remaining eighteen thousand in Far East Mart. Three days later the shares were worth twice that much. It was not to be imagined that things could stop here. Tay Soon secured a loan from his bank and put twenty thousand in OHTE. This was a particularly lucky share; it shot up to four times its value in three days.

"Oh, this is too much, too much," cried Yee Lian in her ecstasy, and she sat down with pencil and paper, and found after a few minutes' calculation that they had made a cool one hundred thousand in a matter of days.

And now there was to be no stopping. The newspapers were full of it, everybody was talking about it, it was in the very air. There was plenty of money to be made in the stock exchange by those who had guts—money to be made by the hour, by the minute, for the prices of stocks and shares were rising faster than anyone could keep track of them! Dr. Soo was said— he laughingly dismissed it as a silly rumour—Dr. Soo was said to have made two million dollars already. If he sold all his shares now, he would be a millionaire twice over. And Yee Yeng, Yee Lian's sister, who had been urged with sisterly good will to come join the others make money, laughed happily to find that the shares she had bought for four twenty on Tuesday had risen to seven ninety-five on Friday—she laughed and thanked Yee Lian who advised her not to sell yet, it was going further, it would hit the ten dollar mark by next week. And Tay Soon both laughed and cursed—cursed that he had failed to buy a share at nine dollars which a few days later had hit seventeen dollars! Yee Lian said reproachfully, "I thought I told you to buy it, darling," and Tay Soon had beaten his forehead in despair and said, "I know, I know, why didn't I! Big fool that I am!" And he had another reason to curse himself—he sold five thousand West Parkes at sixteen twenty-three per share, and saw, to his horror, West Parkes climb to eighteen ninety the very next day!

"I'll never sell now," he vowed. "I'll hold on. I won't be so foolish." And the frenzy continued. Husband and wife couldn't talk or think of anything else. They thought fondly of their shares—going to be worth a million altogether soon. A million! In the peak of good humour, Yee Lian went to her mother-in-law, forgetting the past insults, and advised her to join the others by buying some shares; she would get her broker to buy them immediately for her; there was sure money in it. The old lady refused curtly, and to her son later, she showed great annoyance, scolding him for being so foolish as to put all his money in those worthless shares. "Worthless!" exploded Tay Soon. "Do you know, Mother, if I sold all my shares today, I would have the money to buy fifty terrace houses like the one you have?"

His wife said, "Oh, we'll just leave her alone. I was kind enough to offer to help her make money. But since she's so nasty and ungrateful, we'll leave her alone." The comforting, triumphant thought was that soon, very soon, they would be able to purchase their dream house; it would be even 10 more magnificent than the one they had dreamt of, since they had made almost a—Yee Lian preferred not to say the sum. There was the old superstitious fear of losing something when it is too often or too directly referred to, and Yee Lian had cautioned her husband not to make mention of their gains.

"Not to worry, not to worry," he said jovially, not superstitious like his wife. "After all, it's just paper gains so far."

The downward slide, or the bursting of the bubble as the newspapers dramatically called it, did not initially cause much alarm, for the speculators all expected the shares to bounce back to their original strength and thence continue the phenomenal growth. But that did not happen. The slide continued.

Tay Soon said nervously, "Shall we sell? Do you think we should sell?" but Yee Lian said stoutly, "There is talk that this decline is a technical thing only—it will be over soon, and then the rise will continue. After all, see what is happening in Hong Kong and London and New York. Things are as good as ever.

"We're still making, so not to worry," said Yee Lian after a few days. Their gains were pared by half. A few days later, their gains were pared to marginal.

"There is talk of recovery," insisted Yee Lian. "Do you know, Tay Soon, Dr. Soo's wife is buying up some OHTE and West Parkes now? She says these two are sure to rise. She has some inside information that these two are going to climb past the forty-dollar mark—"

Tay Soon sold all his shares and put the money in OHTE and West 15 Parkes. OHTE and West Parkes crashed shortly afterwards. Some began to say the shares were not worth the paper of the certificates.

"Oh, I can't believe, I can't believe it," gasped Yee Lian, pale and sick. Tay Soon looked in mute horror at her.

"All our money was in OHTE and West Parkes," he said, his lips dry.

"That stupid Soo woman!" shrieked Yee Lian. "I think she deliberately led me astray with her advice! She's always been jealous of me—ever since she knew we were going to build a house grander than hers!"

"How are we going to get our house now?" asked Tay Soon in deep distress, and for the first time he wept. He wept like a child, for the loss of all his money, for the loss of the dream house that he had never stopped loving and worshipping.

The pain bit into his very mind and soul, so that he was like a madman, 20 unable to go to his office to work, unable to do anything but haunt the **broking houses,** watching with frenzied anxiety for OHTE and West Parkes to show him hope. But there was no hope. The decline continued with gleeful rapidity. His broker advised him to sell, before it was too late, but he shrieked angrily, "What! Sell at a fraction at which I bought them! How can this be tolerated!"

And he went on hoping against hope.

He began to have wild dreams in which he sometimes laughed and sometimes screamed. His wife Yee Lian was afraid and she ran sobbing to her sister who never failed to remind her curtly that all her savings were gone, simply because when she had wanted to sell, Yee Lian advised her not to.

"But what is your sorrow compared to mine," wept Yee Lian; "see what's happening to my husband. He's cracking up! He talks to himself, he doesn't eat, he has nightmares, he beats the children. Oh, he's finished!"

Her mother-in-law took charge of the situation, while Yee Lian, wide-eyed in mute horror at the terrible change that had come over her husband, shrank away and looked to her two small children for comfort. Tight-lipped and grim, the elderly woman made herbal medicines for Tay Soon, brewing and straining for hours, and got a Chinese medicine man to come to have a look at him.

"There is a devil in him," said the medicine man, and he proceeded to 25 make him a drink which he mixed with the ashes of a piece of prayer paper. But Tay Soon grew worse. He lay in bed, white, haggard, and delirious, seeming to be beyond the touch of healing. In the end, Yee Lian, on the advice of her sister and friends, put him in hospital.

"I have money left for the funeral," whimpered the frightened Yee Lian only a week later, but her mother-in-law sharply retorted, "You leave everything to me! I have the money for his funeral, and I shall give him the best! He wanted a beautiful house all his life; I shall give him a beautiful house now!"

She went to the man who was well-known on the island for his beautiful houses, and she ordered the best. It would come to nearly a thousand dollars, said the man, a thin, **wizened** fellow whose funereal gauntness and pallor seemed to be a concession to his calling.

"That doesn't matter," she said, "I want the best. The house is to be made of superior paper," she instructed, and he was to make it to her specifications. She recollected that he, Tay Soon, had often spoken of marble flooring, a timbered ceiling, and a kidney-shaped swimming pool. Could he simulate all these in paper?

The thin, **wizened** man said, "I've never done anything like that before. All my paper houses for the dead have been the usual kind—I can put in paper furniture and paper cars, paper utensils for the kitchen and paper servants, all that the dead will need in the other world. But I shall try to put in what you've asked for. Only it will cost more."

The house, when it was ready, was most beautiful to see. It stood seven 30 feet tall, a delicate framework of wire and thin bamboo strips covered with finely worked paper of a myriad colours. Little silver flowers, scattered liberally throughout the entire structure, gave a carnival atmosphere. There was a paper swimming pool (round, as the man had not understood 'kidney') which had to be fitted inside the house itself, as there was no provision for a garden or surrounding grounds. Inside the house were paper figures; there were at least four servants to attend to the needs of the master who was posed beside two cars, one distinctly a Chevrolet and the other a Mercedes.

At the appointed time, the paper house was brought to Tay Soon's grave and set on fire there. It burned brilliantly, and in three minutes was a heap of ashes on the grave.

QUESTIONS FOR DISCUSSION

1. What does the dream house mean to Tay Soon? What does it mean to the rest of the family?

2. Why are the relations between Yee Lian and her mother-in-law strained?

3. Is it sheer greed that leads to the family's bankruptcy, or is it something else? Explain your answer and give examples from the story.

4. Why does Tay Soon's mother insist on buying the funeral house herself?

5. Explain the significance of the story's title.

6. What evidence is there in the story that the family has been influenced by American culture?

In the student essay concluding this chapter, responding to topic 4, the writer reconsiders Richard Rodriguez' question, "Does America Still Exist?" She uses information from the readings to develop her own views. This writer demonstrates how an active response to reading can help us to shape and clarify our own thoughts.

✍ STUDENT ESSAY:

One Out of Many

When I first read the title of Richard Rodriguez' essay "Does America Still Exist?" I shook my head to see if I had read it right. Of course America still exists. Look at the map. But as I read on, and then read some other articles about how the United States and the world are changing, the question began to make more sense. Rodriguez was talking about the *old* America, the white, small-town, Norman Rockwell America. This America probably never did exist, except as the ideal of a certain group of people. However, this image, joined to the idea of the melting pot, influenced the way Americans thought of their country for a long time. Now a new picture is being painted, inspired by changes in America and in its role in the world.

Before the 1960s, the American Dream was the dream of success: moving upward toward a better and better economic life, especially for white men. In those days, according to the myth, hard work and an upright character were all that was needed for success. But times have changed. Life has become more complicated and fast-paced, and many people are wondering what kind of country America is becoming. Traditional ideas of what America is are being questioned from all sides. The old American Dream seems like a fading memory, under pressure from rapid changes in population, technology, and commerce.

Another question Richard Rodriguez asks is, Who are the "real" Americans? He answers that citizens of small towns are the best example of the original idea about who Americans are. William Henry III, in "Beyond the Melting Pot," adds that "White Americans are accustomed to think of themselves as the very picture of their nation." This never was an accurate picture, but as long as non-whites were a small minority and knew their place, it was possible to believe it. Today, changes in population have shifted the balance; white Americans will be in the minority by the end of the century. William Henry III cites statistics which show that by the end of the twentieth century, the Hispanic population will have increased about

21%, Asian about 22%, and African American nearly 12%. At the same time, the increase in white Americans will be little more than 2%. These facts indicate that the perception of white Americans as "the very picture of the nation" is very difficult to maintain. The white, small-town, Norman Rockwell picture looks quaint and out of date, like something you'd see in a museum. As Rodriguez puts it, today's picture is the "cold-hearted city, crowded with races and ambitions, curious laughter, much that is odd."

Shifts in population toward a higher percentage of "people of color" have caused many people to question the traditional "melting pot" image of America. Part of the earlier idea of the American Dream was that an immigrant would shed his old life and ways like a useless skin and "melt" into the great American mainstream. However, because of differences in color and customs, the new immigrants don't melt down quite as easily and are more likely to want to keep much of their native culture. As Rodriguez says, "The melting pot has been retired." Other metaphors are being suggested to replace it: the mosaic, the salad bar, the stew, the patchwork quilt. These images are frightening to those who cling to the old dream, who fear that America is coming apart. But they are hopeful to those who were never allowed to get in the melting pot in the first place. So depending on who you are, you could see the end of the melting pot as either the death or the birth of the American Dream.

While a more diverse population is retiring the melting pot, advances in technology and changes in business and education are making the American Dream harder to achieve. It is now almost impossible for a poor lad with little education to start at the bottom and work his way to the top. Business people today have to understand the complexities of new technologies and international trade. Universities turn out highly-trained M.B.A.'s by the thousands, and many top managers have degrees in engineering or computer science. A person with just a high school degree can't possibly compete with them. These days, the Horatio Alger hero would have to arm himself with much more than a good work ethic and an honest heart. He would need a degree from a good school and considerable technical knowledge to even get a start. The road to success looks rougher now, with more obstacles to overcome and more competition along the way.

America's changing role in the world is also affecting the way Americans see themselves. For example, in business, "Made in America" used to mean what it said. But now it could mean almost anything. In "The Global Village Finally Arrives," Pico Iyer writes, "when an Iowan buys a Pontiac from General Motors, 60% of his money goes to South Korea, Japan, West Germany, Taiwan, Singapore, Britain, and Barbados." Distinctions that were once clear are becoming blurred, and many Americans are frightened because they no longer have a clear sense of what the country is. Bumper stickers that urge us to "Buy American" are starting to look as outdated as Norman Rockwell's paintings. Change is always difficult. Something has to die to make room for something new. Is there a positive side to all of this? There certainly is to many people who never did fit into the Norman Rockwell picture. Richard Rodriguez' image of a city street gives a wider view of the "real" America: "The panhandler at one corner is related to the pamphleteer at the next who is related to the banker who is kin to the Chinese old man wearing an MIT sweatshirt." This is a picture Americans have to accept. It is here. Another point is raised by William Henry III. He writes that "the browning of America offers tremendous opportunity for capitalizing anew on the merits of many peoples from many lands." America has always drawn strength from its immigrants. It is, after all, a country of immigrants. All things considered, it is possible that instead of watching the death of the old dream, we are seeing the birth of the new. But the new is really the old, that is if we really believe the old words written on a dollar bill—*E Pluribus Unum.*

TOPICS FOR WRITING

1. Re-read "Beyond the Melting Pot" and "The Global Village Finally Arrives" and write a letter to the Brentwood Middle School students informing them of what American society will be like when they reach middle-age.

2. Richard Rodriguez writes, "Immigrants come to America and, against hostility or mere loneliness, they recreate a homeland in the parlor. . . ." Andrei Codrescu describes the home of Polish immigrants to show how they "are changing American space and challenging its conventional uses."

   Visit the home of a recent immigrant family or foreign student and write a report for your campus newspaper, focusing on how much these people have "recreated a homeland" in their homes. Pay special attention to details that reflect their previous culture. (If your campus has an ESL department or international student organization, you might ask them for help.)

3. Andrei Codrescu finds in Brâncuşi's "Infinite Column" a symbol of Romanians' desire to "stay close to the earth and to make their own statements about the purpose of space."

   Find an example of art from another culture—it could be a sculpture, painting, textile art, song, or folktale—that represents that culture's view of itself. Consider such things as the totem poles of Northwest Native Americans, African American blues music, or a Chinese New Year celebration. Describe your subject and explain what traits of the culture it embodies.

4. From the information in this chapter, what can you conclude about the ways in which non-European immigrants are re-shaping the earlier European Protestant character of American culture?

5. Using Richard Rodriguez' essay "Does America Still Exist?" as a starting point, write an essay about the effects of American culture on the children of recent immigrants. If you wish, incorporate information from other essays or from your own experience.

6. Is the *mestizo,* as Richard Rodriguez claims, an optimistic symbol of the cultural future of America? Using information from Rodriguez, Pico Iyer, and any other relevant sources, take a position for or against Rodriguez' claim.

7. Angelo Pellegrini and Celeste MacLeod both offer their own definitions of the American Dream. In what ways are they similar, and in what ways are they different? Do they complement or contradict each other?

8. Celeste MacLeod argues that Americans must revise both their perceptions of success and their perceptions of America as a classless society. Do you agree or disagree with her? Take a position for or against her claim and write a paper defending your position.

9. How has a neighborhood in your town or city changed as a result of recent immigration? Spend some time in a particular neighborhood—talk to people and note details of their surroundings—and write a report for your campus paper, describing your findings.

10. Based on the history of your own family, explain the different versions of the American Dream held by family members of different generations.

11. At the end of "Beyond the Melting Pot," William Henry II speculates about the possible consequences of an increasingly multicultural society. Reread his last paragraph, then explain what you think he means when he says, "The 'browning of America' offers tremendous opportunity for capitalizing anew on the merits of many peoples from many lands. Yet this fundamental change in the ethnic makeup of the U.S. also poses risks. The American character is resilient and thrives on change. But, past periods of rapid evolution have also, alas, brought out deeper, more fearful aspects of the national soul."

12. In Catherine Lim's story "Paper," consider Tay Soon's mother's way of life, as exemplified by her house, and then write an argument explaining why Tay Soon's dream house would be a revision of the traditional Singaporean dream of the good life.

Acknowledgments

PHOTO CREDITS

ARCHIVE PHOTOS, page 152.

THOMAS HART BENTON, "Changing West," from *America Today*. 1930. Distemper and egg tempera with oil glaze on gessoed linen. Size 92 x 117 inches. Collection, The Equitable Life Assurance Society of the United States. Photo 1988 by Dorothy Zeidman, page 232.

THE BETTMANN ARCHIVE, page 200.

JOEL GORDON, page 364.

LIBRARY OF CONGRESS, page 264.

NATIONAL ARCHIVES, page 112.

TIMOTHY O'SULLIVAN, the Denver Public Library, Western History Department, page 84.

JERRY UELSMANN, page 294.

UPI/BETTMANN, pages 326 and 392.

TEXT CREDITS

FREDERICK LEWIS ALLEN, excerpts from chapter 4, pages 63–65, from *The Big Change: America Transforms Itself, 1900–1950*. Copyright © 1952 by Frederick Lewis Allen. Reprinted by permission of HarperCollins Publishers., Inc.

MAYA ANGELOU, from *I Know Why the Caged Bird Sings*. Copyright © 1960 by Maya Angelou. Reprinted by permission of Random House, Inc.

ELENA ASURIAS, "Growing Up in the U.S.: A First Generation Look."

PETER SCHUCK, from *Tacoma News Tribune*, June 16, 1991. Reprinted with the permission of the author.

HENRYK SKOLIMOWSKI, "The Language of Advertising." Reprinted from *ETC: A Review of General Semantics*, Vol. 25, No. 1, March 1968 with permission of the International Society for General Semantics, Concord, California.

BRENT STAPLES, "Black Men and Public Space." Reprinted with the permission of the author. *Brent Staples* writes editorials for *The New York Times* and is the author of the memoir *Parallel Time: Growing Up in Black and White.*

STUDS TERKEL, from *American Dreams: Lost and Found.* Copyright © 1980 by Studs Terkel. Reprinted by permission of Pantheon Books, a division of Random House, Inc.

CARLL TUCKER, from *Saturday Review.* Reprinted by permission of the author.

KURT VONNEGUT, JR., "Harrison Bergeron," from *Welcome to the Monkey House.* Copyright © 1961 by Kurt Vonnegut, Jr. Used by permission of Delacorte Press/Seymour Lawrence, a division of Bantam Doubleday Dell Publishing Group, Inc.

E. B. WHITE, from *The New Yorker*, May 31, 1947. Reprinted by permission.

PATRICIA J. WILLIAMS, from *The Alchemy of Race and Rights*, Cambridge, Mass.: Harvard University Press. Copyright © 1991 by the President and Fellows of Harvard College. Reprinted by permission of the publishers.

ANN WORTHAM, "Interview with Bill Moyers," from *Bill Moyers: A World of Ideas.* Copyright © 1989 by Public Affairs Television, Inc. Used by permission of Doubleday, a division of Bantam Doubleday Dell Publishing Group, Inc.

ANZIA YEZIERSKA, "America and I," from *The Open Cage* by Anzia Yezierska. Copyright © 1979 by Louise Levitas Henriksen. Reprinted by permission of Persea Books.

WILLIAM ZINSSER, from *The Lunacy Boom*, published by Harper & Row. Copyright © 1969, 1970 by William K. Zinsser. Reprinted by permission of the author.

Index to the Readings by Rhetorical Strategy (Mode)

Argument

Cause and Effect

Index of Authors and Titles